DAMASCUS

SYRIA

IRAQ

MODERN JERUSALEM
See pp114–123

THE MUSLIM QUARTER
See pp58–73

JORDAN

JERUSALEM

THE CHRISTIAN AND ARMENIAN QUARTERS
See pp84–103

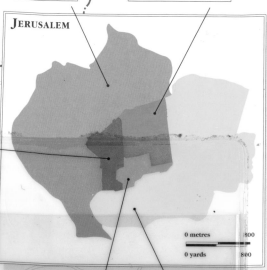

| 0 metres | 800 |
| 0 yards | 800 |

SAUDI ARABIA

FURTHER AFIELD
See pp124–135

THE JEWISH QUARTER
See pp74–83

THE MOUNT OF OLIVES AND MOUNT ZION
See pp104–113

DK TRAVEL GUIDES

JERUSALEM
& THE HOLY LAND

DORLING KINDERSLEY *TRAVEL GUIDES*

JERUSALEM
& THE HOLY LAND

DORLING KINDERSLEY PUBLISHING, INC.
LONDON • NEW YORK • SYDNEY • DELHI
PARIS • MUNICH • JOHANNESBURG
www.dk.com

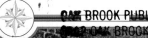

A DORLING KINDERSLEY BOOK

www.dk.com

PROJECT EDITORS Nick Inman, Ferdie McDonald
ART EDITORS Jo Doran, Paul Jackson
COMMISSIONING EDITOR Giovanni Francesio
at Fabio Ratti Editoria S.r.l.
EDITORS Elizabeth Atherton, Cathy Day, Simon Hall,
Freddy Hamilton, Andrew Humphreys
DESIGNERS Chris Lee Jones, Anthony Limerick,
Sue Metcalfe-Megginson, Rebecca Milner, Johnny Pau
PICTURE RESEARCH Monica Allende, Katherine Mesquita
MAP CO-ORDINATOR Dave Pugh
DTP DESIGNER Maite Lantaron
RESEARCHER Karen Ben-Zoor

MAIN CONTRIBUTORS
Fabrizio Ardito, Cristina Gambaro, Massimo Acanfora Torrefranca

PHOTOGRAPHY
Eddie Gerald, Hanan Isachar, Richard Nowitz,
Magnus Rew, Visions of the Land

ILLUSTRATORS
Isidoro Gonzáles-Adalid Cabezas (Acanto Arquitectura y
Urbanismo S.L.), Stephen Conlin, Gary Cross, Chris Forsey,
Andrew MacDonald, Maltings Partnership, Jill Munford,
Chris Orr & Associates, Pat Thorne, John Woodcock

Reproduced by Colourscan, Singapore
Printed and bound by Mondadori, Italy

First American Edition, 2000
2 4 6 8 10 9 7 5 3 1

First published in the United States by Dorling Kindersley
Publishing, Inc., 95 Madison Avenue, New York, New York 10016
Copyright 2000 © Dorling Kindersley Limited, London

Library of Congress Cataloging-in-Publication Data
Jerusalem and the Holy Land
      p. cm. – – (Dorling Kindersley travel guides)
      Includes index.
      ISBN 0-7894-5170-0 (acid-free paper)
      1. Jerusalem–Guidebooks. 2. Jerusalem–Description and travel.
3. Israel–Guidebooks. 4. Israel–Description and travel. I. Series.
DS109.15. J48 2000
915.69404'54–dc21   99-056871

**The information in every
Dorling Kindersley Travel Guide is checked annually**.
Every effort has been made to ensure that this book is as up-to-
date as possible at the time of going to press. Some details,
however, such as telephone numbers, opening hours, prices,
gallery hanging arrangements and travel information are liable to
change. The publishers cannot accept responsibility for any
consequences arising from the use of this book. We value the
views and suggestions of our readers very highly. Please write to:
Senior Managing Editor, Dorling Kindersley Travel Guides,
Dorling Kindersley, 9 Henrietta Street, London WC2E 8PS.

◁ **View over the rooftops of Jerusalem's Christian Quarter**

Mount of Olives, Jerusalem

CONTENTS

HOW TO USE THIS GUIDE 6

INTRODUCING JERUSALEM & THE HOLY LAND

Old Jaffa's attractive waterfront

Middle Eastern handicrafts

Bedouin camel, Western Jordan

Window detail, Dome of the Rock

Moroccan cigars, a favourite snack

The remote St Catherine's Monastery in Sinai

HOW TO USE THIS GUIDE

THIS GUIDE helps you to get the most from your visit to Jerusalem and the Holy Land, by providing detailed practical information. *Introducing Jerusalem and the Holy Land* maps the region and sets it in its historical and cultural context. The Jerusalem section and the four regional chapters describe important sights, using maps, photographs and illustrations. Features cover topics from food to wildlife. Recommended hotels and restaurants are listed in *Travellers' Needs*, while the *Survival Guide* has tips on travel, money and other practical matters.

JERUSALEM AREA BY AREA

The city is divided into five areas, each with its own chapter. A last chapter, *Further Afield*, covers peripheral sights. All sights are numbered and plotted on the chapter's area map. The detailed descriptions of the sights are easy to locate, as they follow the numerical order on the map.

A locator map shows where you are in relation to other areas of the city centre.

Each area of Jerusalem has its own colour-coded thumb tab, as shown inside the front cover.

Sights at a Glance lists the chapter's sights by category: Holy Places, Historic Districts, Museums and Archaeological Sites.

1 Area Map
For easy reference, sights are numbered and located on a map. The central sights are also marked on the Street Finder maps on pages 140–43.

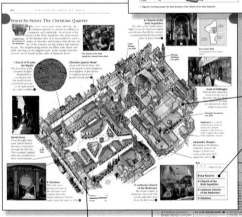

2 Street-by-Street Map
This gives a bird's-eye view of the key area in each chapter.

Stars indicate the sights that no visitor should miss.

Walking routes, shown in red, suggest where to visit on foot.

3 Detailed information
The main sights in the city are described individually. Addresses, telephone numbers and opening hours are given, as well as information on admission charges, guided tours, photography, wheelchair access and public transport.

THE HOLY LAND REGION BY REGION

Apart from Jerusalem, the Holy Land has been divided into four other regions, each of which has a separate chapter. The most interesting cities, towns, historical and religious sites, and other places of interest, are located on a *Pictorial Map*.

1 Introduction
The landscape, history and character of each region is outlined here, showing how the area has developed over the centuries and what it has to offer to the visitor today.

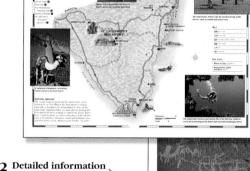

2 Pictorial Map
This shows the road network and gives an illustrated overview of the whole region. Interesting places to visit are numbered and there are also useful tips on getting to and around the region by car and public transport.

Each region of the Holy Land can be quickly identified by its colour-coded thumb tabs (see inside front cover).

3 Detailed information
All the important towns and other places to visit are described individually. They are listed in order, following the numbering on the Pictorial Map. *Within each town or city, there is detailed information on important buildings and other sights.*

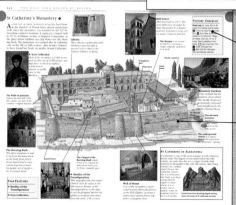

For all major sights, a Visitors' Checklist provides the practical information you will need to plan your visit.

4 The Top Sights
These are given two or more full pages. Historic buildings are dissected to reveal their interiors. Other interesting sights and areas are mapped or shown in bird's-eye view, with the most important features described.

INTRODUCING JERUSALEM & THE HOLY LAND

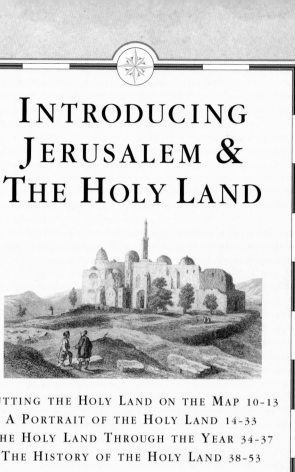

Putting the Holy Land on the Map

Flanked by three continents – Africa to the south, Asia to the east and Europe to the west – the Holy Land is an area which encompasses the whole of Israel and the Palestinian Autonomous Territories, and parts of Jordan and Egypt. Its boundaries could be said to stretch from the Mediterranean in the west, inland to the Jordanian deserts, and from Galilee in the north to the southern tip of the Sinai peninsula. At the core of the Holy Land is Jerusalem, an ancient walled city which stands on the Judaean hills, just to the west of the Dead Sea, the lowest point on earth.

Infrared satellite image of Jerusalem

M E D I T E R R A N E A N

S E A

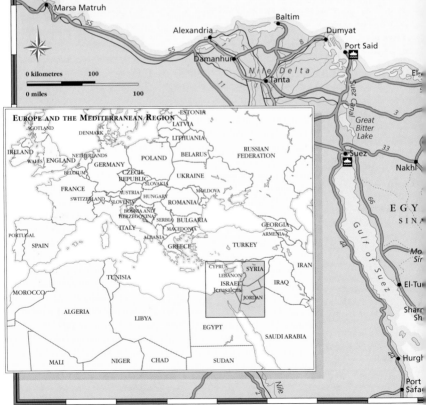

Marsa Matruh

Baltim

Alexandria

Dumyat

Port Said

Damanhur

Nile Delta

Tanta

El-

0 kilometres 100

0 miles 100

Suez Canal

Great
Bitter
Lake

Suez

Nakhl

Europe and the Mediterranean Region

ESTONIA

SCOTLAND

DENMARK

LATVIA

LITHUANIA

IRELAND

WALES ENGLAND

NETHERLANDS

GERMANY

POLAND

BELARUS

RUSSIAN
FEDERATION

BELGIUM

CZECH
REPUBLIC

UKRAINE

FRANCE

AUSTRIA
SLOVAKIA

SWITZERLAND

SLOVENIA HUNGARY

MOLDOVA

ROMANIA

BOSNIA AND
HERZEGOVINA

ITALY

SERBIA BULGARIA

MACEDONIA

GEORGIA

ARMENIA

PORTUGAL

ALBANIA

GREECE

TURKEY

SPAIN

CYPRUS

LEBANON

SYRIA

IRAN

TUNISIA

ISRAEL
Jerusalem

IRAQ

MOROCCO

JORDAN

ALGERIA

LIBYA

EGYPT

SAUDI ARABIA

MALI

NIGER

CHAD

SUDAN

Nile

E G Y

S I N A

Gulf of Suez

Mo
Sir

El-Tu

Sharr
Sh

Hurgh

Port
Safa

◁ **The Monastery at Petra** *(see p206)* in a 19th-century engraving by David Roberts

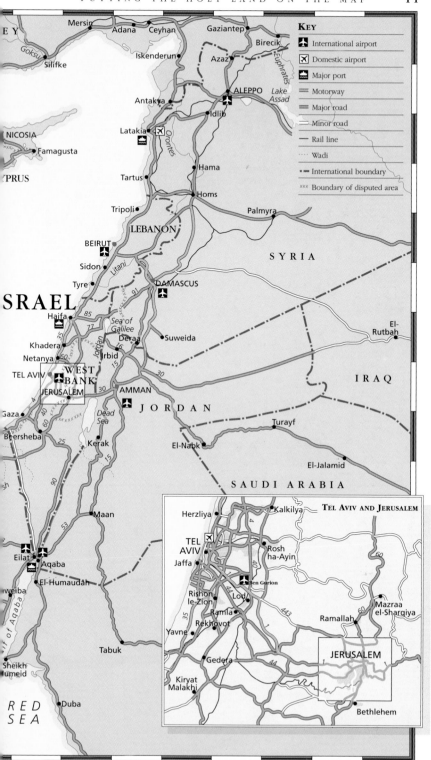

Putting Jerusalem on the Map

JERUSALEM COVERS 125 sq km (48 sq miles). In terms of geographical extent, this makes it Israel's largest city. However, despite its surface area, it is less populous than Tel Aviv. Only 600,000 people live here – 425,000 Jews, 160,000 Muslims and 15,000 Christians. At the core of Jerusalem is the walled Old City, standing 800 m (2,600 ft) above sea level. Dotted on the hilltops around, and strung along the valley floors between, are the ever-expanding modern suburbs. The city limits extend almost to the Palestinian towns of Ramallah in the north and Bethlehem to the south.

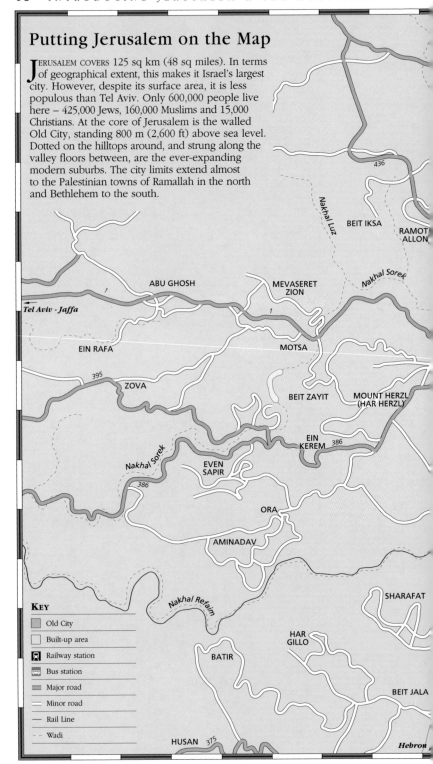

Nakhal Luz

436

BEIT IKSA

RAMOT ALLON

Nakhal Sorek

ABU GHOSH

MEVASERET ZION

◀ *Tel Aviv - Jaffa* 1

1

EIN RAFA

MOTSA

395

ZOVA

BEIT ZAYIT

MOUNT HERZL (HAR HERZL)

EIN KEREM 386

Nakhal Sorek

EVEN SAPIR

386

ORA

AMINADAV

Nakhal Refaim

SHARAFAT

KEY

▨	Old City
☐	Built-up area
🚉	Railway station
🚌	Bus station
▬	Major road
—	Minor road
—	Rail Line
- -	Wadi

HAR GILLO

BATIR

BEIT JALA

HUSAN 375

Hebron

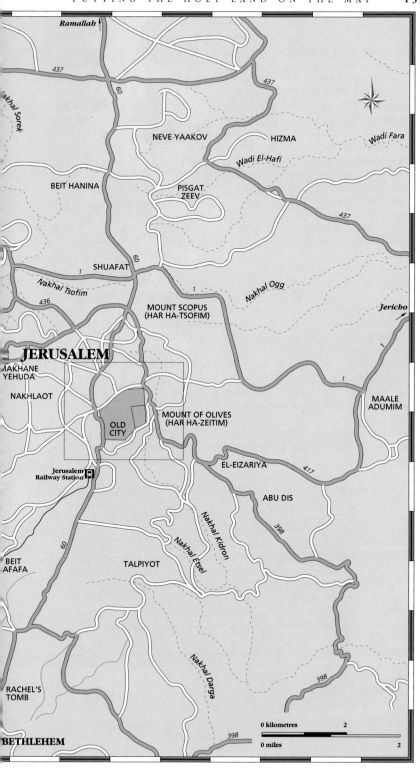

A PORTRAIT OF
THE HOLY LAND

A JEW GROWING UP *in New York, a Christian in Lisbon and a Muslim in Jakarta will have childhoods as different as can be imagined, but one thing they will share is a common set of reference points, which will include names such as Abraham and Moses, and, above all, Jerusalem and the Holy Land.*

For around 2,000 years this narrow corridor of land on the eastern shore of the Mediterranean has exercised an influence on world culture far out of proportion to its modest size. Events that are said to have taken place here in antiquity gave rise to the three great monotheistic religions. As these religions extended their influence throughout the world, so the Holy Land in general, and Jerusalem in particular, became overburdened with spiritual significance. Tradition has it that Jerusalem is where Solomon built his great temple, Christ was crucified, and the Prophet Muhammad visited on his Night Journey. It comes as a

Mural at a Palestinian school in Jerusalem

mild shock to some to discover that this spiritual world centre is no bigger than an average city neighbourhood. Those who come to Jerusalem expecting architectural grandeur to match the stature of these spiritual highlights will be disappointed. The city's churches don't begin to compare with the soaring Gothic cathedrals of Europe. The glorious Dome of the Rock aside, the buildings are quite humble. But the effect this has is to bestow on the city an altogether appropriate air of humility and authenticity, pleasingly at odds with the hyperbole and oversell of the new millennium.

Bedouin encampment in the desert scenery of Wadi Rum, southern Jordan

◁ **Greek Orthodox priest at the Church of the Holy Sepulchre, Jerusalem**

The Old City of Jerusalem, viewed from the Jewish cemetery on the Mount of Olives

While Jerusalem is a city rooted in ancient history, at the same time it lies at the heart of a region which possesses a distinctly youthful nature. Both Israel and Jordan, the two countries which, along with Egypt's Sinai peninsula, make up what we know as the Holy Land, are barely more than half a century old. It is a greatly over-used travel cliché, but here it is difficult to avoid commenting on the striking mix of the ancient and modern. In Jerusalem, ultra-Orthodox Jews wearing clothes that were fashionable in Eastern Europe 300 years ago mingle with Christian pilgrims armed with state-of-the-art digital cameras. In the wilderness of the Negev Desert, Bedouin tribesmen speak nonchalantly on mobile phones, while in Galilee Palestinian farmers lead oxen to fields that lie in the shadow of huge biotechnology plants.

Equally striking is the mix of peoples. The modern state of Israel has drawn its citizens from virtually every continent, embracing a worldwide roll call of Jewry, from Minnesota to Murmansk, Adelaide to Addis Ababa. Side by side with the Jews – and Arabs – are such minority peoples as the Druze, a mysterious offshoot sect of Islam, and the Samaritans, who speak Arabic but pray in Hebrew and number less than 600.

In this land of diversity, even the one common element shared by the majority of Israelis, the Jewish faith, is not the uniting factor it might be. The notion of what it is to be Jewish and, more pertinently, what form a Jewish state should take, are subjects of great contention. There are large, and increasingly influential, sections of society that believe Israel should adhere strictly to the laws prescribed in the Torah. The greater part of society, however, views the notion of a religious state with horror. The gulf between the two standpoints is best

Young boy playing football at the Dome of the Rock

illustrated by the phenomenon of Dana International, the flamboyant transsexual singer who won the 1998 Eurovision Song Contest. It was a victory greeted with pride by a part of the nation, while to the religious sector it served only to confirm "the secular sickness of Israel".

An even more contentious issue is ownership of the land. Israel bases its right to exist on an ancient covenant with God, related in the Old Testament, in which this land was promised to the descendants of the Jewish patriarch Abraham. This is a covenant, needless to say, that is not recognized by the Palestinian Arabs, who have their own claims on the territory, based on centuries of occupancy. During the 20th century four major wars were fought between the Arabs and the Jews. The problem is still far from being resolved. Conflict is no stranger to the region. Since the Hebrew tribes first emerged from the desert around the 12th century BC, this has been one of the world's most turbulent neighbourhoods. Every major Near Eastern empire fought here. This has resulted in a fantastic legacy of historical remains, including Roman cities, Byzantine churches and early Islamic palaces. Archaeologists are constantly at work to uncover what other riches this troubled land might yield. Often, their aims go far beyond the academic: some expeditions search for

Souk stall-holder in the town of Ramallah, a busy centre of Palestinian life and culture

Divisive Dana International

evidence to support territorial claims; others are seeking fabled artifacts such as the Holy Grail or the Ark of the Covenant, which they believe may hold the very key to human existence.

Amidst all this hullabaloo, one should not forget that the Holy Land is a marvellous region for the visitor. It is not necessary to have an advanced grasp of history to appreciate the magnificence of the region's ancient cities, isolated monasteries and hilltop fortresses, while the desert scenery of Wadi Rum is a setting in which to live out fantasies, and the diving in the Red Sea is reckoned by some to be unsurpassed anywhere in the world. Added to this, there is plenty of fine dining and comfortable accommodation. It is quite possible to visit the Holy Land and find that the only issue of concern is getting a decent spot on the beach.

Beach life at Tel Aviv, the vibrant cultural and commercial capital of Israel

Old Testament Sites in the Holy Land

MANY OF THE STORIES recounted in the Old Testament are located within Egypt, Sinai and the "Land of Canaan", which corresponds roughly to present-day Israel. The Bible gives plenty of precise geographical references. Some places, such as Jerusalem and Jericho, still exist and have yielded archaeological evidence confirming some, but by no means all, of the references to them in the Old Testament. Other sites were only attached to their biblical episodes much later. Touring these sites, the visitor cannot but be aware of the contrast between the importance of the events and the often insignificant and all-too-human scale of the places in which they are said to have occurred.

The Destruction of Sodom ①
When Sodom was destroyed by God (see p182) only Lot and his family were spared, but his wife looked back and was turned into a pillar of salt.

The Sacrifice of Isaac ②
God asked Abraham to sacrifice his son, Isaac. The patriarch was about to obey when an angel stayed his hand and instructed him to slaughter a ram instead (Genesis 22). Tradition identifies the place of sacrifice as Mount Moriah, later a part of Jerusalem, and the site on which Solomon's Temple is said to have been subsequently built (see p39).

Gaza

The Tombs of the Patriarchs ③
Acquired as a burial place for his wife Sarah, the Machpelah cave was the first plot in the Land of Canaan purchased by Abraham (Genesis 23). A mosque/synagogue now occupies the traditional site of the tomb, located in the present-day town of Hebron (see p176).

Moses Receives the Ten Commandments ④
Since the 4th century, Mount Sinai (see pp222–3) has been associated with the story of Moses and the Ten Commandments (Exodus 20). The Bible places Mount Sinai in a region called Horeb, but the location of Horeb has never been identified.

0 kilometres   100

0 miles   50

④
Mount Sinai

GULF OF AQ

The Death of Moses ⑤
Moses is said to have seen the Promised Land from the summit of Mount Nebo and died in the same place. Christian tradition identifies Mount Nebo (see p191) as being just southwest of modern-day Amman. As the Bible states, the whereabouts of Moses' tomb is unknown (Deuteronomy 34: 1-7).

Joshua Conquers Jericho ⑥
The Old Testament story tells
how the walls of Jericho (see
p170) fell to the blast of horns
(Joshua 6). This ancient oasis
was the first city conquered by
the Israelites, led by Joshua,
after they emerged from their
40 years in the wilderness.

The Ark of the Covenant ⑦
At Shiloh the Jews built the first
temple and placed in it the Ark
of the Covenant, the sacred
container of the tablets of the
Ten Commandments. The
Ark is shown here in a 13th-
century illumination being
carried by two angels.

Samson and Delilah ⑧
The climax of this story, in which
Samson pulls down the Philistines'
temple, killing himself and his
enemies, is described as taking
place in Gaza (Judges 14–16).

Megiddo •
Mount ⑩ Carmel
SEA OF GALILEE
Jordan River
GILEAD
Shiloh ⑦
Jerusalem ② ⑥ Jericho
⑨ Ha-Ela Valley
⑤ Mount Nebo
bron ③
DEAD SEA
Beersheba
Sodom ①
MOAB

David Defeats Goliath ⑨
As the champion of the Israelites during the reign
of King Saul, David defeated Goliath and routed
the Philistines (I Samuel 17). The site of the battle
is given as the Ha-Ela Valley, northwest of Hebron.

Elijah and the Prophets of Baal ⑩
Elijah challenged the prophets of the Canaanite god
Baal (left). An altar was set up and sacrifices prepared.
Only Elijah's offering burst into flames, showing it
had been acknowledged and proving who the true
God was (I Kings 18). The traditional site of this
event is Mount Carmel, at Haifa (see p157).

THE OLD TESTAMENT AS HISTORY

Unlike Mesopotamia or Egypt, where ancient texts have
allowed the development of a detailed historical framework,
the Holy Land has yielded few written archives. The only
such resource is the Bible. The later books, which describe
events not too far removed from the time they were written,
may be relatively accurate. For example, events recounted
in Kings I and II can be corroborated by contemporary
Assyrian inscriptions. However, the historical basis of stories
such as those relating to Abraham, Moses or Solomon, must
be viewed with caution. The Old Testament as we know
it was compiled from a variety of sources, no earlier than
the 6th century BC. These narratives might well contain
kernels of historical reality, but by the time they came to
be set down they were essentially no more than folk tales.

**Assyrian obelisk (825 BC) showing
Israelite King Jehu (I Kings 19)**

Judaism

JEWISHNESS IS NOT JUST a matter of religion but of belonging to a people. Jews believe themselves to be descended from Abraham, to whom God promised a land "unto thee, and to thy seed after thee". Judaism traditionally passes through the female line or by conversion, different Jewish movements (Orthodox, Conservative, Reform) having different requirements. Practising Jews conduct their life by the *Torah*, which can be translated as "instruction" or "guidance". Its core is the Five Books of Moses, but the Torah also includes all the teachings and laws within the Hebrew Bible (Old Testament) and subsequent interpretations by rabbinic scholars. The creation of the State of Israel has presented the Jewish people with new political and religious challenges.

The menorah, a seven-branched candlestick, derives from the candlestick that originally stood in Solomon's Temple.

THE WESTERN WALL
This is all that remains of the Jews' great Temple *(see pp42–3)*, built to hold the Ark of the Covenant *(see p19)*. It is the holiest of all Jewish sites and a major centre of pilgrimage *(see p83)*.

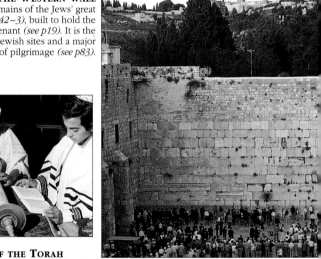

THE SCROLLS OF THE TORAH
The Torah is traditionally inscribed on scrolls. During a synagogue service the scrolls are ceremonially raised to the congregation before being read. It is an honour to be called upon to read the scrolls. A boy of 13 years of age or a girl of 12 is *bar* or *bat mitzu* a "child of the commanc ment", entitled to read from the scroll at a public service.

The Scrolls, when not in use, are placed in the ark. They may be kept in an ornamental box (right) or else tied with a binder inside a decorated cover, adorned with a breast-plate, yad, bells or crown.

The yad ("hand") is a pointer used to avoid touching the sacred text. It is also meant to direct the reader's attention to the precise word and to encourage clear and correct pronunciation.

Traditional Jewish life is measured by the regular weekly day of rest, Shabbat *(from sundown Friday to sundown Saturday), and a great many festivals (see pp34–7). The blowing of the* shofar *(a ram's horn trumpet) marks* Rosh ha-Shanah, *the Jewish New Year.*

DIVISIONS IN JUDAISM

As a result of their history of dispersion and exile, there are Jewish communities in most countries of the world. Over the centuries, different customs have developed in the various communities. The two main strands, with their own distinctive customs, are the Sephardim, descendants of Spanish Jews expelled from Spain in 1492, and the Ashkenazim, descendants of Eastern European Jews. In Western Europe and the US, some Jews adapted their faith to the conditions of modern life, by such steps as improving the status of women. This divided the faith into Reform (modernizers) and Orthodox (traditionalists), with Conservative Jews somewhere in between. Israeli Jews are frequently secular or maintain only some ritual practices. The ultra-Orthodox, or *haredim,* adhere to an uncompromising form of Judaism, living in separate communities.

Yemenite Jewess in wedding dress

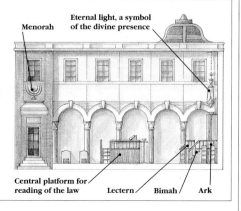

Ultra-Orthodox Jews in Jerusalem's Mea Shearim district in distinctive black garb

THE SYNAGOGUE

Synagogue architecture generally reflects the architecture of the host community, but with many standard elements. There must be an ark, symbolizing the Ark of the Covenant, usually placed against the wall facing Jerusalem. In front of the ark hangs an eternal light *(ner tamid).* The liturgy is read from the lectern at the *bimah,* the platform in front of the ark. The congregation sits around the hall, although in some synagogues women are segregated. Traditionally, a full service cannot take place without a *minyan:* a group of 10 men.

Eternal light, a symbol of the divine presence

Menorah

Central platform for reading of the law

Lectern

Bimah

Ark

Christianity

To HIS FOLLOWERS, Jesus of Nazareth was more than just a prophet, he was the Son of God and bringer of a new covenant replacing the one given by God to Abraham *(see p20)*. His Crucifixion in Jerusalem came to be seen as self-sacrifice for the salvation of humankind and inspired a new religious movement based on his teachings. At first this existed as a subset of Judaism; Jesus came to be known as Christ (*Christos*, the anointed one, in Greek), as he was held to be the Messiah of Jewish prophecies. However, the new religion spread far beyond Judaea. It saw persecution, then recognition by the Roman Empire, eventually becoming its dominant religion in the 4th century AD.

The cross is a symbol of the Crucifixion of Christ. An empty cross shows that he has risen from the dead.

THE EUCHARIST (MASS)

Greek Orthodox priests celebrate the Eucharist, the taking of bread and wine, representing the body and blood of Christ. One of the central sacraments of Christianity, it was instituted by Jesus himself at the Last Supper *(see p113)*.

The Christian Bible is in two parts: the Old Testament consists of Jewish sacred texts; the New Testament relates the life and teaching of Jesus and his Apostles. The latter was written from the mid-1st century. Most early texts were in Greek; a definitive Latin version by St Jerome (see p175) appeared in about AD 404. The Protestant Reformation inspired translations into many other languages, such as this English version, from the 16th century.

...ons play a major role in the Greek and Russian Orthodox churches. This example from St Catherine's Monastery (see pp222–5) shows Christ in Majesty. Usually painted on wood, they are used as aids to devotion, bringing the worshipper into the presence of the subject.

The Virgin and Child is a favourite Christian image. Depictions of the baby Jesus emphasize the human side of his nature, while the cult of his mother, the Virgin Mary, allows the faithful to identify with the joys and suffering of motherhood.

A Palm Sunday procession recreates Christ's entry into Jerusalem. This is a prelude to Holy Week, the most important Christian festival, commemorating the Crucifixion on Good Friday and Christ's Resurrection on Easter Sunday.

CHRISTIAN DENOMINATIONS

Almost all the major Christian churches are represented in Jerusalem. The Greek Orthodox *(see p96)* and Syrian churches were the first to be established in the city. Other ancient Christian communities include the Armenians *(see p103)*, Ethiopians and Copts. The Roman Catholic Church established its own Patriarchate here in the wake of the Crusades, and the most recent arrivals were the Protestants. The Greek Orthodox, Greek Catholic and Roman Catholic churches have large congregations, mostly of Palestinian Arabs, while priests and officials tend to be Greek and Italian.

Syrian Orthodox Christmas in Bethlehem

Procession of Ethiopian priests in Jerusalem

Armenian priests in their black hooded copes

CHURCHES IN THE HOLY LAND

The first churches did not appear in the Holy Land until around AD 200 – the earliest Christians gathered together in each other's homes. Roman suspicion of unauthorized sects kept these churches underground. However, the conversion to Christianity of the Roman emperor Constantine signalled a rash of building on the sites connected with the life of Christ. The usual type of Byzantine church was the basilica, a longitudinal structure with a nave (central aisle) lit by windows in the walls of the side aisles. The apse area, containing the altar, was frequently concealed by an iconostasis, a three-panelled screen adorned with icons.

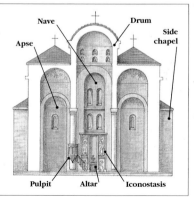

Nave   Drum

Side chapel

Apse

Pulpit   Altar   Iconostasis

Islam

ISLAM WAS FOUNDED by Muhammad, a former merchant from Mecca in Arabia. Born around AD 570, at the age of 40 he began to receive revelations of the word of Allah. These continued for the rest of his life and were transcribed as the Quran. Muhammad's preachings were not well received in Mecca and in 622 he and his followers were forced to flee for Medina. This flight, or *hejira*, constitutes year zero in the Islamic calendar. Before Muhammad died in 632, he had returned to conquer Mecca. Within a further four years, the armies of Islam had swept out of the Arabian desert and conquered the Holy Land.

The crescent moon, the symbol of Islam, has resonances of the lunar calendar, which orders Muslim religious life.

DOME OF THE ROCK
One of the oldest and most beautiful of all mosques, the richly decorated Dome *(see pp68–71)* is the third most holy site of Islam after the Prophet's cities of Mecca and Medina.

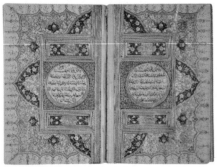

The Quran, the holy book of Islam, is regarded as the exact word of Allah. Muslims believe that it can never be truly understood unless read in Arabic: translations into other languages can only ever paraphrase. The Quran is divided into 114 chapters, or suras, covering many topics, including matters relating to family, marriage, and legal and ethical concerns.

THE FIVE PILLARS OF FAITH
Islam rests on what are known as the "five pillars of faith". The first of these, known as the *Shahada*, is a simple declaration that "There is no god but Allah and Muhammad is his Prophet". The second pillar is the set daily prayers, performed in the direction of Mecca five times a day (in practice, however, few Muslims completely observe this). The third pillar is the fasting during daylight hours that takes place for the whole of the holy month of Ramadan, and the fourth is the giving of alms. The fifth pillar is *Haj*: at least once in their lifetime all Muslims must, if they are able, make the pilgrimage to Mecca, birthplace of Muhammad.

Muslim at prayer

House decorated with pilgrimage scenes, indicating the owner has made the *Haj*

Muslim festivals are relatively infrequent, with just four major dates in the calendar (see p36). The most important of these are Eid el-Adha, marking the time of the pilgrimage, or Haj, and Eid el-Fitr, which marks the end of Ramadan. Celebrations tend to be communal and take the form of great feasts, often out of doors.

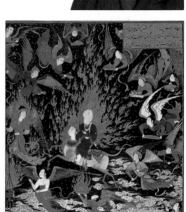

The imam is an Islamic teacher, usually attached to a particular mosque. He delivers the khutba, or sermon, at the midday prayers on Friday. These prayers are always the best attended of the week.

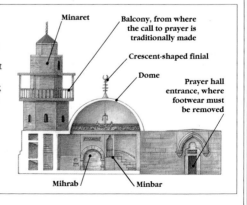

The Night Journey
One of the core episodes in the life of the Prophet Muhammad was his Night Journey, when he was carried from Mecca to Jerusalem and from there made the Miraj, the ascent through the heavens to God's presence, returning to Mecca in the morning.

THE MOSQUE

Mosques come in many shapes and sizes but they all share some common characteristics. Chief of these is the mihrab, the niche that indicates the direction of Mecca. Most mosques also have a *minbar*, from which the imam delivers his Friday sermon. A dome usually covers the prayer hall. The minaret serves as a platform for the delivery of the call to prayer, once made by a *muezzin*, but these days more often a pre-recorded cassette broadcast through a loudspeaker.

Minaret

Balcony, from where the call to prayer is traditionally made

Crescent-shaped finial

Dome

Prayer hall entrance, where footwear must be removed

Mihrab

Minbar

Sites of the New Testament

THE LIFE OF JESUS CHRIST, as narrated in the gospels, was played out in a relatively small geographical arena. He was born in Bethlehem; he grew up in Nazareth; his baptism took place at the Jordan River near Jericho; most of his public activity was carried out around the shores of the Sea of Galilee, where he preached, narrated parables and worked miracles; and his crucifixion, resurrection and ascension all occurred in Jerusalem. Unlike the sites of the Old Testament, those of the New Testament saw the rise of sanctuaries, churches and chapels built within two or three centuries of the death of Jesus. For this reason, a number of these sites have some claim to authenticity, although, as with so much in the Holy Land, nothing is beyond dispute.

The Annunciation ①
At Nazareth Mary was visited by the angel Gabriel and told of her forthcoming child (Luke 1: 26–38). The episode is commemorated by the Basilica of the Annunciation (see p160).

The Birth of Jesus ②
In Bethlehem Jesus was born in a manger and an angel appeared to shepherds in nearby fields, telling them of the birth (Luke 2: 1-20). A church was first built on the site in the 4th century (see pp174–5) and a star marks the alleged site of the Nativity.

The Wedding at Cana ③
Jesus performed his first miracle at this small village near Nazareth, at a wedding where he turned water into wine (John 2: 1–11).

Joppa (Jaffa)•

The Baptism of Christ ④
John the Baptist, a cousin of Jesus, baptized and preached the coming of the Messiah on the shores of the Jordan River. John recognized Jesus as the "Lamb of God" (Matthew 3). The site traditionally identified with the baptism is east of Jericho on the Jordanian border. It lies in a military zone and is only accessible to pilgrims for the Greek Orthodox Epiphany in January and on the third Thursday in October.

0 kilometres 50
0 miles 30

The Temptations ⑤
Following his baptism, Jesus went into the desert, where the Devil tried to tempt him from his 40-day fast (Matthew 4: 1–11). The Greek Orthodox Monastery of the Temptation on Mount Quarntal, just north of Jericho, marks the site of the supposed encounter (see p170).

The First Disciples ⑥
*Christ's first Disciples were fishermen he
encountered on the banks of the Sea of
Galilee. He persuaded them to leave their
nets to become "fishers of men" (Matthew
5: 18–22). In the mid-1980s a fishing
boat was discovered in the mud of the
lake. It dates back to the 1st century AD,
roughly the time of Christ, and is on display
at Kibbutz Ginosar (see pp162–3).*

Tabkha ⑦⑧
⑥ Sea of Galilee
Cana ③
Nazareth ①
GALILEE
aesarea   •Beth Shean
DECAPOLIS
SAMARIA
Jordan River
⑤ Mount Quarntal
④ River Jordan
• JERUSALEM
② Bethlehem
JUDAEA   *DEAD SEA*

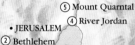

The Multiplication of the Loaves and Fishes ⑦
*The gospels locate this famous miracle, more
colourfully known as the "feeding of the 5,000"
(Matthew 15: 32–39), on the shores of the Sea of
Galilee. The episode is commemorated in a church
at Tabkha on the lake shore (see p164), which has
a mosaic in front of the altar showing a basket of
bread flanked by fish.*

The Sermon on the Mount ⑧
*The longest and one of the key
sermons in the teachings of Jesus,
the Sermon on the Mount, begins
with the Beatitudes: "Blessed are
the meek for they shall inherit the
earth..." (Matthew 5–7). Tradition
has it delivered on a small rise
at Tabkha. It is celebrated by
the nearby, octagonal Church
of the Beatitudes (see p164).*

JESUS IN JERUSALEM

In what was to be the last week of his life, Jesus made
a triumphal entrance into Jerusalem shortly before the
Jewish feast of Passover. He proceeded to the Temple
where he drove out the money changers (Matthew 21:
12–13). He gathered his Disciples to eat a Passover meal;
this was to be the Last Supper. After the meal they went
to the Garden of Gethsemane *(see p110)* where Jesus
was arrested (Matthew 26: 36–56). Condemned by the
Jewish authorities, he was put on trial before Pontius
Pilate, possibly in the Antonia Fortress or the Citadel
(see p63). After being paraded through the city *(see
pp28–9)*, he was crucified and buried at Golgotha,
traditionally identified with the site of the Holy Sepulchre
church. Following his Resurrection, Jesus departed earth
with his Ascension from the Mount of Olives *(see p108)*.

**The Last Supper (Matthew 26: 18–30),
traditionally associated with a room
on Mount Zion *(see p113)***

Via Dolorosa

Via Dolorosa street sign

THE VIA DOLOROSA in Jerusalem traditionally traces the last steps of Jesus Christ *(see pp62–3)*, from where he was tried to Calvary, where he was crucified, and the tomb in the Church of the Holy Sepulchre, where he is said to have been buried. There is no historical basis for the route, which has changed over the centuries. However, the tradition is so strong that countless pilgrims walk the route, identifying with Jesus's suffering as they stop at the 14 Stations of the Cross, each connected with a particular event in the story.

LOCATOR MAP

▨ Via Dolorosa

━ Jerusalem City Walls

Sixth Station
Veronica wipes away Jesus's blood and sweat, and her handkerchief reveals an impression of his face. The Chapel of St Veronica commemorates the story, which is not recorded in the gospels.

Seventh Station
Jesus falls for the second time. A large Roman column in a Franciscan chapel indicates this station.

Eighth Station
Jesus consoles the women of Jerusalem (Luke 23: 28). The spot is marked by a Latin cross on the wall of a Greek Orthodox Monastery.

Fourteenth Station
The last Station of the Cross is the Holy Sepulchre itself. The tomb belonged to Joseph of Arimathea, who asked Pilate for Jesus's body.

Ninth Station
Jesus falls for the third time. The place is marked by part of the shaft of a Roman column at the entrance to the Ethiopian Monastery (see pp89–91).

Steps to Ninth Station

Tenth to Thirteenth Stations
These four Stations (Jesus is stripped of his clothes; he is nailed to the cross; he dies; he is taken down from the cross) are all in the place identified as Golgotha (Calvary) within the Church of the Holy Sepulchre (see pp88–91).

First Station
Jesus is condemned to death. The traditional site of the Roman fortress where this took place lies inside a Muslim college, the Madrasa el-Omariyya (see p66). Franciscan friars begin their walk along the Via Dolorosa here every Friday.

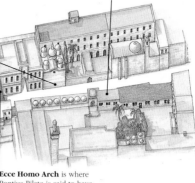

Second Station
Jesus takes up the cross, after being flogged, and crowned with thorns. This station is in front of the Franciscan Monastery of the Flagellation (see p62).

Ecce Homo Arch is where Pontius Pilate is said to have uttered the words "Behold the Man" *(see p62).*

0 metres	50
0 yards	50

Fourth Station
Jesus meets his mother Mary. This point is in front of the Armenian Church of Our Lady of the Spasm, which is built over an earlier Crusader church. This sculpture above the door shows the grief of Mary as she sees her son walking to his death.

Third Station
Jesus falls beneath the weight of the cross for the first time. This is commemorated by a small chapel with a marble relief above the door.

Fifth Station
Simon of Cyrene is ordered by the Roman soldiers to help Jesus carry the cross (Mark 15: 21). A Franciscan oratory marks this point on the Via Dolorosa, which is the start of the ascent to Calvary. This painting also shows St Veronica (see Sixth Station).

Celebrated Visitors

AS A SPIRITUAL OR UTOPIAN concept, Jerusalem has, over the centuries, been celebrated by poets and artists who have never been there, and who would perhaps hardly have known where it was on the map. However, the Holy City and the Holy Land have also been the subject of a no less impressive number of accounts, journals and paintings by a great many well-known travellers, writers and artists who did visit. From the early 19th century, the region also became a magnet for a steady flow of archaeologists and biblical scholars.

Archaeologist Charles Warren

EARLY PILGRIMS AND TRAVELLERS

THE ESTABLISHMENT of Christianity as the religion of the Roman Empire in the 4th century AD triggered a wave of visitors, drawn by the region's biblical associations. One of the first pilgrims we know of is a nun named Egeria, who was perhaps Spanish, and visited the Holy Land from AD 380 to 415. An 11th-century manuscript found in Italy in 1884 contained a copy of her travel diary, which makes frequent mention of places such as Sinai and Jerusalem. Present-day writer William Dalrymple used a similar historical account (the journal of John Moschos, a 5th-century monk who wandered the Byzantine world)

as the basis for his own Holy Land travels recounted in *From the Holy Mountain* (1996).

Early travellers also visited the Holy Land for trade. The most famous of the merchants was Marco Polo who, in the course of his extensive travels, was entertained by the Crusaders in their halls at Acre.

The works of early Muslim travellers include some lively descriptions of the Holy City. The 10th-century historian El-Muqaddasi described Jerusalem as "a golden basin filled with scorpions". The Moroccan scholar Ibn Batuta

Lady Hester Stanhope

who, in the 14th century, travelled over 120,000 km (75,000 miles), also visited Palestine. His journals describe the Tombs of the Prophets in Hebron *(see p176)*, and Jerusalem's Dome of the Rock *(see pp70–71)*, of which he wrote, "It glows like a mass of light and flashes with the gleam of lightning."

REDISCOVERING THE HOLY LAND

IN THE WAKE of Napoleon's invasion of Egypt (1798) and subsequent expedition into Palestine, and the interest it generated in the Orient, Europeans began to visit the Holy Land. First to arrive were the explorers and adventuring archaeologists, typified by Johann Ludwig Burckhardt *(see p198)*, who was one of the first Westerners ever to visit Jerash, and who discovered Petra in 1812. Lady Hester Stanhope was an eccentric British aristocrat who escaped from her high-society existence to live in Palestine. Although she did conduct some haphazard excavations in Ashkelon (north of Gaza) in 1814, she is more famous for wearing men's clothing in order to avoid wearing the veil.

In 1838, Edward Robinson, an American Protestant clergyman with an interest in biblical geography, was the first to make a proper critical study of supposed holy sites; his name is commemorated in Robinson's Arch south of the Western Wall *(see p87)*. In 1867–70, excavations south of the Haram esh-Sharif were carried out by Lieutenant Charles Warren of the Royal Engineers, a man who, some 20 years later, would lead the investigations into the infamous Jack the Ripper serial murders in

Pilgrims in Jerusalem from the *Book of Marvels* on Marco Polo's travels

Jerusalem from the Mount of Olives (1859) by Edward Lear

London. He is remembered in Jerusalem today through "Warren's Shaft", the popular name for the Jebusite well at the City of David archaeological site *(see p111).*

THE WRITERS

As THE GROUND was broken by the early explorers, a steady stream of adventurous travellers followed in their wake, recording their experiences for eager audiences back in the West. François René de Chateaubriand's brief sojourn in Jaffa, Jerusalem, Bethlehem, Jericho and the Dead Sea area as related in his *Journey from Paris to Jerusalem* (1811) initiated the fashion for travel journals and descriptions of the Holy Land among 19th-century literati. The French poet Alphonse de Lamartine followed in his tracks in 1832, recording his experiences in *Remembrances of a Journey to the East.* In 1850 the creator of Madame Bovary, Gustave Flaubert, visited Palestine and Egypt, but found Jerusalem oppressive, writing in his diary, "It seems as if the Lord's curse hovers over the city." American authors Herman Melville and Mark Twain,

both visiting in the mid-19th century were hardly any more enamoured. Melville, author of *Moby Dick*, thought the Holy Sepulchre church "a sickening cheat". Twain was even more caustic, commenting in his 1895 book *The Innocents Abroad*, "There will be no Second Coming. Jesus has been to Jerusalem once and he will not come again." The tradition of scathing comment continued in the 20th century with George Bernard Shaw advising Zionists in the 1930s to erect notices at popular holy sites stating, "Do not bother to stop here, it isn't genuine." More recent writers have been kinder: Nobel laureate Saul Bellow produced a warm-hearted account of the city in *To Jerusalem and Back* (1976).

THE ARTISTS

WITH THE WRITERS came the artists, the best-known and most prolific of whom was David Roberts, a Scot who visited the Holy Land in 1839. He produced an enormous volume of very precise lithographs, collected and published in 1842, which ensured him fame in his own lifetime. His work remains ubiquitous today, adorning almost every book published on the Holy Land *(see pp8–9)*. Better known for his whimsical verse, artist, writer and traveller Edward Lear (1812–63) spent time in the Holy Land, painting a fine series of watercolours.

The English evangelical painter William Holman Hunt, who belonged to the Pre-Raphaelite movement, settled on Ha-Neviim Street in Jerusalem in 1854, where he painted several of his most famous works. This century, Russian-born Jewish artist Marc Chagall (1887–1985) has become closely identified with Jerusalem. His naïve-styled work, with its **Mark Twain** strong Jewish themes can be seen at the Israel Museum *(see pp128–33)*, in tapestry form at the Knesset *(see p127)*, and in stained-glass windows at the synagogue of the Hadassah Hospital *(see p135)*.

The Finding of the Saviour in the Temple (1854–60) by William Holman Hunt

The Landscape and Wildlife of the Holy Land

Asian buttercup

FROM THE LIFE-GIVING Jordan River in the north to the scattered oases of the Negev and Sinai deserts in the south, water is precious in the Holy Land. In Israel it is rare to see water that is not used for irrigating land or creating fishponds. Away from the cultivated areas of Galilee and the coast, visitors will encounter a great variety of environments: mountains in the Golan Heights, green hills in Galilee, stony desert in the Negev and sandy desert in southern Jordan. Then there are the strange lifeless waters of the Dead Sea *(see p177)* and the astonishing abundance of life on the reefs of the Red Sea *(see pp216–17)*.

The Jordan River, which flows from the Golan Heights to the Dead Sea

THE DESERT

Much of the Holy Land is desert. South of the Dead Sea, the landscape changes from scrubby steppe to rocky desert with spectacular craters such as Makhtesh Ramon *(see p183)*. The one common tree is the hardy acacia. Animals such as gazelles, ibexes and hyraxes are found at wadis and oases, but the predators that hunted them, the striped hyena and the wolf, are now extremely rare. A more common sight is that of a wheeling vulture or eagle.

Acacia trees growing in the Negev Desert

The fleet-footed Dorcas gazelle is found in the southern part of Israel and the Sinai peninsula, but in dwindling numbers.

Oases are rare in the deserts of this region. Those with plentiful water, like this one planted with date palms near the Dead Sea, are exploited to the full. Others act as magnets for the wildlife of the region.

A rock hyrax basks in the hot sun. Hyraxes are hard to spot as they remain hidden among the rocks if it is overcast or cold.

Wadis are riverbeds, dry for much of the year. After spring rains, they can fill rapidly with torrents of water, causing a brief explosion of flowers and grasses. Trees that manage to survive in these unpredictable conditions include the acacia and terebinth.

Ice plants are succulents that thrive in desert conditions, surviving drought by storing water in their fleshy leaves.

MOUNTAINS, HILLS AND CLIFFS

The highest mountains in the region are those on the Sinai peninsula and Mount Hermon in the Golan Heights. Trees on the lower slopes in the Golan include Aleppo pine and Syrian juniper. Vegetation in Sinai is very sparse as it is in the spectacular, rocky cliffs and gorges in the Judaean Hills and around the Dead Sea.

Egyptian vultures are found in many of the wilder areas, such as the Negev and the mountains of northern Israel and northwestern Jordan.

The Golan Heights

Ibexes live high in the mountains, descending, in the cool of the morning and late afternoon, to wadis and oases to graze and drink.

The Madonna lily's beautiful white flowers symbolize purity. A number of Holy Land plants have names inspired by the Bible.

Prickly pears thrive in the hot dry climate. Introduced originally from the Americas, they are much appreciated for their sweet refreshing fruit.

Oranges are one of many fruits grown in the fertile areas; they constitute a major export for Israel.

The laughing dove, so called for its rising and falling, laughing cry, has spread dramatically since the 1930s in the cultivated regions of Israel and western Jordan.

CULTIVATED AREAS

Israel makes maximum use of the land available for agriculture, even using irrigation to create artificial oases in the desert. There are extensive plantations of oranges and other citrus fruits, avocados, bananas and dates. Jordan is less fortunate, its only fertile area being along the eastern side of the Jordan Valley. In Sinai there are only rare oases such as Feiran (see p225).

Neatly cultivated fields at Migdal on the western shore of the Sea of Galilee

BIRDWATCHING IN THE HOLY LAND

White pelicans taking off from a field near the Hula Reserve

Migrating stork

Israel lies on one of the most important routes for migratory birds that winter in Africa then return to Europe and Asia to nest in the spring. Larger species include both black and white storks and many birds of prey. In terms of the number of species that can be seen, the area around Eilat (see p215) on the Gulf of Aqaba is reckoned the best place for watching migrating birds in the world. Another popular destination for birdwatchers is the Hula Reserve, an area of protected wetlands north of the Sea of Galilee.

THE HOLY LAND
THROUGH THE YEAR

SHARED AS IT IS by Jews, Christians and Muslims, Jerusalem has an over-abundance of religious holidays. Add to these secular holidays, commemorations and a variety of cultural festivals, and rarely a week passes in the holy city in which some significant event is not taking place. While visitors may well want to time their visit to coincide with some of these happenings, they may equally want to avoid

Kaparot ritual, eve of Yom Kippur

others. During religious holidays such as Passover (and Ramadan in Israel's Arab areas and in Jordan) many shops, cafés, restaurants and museums are closed for the duration or open only for limited hours, and accommodation is hard to find and inflated in price. Its warm climate makes the Holy Land an all-year-round destination, though the extreme heat of July and August is best avoided.

SPRING

SPRING IN Jerusalem usually arrives in the latter part of March. This coincides with the Christian Easter and Jewish Passover celebrations, when the city is filled to bursting with pilgrims. The religious festivities are accompanied by cultural events, which increase in frequency as summer approaches. The weather is mild, and this is the best time for trips to Israel's many parks, even though around the Dead Sea the thermometer is already regularly above 30° C (86° F).

MARCH

International Book Fair, Jerusalem. Held every two years, with the next in 2001.
Easter falls from late March to April *(23 Apr in 2000)* for

Catholics and Protestants; the Orthodox and Armenian churches celebrate a week later. Jerusalem's Easter week begins with a Palm Sunday procession from the Mount of Olives to St Anne's *(see p65)*. The most striking ceremony is the Holy Fire *(see p89)*, held on the Saturday of the Orthodox Easter *(29 Apr in 2000)*.

APRIL

Passover, or Pesach, falls from late March to the second half of April *(20–26 Apr in 2000)*. It celebrates liberation from slavery under the pharaohs in Egypt. During the week-long festival, shops and restaurants are closed, and public transport limited.

Palm Sunday procession in Jerusalem moving along the Via Dolorosa

Armenian Holocaust Day *(24 Apr)*, Jerusalem. Marked with a procession, then a service at St James's Cathedral in memory of the Turkish massacres *(see pp102–3)*.
Mimouna is celebrated the day after Passover ends *(27 Apr in 2000)* by North African Jews. Outdoor festivities are held throughout Israel.
Music Festival *(Passover)*, Jaffa *(see pp154–5)*. A festival of choral music performed by Israeli and foreign choirs.

MAY

Holocaust Day *(2 May in 2000)*. Periodically throughout the day sirens signal for two minutes' silence in remembrance of the victims of the Holocaust.
Remembrance Day *(9 May in 2000)*. In the same fashion as Holocaust Day,

Spring in Israel, the perfect time for exploring the countryside

AVERAGE DAILY HOURS OF SUNSHINE IN JERUSALEM

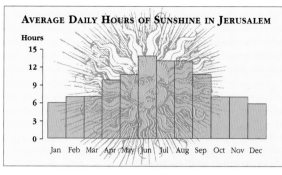

Hours

15 —
12 —
9 —
6 —
3 —
0 —

Jan Feb Mar Apr May Jun Jul Aug Sep Oct Nov Dec

Sunshine Chart
Even during the winter, most days have some sunshine. The summer sun can be very fierce and adequate precautions against sunburn and sunstroke should be taken. Sun screen, a hat and sunglasses are recommended. Drinking plenty of water reduces the risk of dehydration.

this day honours the Israeli dead from past wars.

Independence Day *(10 May in 2000)*. Israeli statehood is commemorated with parades, concerts and fireworks.

Festival of Israel *(May/Jun)*. The most important cultural event in Israel: three weeks of music, dance and theatre in Tel Aviv, Jerusalem, Haifa and the Roman theatres at Caesarea *(see p156)* and Beth Shean *(see p165)*.

Crowds watch an Independence Day air display on Tel Aviv's sea front

SUMMER

W ITH FEWER religious festivals, the attention over summer shifts away from Jerusalem to the coast, where the soaring temperatures are tempered by sea breezes, and to the towns of Galilee, where the altitude partially counteracts the heat.

JUNE

Ascension falls 40 days after Easter *(1 Jun in 2000; a week later for Orthodox)*. It celebrates Christ's ascent to Heaven and in Jerusalem it is marked by prayers on the Mount of Olives *(see pp106–7)*.

Performance by visiting Shakespearean company at the Jerash Festival

Beach Festival *(all summer)*, Tel Aviv *(see pp152–3)*. The city-centre beaches are the venue for rock concerts and free open-air cinema.

JULY

Film Festival *(early Jul)*, Jerusalem. Held at the Cinematheque *(see p118)*, this features the work of Israeli and foreign directors.

Jaffa Nights *(1st week)*, Tel Aviv. Two weeks of open-air concerts and shows in the setting of old Jaffa.

Jazz Festival *(Jul–Aug)*, Eilat *(see p215)*. Held on the shores of the Red Sea, this festival draws an array of international musicians.

Jerash Festival *(late Jul and Aug)*, Jerash. Jordan's most important festival is held in the spectacular setting of the Roman ruins *(see pp188–9)*. It includes folk dance, ballet, opera, poetry competitions, theatre, classical music and displays of local handicrafts.

AUGUST

Puppet Festival, Jerusalem. This is a festival aimed at the young, with shows in various venues, notably the Train Theatre in the Liberty Bell Gardens.

Klezmer Festival, Safed *(see p161)*. A festival devoted to traditional Eastern European Jewish music.

Summer Festival *(Aug–Sep)*, Nazareth *(see p160)*. A festival of theatre, cinema and contemporary Arab music.

JEWISH HOLIDAYS

The Jewish calendar is lunar, meaning that each month begins and ends at the new moon. Jewish holidays therefore fall on a different date each year compared to the Western calendar; however, they do remain roughly fixed about a certain time of the year.

Jewish girl dressed for Mimouna

AVERAGE MONTHLY TEMPERATURE IN JERUSALEM

	°C	°F
	30	85
	25	75
	20	65
	15	55
	10	45
	5	
	0	32

Jan Feb Mar Apr May Jun Jul Aug Sep Oct Nov Dec

Temperature
Summers in Jerusalem are hot, temperatures frequently climbing to over 30° C (86° F). In winter, the thermometer can drop to near freezing, with even the occasional snowfall. The chart (left) shows average daily maximum and average daily minimum temperatures for each month.

AUTUMN

IN TERMS of the weather, autumn is the ideal time to visit Jerusalem. However, several major Jewish holidays occur in September and October, seriously disrupting public transport and reducing opening hours for shops and restaurants. It is also necessary to make hotel reservations well in advance.

SEPTEMBER

Rosh ha-Shanah *(30 Sep in 2000).* The Jewish New Year. It marks the start of ten days of prayer that end with Yom Kippur. On the penultimate day some Jews perform Kaparot, a ceremony in which a live fowl is waved over the head to absorb sins.

OCTOBER

Yom Kippur *(9 Oct in 2000).* The Day of Atonement, the holiest day of the year, which Jews observe by fasting for

Sukkoth booths, in which meals are taken for the feast's duration

26 hours, not having sex and not using cosmetics, the whole country coming to a virtual standstill. The *shofar*, the ram's horn, is sounded at synagogue services.
Sukkoth *(14 Oct in 2000).* This Jewish feast commemorates the Israelites' 40 years in the wilderness after their liberation from slavery in Egypt. Makeshift "booths" are built out of doors, in which all meals are taken for seven days. The ultra-orthodox even sleep in these huts.

Fringe Theatre Festival, Acre *(see pp158–9).* Local and international avant-garde companies perform in venues around the town.

NOVEMBER

Jerusalem Marathon *(late Oct/early Nov).* One of the major sports events in Israel with hundreds of Israelis and foreigners participating.
Palestinian Independence Day *(15 Nov).* Celebrated in the Autonomous Territories, this commemorates the Palestine National Authority's proclamation of the Palestinian state in 1988.

WINTER

CHRISTMAS IS obviously a good time to visit Bethlehem and Nazareth, especially if you can attend one of the special church services. It does occasionally snow in Jerusalem, and snow on the Golan Heights sees the ski-lifts operating.

MUSLIM FESTIVALS

Eid el-Fitr and Eid el-Adha are the major feasts, both lasting two or three days, and celebrated by the slaughter of sheep. The former marks the end of Ramadan, the month of fasting, observed by all devout Muslims. **Muslim at prayer**
Other significant days include the Prophet's Birthday (Moulid en-Nabi) and Islamic New Year (Ras el-Sana). The Islamic year is lunar and 11 days shorter than the Western year. This means that in terms of the Western calendar Islamic festivals fall 11 days earlier each year. Hence, in 2000 Ramadan begins on 27 November, and the following year on 16 November.

AVERAGE MONTHLY RAINFALL IN JERUSALEM

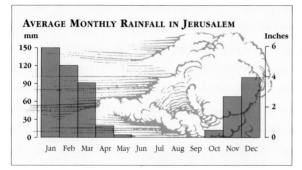

Rainfall
There is virtually no rainfall in Jerusalem from April to October. Showers begin to occur in autumn and winter, and during January and February skies are often filled with threatening grey clouds. Visitors at this time would be wise to go armed with an umbrella.

DECEMBER

Hanukkah *(22–29 Dec in 2000).* The Jewish Festival of Lights, this commemorates the reconsecration of the Temple in 164 BC *(see p40).* It lasts eight days, and is celebrated by the lighting of candles in a special eight-branched menorah.

Christmas *(24–25 Dec).* A Christmas Eve procession from Jerusalem arrives in Bethlehem for midnight mass at the Church of the Nativity *(see pp174–5).* To attend this service you must book in advance at the Christian Information Centre in Jerusalem *(see p97).* The mass is also projected on a huge screen in Manger Square. The service at Abu Ghosh *(see p135)* is also impressive. In Nazareth a colourful procession is held on the afternoon of Christmas Eve,

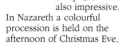

Hanukkah candles

which ends with services held in the town's six churches.

International Choir Festival *(26 Dec),* Nazareth. In the days following the choir festival, the town plays host to sacred music concerts.

Tiberias Marathon *(Dec–Feb).* Less well-known than the Jerusalem Marathon, this attracts many runners because of the scenery along the route *(see pp162–3).*

Skiing on Mount Hermon, possible during January and February

JANUARY

Al-Fatah Day *(1 Jan).* A Palestinian national holiday marking the birth (1965) of the Al-Fatah political party.

Orthodox Christmas *(7 Jan),* Jerusalem. This is celebrated on Christmas Eve with a service at the Holy Trinity Church in the Russian Compound *(see p120).*

Armenian Christmas *(19 Jan),* Jerusalem. This is celebrated by Christmas Eve mass at St James's Cathedral in the Old City *(see pp102–3).*

FEBRUARY

Purim *(21 Mar in 2000).* This festival celebrates the salvation of the Jews in Persia from threatened genocide (related in the Old Testament Book of Esther). Children wear fancy dress, while adults participate with the giving of gifts, feasting and drinking.

Jewish children dressed up as part of Purim festivities

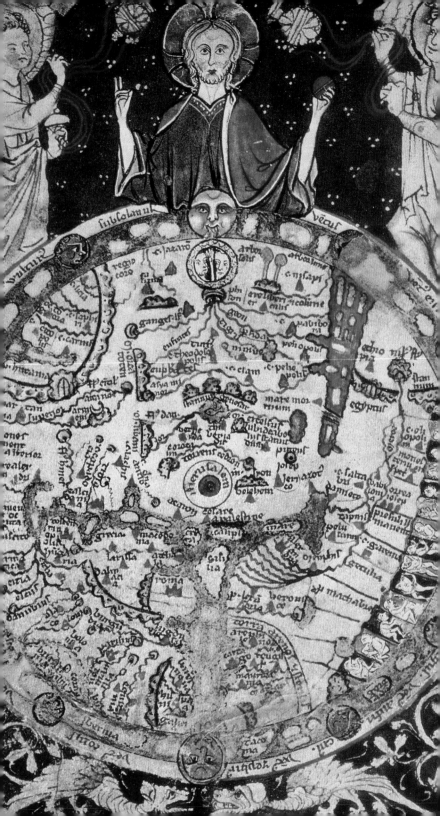

THE HISTORY OF THE HOLY LAND

SINCE PREHISTORIC TIMES *the fertile plains and scattered oases between the Nile and the rivers of Mesopotamia have been colonized by countless different peoples. The ebb and flow of nations continues to this day; as independent countries, both Israel and Jordan are barely half a century old, with the Jewish state composed of a great many nationalities, all united by their shared faith.*

Much of our knowledge of the early prehistory of the Holy Land comes from the site of Jericho, just north of the Dead Sea. Excavations have uncovered a series of settlements dating back to about 10,000 BC, when Stone Age hunters first abandoned their nomadic way of life. In settling, these people took the all-important step which led to cultivating crops and domesticating animals – a process known as the "Neolithic revolution". During the following 3,000 years small farming villages sprang up all over the region.

Philistine sarcophagus lid, 12th century BC

In the 3rd millennium BC the coastal plains witnessed the rise of a fairly uniform culture, known as the Canaanite civilization. There may never have been a single Canaanite nation; rather the Canaanites were probably organized in a series of city-states. A Canaanite army was defeated at Megiddo by the pharaoh Thutmose (1468 BC) and all the city-states were then subject to Egypt. The Canaanites nevertheless survived for two millennia – during which time they developed the world's first alphabet –

until their culture was brought to an end by the rise of two new peoples. The first were invaders who came from the sea around 1200 BC; these were the Philistines, after whom the area was called Palestine ("land of the Philistines"). The second were the Hebrew tribes, who, between about 1200 and 1000 BC, coalesced into a political entity known as Israel.

There are several theories as to how the Hebrews came to control Palestine: through hard-won battles, or possibly by peaceful infiltration. There are no historical sources to verify events, but the Old Testament tells how these tribes formed a confederation that eventually led to the birth of a united kingdom whose first sovereign was Saul. His successors, David (whose rule is traditionally given as from around 1010 to 970 BC) and Solomon (c.970–930 BC), laid the foundations for the Jewish nation. It was David, according to the Bible, who captured Jerusalem and made it the Israelite capital, and Solomon who built the Jews' First Temple there.

TIMELINE

10,000–8000 BC First permanent settlements in the region	**7000 BC** Walled settlement exists at Jericho	*Copper crown from Ein Gedi, c.4000 BC*	**c.1200 BC** Arrival of the Philistines and Hebrew tribes
9000 BC	**7000 BC**	**5000 BC**	**3000 BC**	**1000 BC**

Skull with cowrie shell eyes from Jericho, c. 7000 BC

3200 BC Emergence of Canaanite civilization

c.1010–970 BC Reign of David

c.7000–4000 BC Growth of agricultural communities

c.970–930 BC Reign of Solomon

◁ **Medieval European map, showing the holy city of Jerusalem as the centre of the world**

BABYLONIAN CAPTIVITY

According to the Bible, after Solomon died, conflicts led to the division of the Jewish nation into two separate parts: the Kingdom of Israel in the north and the Kingdom of Judaea in the south. Two centuries later, the Assyrians conquered the north, and many of the Jews of Israel were deported. When Judaea withheld tribute, it too was invaded and defeated at the battle of Lachish. The Assyrians, in turn, were defeated by the Babylonians who, in 586 BC, captured Jerusalem and destroyed Solomon's Temple, forcing the Jews of Judaea into exile. During the brief period of Babylonian captivity the Jews maintained and even strengthened their cultural and religious identity. Defeated by the Persians under Cyrus the Great in 539 BC, the Babylonians disappeared from history and the Jews were allowed to return to their land.

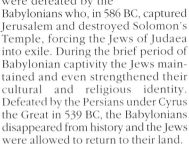

Israelite prisoners leaving Lachish after its fall to the Assyrians in 701 BC

THE SECOND TEMPLE

Returning to Jerusalem, in the 6th century BC, the Jews built a new temple on the same site as the first. This event in the history of Jerusalem marks the beginning of what is referred to as the "Second Temple" period.

The Persians remained dominant in the region until their empire was torn apart by the armies of Alexander the Great. Judaea was swallowed up in the wake of the Macedonian's triumphant progress into Egypt. On the death of Alexander, his empire was split between three generals; the dynasties they founded proceeded to fight over the spoils, with Palestine eventually going to the Syria-based Seleucids. The culture of the Greeks spread throughout the region. This era saw the rise of the Decapolis ("ten cities" in Greek), a loose grouping of Hellenistic city-states in an otherwise Semitic landscape, which included Philadelphia (Amman), Gerasa (Jerash) and Scythopolis (Beth Shean). But Jerusalem resisted. The response of the Seleucid king Antiochus IV Epiphanes (175–164 BC) was to rededicate the Jews' temple in Jerusalem to Zeus and make observance of Hebrew law punishable by death. Led by Judas Maccabeus, a priest of the Hasmonean family, the Jews rebelled in 164 BC. They defeated the Seleucids, took complete control of Jerusalem and reconsecrated their Temple.

Rule of Judaea was assumed by the Hasmoneans. However, independence for the Jews did not ensure peace. There was bitter conflict between the Hasmoneans and the Pharisees, a rival priestly sect who propounded strict observance of Hebrew religious tradition. In the struggle for influence,

The recapture of the Temple by Judas Maccabeus in his successful revolt against the Seleucids, 164 BC

TIMELINE

722 BC Assyria conquers the Kingdom of Israel and sends the Israelites into exile

586 BC The Babylonians conquer Jerusalem and destroy the First Temple

515 BC The founding of the Second Temple

 Alexander the Great whose successors Hellenized Palestine

800 BC	700 BC	600 BC	500 BC	400 BC

 The seal of Jeroboam, a 9th-century Jewish king

539 BC Cyrus the Great frees the Jews in exile in Babylon

332 BC Alexander the Great conquers Palestine

both factions asked for help from the new political and military power of the period – Rome.

THE ROMANS AND JEWISH UPRISINGS

The Romans lost no time in taking advantage of this opportunity: in 63 BC their legions took Jerusalem. The Hasmoneans were superseded by a series of Roman governors, known as procurators. Anxious not to offend local religious sensibilities, the Romans had the Jewish Herod (the Great) rule as a client king in Palestine (37–4 BC). Allowed a relatively free hand in domestic affairs, the ambitious Herod expanded his frontiers and promoted architectural projects such as the Masada and Herodion fortress complexes, the port-city of Caesarea and the grand reconstruction of the Jews' Second Temple in Jerusalem.

On Herod's death his kingdom was ruled for a brief period by his three sons before being governed directly by the Romans. A heavy tax burden, insensitive administration and the imposition of Roman culture were responsible for growing discontent among the Jews. Large numbers of Messianic claimants, revolutionary prophets and apocalyptic preachers only served to inflame the situation further. This was the political climate into which Jesus Christ was born, as described in the biblical New Testament.

Jewish clashes with Rome broke out repeatedly, culminating in a full-scale revolt in AD 66. It took the Romans four years to gain victory in this First Jewish War. When in AD 70 they finally captured Jerusalem, they destroyed the city and demolished the Temple *(see pp42–3)*. The final subjugation of the Jews occurred three years later at Masada. Judaea once again became a

Jerash, a former Decapolis city which flourished under the Romans

Roman province, but the Jews refused to be subdued and before long a second major revolt broke out.

THE EXILE OF THE JEWS

After the Second Jewish War (AD 132–5), Hadrian rebuilt Jerusalem as Aelia Capitolina, a Roman city, which Jews were forbidden to enter. Their communities were broken up and great numbers were sold into slavery and sent to Rome. Others fled, south into Egypt and across North Africa, or east to join the existing Jewish community in Babylon who had settled there after the destruction of the First Temple. This great scattering of the Jews is known as the Diaspora.

Hadrian, builder of Aelia Capitolina

BC	200 BC	100 BC	AD 1	AD 100	AD 200

164 BC The Maccabean Revolt results in Jewish independence

37–4 BC Herod the Great reigns in Judaea

AD 66–70 First Jewish War and the destruction of the Second Temple

132–5 Second Jewish War led by Simon Bar-Kokhba

3rd century BC Growth of the Decapolis

1st century BC Petra-based Nabataean empire at its height

63 BC Roman legions under Pompey conquer Jerusalem

AD 73 Fall of Masada

Coin minted by the Jewish rebels at Masada

The Destruction of the Second Temple

Titus

DURING THE JEWISH REVOLT of AD 66, the Romans suffered early defeats until the emperor Vespasian sent his son Titus to Jerusalem with four legions. The siege of the city was bitterly fought. Eventually, after five months, on 29 August AD 70, the city's defenders were forced to surrender. In *The Jewish War*, historian Flavius Josephus describes how the Temple was set ablaze in the heat of battle. "When the flames rose up," he writes, "the Jews let out a terrific cry and, heedless of mortal danger, ran to put it out." But it was in vain, and the Second Temple was razed to the ground.

ROMAN EMPIRE AD 117

▨ *Maximum extent of the Empire*

Arch of Titus
The Romans built the triumphal Arch of Titus in the Forum in Rome, with friezes showing the victorious troops with their booty from the destroyed Temple.

The Antonia Fortress was built by Herod the Great around 37–35 BC to protect the Temple, and named for his patron, Mark Antony. It was the last stronghold of the Jewish rebels in AD 70.

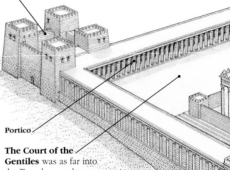

Portico

The Court of the Gentiles was as far into the Temple complex as non-Jews could venture.

The Causeway linked the Temple with the main city gate to the west. Evidence of it remains today in Wilson's Arch *(see p83)*.

Ossuary of Caiaphas
Carved from limestone, ossuaries held the bones of the dead. This particular ossuary bears the name Caiaphas, which was the name of the Temple High Priest at the time of the crucifixion of Jesus.

The Western Wall
Herod's engineers created the Temple platform by building four walls around a natural hill and filling in. The Western Wall (see p83) is part of one of those retaining walls.

Destruction and Sack of the Temple of Jerusalem
Painted by Nicolas Poussin in 1625–6, and now in the collection of the Israel Museum (see pp128–33), this shows Roman soldiers, directed by Titus on his white horse, emerging from the Inner Temple carrying the Jewish menorah and other treasures.

The Inner Temple
contained the Holy of Holies, an empty chamber meant for the Ark of the Covenant, which was lost when the First Temple was destroyed.

Bronze Helmet
Archaeologists' finds such as this legionary's helmet (c. AD 100) indicate that Rome maintained a strong military presence after the Jewish Revolt.

The Hulda Gates

The Royal Stoa was a covered colonnade, 162 columns in length, used for teaching.

The Lower City Steps
led to the area known as the City of David. Evidence of them exists in Robinson's Arch *(see p83).*

"Judaea Capta" Coin
A commemorative coin issued after the defeat of the Jewish rebels depicting, on one side, Vespasian and, on the other, Rome standing triumphant over a subdued Judaea.

THE SECOND TEMPLE
Built in the 6th century BC on the same site as the First Temple, which was destroyed by the Babylonians in 586 BC, the Second Temple was greatly expanded by Herod the Great (37–4 BC). He nearly doubled the size of the Inner Temple.

Constantine the Great, the first Christian Roman emperor

Constantine – and Jerusalem regained its former importance. The first Christian churches were built on the sites connected with the life of Christ, and monasticism spread both in the towns and in the deserts of Palestine and Egypt. The first Holy Sepulchre church was dedicated in Jerusalem in 335.

During the rule of Theodosius (379–95) Christianity became the official state religion. Not long after the Roman Empire was divided in 395 between Theodosius's two sons, the Latin-speaking Western Empire fell to Germanic invaders but the Greek-speaking Eastern Empire, thereafter known as the Byzantine Empire, survived.

PALESTINE UNDER ROMAN RULE

Despite the Jews being banned from Jerusalem, during the 2nd and 3rd centuries their religion and traditions remained very much alive in Palestine, and scholars and religious schools were active throughout Galilee. This was the period in which the academies wrote down Jewish oral law and the commentaries on it, known collectively as the Talmud.

In the early 4th century, the Christians, who had also suffered Roman persecution, were granted freedom of worship by the Emperor Constantine (306–37), himself a convert to the religion. Constantine moved his capital from Rome to Byzantium, which was renamed Constantinople.

This turn of events opened the doors of the Holy Land to pilgrims – first and foremost the devout Helena, mother of

Byzantine icon of the Madonna and Child, 6th century

THE BYZANTINE ERA

Despite a long series of schisms within the Eastern Church over the nature of Christ (see p96), the Byzantine period was an age of relative stability and prosperity in the Holy Land. The flow of pilgrims continued and monastic life drew ever more adherents. The construction of two important religious buildings, St Catherine's Monastery (see pp222–4) in Sinai and the enormous Nea Basilica (see p80) in Jerusalem, reflected the confidence of the era. The Holy Land became the land we can see on the early medieval mosaic map at Madaba (see pp192–3). However, upheaval was to arrive in

TIMELINE

AD 313 Constantine grants freedom of worship to Christians in the Edict of Milan	**527–65** Reign of Byzantine emperor Justinian	**661** Omayyad dynasty established in Damascus
AD 300 **400** **500** **600**		
395 The Roman Empire splits into East and West	**638** Battle of Yarmuk River; beginning of Arab dominion in the Holy Land	
Coin of Constantine, AD 320		**691** Dome of the Rock completed in Jerusalem

614 in the form of an invading Persian army. Welcomed and supported by the Jews, who hoped for greater religious freedom, the Persians massacred the Christians and desecrated their holy sites before being driven off in 628 by the forces of the Byzantine Empire.

In the same year that the Byzantines reconquered Palestine, in neighbouring Arabia an army led by the Prophet Muhammad conquered Mecca, marking the emergence of a new force in the Near East which, in a little over ten years, would change the face of the Holy Land.

Pilgrimage scroll showing the Haram esh-Sharif

THE ARABS AND ISLAM

In AD 638, only six years after Muhammad's death, the troops of his successor, or *caliph*, Omar defeated the Byzantines at the Yarmuk River, in modern-day Syria. The Muslims became the new rulers of Palestine.

Islam recognizes many of the prophets of the Old Testament, such as Abraham (Ibrahim), and so the Arabs regarded Jerusalem as holy in the same way as the Jews and Christians. The Arabs also believed that the Prophet Muhammad had ascended to Heaven on his Night Journey *(see p25)* from the same rock in Jerusalem on which, according to the Bible, Abraham had been about to sacrifice his son, and over which the Jews had built their temples. Consequently, the rubble in the Temple area was cleared and construction of two mosques began there: the Dome of the Rock (691) and El-Aqsa (705). Access to this "sacred precinct" *(Haram esh-Sharif)*, was forbidden to non-Muslims, but Christians and Jews were permitted to live in the city of Jerusalem on payment of an "infidels" tax.

Groups of Christian pilgrims regularly arrived in the Holy Land from Byzantium and Europe and were given safe passage under the successive Arab dynasties of the Omayyads (661–750), Abbasids (750–974) and, initially, the Fatimids (975–1171). This happy state of affairs ended in 1009 when the third Fatimid caliph El-Hakim initiated the violent persecution of non-Muslims and destroyed the Holy Sepulchre. The situation became critical in 1071 when Jerusalem fell to the Seljuk Turks, who forbade Christians access to the Holy City.

The outraged response of Christian Europe was to take up arms and set off on the first of a series of crusades spread over almost 200 years to recapture the Holy City and biblical sites of Palestine *(see pp46–7)*.

Muslims celebrating the end of the feast of Ramadan

747 Earthquake drives dwindling populations from Petra and Jerash

Fatimid jewellery

1071 Seljuk Turks capture Jerusalem and bar Christian pilgrims

800 900 1000 1100

1099 The Crusaders take Jerusalem

Dome of the Rock

975 North African Fatimid dynasty rules the Holy Land from Cairo

The Crusades

"**G**OD WILLS IT!**" With these words, on 27 November 1095 at the Council of Clermont, Pope Urban II launched an appeal to liberate Jerusalem and the Holy Land from the Muslims. His preachings inspired more than 100,000 men and women from all over Europe to join the armies heading east. They succeeded in creating a Latin kingdom of Jerusalem, but a series of further Crusades meant to reinforce the Western Christian presence in the east were ever less successful. Within 200 years the Crusaders were gone from the Holy Land, leaving a legacy of fine ecclesiastical and military architecture.

Crusading emperor Frederick I

THE HOLY LAND

Crusader domains 1186

The First Crusade
Passing through Constantinople, the Crusaders first engaged the Muslim Seljuks in Anatolia (Turkey). They conquered Nicaea and Antioch before marching down through Syria to Palestine.

Church of the Holy Sepulchre

Scenes from the life of Christ

Stylized Gothic gates of Jerusalem

The Second Crusade
Most of the Second Crusaders never made it to the Holy Land. Those that did launched a disastrous attack on Damascus and had to withdraw.

THE CAPTURE OF JERUSALEM
On 7 June 1099, the Crusaders laid siege to Jerusalem. The Muslims held out for five weeks until on 15 July the Christian troops breached the walls unleashing a massive slaughter in the streets.

TIMELINE

1119 Founding of the Knights Templar

Templar Knight

1148 Second Crusade defeated while besieging Damascus

1187 Saladin defeats the Crusaders at the Horns of Hattin and takes Jerusalem

| 1100 | 1120 | 1140 | 1160 | 1180 | 1 |

1099 Crusaders capture Jerusalem; Godfrey of Bouillon becomes "Protector of the Holy Sepulchre"

Saladin, founder of the Ayyubid dynasty (1169–1250)

1188–92 Third Crusade; after reconquering much of the coa Richard I fails to retake Jerusalem

The Third Crusade

The retaking of Jerusalem by Saladin in 1187 prompted the Third Crusade. The Crusade failed to regain the Holy City, but Richard I "the Lionheart" negotiated the right of access for pilgrims.

Richard I and Saladin

The Crucifixion was believed to have taken place on the site occupied by the Holy Sepulchre church.

The burial of Christ

The city walls were finally breached by the Crusaders in the north, near Herod's Gate, and also on Mount Zion.

Siege warfare was a major element of the Crusades; siege engines were built on site.

The Fall of Acre

Following a succession of defeats by the Mamelukes, the Crusaders were forced to leave the Holy Land for good in 1291. The last stronghold to fall was Acre, where this coat of arms was discovered.

THE TEMPLARS AND HOSPITALLERS

Much of the defence of Crusader gains in the Holy Land fell to two elite Military Orders of monastic knights, the Hospitallers (see p95) and the Templars, so named because they were headquartered in the former Temple area of Jerusalem. The Orders occupied and refortified Crusader castles in the Holy Land, as well as building new ones of their own.

The Hospitaller castle of Belvoir in the Jordan Valley

1244 Jerusalem falls to Muslim mercenaries in the employ of Egypt		**1270** Last major Crusade, led by Louis IX, ends in his death in Tunis		*Louis IX embarking on the last Crusade*	
1220	**1240**	**1260**	**1280**	**1300**	
1217–21 Fifth Crusade	**1249–50** Louis IX of France leads unsuccessful invasion of Egypt	**1260** Mamelukes defeat invading Mongols; Baybars becomes Sultan of Egypt		**1291** Last Latin strongholds in Holy Land, including Acre, fall to Mamelukes	

Mameluke horsemen training for battle, from a 15th-century manuscript

PALESTINE UNDER THE MAMELUKES

In the wake of the Crusades, Jerusalem slowly declined to the status of a provincial city. The Mamelukes (former slave guards of Saladin's Ayyubid dynasty) ruled the Holy Land from Egypt, and the Holy City became a place of banishment for officials who fell from court favour in Cairo.

While the Mamelukes had driven the Christian knights from the Holy Land, they did make allowance for Christian pilgrims. In 1333 the Franciscan Friars were permitted a presence in Jerusalem, living in the supposed Hall of the Last Supper. In 1342 Pope Clement VI ratified this mission, which took on the name of the Franciscan Custody of the Holy Land.

The following century saw the beginning of a flow of Jews into Palestine escaping persecution in Europe, a movement that has continued through into the 20th century. In this case, the defeat of the Moors in Spain had given way to the Inquisition and the resultant expulsion of some 100,000 Jews from the country, accused of having too close ties with the vanquished Arabs.

THE OTTOMAN EMPIRE

Mameluke control of Palestine ended in 1516 with defeat at the hands of the Ottoman army. Originating in northwest Turkey, the Ottoman Turks had captured Constantinople in 1453, renaming it Istanbul. Under the rule of their greatest sultan, Suleyman the Magnificent (1520–66), vast architectural projects were carried out in Jerusalem, most notably the construction of the city walls and gates.

However, a series of weak sultans meant that by the 18th century the enormous Ottoman empire was no longer so secure, particularly in the provinces where corruption was often a system of administration. This was the case in Palestine, where the people frequently suffered heavy taxes and poor government. But the Jews continued to return, largely because they were safer under Turkish rule than they were in Europe. Many chose to settle in Galilee, around Tiberias and Safed, joining the Sephardic Jewish communities that had fled Spain several centuries earlier. At the same time, Europe was making its first real entry into the region since the Crusades; Napoleon landed in Egypt in 1798 and the following year he had to be repelled from invading at Acre by the Ottoman governor, Ahmed Pasha el-Jazzar.

Suleyman I, the Magnificent, Ottoman sultan, 1520–66

TIMELINE

14th century Development of the area round the Haram esh-Sharif in Jerusalem	**1492** Edict signed by King Ferdinand expelling all professing Jews from Spain	**1516** Ottomans defeat the Mamelukes and seize control of Palestine and Egypt	
1300	**1400**	**1500**	1(
1333 Franciscans permitted to settle in Jerusalem	**1400** Mamelukes halt westward advance of Mongol ruler Tamerlane	*Jaffa Gate, one of seven gates built by Suleyman's engineers*	**1537** Suleyman the Magnificent orders the construction of the walls of Jerusalem

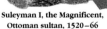

Acre, rebuilt by successive Ottoman governors

JERUSALEM AND THE COLONIAL POWERS IN THE 19TH CENTURY

With the continuing decline of the Ottoman Empire the European nations, newly empowered by their Industrial Revolution, began to follow in Napoleon's wake – unsuccessful though he had been. When in 1831 the Egyptian ruler Muhammad Ali, the supposed vassal of Istanbul, seized Palestine, it was only with British military help that the Turks regained the territory. A British consul arrived in Jerusalem in 1838, followed closely by diplomatic representatives of France and Prussia. One of the causes of the Crimean War (1854) was the French claim to holy sites at that time in Russian hands.

All the while, Jewish immigration continued, propelled by virulent anti-Semitism and pogroms in eastern Europe and throughout the Russian Empire. A result of this influx was that in the mid-19th century, Jerusalem overspilled

the bounds of its medieval walls with the establishment of a series of small Jewish settlements outside the city gates. The city began to emerge from the lethargy that had characterized it in the preceding centuries.

Over in Europe there had been a growing, but not yet unified, Jewish national movement. In 1839 the British Jew Sir Moses Montefiore had first called for the creation of a Jewish state. This culminated in 1896 with the publication by an Austro-Hungarian Jewish journalist named Theodor Herzl of *Der Judenstat (The Jewish State)*, which proved a rallying cry for Jews worldwide. The following year saw the formation of the World Zionist Organization, with Herzl at its head. Its stated aim was "to create for the Jewish people a home in Palestine". A Jewish National Fund was set up to purchase land for settlement.

However, the Zionist immigrants were also laying the foundations for a century of conflict to come; slogans such as "A land without a people for a people without a land" conveniently ignored the fact that Palestine was already home to a large indigenous Arab population with aspirations to self-rule of its own.

The American Colony, one of a great many Western outposts established in 19th-century Jerusalem

Ottoman janissary, soldier of the sultan's guard	**1831** Egypt's Muhammad Ali takes control of Palestine	**1839** British Jew Sir Moses Montefiore first proposes the idea of a Jewish state	**1909** Founding of Tel Aviv and first kibbutz
1700	**1800**		**1900**
	1860 Jerusalem's first new Jewish settlements since the Diaspora		*Theodor Herzl*
1812 Petra rediscovered by Swiss explorer Jean Louis Burckhardt			**1896** Herzl publishes *The Jewish State*

THE COLLAPSE OF THE OTTOMANS AND THE BRITISH MANDATE

Turkish rule in Palestine ended in 1917, during World War I, when British troops under the command of General Allenby took Jerusalem.

The Arabs, under their leader Faisal, had fought alongside the British and expected Palestine in return. However, with the Balfour Declaration of 1917 the British had let it be known that "His Majesty's government favourably views the creation of a national Jewish home in Palestine". In the event, peace talks in 1920 put Palestine under British authority and this was ratified by the League of Nations on 24 July 1922.

Zionist poster soliciting funds for a homeland in Palestine

The following year, in order to placate Arab discontent, the British recognized Trans-Jordan as an autonomous Arab emirate, ruled by the emir Abdullah, the eldest brother of Faisal, with Amman as its capital. Initially under the supervision of the British in Jerusalem, the territory became totally independent in 1946, with Abdullah confirmed as its king.

ARAB-JEWISH CONFLICT

At the time of World War I, some 500,000 Palestinian Arabs and about 85,000 Jews were living in the Holy Land. In the 20 years between then and the outbreak of World War II about 250,000 more Jews arrived at the ports of Jaffa and Haifa to settle in Palestine. Each new wave of immigrants served to increase the tension between the Palestinian and Jewish communities.

In 1929 Palestinian riots culminated in a series of pogroms in Jerusalem, Hebron and Safed. An Arab "revolt" proclaimed in 1936 led to a six-month general strike that brought the country to a standstill.

The *Theodor Herzl* about to dock at Haifa, decks crowded with Jewish immigrants, 1947

TIMELINE

TE Lawrence "of Arabia"

1916 Faisal and the Arabs, encouraged by TE Lawrence, join the British in a desert war against the Turks

24 July 1922 League of Nations ratifies British mandate in Palestine

1900	1905	1910	1915	1920

1909 Founding of Tel Aviv and first kibbutz in Palestine

1914 War breaks out in Europe; the Ottoman Turks side with Germany

1917 General Allenby captures Jerusalem from the Ottoman Turks

General Allenby

Proposals for Partition

By this time, the British were finding rule in Palestine extremely uncomfortable. In 1937, following the deliberations of the Peel Commission, they proposed ending the Mandate and partitioning the country. The Jews accepted but the Arabs refused, claiming that the proposed Jewish homeland occupied the region's most fertile zones.

Elsewhere, the world was much more concerned with developments in Europe, where war seemed inevitable. In a brazen attempt to improve relations with its potential allies, the Arabs, in 1939, on the eve of war, Britain published a "White Paper" drastically limiting Jewish immigration to Palestine. However, faced with the dangers of Nazism, tens of thousands of Jews continued to arrive, often sneaking in clandestinely by sea. British attempts to check the immigration were, for the most part, in vain.

Allenby Street, in the rapidly expanding Jewish Tel Aviv of the 1930s

Nations. On 29 November 1947 the UN voted for the partition of the Holy Land into an Arab state and a Jewish state, with Jerusalem under international administration. Britain announced its intention to pull out of Palestine on 15 May 1948 and leave the Arabs and Jews to fight among themselves.

Ben Gurion witnessing the departure of British troops from Haifa port in 1948

The main Jewish response to the White Paper was to inspire extremists to attacks on the British. On 22 July 1946 the Jewish military organization Irgun – one of whose leaders was the future prime minister Menachem Begin – bombed British headquarters at the King David Hotel in Jerusalem, killing more than 80 and wounding hundreds more.

Trapped in a no-win situation, the British placed the "Palestine question" before the newly-formed United

The Creation of Israel

Skirmishing between the Palestinians and Jews escalated as both sides manoeuvred to control as much territory as possible before the end of the Mandate. Jewish extremists attacked Palestinian villages (most infamously at Deir Yassin, on the road between Tel Aviv and Jerusalem), while armed Palestinians made raids against Jewish settlements.

As the British prepared to leave, the Jews were ready to replace them. On 14 May 1948, the eve of departure, David Ben Gurion declared the birth of the State of Israel.

1934 Jews flee central Europe and the threat of Hitler's Germany

1936 Arab Revolt in Palestine

1939 Great Britain publishes the "White Paper"

1947 Discovery of the Dead Sea Scrolls at Qumran

| 1930 | 1935 | 1940 | | 1950 |

1929 Arab attacks on Jews in Jerusalem, Hebron and Safed

1937 Peel Commission proposes partition of Palestine

14 May 1948 State of Israel declared in Tel Aviv

One of the Dead Sea Scrolls

Refugees crossing the border into Jordan in 1967

THE 1948 WAR

The Arab reaction to the creation of Israel was swift. Lebanon, Syria, Iraq, Jordan and Egypt launched a combined attack with the avowed aim of casting the new-born state into the sea. Fighting continued until an armistice was signed in December 1949. At the cease of hostilities, the Israelis had made great territorial gains at the expense of the Palestinians. Prior to 1948 the Jews owned less than seven per cent of Palestine but at the war's end they occupied about 80 per cent. As a result, some 500,000 to 750,000 Palestinians were made refugees in neighbouring Arab countries and in camps in the Egyptian-controlled Gaza Strip and in the Jordanian-held territories on the west bank of the Jordan River.

One of the main objectives of the opposing sides had been the capture of Jerusalem. Neither side had achieved this; the Israelis held the modern quarters of West Jerusalem,

Pre-1967 poster, with the West Bank shown as part of Jordan

the Jordanians held the Old City and East Jerusalem. The city was to remain divided, along what came to be known as the Green Line, for almost 20 years.

THE ARAB-ISRAELI WARS AFTER 1949

After the violent birth of Israel, the infant state sought to consolidate its position by passing the Law of Return. This extended to all Jews throughout the world the right to live in Israel. The first to heed the invitation were Jews from the Arab world, but those that followed came from everywhere from South America to Siberia.

Relations with the Arabs remained on a war footing. In 1956, the Israeli army swept into Sinai in support of the French and British attempt to seize the Suez Canal, newly nationalized by Egypt's President Nasser. On this occasion, under pressure from the United States and the United Nations, they were forced to retreat. Eleven years later, in 1967, Israeli tanks rolled into Sinai once again. Alarmed by a build-up of Egyptian forces on the border, Israel launched a pre-emptive attack. Despite then facing the combined forces of all its Arab neighbours, in six days Israel's army had taken the Golan Heights from Syria, the Gaza Strip and Sinai from Egypt, and the West Bank from Jordan. The Israelis also captured the whole of Jerusalem. In what amounted to a face-saving exercise, on 6 October 1973, the Jewish feast of Yom Kippur, Egypt and Syria launched a surprise attack on

TIMELINE

1951 Assassination of King Abdullah of Jordan in Jerusalem by Palestinian extremists

Hussein, crowned king of Jordan in May 1953

6 October 1973 Yom Kippur War breaks out

1950	1955	1960	1965	1970

14 May 1948 On the declaration of the State of Israel war breaks out with the Arabs

1956 Suez crisis

5–11 June 1967 Six Day War results in reunification of Jerusalem under the Israelis

Golda Meir, Israeli prime minister 1969–74

Israeli positions. Caught off guard, the Israelis suffered initial losses but they managed to counterattack and reverse early Arab gains. At the cease of hostilities the action had failed to alter the territorial state of affairs set six years previously.

What the 1973 War did do was to pave the way for the first talks between Egypt and Israel. In 1979 the two countries formally agreed to peace by signing the Camp David agreement. In 1982 Sinai was returned to Egypt.

The historic handshake between Rabin and Arafat in Washington

THE QUEST FOR PEACE

The peace treaty was not welcomed by all parties. The Palestinians saw it as undermining their campaign for self-rule. Groups such as the Palestine Liberation Organization (PLO) stepped up their anti-Israel guerrilla war. Their terror tactics won them little sympathy with the international community. That changed in late 1987 with the beginning of the *intifada* ("shaking off"), a grass-roots Palestinian revolt against Israeli occupation in the Gaza Strip and West Bank. Television screens worldwide were filled almost nightly with images of stone-throwing young Arab boys facing up to well-armed Israeli soldiers. The world's response was to call for the resolution of the Palestinian issue. In the wake of 1991's Gulf War, the Americans brokered

a meeting between Israeli and Palestinian delegations in Madrid. This seemed to achieve little, but in 1993 it was revealed that the two parties had been meeting in Norway where an agreement had been formulated. The signing of the "Oslo Accords" was capped that year by a handshake between Israeli prime minister Yitzhak Rabin and PLO president Yasser Arafat in front of the world's press on the lawn of the White House. The following year saw Jordan and Israel formally end the state of war that had existed between the two countries since 1948.

Since then, Israel has celebrated 50 years of statehood. In that short time it has developed into a dynamic, multi-racial nation, and become a world leader in certain specialized areas of agriculture, computer software and armaments. The Palestinians remain without a state of their own. They have only limited authority over parts of the Gaza Strip and West Bank. A solution to this issue has yet to be found, but it does seem possible that that solution may well come sooner rather later, and from talking rather than fighting.

Watching Independence Day celebrations on the seafront, Tel Aviv

1980	1985	1990	1995	2000

1982 Sinai returned to the Egyptians

1993 Oslo Accords lead to Rabin and Arafat shaking hands

1995 Israeli prime minister Yitzhak Rabin assassinated

1999 King Hussein of Jordan dies

1979 Camp David peace treaty signed between Egypt and Israel

1987 Eruption of Palestinian *intifada* against Israeli occupation

1994 Palestinians granted limited autonomy

First issue of Palestinian stamps, 1994

JERUSALEM
AREA BY AREA

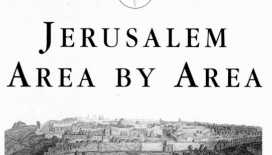

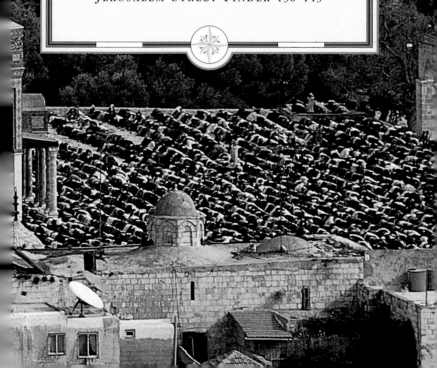

Jerusalem at a Glance

THE OLD CITY of Jerusalem has a history that
stretches back more than 3,000 years,
although the present street plan dates largely
from Byzantine times, and the encircling walls
are from the 16th century. Within the walls,
the Old City divides into four vaguely defined
quarters – one each for the Christians, Jews
and Muslims, and the fourth occupied by the
Armenians. East and south of the Old City are
the Mount of Olives and Mount Zion, both
places traditionally linked with the last acts of
Jesus Christ. To the north and west is modern
Jerusalem, liberally endowed with fine examples
of late 19th-century architecture.

The Church of the Holy Sepulchre
(see pp88–91) *is the most important
of the Holy Land's Christian sites.
Tradition has it that the church occupies the site of Golgotha, where Jesus
Christ was crucified and buried.*

The Citadel (see
pp98–100) *is an
impressively restored,
fortified complex, which
has its origins in the
2nd century BC. It now
houses an excellent
museum devoted to the
history of Jerusalem.
There are also splendid
views of the city from
its ramparts.*

**MODERN
JERUSALEM**
(See pp114–123)

**THE CHRISTIAN
AND ARMENIAN
QUARTERS**
(See pp84–103)

The Israel Museum (see pp128–33) *was
purpose-built in the 1960s to house the
country's most significant archaeological
finds, including the Dead Sea Scrolls, which
are displayed in this uniquely shaped hall.
The museum is situated a short distance
west of the city centre.*

Yemin Moshe (see pp116–7) *is one of several
attractive old quarters in modern Jerusalem,
developed in the mid-19th century to escape
overcrowding in the Old City. It is distinguished
by its windmill and by this communal housing
block, known as Mishkenot Shaananim.*

The **Haram esh-Sharif** (see pp66–71) is the focus of the Muslim faith in Jerusalem. A large plateau on the eastern edge of the Old City, it contains some fine Islamic buildings, including the 8th-century El-Aqsa Mosque, and the magnificent Dome of the Rock, with its dazzling interior.

THE MUSLIM QUARTER
(See pp58–73)

The **Western Wall** (see p83) is Judaism's holiest site. It is believed to be part of the great Temple enclosure built by Herod in the 1st century BC. The plaza in front is busy, day and night, with supplicants at prayer.

THE JEWISH QUARTER
(See pp74–83)

THE MOUNT OF OLIVES and MOUNT ZION
(See pp104–113)

Hurva Square (see pp76–7) lies at the centre of the Jewish Quarter. This area was largely rebuilt following its capture by the Israeli army in 1967. The square's main landmark is the free-standing arch of the ruined Hurva Synagogue.

The Mount of Olives (see pp106–110) has several fine churches, including the richly decorated Russian Orthodox Church of St Mary Magdalene.

| 0 metres | 300 |
| 0 yards | 300 |

THE MUSLIM QUARTER

Street sign for a Quranic recitation school

THIS IS THE LARGEST and most densely populated quarter of the Old City. It was first developed under Herod the Great and delineated in its present form under the Byzantines. In the 12th century it was taken over by the Crusaders, hence the quarter's wealth of churches and other Christian institutions, such as the Via Dolorosa (see pp28–9). In the 14th and 15th centuries the Mamelukes rebuilt extensively, especially in the areas abutting the Haram esh-Sharif. The quarter has been in decay since the 16th century. Today it contains some of the city's poorest homes. It is also one of the most fascinating and least explored parts of Jerusalem.

SIGHTS AT A GLANCE

**Historic Streets,
Buildings and Gates**
Chain Street ❻
Damascus Gate ❽
Ecce Homo Arch ❷
Herod's Gate ❾
Lady Tunshuq's Palace ❹
St Stephen's Gate ⓫
Via Dolorosa ❸

Souks and Markets
Central Souk ❼
Cotton Merchants'
  Market ❺

Holy Places
Haram esh-Sharif
  pp66–71 ⓬
Monastery of the
  Flagellation ❶
St Anne's Church ❿

GETTING THERE
The Muslim Quarter is served by Damascus, Herod's and St Stephen's gates. There are buses from the New City to Damascus Gate (see p281). Alternatively, for visitors with their own transport, there is a car park just inside St Stephen's Gate.

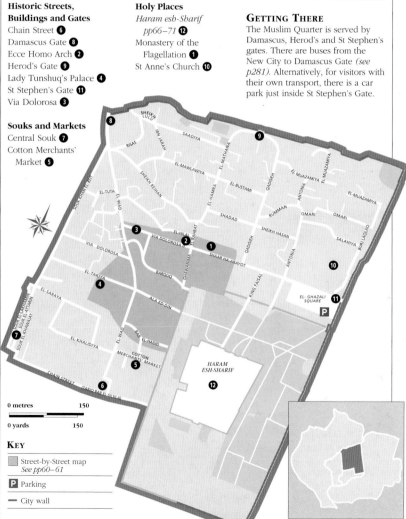

KEY

Street-by-Street map
See pp60–61

P Parking

City wall

0 metres 150
0 yards 150

◁ Muslim women entering the Dome of the Rock, centrepiece of the Haram esh-Sharif

Street-by-Street: The Muslim Quarter

T HE MAIN ROUTES through this busy quarter are along the Via Dolorosa and up and down El-Wad. Both streets are lined with a gaudy array of shops, whose salesmen eagerly press on visitors all manner of ornaments and kitsch, from plastic crucifixes to glass-bowled water pipes. Few people stray from the main thoroughfares, but those who do are richly. rewarded.

Studium Museum artifact The quiet, winding back alleys contain a wealth of fine medieval Islamic architecture, much of it dating from the Mameluke era (1250–1516). Not all of it is in good condition, but many of these buildings still perform the functions for which they were intended.

The Austrian Hospice was built in 1869 to accommodate Christian pilgrims.

Damascus Gate

VIA DOLORO

EL-WAD

Via Dolorosa
Crossing the quarter from east to west, this street is revered by Christian pilgrims as the route taken by Christ as he was led to his crucifixion ❸

Holy Sepulchre church and the Christian Quarter

Abu Shukri restaurant (see p246)

El-Takiya Street
A narrow, stepped street at the heart of the quarter, El-Takiya contains some of the city's finest examples of Mameluke architecture.

Lady Tunshuq's Palace
The banding of different coloured stone and panels of intricate marble inlay typify the decorative style of the Mamelukes ❹

KEY

– – – Suggested route

STAR SIGHTS

★ **Monastery of the Flagellation**

★ **Ecce Homo Arch**

★ Monastery of the Flagellation
Built on the site traditionally associated with the flogging of Christ, this Franciscan complex includes two attractive chapels and the Studium Museum ❶

LOCATOR MAP
See Jerusalem Street Finder, map 4

St Stephen's Gate and the Mount of Olives →

Convent of the Sisters of Zion
The convent, which runs a pilgrims' hospice, dates from the 19th-century Christian building boom.

★ Ecce Homo Arch
The arch, which spans the Via Dolorosa, is the main section of a Roman triple arch. One of the smaller, flanking arches (left) is incorporated into the structure of the Convent of the Sisters of Zion ❷

Madrasa el-Araghonia (1358)

↓ Jewish Quarter

0 metres   50
0 yards   50

Bab el-Hadid Street
Though badly neglected, this street has a number of madrasas (see p69) from the 14th and 15th centuries.

Monastery of the Flagellation, with the Via Dolorosa behind

Monastery of the Flagellation **❶**

Via Dolorosa. **Map** 4 D2. ⬜ 8am–
6pm (Oct–Mar: 5pm) daily.
Studium Museum 📞 (02) 628
0271. ⬜ 9–11:30am Mon–Sat.

OWNED BY the Franciscans,
this complex embraces
the simple and striking Chapel
of the Flagellation, designed
in the 1920s by the Italian
architect Antonio Barluzzi,
who was also responsible for
the Dominus Flevit Chapel on
the Mount of Olives (see p109).
It is located on the site
traditionally held to be where
Christ was flogged by Roman
soldiers prior to his
Crucifixion (Matthew 27:
27–30; Mark 15: 16–19).

On the other side of the
courtyard is the Chapel of the
Condemnation, which also
dates from the early 20th
century. It is built over the
remains of a medieval chapel,
on the site popularly identified with the trial of Christ
before Pontius Pilate.

The neighbouring monastery
buildings house the Studium
Biblicum Franciscanum, a
prestigious institute of biblical,
geographical and archaeo-
logical studies. Also part of
the complex, the **Studium
Museum** contains objects
found by the Franciscans in
excavations at Capernaum,
Nazareth, Bethlehem and
various other sites. The most
interesting exhibits are
Byzantine and Crusader

objects, such as fragments of
frescoes from the Church of
Gethsemane, precursor of the
present-day Church of All
Nations (see p110), and
a 12th-century crozier
from the Church of
the Nativity in Bethle-
hem (see pp174–5).

**Crusader-era angel's
head, Studium Museum**

Ecce Homo Arch **❷**

Via Dolorosa. **Map** 4 D2. **Convent of
the Sisters of Zion** 📞 (02) 627
7292. ⬜ 8:30am–12:30pm &
2–5pm Mon–Sat. 🖼 🎞

THIS ARCH that spans the Via
Dolorosa was built by the
Romans in AD 70 to support
a ramp being laid against the
Antonia Fortress, in which
Jewish rebels were barricaded
(see p42). When the Romans

The Ecce Homo Arch bridging
the Via Dolorosa

rebuilt Jerusalem in AD 135 in
the wake of the Second Jewish
War (see p41), the arch was
reconstructed as a monument
to victory, with two smaller
arches flanking a large central
bay. It is the central bay that
you see spanning the street.

One of the side arches is
also still visible, incorporated
into the interior of the neighbouring **Convent of the
Sisters of Zion**. Built in the
1860s, the convent also
contains the remains of the
vast Pool of the Sparrow
(Struthion), an ancient reservoir which collected rainwater
directed from the rooftops.
The pool was originally covered with a stone pavement
(lithostrothon) and it was on
this flagstone plaza, Christian
tradition has it, that Pilate
presented Christ to the
crowds and uttered
the words "Ecce homo"
(Latin for "Behold the
man"). However,
archaeology refutes
this, dating the pave-
ment to the 2nd century
AD, long after the time
of Christ. Within a railed
section you can see marks
scratched into the stone.
Historians speculate that they
may have been carved by
bored Roman guards as part
of some kind of street game.

Via Dolorosa **❸**

Map 3 C3 & 4 D2.

THE IDENTIFICATION of the Via
Dolorosa (see pp28–9) with
the ancient "Way of Sorrows"
walked by Christ on the way
to his Crucifixion has more to
do with religious tradition than
historical fact. It nevertheless
continues to draw huge numbers of pilgrims every day.
The streets through which they
walk are much like any others
in the Muslim Quarter, lined
with small shops and stalls, but
the route is marked out by 14
"Stations of the Cross", linked
with events that occurred on
Christ's last, fateful walk. Some
of the Stations are commemorated only by wall plaques,
which can be difficult to spot
among the religious souvenir
stalls. Others are located

inside buildings. The last five Stations are all within the Holy Sepulchre church (see pp88–91).

Friday is the main day for pilgrims, when, at 3pm, the Franciscans lead a procession along the route.

In fact, the more likely route for the original Via Dolorosa begins at what is now the Citadel (see pp98–9) but was at the time the royal palace. This is where Pontius Pilate resided when in Jerusalem, making it a more likely location for the trial of Christ. From here, the condemned would probably have been led down what is now David Street, through the present-day Central Souk (see p64), out of the then city gate and to the hill of Golgotha, the presumed site of which is now occupied by the Holy Sepulchre church.

An unusually quiet Via Dolorosa, leading down from Ecce Homo Arch to El-Wad Road

Stalactite stone carvings above a window on Lady Tunshuq's Palace

Lady Tunshuq's Palace ❹

El-Takiya St. **Map** 4 D3.
⬤ to public.

LADY TUNSHUQ, of Mongolian or Turkish origin, was the wife, or mistress, of a Kurdish nobleman. She arrived in Jerusalem some time in the 14th century and had this edifice built for herself. It is one of the loveliest examples of Mameluke architecture in Jerusalem. Unfortunately the narrowness of the street

prevents you from standing back and appreciating the building as a whole, but you can admire the three great doorways with their beautiful inlaid-marble decoration. The upper portion of a window recess also displays some fine carved-stone, stalactite-like decoration, a form known as muqarnas. The former palace now serves as an orphanage and is not open to the public.

When Lady Tunshuq died, she was buried in a small tomb across from the palace. The fine decoration on the tomb includes panels of different coloured marble, intricately shaped and slotted together like a jigsaw – a typical Mameluke feature known as "joggling".

If you head east and across El-Wad Road, you will enter a narrow alley called Ala ed-Din, which contains more fine Mameluke architecture. Most

of the façades are composed of bands of different hues of stone, a strikingly beautiful Mameluke decorative technique known as ablaq.

Cotton Merchants' Market ❺

Off El-Wad Rd. **Map** 4 D3.

KNOWN IN ARABIC as the Souk el-Qattanin, this is a covered market with next to no natural light but lots of small softly-lit shops. It is possibly the most atmospheric street in all the Old City. Its construction was begun by the Crusaders. They intended the market as a free-standing structure but later, in the first half of the 14th century, the Mamelukes connected it to the Haram esh-Sharif (see pp66–71) via a splendidly ornate gate facing the Dome of the Rock. (But note, non-Muslims are not allowed to enter the Haram esh-Sharif by this gate, although you can depart this way.)

As well as some 50 shop units, the market also has two bathhouses, the Hammam el-Ain and the Hammam el-Shifa. One of these has been undergoing restoration with a view to its being eventually opened to the public. Between the two bathhouses is a former merchants' hostel called Khan Tankiz, also being restored.

Less than 50 m (160 ft) south of the Cotton Merchants' Market on El-Wad Road is a small public drinking fountain, or sabil, one of several such erected during the reign of Suleyman the Magnificent.

The tunnel-like interior of the Cotton Merchants' Market

Chain Street ❻

Map 4 D4.

THE ARABIC NAME for this street is Tariq Bab el-Silsila, which means "Street of the Gate of the Chain". The name refers to the magnificent entrance gate to the Haram esh-Sharif (see pp66–71) situated at its eastern end. The street is a continuation of David Street, and together the two streets run the width of the Old City from Jaffa Gate to the Haram esh-Sharif.

Chain Street has several noteworthy buildings commissioned by Mameluke emirs in the 14th century. Heading eastwards from David Street, the first is the Khan el-Sultan caravanserai, a restored travellers' inn. Further along on the right is Tashtamuriyya Madrasa, with its elegant balcony. It houses the tomb of the emir Tashtamur, and is one of many final resting places built here in the 14th and 15th centuries in order to be close to the Haram esh-Sharif. On the same side of the street is the tomb of the brutal Tartar emir Barka Khan, father-in-law of the Mameluke ruler Baybars, who drove the Crusaders out of the Holy Land (see pp46–7). This building, with its intriguing façade decoration, now houses the Khalidi Library.

Opposite the Khalidi Library are two small mausoleums. Of the two, that of emir Kilan stands out for its austere, well-proportioned façade. Further

Window on Khalidi Library

along on the same side is the tomb of Tartar pilgrim Turkan Khatun, easily recognizable by the splendid arabesques on its façade. Opposite the Gate of the Chain is the impressive entrance to the 14th-century Tankiziyya Madrasa. In the inscription, three symbols in the shape of a cup show that emir Tankiz, who built the college, held the important office of cupbearer. Nearby is a drinking fountain, or *sabil*, from the reign of Suleyman the Magnificent, which combines Roman and Crusader motifs.

Central Souk ❼

David St/Chain St. **Map** 3 C4. ⬜ 8am–7pm Sat–Thu.

THE CENTRAL SOUK (see pp256–7) consists of three parallel covered streets at the intersection of David Street and Chain Street. They once formed part of the Roman Cardo (see p78). Today's

Some of the many and varied spices on sale at the Central Souk

markets sell mostly clothes and souvenirs, although the section called the Butchers' Market (Souk el-Lakhamin in Arabic), restored in the 1970s, still offers all the excitement of an eastern bazaar. It is not for the faint-hearted, however, as the pungent aromas of spices and freshly slaughtered meat can be overwhelming.

Damascus Gate ❽

Map 3 C1. 🚌 1, 2, 23. **Roman Square Excavations** ⬜ 9am–5pm Sat–Thu, 9am–3pm Fri. 🅹

SPOTTING THIS GATE is easy, not only because it is the most monumental in the Old City, but also because of the perpetual bustle of activity in the area outside the gate.

Arabs call it Bab el-Amud, the Gate of the Column. This could refer to a large column topped with a statue of the emperor Hadrian (see p41) which, in Roman times, stood just inside the gate. For Jews it is Shaar Shkhem, the gate which leads to the biblical city of Shechem, better known by its Arabic name – Nablus.

The present-day gate was built over the remains of the original Roman gate and parts of the Roman city. Outside the gate and to the west of the raised walkway, steps lead down to the excavation area. In the first section are remains of a Crusader chapel with frescoes, part of a medieval roadway and an ancient sign marking the presence of the Roman 10th Legion. Further in, metal steps lead down to the single surviving arch of

Crowds of visitors and market traders outside Damascus Gate

the Roman gate, which gives access to the **Roman Square Excavations**. Here, the fascinating remains of the original Roman plaza, the starting point of the Roman Cardo, include a gaming board engraved in the paving stones. A hologram depicts Hadrian's column in the main plaza. This is also a starting point for walks along the ramparts of the city walls *(see p101)*.

Herod's Gate ⑨

Map 4 D1.

THE ARABIC and Hebrew names for this gate, Bab el-Zahra and Shaar ha-Prakhim respectively, both mean "Gate of Flowers", referring to the rosette above the arch. It came to be known as Herod's Gate in the 1500s, when Christian pilgrims wrongly thought that the house inside the gate was the palace of Herod the Great's son. It was via the original, now closed, entrance further east that the Crusaders entered the city and conquered it on 15 July 1099 *(see pp46–7)*.

St Anne's Church ⑩

2 Shaar ha-Arayot St. **Map** 4 E2.
📞 *(02) 628 3285.* ⏱ *8am–noon & 2–6pm (winter: 4pm) Mon–Sat.* 📷

THIS BEAUTIFUL Crusader church is a superb example of Romanesque architecture. It was constructed between 1131 and 1138 to replace a previous Byzantine church, and exists today in more or less its original form. It is traditionally believed that the church stands on the spot where Anne and Joachim, the

The 16th-century St Stephen's Gate, in the Old City's eastern wall

parents of the Virgin Mary, lived. The supposed remains of their house are in the crypt, which is also noted for its remarkable acoustics.

Shortly after the church was built, it was made larger by moving the façade forwards by several metres. The connection with the original church can still be seen in the first row of columns. In 1192, Saladin *(see pp46–7)* turned the church into a Muslim theological school. There is an inscription to this effect above the church's entrance. Later abandoned, the church fell into ruins, until the Ottomans donated it to France in 1856 and it was restored.

Next to the church are two cisterns that once lay outside the city walls. They were built in the 8th and 3rd centuries BC to collect rainwater. Some time later, under Herod the Great they were turned into curative baths. Ruins of a Roman temple, thought to have been to the god of medicine, can be seen here, as can those of a later Byzantine church built over the temple. It is also widely believed that this is the site of the Pool of Bethesda, described in St John's account of Christ curing a paralysed man (John 5: 1–15).

Lion detail from St Stephen's Gate

St Stephen's Gate ⑪

Map 4 F2.

SULEYMAN THE Magnificent built this gate in 1538. Its Arabic name, Bab Sitti Maryam (Gate of the Virgin Mary), refers to the Tomb of the Virgin in the nearby Valley of Jehoshaphat *(see p111)*. The Hebrew name, Shaar ha-Arayot, or Lions' Gate, refers to the two emblematic lions on either side of the gateway, although one school of thought insists that they are panthers. There are many different stories to explain the significance of the lions. One is that Suleyman the Magnificent had them carved in honour of the Mameluke emir Baybars and his successful campaign to rid the Holy Land of Crusaders. The name St Stephen's Gate was adopted in the Middle Ages by Christians who believed that the first Christian martyr, St Stephen, was executed here. Prior to that, however, it had been generally accepted that St Stephen had been stoned to death outside Damascus Gate.

The gate is also significant because of its more recent history, for it was through it that the Arab Legion penetrated the Old City in 1948 *(see p52)* and where Israeli paratroopers entered in 1967 *(see p52)*. It is an excellent starting point for the walk along the Via Dolorosa *(see p62)*.

Archaeological site in front of St Anne's Church

Haram esh-Sharif ⑫

Dome of the Prophet

Haram esh-sharif, the "Noble Sanctuary" or Temple Mount, is a vast rectangular esplanade in the south-eastern part of the Old City. Traditionally the site of Solomon's Temple, it later housed the Second Temple, enlarged by Herod the Great and destroyed by the Romans *(see pp42–3)*. Left in ruins for more than half a century, the site became an Islamic shrine in AD 691 with the building of the Dome of the Rock. Over the centuries other buildings have been added to this, the third most important Islamic religious sanctuary.

★ Dome of the Rock
This is the crowning glory not just of the Haram esh-Sharif but of all Jerusalem (see pp70–71).

Madrasa el-Omariyya is one of several Mameluke-era schools on the Haram.

Madrasa el-Isardiyya

Dome of the Prophet

Sabil of Qaitbey
This public fountain was built on the order of the Mameluke sultan Qaitbey (ruled 1468–98). It has a superb carved stone dome, the only one of its kind in the Holy Land.

Cotton Merchants' Gate is a strikingly decorated Mameluke portal giving access to the market of the same name *(see p63)*.

Chain Gate

Western Wall (see p83)

Moors' Gate (Bab el-Maghariba) is one of only two gates that non-Muslims may use to enter the Haram.

Grammar College
Also known as "The Dome of Learning", this still serves as a Quranic teaching school. The doorway on the north side is flanked by some unusual candy-twist columns dating from the Ayyubid era (1169–1250).

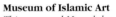

Museum of Islamic Art
This engraved Mameluke vessel is part of a collection of artifacts, largely from the Middle Ages, that includes Qurans, textiles, ceramics and weaponry (see p68).

★ Dome of the Chain
This small dome (see p69) *stands at the approximate centre of the Haram esh-Sharif, which, according to one theory, equated to the centre of the world. The 13th-century tiling on the interior surpasses even that of the Dome of the Rock.*

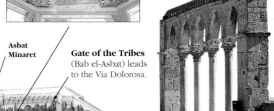

Asbat Minaret

Gate of the Tribes
(Bab el-Asbat) leads to the Via Dolorosa.

Qanatir
Each of the eight flights of steps up to the platform of the Dome of the Rock is topped by a qanatir, *or freestanding arcade (see p68). The column capitals have been recycled from Roman-era buildings.*

Golden Gate is one of the original city gates *(see p69)* but was sealed up by the Muslims in the 7th century. The area is out of bounds.

★ El-Aqsa Mosque
Originally built in the early years of the 8th century (see p68), El-Aqsa remains the main place of Islamic worship in Jerusalem and draws huge crowds of devout Muslims each Friday for noon prayer.

Crusader-built tower

Women's mosque

El-Kas Fountain
Carved from a single block of stone and dating from 1320, this is the largest of the Haram's many old but still functioning ablutions fountains.

STAR FEATURES

★ **Dome of the Rock**

★ **Dome of the Chain**

★ **El-Aqsa Mosque**

Exploring the Haram esh-Sharif

Stone
window,
El-Aqsa

ALTHOUGH THE UNDOUBTED main attraction is the Dome of the Rock, the Haram esh-Sharif has a great many other features that are worthy of attention. The esplanade acts as a virtual museum of Islamic architecture, beginning with the Dome, which dates back to the Omayyad era and is the earliest structure, and running through the Ayyubid (Grammar College), Mameluke (numerous *madrasas*) and Ottoman periods. Visitors should be aware that certain parts of the Haram esh-Sharif are out of bounds, notably the area south of the Gate of the Tribes and east of El-Aqsa.

Antiquity-strewn area in front of
the Museum of Islamic Art

The much reconstructed interior of the El-Aqsa Mosque

EL-AQSA MOSQUE

CONSTRUCTION OF El-Aqsa was begun less than 20 years after the completion of the Dome of the Rock. However, unlike the Dome, whose structure and interior have remained intact over the centuries, El-Aqsa has undergone great changes. In the first 60 years of its existence the mosque was twice razed to the ground by earthquakes. Its present form dates from the early 11th century. When the Crusaders captured Jerusalem in 1099, El-Aqsa became the headquarters of the Templars *(see p47)*; their legacy remains in the three central bays of the main façade. As it appears today, the façade has seven bays; in the mid-14th century the Mamelukes added an extra two on either side of the original Crusader porch.

The interior is dominated by mid-20th century additions, notably ranks of marble columns, donated by Benito Mussolini, and an elaborately painted ceiling paid for by King Farouk of Egypt. Older elements include the mihrab, decorated in 1187 under the patronage of Saladin, and the mosaics above the central aisle arch and around the drum of the dome, dating from 1035. Until 1969, the mosque had a fine carved pulpit *(minbar)*, also dating from the time of Saladin, but this was lost in a fire started by a deranged visitor.

A *qanatir*, topping a flight of steps up to the Dome

MUSEUM OF ISLAMIC ART

HOUSED IN the Crusader-era refectory of the Knights Templar, this sparsely-filled museum contains objects donated to the Haram esh-Sharif over the centuries, as well as architectural remnants from many of the Haram's buildings. Worthy of mention are the precious large Qurans, with pages adorned by fine Islamic calligraphy; part of a carved cypress-wood ceiling from El-Aqsa, dating from the 7th century and removed in 1948; and fine 15th-century copper doors from the Dome of the Rock. Admission to the museum is included in the fee for the Dome of the Rock and El-Aqsa Mosque.

Visitors with an interest in Islamic art should also visit the LA Mayer Museum in the new city *(see p126)*.

THE QANATIRS

EIGHT SHORT FLIGHTS of steps lead up to the platform on which the Dome of the Rock sits. All these stairways are of different sizes and lengths, and they all date from different periods. The flight opposite the Sabil of Qaitbey, leading up to the main entrance of the Dome, is unique in that it is carved out of the stone of the platform. Each flight is crowned by a slender arcade known as a *qanatir*. An alternative name for the arches is *mawazin*, or scales, because according to a widely-accepted Muslim belief, on the day of the Last Judgment, the scales used by God to weigh the souls of humankind will be hung from these arches on the Haram.

DOME OF THE CHAIN

BESIDE THE DOME of the Rock, the Haram has many other, smaller domes. The most impressive is the Dome of the Chain, immediately to the east of the Dome of the Rock. It is a simple structure of a domed roof supported on 17 columns. It originally had 20 columns but was remodelled to its current form by the Mameluke emir Baybars in the 13th century. The interior tiling is splendid (see p67). Some mystery exists over the purpose of the dome, but it is likely that it was a treasury. Its name derives from the legend that a chain once hung from the roof, and whoever told a lie while holding it would be struck dead by lightning.

THE MADRASAS

MOST OF the buildings fringing the Haram are madrasas – Islamic colleges. Of these, the **Ashrafiyya** on the western side of the Haram, built in 1482 by Sultan Qaitbey, is a masterpiece of Islamic architecture. It has an especially ornate doorway exhibiting all the best elements of Mameluke design, including bands of different

JERUSALEM AND ISLAM

The Dome of the Rock and neighbouring El-Aqsa Mosque represent the first great religious complex in the history of Islam. Although Muslims venerate many of the same prophets as the Jews and Christians, notably Abraham (Ibrahim to the Muslims), Jerusalem itself is never mentioned in the Quran. The choice of this site was more likely a political issue. In locating his mosque on the site of the Temple, the caliph Abd el-Malik meant to reinforce the idea that the new religion of Islam, and its worldly empire, was the successor and continuation of those of the Jews and the Christians. It was only later that Jerusalem came to be tied into Islamic tradition through the story of the Night Journey (see p25). In this, Muhammad visits el-masjid el-aqsa, which means literally "the most distant mosque", and this name was retroactively applied to the whole Haram esh-Sharif before later being restricted to the mosque only.

Angel with Muhammad's robe on the Night Journey

coloured stone, stalactite carvings above the doorway and, on the benches on either side, intricate, interlocking stones known as "joggling".

Adjoining the Ashrafiyya to the north, close to the Sabil of Qaitbey, is another madrasa, the **Uthmaniyya**. Its upper section has beautiful wheel-shaped decorations formed by inlays of yellow and red stone. Along the northern edge of the Haram are two more, the triple-domed **Isardiyya** and adjacent **Malekiyya**. Both date from the 14th century. West of these two, in the corner, is the **Omariyya** college, which is held to contain the First Station of the Cross, but can only be entered from the Via Dolorosa (see pp28–9).

GOLDEN GATE

ALSO KNOWN as the Gate of Mercy (Bab el-Rahma), the Golden Gate was one of the original Herodian city gates. According to Jewish tradition, the Messiah will enter Jerusalem through this gate, which is said to be the reason why the Muslims walled it up in the 7th century. The existing structure dates to the Omayyad period and is best viewed from outside the city walls.

The domed fountain, the Sabil of Qaitbey, with part of the Ashrafiyya Madrasa in the background

Dome of the Rock

Tile above the south entrance

Oᴺᴱ ᴼᶠ ᵀʜᴱ first and greatest achievements of Islamic architecture, the Dome of the Rock was built in AD 688–91 by the Omayyad caliph Abd el-Malik. Intended to proclaim the superiority of Islam and provide an Islamic focal point in the Holy City, the majestic structure now dominates Jerusalem and has become a symbol of the city. More a shrine than a mosque, the mathematically harmonious building echoes elements of Classical and Byzantine architecture, including the rotunda of the Holy Sepulchre *(see pp88–91)*.

View of the Dome of the Rock with the Muslim Quarter in the background

The drum is decorated with tiles and verses from the Quran which tell of Muhammad's Night Journey.

★ **Tilework**
The multicoloured tiles that adorn the exterior are faithful copies of Persian tiles that Suleyman the Magnificent added in 1545 to replace the badly damaged original mosaics.

Quranic verses

The octagonal arcade is adorned with original mosaics (AD 692) and an inscription inviting Christians to recognize the truth of Islam.

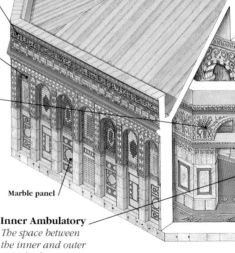

Marble panel

Inner Ambulatory
The space between the inner and outer arcades forms an ambulatory around the Rock. The shrine's two ambulatories recall the ritual circular movement of pilgrims around the Qaaba in Mecca.

Sᴛᴀʀ Fᴇᴀᴛᴜʀᴇꜱ

★ **Interior of Dome**

★ **Tilework**

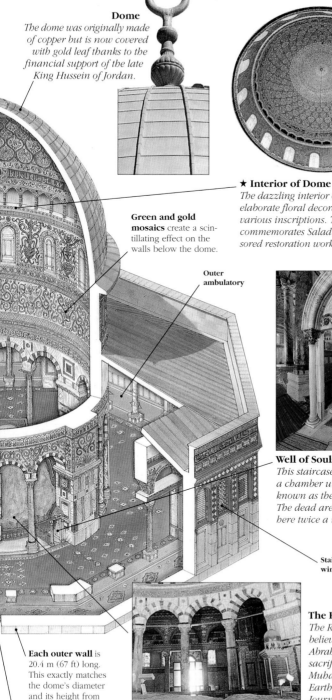

Dome
The dome was originally made of copper but is now covered with gold leaf thanks to the financial support of the late King Hussein of Jordan.

★ **Interior of Dome**
The dazzling interior of the cupola has elaborate floral decoration as well as various inscriptions. The large text commemorates Saladin, who sponsored restoration work on the building.

Green and gold mosaics create a scintillating effect on the walls below the dome.

Outer ambulatory

Well of Souls
This staircase leads down to a chamber under the Rock known as the Well of Souls. The dead are said to meet here twice a month to pray.

Stained-glass window

Each outer wall is 20.4 m (67 ft) long. This exactly matches the dome's diameter and its height from the base of the drum.

South entrance

The Rock
The Rock is variously believed to be where Abraham was asked to sacrifice Isaac, where Muhammad left the Earth on his Night Journey (see p25), *and the site of the Holy of Holies of Herod's Temple* (see pp42–3).

Geometric tiling and verses from the Quran on the exterior of the Dome of the Rock ▷

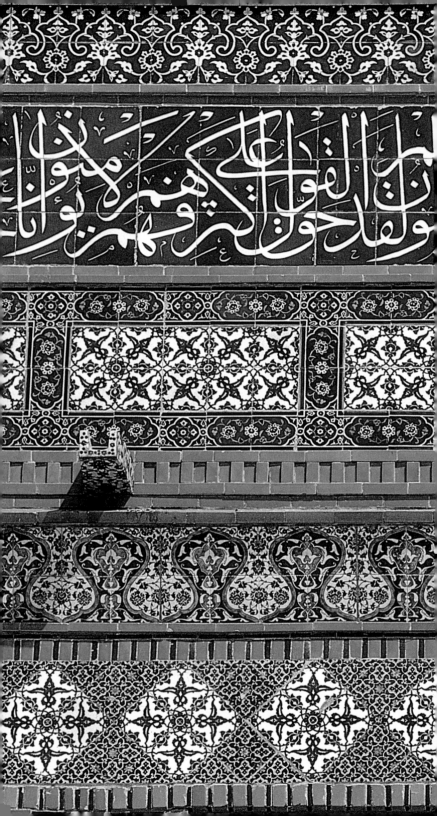

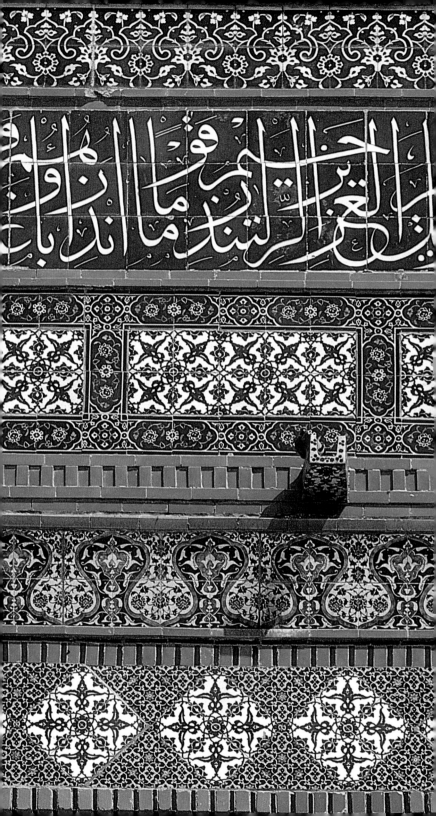

THE JEWISH QUARTER

IN HERODIAN TIMES this area abutted the Temple enclosure *(see pp42–3)* and was occupied by the priestly elite. In the late Roman period, Jews were forbidden from living in Jerusalem and it was not until the 13th century that a small community was re-established here. The district became prevalently Jewish during Ottoman rule, when it acquired its present name. By the 16th century, pilgrimage to the Western Wall – the only surviving remnant of the Temple – had become

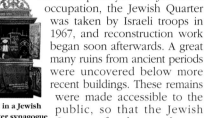
Ark in a Jewish Quarter synagogue

a strong tradition. After the destruction wrought in the 1948 War and the subsequent years of Jordanian occupation, the Jewish Quarter was taken by Israeli troops in 1967, and reconstruction work began soon afterwards. A great many ruins from ancient periods were uncovered below more recent buildings. These remains were made accessible to the public, so that the Jewish Quarter of today stands as a fascinating, living mix of more than 2,000 years of Jerusalem Jewry.

SIGHTS AT A GLANCE

Archaeological Sites
The Broad Wall ❷
The Cardo ❶
Israelite Tower ❿
Ophel Archaeological Park ⓮
St Mary of the Germans ⓭

Museums
The Burnt House ⓬
Old Yishuv Court Museum ❾
Rachel Ben Zvi Centre ⓫
Wohl Archaeological Museum ❻

Holy Places
Ramban Synagogue ❹
The Sephardic Synagogues ❽
The Western Wall ⓯

Streets and Squares
Batei Makhase Square ❼
Hurva Square ❸
Tiferet Yisrael Street ❺

KEY

- Street-by-Street map *See pp76–7*
- Tourist information
- Parking
- Taxi rank
- Bus station
- City wall

GETTING THERE
The Jewish Quarter is most easily reached on foot via Jaffa Gate and the Armenian Quarter. Bus No. 1 stops at Western Wall Plaza. Drivers can enter the Old City by Jaffa, Zion or Dung gates and park at the bottom of Khabad Street.

◁ **Orthodox Jews praying at the Western Wall**

Street-by-Street: Around Hurva Square

Jewish Quarter sign

Extensively reconstructed since 1967 and largely residential, the Jewish Quarter is noticeably more orderly than the rest of the Old City. It is also relatively free of large groups of tourists. The focal point for the local community is Hurva Square. This has a few small shops and cafés with outdoor seating. Most of the interesting sights in the quarter are just a few minutes' walk from here. Another hub of the district is the Cardo and Jewish Quarter Road area, which is filled with souvenir shops and more places to eat.

Looking towards Hurva Square from Jewish Quarter Road

Cardo shopping arcade

The Sidna Omar minaret is all that remains of a 14th-century mosque.

★ The Cardo
This is an excavated and partially reconstructed section of the main street of Byzantine-era Jerusalem ❶

The Sephardic Synagogues
Two of these four synagogues date back to the early 17th century. They all contain much ornate decoration ❽

Rothschild House

Batei Makhase Square
A small secluded square, this is favoured by local children as a play area. Its most notable feature is the elegant 19th-century Rothschild House, with its arcaded façade ❼

Shelter Houses *(see p80)*

MISHMEROT HA KEHUNA

BATEI MAKHA SQUAR

Hurva Synagogue
(see pp78–9)

Muslim Quarter

Ramban Synagogue
Founded around 1400, the Ramban was the first synagogue to be built here since the Roman expulsion of the Jews from Jerusalem ❹

The Broad Wall
Archaeologists have dated these remains to the 8th century BC ❷

LOCATOR MAP
See Jerusalem Street Finder, maps 3 and 4

MUSLIM QUARTER

JEWISH QUARTER

MOUNT OF OLIVES AND MOUNT ZION

★ **Hurva Square**
Dominated by the arch of Hurva Synagogue, the quarter's main square is a good place to sit and watch the locals going about their business ❸

Western Wall

Western Wall and St Mary of the Germans

Tiferet Yisrael Street
This lively street heads towards the Western Wall, passing the ruined 19th-century Tiferet Yisrael Synagogue ❺

★ **Wohl Archaeological Museum**
Located under a modern housing block, the Wohl contains archaeo-logical remains of Jewish dwellings from the era of Herod the Great ❻

KEY

– – – Suggested route

STAR SIGHTS

★ **The Cardo**

★ **Hurva Square**

★ **Wohl Archaeological Museum**

0 metres   25
0 yards   25

The Cardo ❶

Map 3 C4.

Now in part an exclusive shopping arcade, the Cardo was Jerusalem's main thoroughfare in the Byzantine era. It was originally laid by the Romans, then extended in the 4th century as Christian pilgrims began to flock to Jerusalem and the city expanded accordingly. The Byzantine extension, which remains in evidence today, linked the two major places of worship of the time, the Church of the Holy Sepulchre *(see pp88–91)* in the north and the long since vanished Nea basilica in the south.

The central roadway of the Byzantine Cardo was 12.5 m (41 ft) wide. This was flanked by broad porticoed pavements and lined with shops. Visitors can get a good idea of how the whole once looked by descending to a reconstructed section, which runs for almost 200 m (650 ft) alongside Jewish Quarter (Ha-Yehudim) Road. At the southern end are the remains of original shops that were partly hewn out of the rock on the west side of the street.

The Cardo's continued importance during the reign of Justinian in the 6th century is attested to by its prominent appearance on the famous Madaba map *(see pp192–3)*. Some 500 years later, in the Crusader era, the Cardo was converted into a covered market, which is how the northern section has now been preserved, as an arcade of smart galleries and boutiques.

The ancient Broad Wall, cutting through the new Jewish Quarter

The Broad Wall ❷

Plugat ha-Kotel St. **Map** 3 C4.

The Jewish Quarter was largely destroyed during the 1948 War and allowed to deteriorate further under 19 years of subsequent Jordanian occupation. Following the 1967 Israeli victory, a vast reconstruction programme resulted in many important archaeological finds. One of the most significant was the unearthing of the foundations of a massive wall 7 m (22 ft) thick and 65 m (215 ft) long. This was possibly part of fortifications built by King Hezekiah in the 8th century BC to enclose a new quarter outside the previous city wall. The need for expansion was probably brought about by a flood of refugees from Samaria after the Assyrian invasion of 722 BC.

On the building next to the exposed wall, a clearly visible line indicates what archaeologists think was the original height of the wall. Also visible are the remains of housing from the same period, demolished to make way for the wall, as described in the Book of Isaiah (22: 10), "And ye have numbered the houses of Jerusalem, and the houses have ye broken down to fortify the wall".

Hurva Square ❸

Map 3 C4.

This is the heart and social centre of the present-day Jewish Quarter. In the maze of narrow, winding streets which, though modern, follow the topography of the quarter before its destruction, Hurva Square is one of the few open spaces in the area. It has cafés, souvenir shops and a few snack bars that have small tables outside when the weather is good. Also here is the Jewish Students' Information Centre, which provides help with accommodation and invitations to Shabbat (Sabbath) dinners for young Jews.

Sidna Omar minaret

On the west side of the square is the minaret of the vanished 14th-century mosque of Sidna Omar, along with the Hurva and Ramban synagogue complexes. Hurva means "ruins" and the history of the Hurva Synagogue more than justifies its name. In the 18th century a group of a few hundred Ashkenazi Jews from Poland followed the rabbi Yehuda Hassid to Jerusalem and founded a synagogue on this site. However, it was burnt down by creditors inflamed by the community's unpaid debts. The synagogue was rebuilt in 1864 in a grand Neo-Byzantine style. At the time, it was one of the largest buildings in the Old City. However, during the fighting that took place in 1948

The Cardo, the main street of Byzantine-era Jerusalem

Hurva Arch, all that has been reconstructed of the former synagogue

between the Arab and Jewish armies, the synagogue was destroyed. Since the Israelis recaptured the Old City in 1967, there have been many proposed schemes for its rebuilding, but to date it remains a shell, marked only by a single reconstructed arch of the synagogue's former main façade. The ruins have been made safe for visitors to wander around, and information boards help one visualize the edifice that once stood here.

Ramban Synagogue ❹

Hurva Square. **Map** 3 C4. ◯ *for morning and evening prayers.* ♿

WHEN THE SPANISH rabbi and scholar Moses Ben Nahman (Nahmanides) arrived in Jerusalem in 1267, he was shocked to find only a handful of Jews in the city. He dedicated himself to nurturing a Jewish community and bought land near King David's Tomb *(see p113)* on Mount Zion in order to build a synagogue. Some time around 1400, the synagogue was moved to its present site. It was the first time there had been a Jewish presence in this quarter of the Old City since the exile of the Jews in AD 135 and marked the start of their gradual return. The synagogue had to be rebuilt in 1523 after it collapsed. It is believed that, at this time, it was probably the only Jewish place of worship in what was then Ottoman-controlled Jerusalem. In 1599 the authorities banned the Jews from worship in the synagogue and the building became a workshop instead.

It was not until the Israelis took control of the Old City in 1967 that, after a hiatus of nearly 400 years, the synagogue was restored as a place of regular worship.

Tiferet Yisrael Street ❺

Map 4 D4.

THIS IS ONE of the busiest streets in the Jewish Quarter. It connects Hurva Square with the stairs that descend towards the Western Wall. Partway along is the shell of the ruined Tiferet Yisrael Synagogue, destroyed in the 1948 War and left gutted as a memorial. Sectarian feelings run high around here, and local souvenir shops stock some dubious merchandise, such as Israeli Army T-shirts and postcards of the Haram esh-Sharif with its mosques replaced by the "future Third Temple". The street ends in an attractive tree-shaded square which has several snack bars and cafés, including the popular Quarter Café,

Tiferet Yisrael Street, one of the liveliest in the Jewish Quarter

which serves kosher food and offers great views of the Haram esh-Sharif and Dome of the Rock from its terrace.

Wohl Archaeological Museum ❻

1 Ha-Karaim St. **Map** 4 D4. 📞 *(02) 628 3448.* ◯ *9am–5pm Sun–Thu, 9am–1pm Fri.* 📷 🚫

IN THE ERA of Herod the Great (37–4 BC), the area of the present-day Jewish Quarter was part of a wealthy "Upper City", occupied for the most part by the families of important Jewish priests. During post-1967 redevelopment, the remains of several large houses were unearthed here. This rediscovered Herodian quarter now lies from 3 to 7 m (10 to 22 ft) below street level, underneath a modern complex, and is preserved as the Wohl Archaeological Museum.

The museum is remarkable for its vivid evocation of everyday life 2,000 years ago. All the houses had an inner courtyard, ritual baths, and cisterns to collect rain, which was the only source of water at the time. The first part of the museum, called the Western House, has a mosaic in the vestibule and a well-preserved ritual bath *(mikveh)*. Beyond this is the Middle Complex, the remains of two separate houses where archaeologists found a maze-pattern mosaic floor covered in burnt wood; this, they surmised, was fire damage from the Roman siege of Jerusalem led by Titus in AD 70 *(see pp41–3)*. The largest and most complete of all the Herodian buildings is the Palatial Mansion. This, too, has signs of fire damage, as well as more splendid mosaic floors and ritual baths.

The entrance fee to the Wohl Museum also covers admission to the Burnt House, another building from the same era *(see p82)*.

Batei Makhase Square ❼

Map 4 D5.

THIS QUIET SQUARE is named after the so-called Shelter Houses (Batei Makhase), which lie just south of it. They were built in 1862 by Jews from Germany and Holland for destitute immigrants from central Europe. Tenants were chosen by lottery and charged little or no rent. Severe damage in the 1948 and 1967 wars *(see p52)* made restoration necessary.

The work brought to light the first remains of the Nea (New) Basilica, whose existence had previously been known only from the Madaba map *(see pp192–3)* and literary sources. Built by Byzantine emperor Justinian in AD 543, it was at the time the largest basilica in Palestine. The remains of one of the apses can be seen near the square's southwest corner. Although other remains are sparse, archaeologists have now been able to trace the basilica's full extent – an enormous 100 m (328 ft) by 52 m (171 ft).

The handsome, arcaded building on the western side of the square was built for the Rothschild family in 1871. In front of it are parts of Roman columns, whose original provenance is unknown.

The 17th-century Ben Zakkai Synagogue

The Sephardic Synagogues ❽

Ha-Tupim St. **Map** 3 C5. ⬜ *9:30am–4pm Sun–Thu, 9:30am–2pm Fri.*

THE FOUR SYNAGOGUES in this group became the spiritual centre of the area's Sephardic community in the 17th century. The Sephardim were descended from the Jews expelled from Spain in 1492 and Portugal in 1497. They had first settled in the Ottoman Empire and then moved to Palestine when the latter was conquered by the Turks in 1516. When the first two synagogues were built, the Sephardim formed the largest Jewish community in Jerusalem. The synagogue floors were laid well below street level to allow sufficient height for the buildings, as Ottoman law stated

Bimah (see p21),
Istambuli Synagogue

that synagogues should not rise above the surrounding houses.

The Ben Zakkai Synagogue was built in 1610. Its courtyard, with a matroneum, or gallery for women worshippers, was converted into the Central Synagogue, whose present form dates from the 1830s. The Prophet Elijah Synagogue, created from a study hall built in 1625, was consecrated in 1702. Legend has it that during prayers to mark Yom Kippur, Elijah appeared as the 10th adult male worshipper needed for synagogue prayer – hence the building's name. The Istambuli Synagogue was built in 1857 and, like the other three, contains furnishings salvaged from Italian synagogues damaged in World War II.

Old Yishuv Court Museum ❾

6 Or ha-Khayim St. **Map** 3 C5. 🆑 *(02) 627 6319.* ⬜ *9am–2pm Sun–Thu.*

THIS SMALL MUSEUM, devoted to the history of the city's Jewish community from the mid-19th century to the end of Ottoman rule in 1917, occupies one of the oldest complexes of rooms in the Jewish Quarter. Of Turkish construction, thought to date from the 15th or 16th centuries, it was once part of a private home. The exhibits, consisting largely of reconstructed interiors, memorabilia and photographs, also include the Ari Synagogue on the ground floor. This was used by a Sephardic congregation during most of the Ottoman period. Badly damaged in the fighting of 1936, it fell into disuse until 1967, when it was restored. On

Rothschild House and a Roman column base and capital in Batei Makhase Square

Household objects on display at the Old Yishuv Court Museum

Rachel Ben Zvi Centre ⓫

Shonei Halakhot St. **Map** 4 D4.
 (02) 628 6288. *9am–4pm
(Jul & Aug: 6pm) Sun–Thu, 9am–
1pm Fri.*

T HE PRINCIPAL EXHIBIT here is
a model of all the archaeological remains of First Temple
Period Jerusalem (around the
8th century BC). It clearly illu-
strates the relationship between
remains which can be difficult
to interpret when they are seen
on the ground, surrounded by
other buildings. It also shows
the original topography of the
area before valleys were filled
in and occupation layers built
up. Water-supply systems,
including Warren's Shaft and
Hezekiah's Tunnel *(see p111)*,
are also shown. An audiovisual
show describes the city's
history from 1000 to 586 BC.

There is also a fascinating
display of finds from a secret
dig carried out in 1909–11 by
English archaeologist Captain
Montague Parker. His team of
excavators penetrated underneath the Haram esh-Sharif
(Temple Mount) in search of
a chamber that reputedly contained King Solomon's treasure.
When news of the dig got
out, violent demonstrations
by Jews and Muslims, united
in their opposition to the
desecration of their holy site,
forced Parker to flee the city
and return to England.

the top floor is the 18th-century
Or ha-Khayim Synagogue, used
by Ashkenazi Jews in the 19th
century. Closed between 1948
and 1967, it is now a functioning synagogue once more.

Israelite Tower ⓾

Shonei Halakhot St. **Map** 4 D4.
 *9am–5pm Sun–Thu, 9am–1pm
Fri.*

S TEPS AT THE CORNER of Shonei
Halakhot and Plugat ha-
Kotel streets lead underneath
a modern apartment block to
the remains of a tower of the
7th century BC. The tower,
the walls of which are over
4 m (13 ft) thick and survive
to a height of 8 m (26 ft), is
believed to have been part of
a gateway in the Israelite city
wall. At its foot were found

the heads of Israelite and
Babylonian arrows, as well as
evidence of burning. These
finds are thought to date from
the Babylonian conquest of
Jerusalem in 586 BC *(see p40)*
and may identify the gate as
the one through which
Babylonian troops entered the
city (Jeremiah 39: 3). The other
visible remains belong to the
2nd-century BC Hasmonean
city wall, another section of
which can be seen at the
Citadel *(see pp98–100)*.

The apartment block above
was built on stilts, as were
other modern buildings in the
Jewish Quarter, to allow access
by archaeologists. However,
the need to rebuild rapidly
after the 1948 War meant that
there was insufficient time to
uncover many of the remains
and draw a complete plan
of the area's fortifications.

JEWISH QUARTER ARCHITECTURE

Heavily damaged during the 1948 War, the
Jewish Quarter has been almost totally
reconstructed in recent times. While there is
no distinct "Jewish style", the quarter's modern architecture belongs to a well-defined
Jerusalem tradition. First and foremost,
everything is constructed of the pale local
stone. Use of this stone has been mandatory
in Jerusalem since a law to this effect was
passed by the British military governor,
Ronald Storrs, in 1917. Buildings and street
patterns are deliberately asymmetrical to
evoke haphazard historical development.
Streets are also narrow and cobbled, with
many small courtyards and external staircases to upper levels. Buildings make great
use of traditional Middle Eastern elements
such as arches, domes and oriels (the high
bay windows supported on brackets, much
favoured by Mameluke builders). A jumble

Courtyard in the Jewish Quarter near The Cardo

of different heights means that the roof of one
building is often the terrace of another. The
result is a very contemporary look, which is
at the same time firmly rooted in the past.

The Burnt House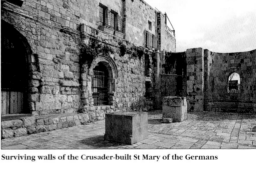

13 Tiferet Yisrael St. **Map** 4 D4.
📞 (02) 628 7211. 🕐 9am–4:30pm
Sun–Thu, 9am–12:30pm Fri. 🏛 ♿
📷 phone in advance.

WHEN THE ROMANS took Jerusalem in AD 70 (see pp41–3), they destroyed the Temple and Lower City to the south. A month later they rampaged through the wealthy Upper City, setting fire to the houses and killing the Jewish inhabitants sheltering inside them. The charred walls and a coin dated to AD 69 discovered during excavations show that this was one of those houses.

A stone weight found among the debris bears the inscription "son of Kathros", indicating that the house belonged to a wealthy family of high priests. They are known from a subsequent reference to them in the Babylonian Talmud, the codification of Jewish law developed by Babylonian Jews in the 3rd century AD.

The rooms on view, introduced by a slide show with commentary, comprise a kitchen, four rooms that may have been bedrooms, and a bathroom with a ritual bath, all leading off a long entrance hall. It is believed that these formed part of the basement of a much larger residence, but further excavations cannot be undertaken as the remains lie beneath present-day neighbouring houses.

The entrance fee also covers admission to the Wohl Archaeological Museum (see p79).

Storage vessel found in the Burnt House

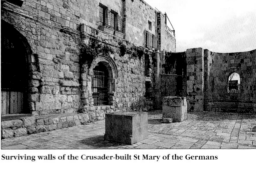

Surviving walls of the Crusader-built St Mary of the Germans

St Mary of the Germans

Misgav la-Dakh St. **Map** 4 D4.
🕐 daily.

IMMEDIATELY BELOW the terrace of the Quarter Café (see p246) are the original walls of St Mary of the Germans. This early 12th-century Crusader church was part of a complex that included a pilgrims' hospice (no longer in existence) and a hospital. It was built by the Knights Hospitallers (see p47) and run by their German members. This was in response to the influx of German-speaking pilgrims unfamiliar with French, the lingua franca, or Latin, the official language, of the new Latin Kingdom of Jerusalem. Activity ceased when Jerusalem fell to the Muslims in 1187, but the church and the hospital were again used during the brief period when Jerusalem was once more under Christian rule (1229–44).

Today the church is roofless. However, the walls survive to a considerable height, clearly showing the three apses of the typical basilica plan so widely used in the Holy Land from early Byzantine times.

Beside the church the steps down to the Western Wall Plaza provide wonderful views of the Western Wall, the Dome of the Rock and the Mount of Olives behind.

Ophel Archaeological Park

Dung Gate. **Map** 4 E4. 📞 (02) 625 4403. 🕐 9am–5pm Sun–Thu, 9am–3pm Fri. 🏛 ♿ 📷 phone in advance.

THIS AREA on the southern and southwestern side of the Haram esh-Sharif (Temple Mount) was built over, razed, and rebuilt several times over the centuries. The first dwellings were built here in the 8th century BC, though the remains on view are

Herodian and Omayyad remains at the southwestern corner of the Haram esh-Sharif, Ophel Archaeological Park

mainly Herodian (34–4 BC), Byzantine (AD 395–661) and Omayyad (AD 661–750).

Left from the entrance, the way leads between the walls of two Omayyad buildings to an area where another Omayyad structure has been removed to show Herodian remains. Also Herodian are the beginnings of a great arch, known as Robinson's Arch, which spring from the Temple wall and a pier opposite. The arch once supported an entrance to the Temple courtyard *(see pp42–3)*.

Back near the entrance is a much-restored, 8th-century Omayyad palace built around a courtyard. In the palace's far left-hand corner a tower abutting the Temple walls was inserted by the Crusaders, then rebuilt by the Mamelukes. The south and east palace walls are topped by 16th-century ramparts.

Beyond the palace, whose exit leads under the present city wall, are more Herodian and Omayyad remains, some Jewish ritual baths and several Byzantine houses. In the Temple wall can be seen traces of the Double Gate, Triple Gate and Single Gate – ancient city gates that had all been blocked up by the late 12th century.

The Western Wall ⑮

Western Wall Plaza. **Map** 4 D4. 🚌 *1.* ♿ 🚫 *on Sabbath.* **Western Wall Tunnel** ☎ *(02) 627 3515.* ⏱ *9:30am–12:30pm Mon–Wed (only by prior telephone booking).* ⬤ *Jewish hols.* 📷 📹 *compulsory.*

A MASSIVE, blank wall built of huge stone blocks, the Western Wall (Ha-Kotel ha-Maaravi in Hebrew) is Judaism's holiest site, and the plaza in front of it is a permanent place of worship. The wall is part of the retaining wall of the Temple Mount and was built by Herod the Great in 20 BC during his expansion of the Temple enclosure *(see pp42–3)*. The huge, lower stones are Herodian, while those higher up date from Omayyad and Fatimid times.

During the Ottoman period *(see p48)*, the wall became the

Jews' chief place of pilgrimage, where they came to lament the destruction of the Temple in AD 70. For this reason it was for centuries known as the Wailing Wall. As the Jews had been forbidden access to the Temple Mount, this was the only part of the ruins they were allowed to approach.

Houses covered the adjoining land until relatively recently. When the Israelis gained control of the Old City after the 1967 war *(see p52)*, they levelled the neighbouring Arab district to create the Western Wall Plaza.

The area in front of the wall is partly divided by a screen. Men pray on the left, women on the right. Non-Jews can also approach the wall, provided they cover their heads, dress appropriately *(see pp268–9)* and behave with decorum.

At the left-hand corner of the men's prayer section is Wilson's Arch (named after a 19th-century archaeologist). Now contained within a building which functions as a synagogue, it originally carried the Causeway to the Temple. From the arch, archaeologists have dug the **Western Wall Tunnel** to explore the wall's foundations. It runs north, following the base of the outside face of the Temple wall along a Herodian street, below today's street level, and emerges on the Via Dolorosa *(see p62)*.

Men's prayer section, Western Wall

THE CHRISTIAN AND ARMENIAN QUARTERS

U NDER BYZANTINE RULE the Christian community of Jerusalem expanded rapidly. Settlement was concentrated in the northwest corner of the city, in the shadow of the great basilica of the Holy Sepulchre. Bounded by Souk Khan el-Zeit and David Street,

Old City sign made of Armenian tiles

the modern quarter remains filled with the churches, patriarchates and hospices of the city's many Christian denominations. To the south is the area traditionally inhabited by the Armenians, who have a long history in Jerusalem. It is one of the quietest parts of the Old City.

SIGHTS AT A GLANCE

Museums
The Citadel pp98–100 **9**
Mardigian Museum **14**
Museum of the Greek
   Orthodox Patriarchate **7**

Churches
Alexander Hospice **2**
Church of the Holy Sepulchre
pp88–91 **1**
Church of St John
   the Baptist **5**
Lutheran Church of
   the Redeemer **3**
St James's Cathedral **13**
St Mark's Church **12**

Historic Areas, Streets and Gates
Christian Quarter Road **6**
Jaffa Gate **8**
Muristan **4**
Omar ibn el-Khattab Square **10**
Zion Gate **15**

Walks
A Walk on the Roofs **11**

GETTING THERE
These two quarters are served mainly by Jaffa Gate; a great many buses from the New City halt just outside. The area can also be entered from Zion and New gates. Zion Gate has parking just outside.

KEY
▨ Street-by-Street map
   See pp86–7
ℹ Tourist information
🚖 Taxi rank
— City wall

0 metres   150
0 yards   150

◁ **Pilgrims crowding outside the main doorway of the Church of the Holy Sepulchre**

Street-by-Street: The Christian Quarter

Capital from the Church of the Redeemer

THE MOST VISITED PART of the Old City, the Christian Quarter is a head-on collision between commerce and spirituality. At its heart is the Church of the Holy Sepulchre, the most sacred of all Christian sites. It is surrounded by such a clutter of churches and hospices that all one can see of its exterior are the domes and entrance façade. The nearby streets are filled with shops and stalls that thrive on the pilgrim trade. Respite from the crowds can be found in the cafés of Muristan Road.

The Christian Quarter, centred on the Holy Sepulchre

Church of St John the Baptist
The founding of the Crusader Knights Hospitallers is connected with this small church. A carved stone cross echoes the order's historic emblem ❺

Christian Quarter Road
Along with David Street, this is the quarter's main shopping thoroughfare. It specializes in religious items and quality handicrafts ❻

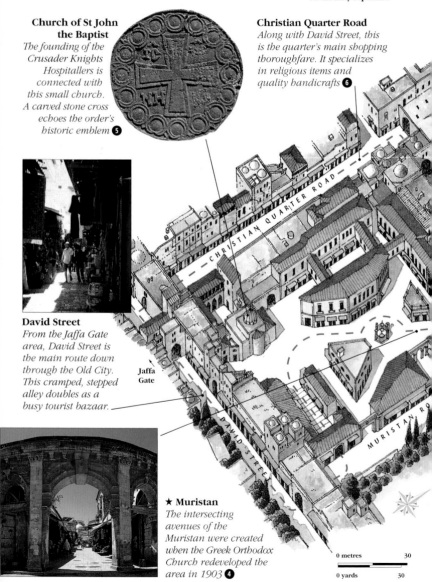

David Street
From the Jaffa Gate area, David Street is the main route down through the Old City. This cramped, stepped alley doubles as a busy tourist bazaar.

Jaffa Gate

★ **Muristan**
The intersecting avenues of the Muristan were created when the Greek Orthodox Church redeveloped the area in 1903 ❹

0 metres   30
0 yards   30

★ Church of the Holy Sepulchre
The Stabat Mater Altar is one of numerous chapels and shrines that fill the church, which commemorates the Crucifixion and burial of Christ ❶

Omar Mosque
(see p95)

Khanqa Salahiyya
(see p95)

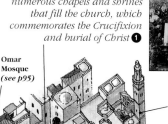

LOCATOR MAP
See Jerusalem Street Finder, map 3

Souk el-Dabbagha
With the Holy Sepulchre church at the end of the street, the few shops here have no shortage of customers for their religious souvenirs.

Ethiopian Monastery
(see p91)

Zalatimo's is a famed confectionery shop; its storeroom contains remains of the doorway of the original 4th-century Holy Sepulchre church.

Alexander Hospice
Belonging to the Russian Orthodox Church, the hospice is built over ruins of the early Holy Sepulchre church ❷

SOUK EL-DABBAGHA

SOUK KHAN EL-ZEIT

KEY
– – – Suggested route

★ Lutheran Church of the Redeemer
This church has an attractive medieval cloister, but most people visit for the views from the bell tower ❸

STAR SIGHTS

★ **Church of the Holy Sepulchre**

★ **Lutheran Church of the Redeemer**

★ **Muristan**

Church of the Holy Sepulchre ❶

BUILT AROUND WHAT IS BELIEVED to be the site of Christ's
Crucifixion, burial and Resurrection, this complex
church is the most important in Christendom. The first
basilica here was built by Roman emperor Constantine
between AD 326 and 335 at the suggestion of his mother,
St Helena. It was rebuilt on a smaller scale by Byzantine
emperor Constantine Monomachus in the 1040s following
its destruction by Fatimid sultan Hakim in 1009, but was
much enlarged again by the Crusaders between 1114
and 1170. A disastrous fire in 1808 and an earthquake
in 1927 necessitated extensive repairs.

**The mosaic of roofs and domes of the
Church of the Holy Sepulchre**

The Rotunda,
heavily rebuilt after
the 1808 fire, is the
most majestic part
of the church.

★ **Christ's Tomb**
*For Christians, this is the most
sacred site of all. Inside the 1810
monument, a marble slab covers
the rock on which Christ's body
is believed to have been laid.*

**The Crusader bell
tower** was reduced by
two storeys in 1719.

**Chapel of
the Franks**

The main entrance is early
12th century. The right-hand
door was blocked up late in
the same century.

Stone of Unction
*This is where the anointing
and wrapping of Christ's
body after his death has
been commemorated since
medieval times. The present
stone dates from 1810.*

Courtyard
*The main entrance court-
yard is flanked by chapels.
The disused steps opposite
the bell tower once led to
the Chapel of the Franks,
the Crusaders' ceremonial
entrance to Golgotha.*

THE HOLY FIRE

On the Saturday of Orthodox Easter, all the church's lamps are put out and the faithful stand in the dark, a symbol of the darkness at the Crucifixion. A candle is lit at Christ's Tomb, then another and another, until the entire basilica and courtyard are ablaze with light to symbolize the Resurrection. Legend says the fire comes from heaven.

The Easter ceremony of the Holy Fire

VISITORS' CHECKLIST

Entrance from Souk el-Dabbagha.
Map 3 C3. ☎ (02) 627 3314.
☐ summer: 5am–9pm daily;
winter: 4am–7pm daily.

The Seven Arches of the Virgin are the remains of an 11th-century colonnaded courtyard.

Catholikon Dome
Rebuilt after the 1927 earthquake and decorated with an image of Christ, this dome covers the central nave of the Crusader church. This part of the building is now used for Greek Orthodox services.

The Centre of the World, according to ancient map-makers *(see p38)*, is marked here by a stone basin.

★ **Golgotha**
Through the glass around the Greek Orthodox altar can be seen the outcrop of rock venerated as the site of the Crucifixion.

Chapel of Adam *(see p90)*

Rock of Golgotha *(see p90)*

The Chapel of St Helena is now dedicated to St Gregory the Illuminator, patron of the Armenians.

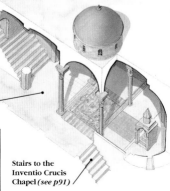

Ethiopian Monastery
A cluster of small buildings on the roof of the Chapel of St Helena is inhabited by a community of Ethiopian monks.

STAR FEATURES

★ **Christ's Tomb**

★ **Golgotha**

Stairs to the Inventio Crucis Chapel *(see p91)*

Exploring the Church of the Holy Sepulchre

Chapel door, main courtyard

THE RECONSTRUCTIONS and additions that have shaped this church over the centuries make it a complex building to explore. Its division into chapels and spaces allotted to six different denominations adds a further sense of confusion. The interior is dimly lit, and queues often form at Christ's Tomb, so that the time each person can spend inside the shrine may be limited to just a few minutes. Nonetheless, the experience of standing on Christianity's most hallowed ground inspires many visitors with a deep sense of awe.

show that the site lay outside the city walls until new ones encompassed it in AD 43; that in the early 1st century it was a disused quarry in which an area of cracked rock had been left untouched; and that rock-hewn tombs were in use here in the 1st centuries BC and AD. This all tallies with Gospel accounts of the Crucifixion.

CHAPEL OF ADAM

IMMEDIATELY beneath the Greek Orthodox chapel on Golgotha, this chapel is built against the Rock of Golgotha. It is the medieval replacement of a previous Chapel of Adam that was part of Constantine's 4th-century basilica. It was so called because tradition told that Christ was crucified over the burial place of Adam's skull – a tradition first recorded by the Alexandrian theologian Origen (c. AD 185–245).

The crack in the Rock of Golgotha, clearly visible in the apse, is held by believers to have been caused by the earthquake that followed Christ's death (Matthew 27: 51).

The Greek, Stabat Mater and Roman Catholic altars on Golgotha

GOLGOTHA

JUST INSIDE the church's main entrance, on the right, two staircases lead up to Golgotha, which in Hebrew means "Place of the Skull" and was translated into Latin as Calvary. The space here is divided into two chapels. On the left is the Greek Orthodox chapel, with its altar placed directly over the rocky outcrop on which the cross of Christ's Crucifixion is believed to have stood. The softer surrounding rock was quarried away when the church was built and the remaining, fissured, so-called Rock of Golgotha can now be seen through the protective glass around the altar. It can be touched through a hole in the floor under the altar. The 12th Station of the Cross *(see p28)* is commemorated here.

To the right is the Roman Catholic chapel, containing the 10th and 11th Stations of the Cross. The silver and bronze altar was given by Ferdinand de Medici in

1588. The 1937 mosaics encircle a Crusader-era medallion of the Ascension on the ceiling. The window looks into the Chapel of the Franks *(see p88)*.

Between these altars is the Altar of the Stabat Mater, commemorating Mary's sorrow as she stood at the foot of the cross. It marks the 13th Station of the Cross. The wooden bust of the Virgin is 18th century.

Archaeological evidence that the church rests on a possible site of the Crucifixion is scant, but positive. Excavations

11th-century apse, Chapel of Adam, built against the Rock of Golgotha

THE STATUS QUO

Fierce disputes, lasting centuries, between Christian creeds *(see p96)* over ownership of the church were largely resolved by an Ottoman decree issued in 1852. Still in force and known as the Status Quo, it divides custody among Armenians, Greeks, Copts, Roman Catholics, Ethiopians and Syrians. Some areas are administered communally. Every day, the church is unlocked by a Muslim keyholder acting as a "neutral" intermediary. This ceremonial task has been performed by a member of the same family for several generations.

Coptic priest in ceremonial vestments

CHRIST'S TOMB

THE PRESENT-DAY shrine around the tomb of Christ was built in 1809–10, after the severe fire of 1808. It replaced one dating from 1555, commissioned by the Franciscan friar Bonifacio da Ragusa. Before that, there had been a succession of shrines replacing the original 4th-century one destroyed by the sultan Hakim in 1009. Constantine's builders had dug away the hillside to leave the presumed rock-hewn tomb of Christ isolated and with enough room to build a church around it. They had also had to clear the remains of an AD 135 Hadrianic temple from the site, as well as the material with which an old quarry had been filled to provide the temple's foundations. In so doing, the Rock of Golgotha was also found.

Today the shrine, owned by the Greek, Armenian, Coptic, and Roman Catholic communities, contains two chapels. The outer Chapel of the Angel has a low pilaster incorporating a piece of the stone said to have been rolled from the mouth of Christ's Tomb by angels. It serves as a Greek Orthodox altar. A low door leads to the tiny inner Chapel of the Holy Sepulchre with the 14th Station of the Cross. A marble slab covers the place where Christ's body was supposedly laid. The slab was installed here in the 1555 reconstruction and purposely cracked to deter Ottoman looters.

SITE OF CHRIST'S TOMB

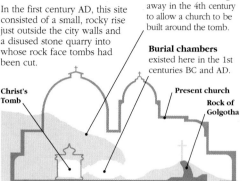

In the first century AD, this site consisted of a small, rocky rise just outside the city walls and a disused stone quarry into whose rock face tombs had been cut.

The hillside was dug away in the 4th century to allow a church to be built around the tomb.

Burial chambers existed here in the 1st centuries BC and AD.

Christ's Tomb

Present church

Rock of Golgotha

In the Coptic chapel behind the shrine, a piece of polished stone is shown as being part of the tomb itself, but it is granite and not limestone, as the tomb here is known to be.

ROTUNDA AND SYRIAN CHAPEL

THE ROTUNDA is built in Classical Roman style. The outer back wall (now hidden by interior partitions) survives from the 4th-century basilica up to a height of 11 m (36 ft). The 11th-century dome was replaced after the 1808 fire and the two-storey colonnade built. The first two columns on the right, standing with your back to the nave, are replicas of two that survived the fire, but were judged unstable. The originals were made in the 11th century from the two halves of a single, gigantic Roman column – part either of the 4th-century basilica or of the previous Hadrianic temple.

In the Rotunda's back wall is the Syrian Chapel. It contains Jewish rock tombs (c.100 BC– AD 100), marking the limit to which the hillside was dug away when the first church was built.

Carvings in St Helena's Chapel

CHAPELS OF ST HELENA AND THE INVENTIO CRUCIS

FROM THE AMBULATORY in the Crusader-period apse, now the choir in the Greek Catholikon, steep steps lead down to St Helena's Chapel. The crosses on the walls were carved by pilgrims. Although this crypt was built by the Crusaders, who reused Byzantine columns, the side walls are, in fact, foundations of the 4th-century basilica. More stairs go down to the Inventio Crucis (Finding of the Cross) Chapel, a former cistern, in which St Helena is said to have found the True Cross. The statue of her is 19th century.

ETHIOPIAN MONASTERY

THIS SIMPLE MONASTERY is approached either through the Coptic chapel in the corner of the courtyard, to the right of the main entrance, or from Souk Khan el-Zeit (see p87), up steps beside Zalatimo's, a famous pastry shop.

It occupies a series of small buildings on the roof of St Helena's Chapel, among the ruins of the former Crusader cloister. The Ethiopians were forced up here in the 17th century, when, unable to pay Ottoman taxes, they lost ownership of their chapels in the main church to the Copts.

People queuing to enter the shrine containing Christ's Tomb in the church's Rotunda

View of the Holy Sepulchre church from the roof of St Helena's Chapel ▷

Alexander Hospice ❷

Souk el-Dabbagha. **Map** 3 C3.
☎ (02) 627 4952. **Excavations**
◯ 9am–1pm & 3–5pm Mon–Sat;
ring the bell. 📷 ♿ ✍

HOME TO St Alexander's Church, the central place of worship for Jerusalem's Russian Orthodox community, the Alexander Hospice also houses some important excavations. When the hospice was founded in 1859, the site was already known to contain ruins of the original church of the Holy Sepulchre, built in AD 335. In 1882, however, excavations revealed remains of a Herodian city wall. This finally proved that the site of the Holy Sepulchre church was outside the ancient city walls, which added credence to the claim that it was on the true site of Christ's crucifixion (see pp88–93).

Alexander Hospice doorway

Also preserved here are remnants of a colonnaded street and, in the church, part of a triumphal arch from Hadrian's forum, begun in AD 135. The excavations are open to the public, but only parts of the church can be visited.

Lutheran Church of the Redeemer ❸

24 Muristan Rd. **Map** 3 C3.
☎ (02) 627 6111. ◯ 9am–1pm & 1:30–5pm Mon–Sat. 📷 for bell tower only.

THIS NEO-ROMANESQUE church was built for the German Kaiser Wilhelm II, and completed in 1898. Renewed interest in the Holy Land by Europe during the late 19th century had ushered in a period of restoration and church building, with many nations wanting to establish a religious presence in Jerusalem. The Lutheran Church of the Redeemer was constructed over the remains of the 11th-century church of St Mary of the Latins, built by wealthy merchants from Amalfi in Italy. An even earlier church is thought to have existed on the site from the 5th century. Many details from the medieval church have been incorporated into the new building, and the entrance way, decorated with the signs of the zodiac and symbols of the months, is largely original. The attractive cloister, which is inside the adjacent Lutheran hospice, has two tiers of galleries and dates from the 13th–14th centuries. Perhaps the most interesting part of the church though is the bell tower. After climbing the 177 steps, visitors are rewarded with some great views over the Old City.

One of the many souvenir shops in the Muristan

Muristan ❹

Muristan Rd. **Map** 3 C3.

THE NAME MURISTAN derives from the Persian word for a hospital or hospice for travellers. For centuries the area known as the Muristan, south of the Holy Sepulchre, was the site of just such a hospice for pilgrims from Latin-speaking countries. It was built by Charlemagne in the early 9th century, with permission from the caliph Haroun el-Rashid. Partly destroyed in 1009 by the Fatimid caliph El-Hakim, it was restored later in the 11th century by merchants from Amalfi. They also built three churches here: St Mary Minor for women, St Mary of the Latins for men, and St John the Baptist for the poor.
St John the Baptist still stands today, and was where the Knights of the Hospital of St John (or the Knights Hospitallers) were founded. They were to take over much of the Muristan area as their

The dominating tower of the Lutheran Church of the Redeemer

The fountain square, at the heart of the Muristan

headquarters, later building their own huge hospital to the north of the church. During the Crusades it was reported that there could often be up to 2,000 people under their care here at any one time.

By the 16th century the Muristan had fallen into ruins and Suleyman the Magnificent had its stones used to rebuild Jerusalem's city walls.

Today the Muristan is very different from how it once looked, most traces of the original buildings having long since disappeared. It is now characterized by its quiet lanes and attractive pink-stone buildings. The lanes converge at the ornate fountain in the main square – site of the original hospice. The surrounding streets are packed with small shops selling souvenirs, handicrafts and antiques. Along the nearby Muristan Road you will also find a number of outdoor cafés where you can sit and absorb the atmosphere.

The distinctive dome of the
Church of St John the Baptist

Church of St John the Baptist ❺

Christian Quarter Rd. **Map** 3 C4.
⬤ to the public.

THE SILVERY DOME of the Church of St John the Baptist is clearly visible above the rooftops of the Muristan, but the entrance is harder to spot among the hordes of people along busy Christian Quarter Road. A small doorway leads into a courtyard, which in turn gives access to the neighbouring Greek Orthodox monastery and the church proper.

Founded in the 5th century, the Church of St John the Baptist is one of the most ancient churches in Jerusalem. After falling into ruin, it was extensively rebuilt in the 11th century, and aside from the two bell towers which are a later addition, the modern church is little changed.

In 1099 many Christian knights who were wounded during the siege of Jerusalem were taken care of in this church. After their recovery they decided to dedicate themselves to helping the sick and protecting the pilgrims visiting Jerusalem. Founding the Knights of the Hospital of St John, they later developed into the military order of the Hospitallers and played a key role in the defence of the Holy Land (see pp46–7).

Christian Quarter Road ❻

Map 3 B3.

TOGETHER WITH David Street, which runs from Jaffa Gate towards the Muristan, Christian Quarter Road is one of the main streets in the Christian Quarter. Marking off the Muristan zone, it passes by the western side of the Holy Sepulchre, and parallel to Souk Khan el-Zeit. This busy road is lined with shops selling antiques, Palestinian handicrafts (embroidery, leather goods and Hebron glass), and religious articles (icons, carved olive-wood crucifixes and rosaries).

Midway up the road on the right, down an alley signposted for the Holy Sepulchre, a short stairway descends to the modest **Omar Mosque**, with its distinctive square minaret. Its name commemorates the caliph Omar, the person generally credited with saving the Holy Sepulchre from

Glassware on
sale on Christian
Quarter Road

falling into Muslim control after Jerusalem passed under Muslim dominion in February 638. Asked to go and pray inside the church, which would almost certainly have meant its being converted into a mosque, he instead prayed on the steps outside, thus allowing the church to remain a Christian site. The Omar mosque was built later, in 1193, by Saladin's son Aphdal Ali, beside the old Hospital of the Knights of St John.

The unassuming **Khanqa Salahiyya** is at the top of Christian Quarter Road. Built by Saladin between 1187 and 1189 as a monastery for Sufi mystics, it is on the site of the old Crusader Patriarchate of Jerusalem. Its ornate entrance way may be as close as you are allowed, however, as it is not open to non-Muslims. Along the north side of the mosque is El-Khanqa Street. This attractive, old, stepped street is lined with interesting shops, and runs up one of the Old City's many hills.

Museum of the Greek Orthodox Patriarchate ❼

Greek Orthodox Patriarchate Rd.
Map 3 B3. 🄲 (02) 628 2048.
⬜ 8am–3pm Mon–Sat. 📷 **Greek Catholic Patriarchate** 🄲 (02) 627 1968. ⬜ 8am–noon Mon–Sat. 📷

TUCKED AWAY in the back alleys of the Christian Quarter, this museum houses a collection of ecclesiastical items, which includes icons, embroidered vestments, mitres, chalices and filigree objects. It also has a fine array of archaeological finds. Of most interest are two white-stone sarcophagi found at the end of the 19th century in a tomb near the present-day King David Hotel. They are considered to belong to the family of Herod the Great (see p116), and are covered in wonderfully elaborate floral decoration, which represents some of the finest Herodian-era funerary art ever found. The museum also displays Crusader objects, including a 12th-century carved capital from Nazareth, and artifacts found in the tomb of Baldwin I (king of Jerusalem, 1100–18) in the Church of the Holy Sepulchre.

Among a collection of historical firmans (imperial edicts), is one that purports to have been issued by the caliph

Illuminated medieval codex from the Museum of the Greek Orthodox Patriarchate

Omar in AD 638, granting the Greek Orthodox Church custody of the holy places.

The nearby **Greek Catholic Patriarchate**, on the street of the same name that leads towards Jaffa Gate, has a small museum containing a collection of religious vestments and liturgical objects.

Jaffa Gate ❽

Map 3 B4. 🚌 1, 13, 20. 🄲 (02) 628 2048.

THIS IS THE BUSIEST of the seven Old City gates. It is the main gate for traffic and pedestrians coming from

modern West Jerusalem. Despite the gate's great size, the entrance tunnel is narrow; it is also L-shaped – both measures meant to slow attackers. It was constructed during the reign of Suleyman the Magnificent – an exact date of 1538 is given in a dedication within the arch on the outside of the gate. The breach in the wall through which cars now pass was made in 1898, in order to allow the visiting Kaiser Wilhelm II of Germany to enter the city in his carriage.

Immediately inside the gate, set into the wall behind some railings on the left, are two graves. Tour guides like to tell how these belong to Suleyman's architects, executed because they failed to incorporate Mount Zion within the city walls. An alternative legend has it that they were killed to prevent them ever building such grand walls for anyone else. In fact, they are the graves of a prominent citizen and his wife.

Jaffa Gate is also one of the places where visitors can climb up to the ramparts to walk along the city walls (see p101).

EASTERN CHRISTIANITY AND THE PATRIARCHATES

Jerusalem's Greek Orthodox Patriarch

There are no fewer than 17 churches represented in Jerusalem, a result of a great many historical schisms. As Christianity spread in the 2nd and 3rd centuries, patriarchates were established in Alexandria, Antioch, Constantinople, Jerusalem and Rome. Their heads, the patriarchs, claimed lineage from the Apostles, which gave them the authority to pronounce on correct doctrine. The first major schism came when the Council of Chalcedon (AD 451) proclaimed the dual "divine and human" nature of Christ, and in so doing estranged the Armenian, Ethiopian, Coptic and Syrian churches from the Roman Catholic and mainstream Orthodoxy. Eastern and Western Christianity split in 1054, when the Eastern churches refused to acknowledge the primacy of the Pope and the Roman church. Today there are four patriarchs (a position akin to that of an archbishop) resident in Jerusalem: those of the Greek Orthodox, Armenian, Greek Catholic and Latin (Roman Catholic) churches. The Ethiopians and Copts have a building called a patriarchate, but without the figure of the patriarch.

Syrian Orthodox priest

Armenian priest

Jaffa Gate, the main way into the Old City from West Jerusalem

To the Arabs this gate is known as Bab el-Khalil, from the Arabic name for Hebron (El-Khalil). The old road to the town started here.

The Citadel ❾

See pp98–100.

Omar ibn el-Khattab Square ❿

Map 3 B4.

NOT SO MUCH a square as a widening of the road as it passes around the Citadel, this area just inside Jaffa Gate is a focal point of Old City life. Arab boys selling street food solicit black-garbed Orthodox Jews heading for the Western Wall, and priests in cassocks pose for the cameras of the tourist groups, who pick up their tour guides here.

The square takes its name from the caliph Omar, who captured Jerusalem for Islam in AD 638. The Muslim name

is misleading, as most of the property around the square is owned by the Greek Orthodox Patriarchate. In the late 19th century, the patriarchate built the hotels and shops on the north side, including the Neo-Classical Imperial Hotel. These days the hotel suffers badly from neglect and has appeal only for those who value atmosphere over comfort.

At a street junction behind the hotel is a Roman column, erected around AD 200 in honour of the prefect of Judaea and commander of the 10th Legion. This was one of the legions that participated in the recapture of Jerusalem in AD 70 *(see p41)*, and was subsequently quartered in the city. The column now supports a street light.

Several cafés with pavement tables fringe the east side of the square. Next to the cafés is the Christian Information Centre, and, opposite the entrance to the Citadel, the Anglican Christ Church compound. Its Neo-Gothic church (1849) was the first Protestant building in the Holy Land.

A Walk on the Roofs ⓫

Map 3 C4.

AT THE CORNER of St Mark's Road and Khabad Street, in an area where the Jewish, Christian and Muslim Quarters all overlap, a shaky staircase leads up to the Old City rooftops. From here it is possible to walk above the central souk area, peering down through ventilation grilles to the

bustling street below. The terrace extends for a considerable distance, running between satellite dishes and dividing walls. Locals use the rooftops as a short cut, appearing and disappearing through doors and gates; for visitors, the appeal is in the unusual views the terrace affords of the Holy Sepulchre church and the Dome of the Rock. It is also worth coming up here in the evening to see the rooftop skyline thrown into silhouette by moonlight. A second set of stairs leads down into the courtyard of the Khan el-Sultan, which allows exit onto Chain Street *(see p64)*.

The pulpit in the Syrian Orthodox church of St Mark's

St Mark's Church ⓬

5 Ararat St. **Map** 3 C4. ☎ (02) 628 3304. ◻ 8am–5pm (winter: 4pm) daily.

THIS SMALL CHURCH is the centre of the Syrian Orthodox community in Jerusalem. It is a place rich in biblical associations, albeit of suspect authenticity. According to tradition the church was built on the site of the house of Mary, mother of St Mark the Evangelist. A stone font in the church is supposedly that in which the Virgin Mary was baptized, and the church also has a painting on parchment of the Virgin and Child that is often attributed to St Luke. Of course, historians identify it as dating from a much later period. Some scholars do believe, however, that a small cellar room here was the true site of the Last Supper, not Mount Zion *(see p113)*.

Tourists enjoying a walk across the rooftops of the Old City

The Citadel ❾

Ruined arch in the courtyard

View of the Citadel and the Dome of the Rock behind, from the New City

NOW OCCUPIED BY the Tower of David Museum of the History of Jerusalem *(see p100)*, the Citadel is an imposing bastion just inside the city wall. The present-day structure dates principally from the 14th century and includes additions made in 1532 by Suleyman the Magnificent. However, excavations have revealed remains dating back to the 2nd century BC, and indicate that there was a fortress here from Herodian times. This supports the view that this is the most likely site of Christ's trial and condemnation.

Base of an early Islamic tower

The mosque was built by the Mamelukes above a Crusader hall.

The Hasmonean city wall (2nd century BC) is one of the oldest finds. Part of the same wall can be seen in the Jewish Quarter *(see p81)*.

Southeast Tower

East Tower

The entrance was built with an L-shaped hallway to impede the progress of attackers.

Open-air mosque

Tower of David
The Citadel is also called the Tower of David. The misnomer dates back to Byzantine confusion over the geographical layout of the city. Today it is also applied to this minaret, added in 1655.

Triple-arched Gateway
This ornamental gate was built in the 16th century. It was on the steps in front that General Allenby accepted the city's surrender in 1917 (see p50).

★ **Ramparts**
The crenellated walls have the same outline as in Crusader times, but date largely from the 14th century. It is possible to walk almost the whole circuit, taking in views of the city in all directions.

An 1873 model of Jerusalem is on display in an underground cistern.

The courtyard within the Citadel has archaeological remains from almost every era from the 2nd century BC to the 12th century AD.

Entrance to café

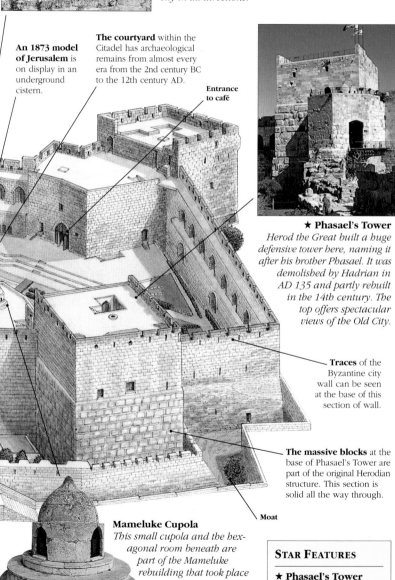

★ **Phasael's Tower**
Herod the Great built a huge defensive tower here, naming it after his brother Phasael. It was demolished by Hadrian in AD 135 and partly rebuilt in the 14th century. The top offers spectacular views of the Old City.

Traces of the Byzantine city wall can be seen at the base of this section of wall.

The massive blocks at the base of Phasael's Tower are part of the original Herodian structure. This section is solid all the way through.

Moat

Mameluke Cupola
This small cupola and the hexagonal room beneath are part of the Mameluke rebuilding that took place around 1310. The tour of the museum starts on this rooftop.

STAR FEATURES

★ **Phasael's Tower**

★ **Ramparts**

Exploring the Citadel

Statue of a Crusader

THERE IS A LOT to see in the Citadel's Tower of David Museum. To help the visitor, there are three well-signposted routes: the Observation Route runs along the ramparts for the best panoramic views of the city, both Old and New; the Excavation Route concentrates on the archaeological remains in the courtyard; and the Exhibition Route takes visitors through a series of display rooms in which the history of the city of Jerusalem is presented. This presentation takes the form of displays, dioramas and models, rather than a collection of historical artifacts. The Exhibition Route begins in Phasael's Tower with a short, animated film.

Saladin in his tent, illustrated in a richly coloured diorama

19th-century model of Jerusalem, displayed in the Citadel

THE CANAANITES AND THE FIRST TEMPLE

HEADING CLOCKWISE from Phasael's Tower, the first two sections deal with the origins of Jerusalem, covering the period from 3150 to 586 BC, the year the First Temple was destroyed. Exhibits include a model of a 19th-century BC Egyptian statuette bearing the first written reference to Jerusalem. There is also a model of the 10th-century City of David, prior to the building of the Temple, a hologram of the Temple itself, and an informative animation showing how the ancient city's water system worked. The latter is very useful for those who intend later visiting Hezekiah's Tunnel and the Pool of Siloam *(see p111)*.

THE SECOND TEMPLE TO THE BYZANTINES

THE NEXT SERIES of rooms, in the east and southeast towers, traces the return of the Jews to Jerusalem from exile in Babylon, and the periods of rule of the Roman and Byzantine empires. One room features a large-scale model of the Second Temple, while the Roman conquerors are represented by a reproduction "Judaea Capta" coin *(see p43)*. The following rooms have floors based on mosaics from Hadrian's Villa in Rome and the St Martyrius Monastery near Jerusalem. There is also a splendid model, 1.5 m (5 ft) long, of the Church of the Holy Sepulchre as it is thought to have looked when first built in the 4th century.

ISLAM AND THE CRUSADES

APPROPRIATELY ENOUGH, the early Islamic exhibits are housed in the Citadel's former mosque. It still has its mihrab (niche indicating the direction of Mecca) and *minbar* (pulpit). At the centre of the room is a large, detailed, sectioned model of the Dome of the Rock. The model apparently took two years to construct. There is also a model of the Crusader church of St Anne's *(see p65)* and life-size statues of Crusader knights, as well as a diorama showing Saladin in his tent outside the city walls.

THE MAMELUKES TO THE BRITISH MANDATE

THE FINAL exhibition rooms are in the large, northwest tower. Mameluke Jerusalem is represented by a small scale reconstruction of a street of distinctive striped-stone architecture. For the Ottoman era, there is a beautiful model of the *sabil* (fountain) of Suleyman the Magnificent on Chain Street, at the entrance to the Haram esh-Sharif *(see p64)*. The chronological sequence ends with a superb model of Jerusalem as it was at the time, made by a Hungarian artist in 1873. It was exhibited throughout Europe before going into storage and being forgotten for a century until its rediscovery in the early 1980s.

The Citadel courtyard, as seen from the top of Phasael's Tower

The Old City Gates and the Ramparts Walk

JERUSALEM'S WALLS were built in the first half of the 16th century (in part on the line of earlier walls) on the order of the Ottoman sultan Suleyman the Magnificent. The 4-km (2.5-mile) circuit is pierced by eight gates, of which seven remain in current use. Until as recently as 1870, the gates were closed at sunset and opened again each sunrise. Visitors can walk along two sections of the ramparts,

The crenellations of Damascus Gate

from Jaffa Gate clockwise via Damascus Gate to St Stephen's Gate, and from Jaffa Gate anticlockwise to Dung Gate. The section between St Stephen's and Dung gates, around the Haram esh-Sharif, is closed. Access to the ramparts is only possible at Jaffa and Damascus gates, although walkers can descend at any gate. The ramparts are open daily from 9am to 4pm (2pm on Fridays), and there is an admission fee.

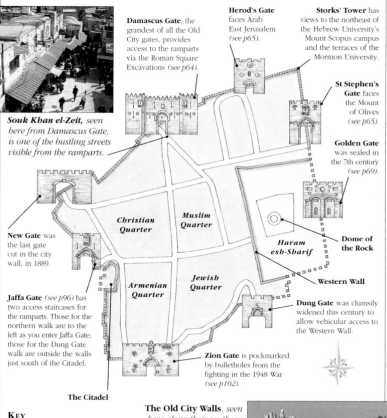

Souk Khan el-Zeit, seen here from Damascus Gate, is one of the bustling streets visible from the ramparts.

Damascus Gate, the grandest of all the Old City gates, provides access to the ramparts via the Roman Square Excavations *(see p64)*.

Herod's Gate faces Arab East Jerusalem *(see p65)*.

Storks' Tower has views to the northeast of the Hebrew University's Mount Scopus campus and the terraces of the Mormon University.

St Stephen's Gate faces the Mount of Olives *(see p65)*.

Golden Gate was sealed in the 7th century *(see p69)*.

New Gate was the last gate cut in the city wall, in 1889.

Jaffa Gate *(see p96)* has two access staircases for the ramparts. Those for the northern walk are to the left as you enter Jaffa Gate; those for the Dung Gate walk are outside the walls just south of the Citadel.

Christian Quarter

Muslim Quarter

Haram esh-Sharif

Dome of the Rock

Western Wall

Armenian Quarter

Jewish Quarter

Dung Gate was clumsily widened this century to allow vehicular access to the Western Wall.

Zion Gate is pockmarked by bulletholes from the fighting in the 1948 War *(see p102)*.

The Citadel

KEY

▭▭▭ Accessible ramparts

▫ ▫ ▫ Ramparts closed to public

0 metres	300
0 yards	300

The Old City Walls, seen here along their southern stretch, sharply defined Jerusalem until as late as the mid-19th century. It was only in the 1860s that the first tentative settlements began to develop outside the shelter and security offered by Suleyman's splendid fortifications.

Wrought-iron gate framing the ornate main entrance to St James's Cathedral

St James's Cathedral ⑬

Armenian Patriarchate Rd. **Map** 3 B5.
📞 (02) 628 2331. ⏰ 6:30–7:30am & 3–3:40pm Mon–Fri, 6:30–9:30am Sat & Sun.

THE ARMENIAN CATHEDRAL is one of the most beautiful of all Jerusalem's sacred buildings. It was originally constructed in the 11th and 12th centuries over the reputed tomb of St James the Great, the Apostle, killed by Herod Agrippa I (AD 37–44). Many alterations and additions have since been made, most notably in the 18th century, when much of the existing decoration was added.

Entrance to the cathedral is via a small courtyard with a 19th-century fountain. On the western wall of the courtyard are inscriptions in Armenian, one of which dates from 1151. Hanging in the vaulted porch are wooden bars. Each afternoon a priest strikes these with a wooden mallet known as a *nakus*, to signal the start of the service.

The cathedral interior is enchanting. It is only dimly illuminated by a forest of oil lamps hung from the ceiling. There are no seats; instead the floors are thickly laid with Oriental rugs. Four great square piers divide the main space into three aisles. These piers, along with the walls, are covered in blue-and-white tiles with floral and abstract patterns. In the apses at the end of each of the three aisles are altars, separated from the rest of the church by the iconostasis screen. Two thrones stand in the choir; the one nearest the pier is said to be that of St James the Less, traditionally held to have been a step-brother of Christ and the first bishop of Jerusalem. It is used only once a year, in early January, on the occasion of his feast day. The other throne is the one normally used by the patriarch.

The cathedral contains many small shrines and chapels. The third on the left as you enter is the most important: it supposedly holds the head of St James the Great. Off to the right, the Etchmiadzin Chapel has some beautiful tiling.

Mardigian Museum ⑭

Armenian Patriarchate Rd. **Map** 3 B5.
📞 (02) 628 2331. ⏰ 9am–4:30pm Mon–Sat. 🎫

DATING FROM 1863, this was originally the seminary of the nearby Armenian patriarchate. It is now a museum dedicated to the history and culture of the Armenian people. The building is attractive, with a long central courtyard flanked by porticoes. The oldest finds in the collection are fragments of 1st-century frescoes from the courtyard of the so-called House of Caiaphas on Mount Zion, and remains from Byzantine-period Armenian

17th-century jug, Mardigian Museum

churches unearthed near Damascus Gate. The pride of the museum is its collection of early manuscripts. In addition, there are also a great many liturgical objects, many of which were donated to St James's Cathedral by Armenian pilgrims. There are also examples of the pottery for which the Armenians have always been famous.

Other interesting objects are examples of the first books printed in the first print shop in Jerusalem, which has been active since 1833 inside the Armenian monastery.

Battle-scarred Zion Gate

Zion Gate ⑮

Map 3 C5.

ZION GATE was constructed by Suleyman the Magnificent's engineers (see p101) in 1540. It allowed direct access from the city to the holy sites on Mount Zion. Fighting was particularly fierce here in 1948, when Israeli soldiers were desperate to breach the walls to relieve the Jewish Quarter inside, under siege by the Jordanians. The outside of the gate is terribly pockmarked by bulletholes. A short distance to the west of the gate there is conspicuous damage to the base of the wall where soldiers tried to blast their way through with explosives.

In Arabic, the gate is known as Bab el-Nabi Daud (Gate of the Prophet David), because of its proximity to the place traditionally known as King David's Tomb (see p113).

The Armenians in Jerusalem

Detail from an Armenian carpet

THE KINGDOM of Armenia was the first country to make Christianity the state religion, when in AD 301 its king was converted. Armenian pilgrims began to visit the Holy City soon after. In the 12th century they purchased St James's Cathedral from the Georgians, and this became the focal point of their community in Jerusalem. The Armenian Quarter grew to its current size in the 17th and 18th centuries, during the rule of the Turks. In the early 20th century Armenian numbers were swollen by refugees who had fled from the 1915 persecution in Turkey, a terrible genocide in which some one and a half million Armenians were exterminated. But from a peak of around 16,000 in 1948, the Armenian population of Jerusalem has since dwindled to less than 2,000, largely due to emigration. After the 1967 war, the Jews also started to encroach into the area, and the fear now is that other than in name, the Armenian Quarter may one day disappear altogether.

Tiling adorns the interior of St James's Cathedral. The tiles were made in the early 18th century in Kütahya, a town around 125 km (75 miles) southeast of Constantinople, and renowned as the foremost Armenian ceramic centre in the Ottoman Empire.

The Armenian Church *is one of the three major guardians of the Christian places in the Holy Land. Among the sites they have at least partial jurisdiction over are the Church of the Holy Sepulchre, the Mosque of the Ascension and the Tomb of the Virgin on the Mount of Olives, the Church of the Nativity in Bethlehem and, of course, St James's Cathedral (above).*

Mosaics *represent the finest legacy of ancient Armenian art. This 5th- or 6th-century example was unearthed just outside Damascus Gate.*

Armenian-language manuscripts, such as this 13th-century example, are held in huge numbers at the Gulbenkian Library, next to St James's Cathedral.

Giant pots *for wine or oil, dating from around 1700, are displayed at the Mardigian Museum.*

TCHEQUE

Otče náš,
jenž jsi na nebesích,
posvěť se jméno tvé.
Přijď království tvé.
Buď vůle tvá, jako
v nebi tak i na zemi.
Chléb náš vezdejší
dej nám dnes. A odpusť
nám naše viny, jako
i my odpouštíme našim
viníkům. A neuveď nás
v pokušení, ale zbav
nás od zlého.

Amen.

THE MOUNT OF OLIVES AND MOUNT ZION

Belfry at the Tomb of the Virgin

T HE MOUNT OF OLIVES is the hill that rises to the east of the Old City. Its slopes have been used as a place of burial since the 3rd millennium BC. The hill is also dotted with sites connected with the last days of Jesus Christ, but the highlight for many visitors is the superb view of the Old City from the summit. Between the city walls and the hill is the Valley of Jehoshaphat, with several tombs from the 1st and 2nd centuries BC. At the southern end of the valley is the site of the 3,000-year-old settlement that was to become Jerusalem (the City of David). The land rises again to the west to Mount Zion, an area of the city traditionally linked with the Last Supper.

SIGHTS AT A GLANCE

Holy Places
Church of All Nations **7**
Church of the Dormition **13**
Church of the Paternoster **3**
Church of St Mary Magdalene **6**
Dominus Flevit Chapel **5**
Hall of the Last Supper **14**
Mosque of the Ascension **2**
Russian Church of the
    Ascension **1**
St Peter in Gallicantu **11**
Tomb of the Virgin **8**

Archaeological Sites
City of David **10**

Historic Areas
Mount Zion **12**

Tombs
King David's Tomb **15**
Schindler's Tomb **16**
Tombs of the Prophets **4**
Valley of Jehoshaphat **9**

KEY

▒	Mount of Olives See pp106–7
P	Parking

GETTING THERE
The best way to see the Mount of Olives is to take a bus (No. 75 from the station on Sultan Suleyman Street) or a taxi to the summit and walk down. Walking from the Old City involves a strenuous uphill climb. Mount Zion is most easily reached via Zion Gate in the Old City.

0 metres   400
0 yards   400

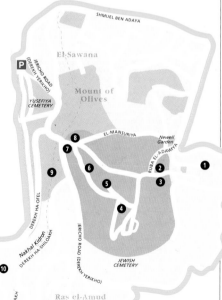

◁ **The cloister of the Church of the Paternoster, which displays the Lord's Prayer in over 60 languages**

The Mount of Olives

Mosaic, Dominus Flevit Chapel

RISING ON THE EASTERN SIDE of Jerusalem, the Mount of Olives offers magnificent views of the Dome of the Rock and the Old City. Now best known as the scene of Christ's Agony and betrayal in the Garden of Gethsemane and his Ascension into Heaven, this prominent hill has always been a holy place to the inhabitants of the city. The Jebusites dug tombs here as early as 2400 BC, as later did Jews, Christians and Muslims. To take in all the sights it is wisest to start at the top, near the Mosque of the Ascension, and walk downhill to the Tomb of the Virgin. The Old City views are best in the morning.

Dominus Flevit Chapel
The chapel's west window frames a breathtaking view of the Old City ❺

The Cave of Gethsemane is the traditional site of Christ's betrayal by Judas.

Garden of Gethsemane

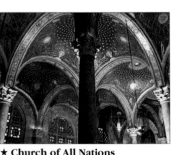

★ Tomb of the Virgin
An impressive flight of Crusader steps leads into the cruciform underground church. Tradition says this is where the Virgin Mary was laid to rest ❽

★ Church of All Nations
Mosaics, predominantly in blues and greens, decorate the 12 domes of this church, built in 1924 with donations from many countries ❼

Jericho Road

STAR SIGHTS
★ Tomb of the Virgin
★ Church of All Nations
★ Church of the Paternoster

Church of St Mary Magdalene
This Russian Orthodox Church, with typically Muscovite gilded onion domes, was built by Tsar Alexander III in memory of his mother, whose patron saint was Mary Magdalene ❻

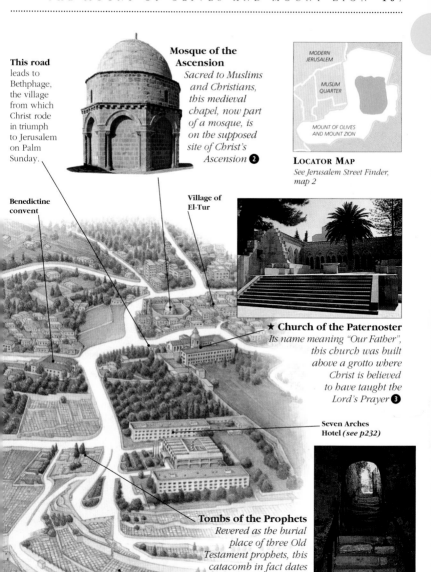

This road leads to Bethphage, the village from which Christ rode in triumph to Jerusalem on Palm Sunday.

Mosque of the Ascension
Sacred to Muslims and Christians, this medieval chapel, now part of a mosque, is on the supposed site of Christ's Ascension ❷

MODERN JERUSALEM
MUSLIM QUARTER
MOUNT OF OLIVES AND MOUNT ZION

LOCATOR MAP
See Jerusalem Street Finder, map 2

Benedictine convent

Village of El-Tur

★ **Church of the Paternoster**
Its name meaning "Our Father", this church was built above a grotto where Christ is believed to have taught the Lord's Prayer ❸

Seven Arches Hotel *(see p232)*

Tombs of the Prophets
Revered as the burial place of three Old Testament prophets, this catacomb in fact dates from a much later period, the 1st century AD ❹

Jewish Cemeteries
Many Jews wish to be buried on the Mount of Olives so as to be close to the Valley of Jehoshaphat, where it is said mankind will be resurrected on the Day of Judgment.

Church of the Ascension's bell tower in the quiet convent gardens

Russian Church of the Ascension ❶

Off Ruba el-Adawiya St, Mount of
Olives. **Map** 2 F3. ☎ (02) 628 4373.
◐ 9am– noon Tue & Thu. 📷

THIS IS THE CHURCH of a still
active Russian Orthodox
convent built between 1870
and 1887. The bell tower, a
prominent landmark on the
Mount of Olives, was built tall
enough to allow pilgrims too
infirm to walk to the River
Jordan to see it from afar. The
8-tonne bell was hauled from
Jaffa by Russian pilgrims.

Two Armenian mosaics were
found during construction. A
small museum was built over
the most beautiful, which is
fragmentary and dates from the
5th century AD; the other, complete and of slightly later date,
is in the Chapel of the Head
of John the Baptist, inside the
church. An iron cage on the
floor shows where John's
head was supposedly found.

Mosque of the Ascension ❷

Off Ruba el-Adawiya St, Mount of
Olives. **Map** 2 F3. ◐ daily (if closed,
ring bell). 📷

POEMENIA, a Christian noble-
woman, built the first
chapel here around AD 380 to
commemorate Christ's Ascension. It had three concentric
porticoes around an uncovered
space, where the dust miracu-
lously formed the image of
Christ's footprints. The Crusaders rebuilt the chapel as an
octagon and the column bases
of a surrounding Crusader portico are still visible outside. By
this time, the footprints, now
set in stone, were venerated
here and the right imprint remains to this day. The capitals
were carved in the 1140s and
the two depicting animals and
leaves are particularly beautiful.

The chapel became a Muslim
shrine after Saladin's conquest
in 1187. In 1200 it was roofed
with a dome, the arches were
walled in, a mihrab added and
a surrounding wall built. The
outer wall today is largely rebuilt. The adjacent minaret
and mosque are 17th century.

The underground tomb near
the entrance is venerated by
Jews as belonging to the Old
Testament prophetess Huldah,
by Christians as St Pelagia's and
by Muslims as that of the holy
woman Rabia el-Adawiya.

Church of the Paternoster ❸

Mount of Olives. **Map** 2 F4. ☎ (02)
628 3143. ◐ 9 –11:30am & 3 –5pm
Mon –Sat.

THIS CHURCH stands next to
the partly restored ruins
of one commissioned by the
Emperor Constantine, who
sent his mother, St Helena,
to supervise construction in

**Site of Christ's footprint in the
Mosque of the Ascension**

AD 326. Called Eleona (*elaion*
in Greek meaning "of olives"),
it was sited above a grotto
where the Ascension was
commemorated. By Crusader
times, the church had been
rebuilt three times and the
grotto was known as the
place where Christ had taught
the Disciples the Paternoster
(meaning "Our Father"), or
Lord's Prayer.

The present church and a
Carmelite monastery were built
close by between 1868 and
1872 by the French Princesse
de la Tour d'Auvergne. Excavations of the Byzantine church
in 1910–11 unearthed a marble
plaque engraved in Latin with
the Paternoster. In 1920, the
grotto was restored, but plans
to reconstruct the Byzantine
church were never realized
through lack of funds.

Today, the 19th-century
church and its cloister are
famous for the tiled panels
inscribed with the Paternoster
in more than 60 languages.

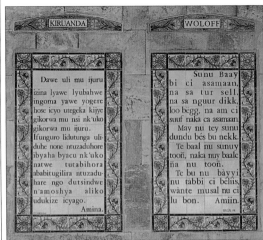

Panels inscribed with the Lord's Prayer, Church of the Paternoster

Tombs of the Prophets ❹

Mount of Olives. **Map** 2 F4.
⬤ 9am–3:30pm Mon–Fri.

THE SOUTHWESTERN SLOPE of the Mount of Olives, facing the Kidron Valley (also known along this stretch as the Valley of Jehoshaphat – *see p111*), is densely occupied by Jewish cemeteries. At the top of the slope, an unusual, fan-shaped catacomb containing *kokhim* (oven-shaped) graves is held by Christian and Jewish tradition to enclose the tombs of the 5th-century BC prophets Haggai, Malachi and Zechariah. The graves actually date from the 1st century AD and were reused in the 4th or 5th.

Dominus Flevit Chapel ❺

Mount of Olives. **Map** 2 F4. 📞 (02) 627 4931. 🚌 99. ⬤ 8–11:45 am & 2:30–5pm daily.

ITS NAME MEANING "The Lord Wept", this chapel stands where medieval pilgrims identified a rock as the one on which Jesus sat when he wept over the fate of Jerusalem. The chapel was designed in the shape of a teardrop by Italian architect Antonio Barluzzi and built in 1955 over a 7th-century chapel. Part of the original apse is preserved in the new one. The view of the Dome of the Rock from the altar window is justly famous. A mosaic floor preserved in situ outside is from a 5th-century monastery. The graves on view nearby

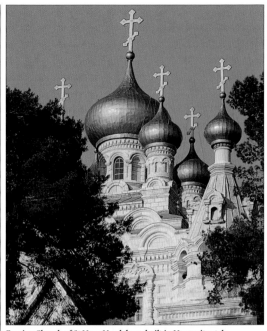

Russian Church of St Mary Magdalene, built in Muscovite style

show the types found in the 1950s in a vast cemetery here, in use periodically from 1600 BC to AD 70. Also on show are some carved stone ossuaries.

Church of St Mary Magdalene ❻

Mount of Olives. **Map** 2 E3. 📞 (02) 628 4371. 🚌 99. ⬤ 10am–noon Tue & Thu.

IN 1885, Tsar Alexander III had this Russian Orthodox church built in memory of his mother, Maria Alexandrovna.

It is pleasantly set among trees, and the seven gilded onion domes are among the most striking features of Jerusalem's skyline when viewed from the Old City. The domes and other architectural and decorative features are in 16th–17th-century Muscovite style.

The church was consecrated in 1888 by Grand Duke Sergei Alexandrovich (Tsar Alexander III's brother) and his wife, Grand Duchess Elizabeth Feodorovna. In 1920, after her murder during the Russian Revolution, her remains were brought here for burial.

THE RUSSIANS IN JERUSALEM

Russia's Christians belong to the Eastern Orthodox church, the centre of which was once Constantinople. In the 19th century, when the European powers were competing to stake their claims on pieces of the crumbling Ottoman Empire, the Russians thus presented themselves as the successors to the Byzantine Empire and the true "defenders of Christianity and the Holy Places". At this time some 200,000 Russian pilgrims were

Russian Orthodox nuns embroidering vestments, Church of the Ascension

visiting Jerusalem each year. The Russian government purchased land on a grand scale, notably on the Mount of Olives and just west of the Old City, where they built a great cathedral, a consulate, a hospital and several hospices, all enclosed in a walled compound, like a city within a city (*see p120*). But in World War I, when the British captured Jerusalem they declared all Russia's properties to be "enemy institutions" and confiscated everything.

Mosaic-decorated, vaulted ceiling in the Church of All Nations

Church of All Nations ❼

Jericho Rd. **Map** 2 E3. 📞 *(02) 628 3264.* 🚌 *99.* ⏰ *8am–noon & 2:30–5pm (summer: 6pm) daily.*

THE CHURCH of All Nations is also known as the Church of the Agony because it is built over the rock in the Garden of Gethsemane on which it is believed Christ prayed the night before he was arrested.

The 4th-century church built here was destroyed in an earthquake in 747. The Crusaders built a new one, aligned differently to cover three outcrops of rock, recalling Christ's three prayers during the night. It was consecrated in 1170, but fell into disuse after 1345.

After excavation of the site in the early 20th century, the present church was designed by Antonio Barluzzi *(see p109)* and built in 1924 with financial contributions from 12 nations – hence the church's name and its 12 domes decorated with national coats of arms. In the centre of the nave is the rock of the Byzantine church, surrounded by a wrought-iron crown of thorns. The mosaic in the apse represents Christ's agony, while others depicting his arrest and Judas's kiss are at the sides. The plan of the Byzantine church is traced in black marble on the floor, and sections of Byzantine mosaic pavement can also be seen.

Outside, the gilded mosaic scene decorating the pediment also depicts the Agony. Next to the church is the surviving part of the Garden of Gethsemane with its centuries-old olive trees.

Tomb of the Virgin ❽

Jericho Rd. **Map** 2 E3. 📞 *(02) 628 4054.* 🚌 *99.* ⏰ *8am–noon & 2:30–5pm daily.* **Cave of Gethsemane** 📞 *(02) 628 3264.* ⏰ *8:30am–noon & 2:30–5pm daily.*

BELIEVED TO BE where the Disciples entombed the Virgin Mary, this underground sanctuary in the Valley of Jehoshaphat is one of the most intimate and mystical holy

places in Jerusalem. The façade, the impressive flight of 47 steps and the royal Christian tombs in side niches half-way down all date from the 12th century. The tomb on the right, going down, was originally the burial place of Queen Melisande of Jerusalem, who died in 1161. Her remains were moved into the crypt in the 14th century and the tomb has been venerated since about that time as that of St Anne and St Joachim, Mary's parents.

The first tomb was cut in the hillside here in the 1st century AD. The cruciform crypt as seen today, much of it cut into solid rock, is Byzantine. By the 5th century, an upper chapel had also been built. This was destroyed by the Persians in 614, rebuilt by the Crusaders,

The 12th-century entrance to the atmospheric Tomb of the Virgin

but again destroyed by Saladin in 1187. He left the crypt, however, largely intact.

The Tomb of Mary stands in the eastern branch of the crypt, which is decorated with icons and sacred ornaments typical of Orthodox Christian tradition. Today, religious services are held here by Greek, Armenian, Coptic and Syrian Christians.

In the southwestern wall beside the Tomb of Mary is a mihrab installed after Saladin's conquest. The place was sanctified by Muslims because, according to the 15th-century scholar Mujir al-Din, Muhammad saw a light over the tomb of his "sister Mary" during his Night Journey to Jerusalem *(see p25)*. In the opposite wall, a 1st-century tomb is evidence of the site's earliest use for burials.

Outside, to the right of the façade, is the **Cave of Gethsemane**, or Cave of the Betrayal, the traditional place of Judas's betrayal. It was once used for oil pressing, but fragments of 4th–5th-century mosaics bear

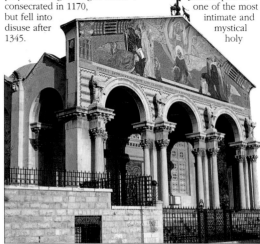

The Church of All Nations in the Garden of Gethsemane

The Tomb of Bnei Hezir (left) and the pyramid-roofed Tomb of Zechariah in the Valley of Jehoshaphat

witness to its transformation into a place of worship. The stars on the vaults were painted in Crusader times.

Valley of Jehoshaphat ❾

Map 2 E3.

THE KIDRON VALLEY separates the Old City from the Mount of Olives. Near Gethsemane the valley is also known by its Old Testament name, the Valley of Jehoshaphat (meaning "Yahweh judges", Yahweh being the Hebrew name for God), where it was believed the dead would be resurrected on the Day of Judgment (Joel 3: 1–17). For this reason, the valley sides are densely covered with Christian, Jewish and Muslim cemeteries.

At the southern end are several Jewish rock-hewn tombs of the 1st and 2nd centuries BC. Four are particularly fine. Absalom's Tomb, like an inverted funnel, was ascribed in medieval times to King David's rebellious son, Absalom. The so-called Tomb of Jehoshaphat (the 9th-century BC King of Judah) behind it has a carved frieze above the doorway. The pyramid-topped Tomb of Zechariah is actually the above-ground monument of the adjacent Tomb of Bnei Hezir. The latter has a rectangular opening with two Doric columns and was identified by an inscription referring to the "sons of Hezir", a Jewish priestly family.

City of David ❿

Maalot Ir David. **Map** 2 D4. ☎ (02) 626 2341. ◐ 9am–5pm Sun–Thu (Shaft & Tunnel: 4pm in winter), 9am– 1pm Fri. 🎫 for Shaft & Tunnel. 🎫 phone in advance.

SOUTH OF the Temple Mount (Haram esh-Sharif) a rocky ridge runs beside the Kidron Valley. Its summit was already settled by the Jebusites, a Canaanite (see p39) people, in the 20th century BC, making this the oldest part of Jerusalem. It was from them that David supposedly took the city for his capital in about 1000 BC (2 Samuel 5: 6–17).

On the site are remains of buildings up to the city's capture by the Babylonians in 586 BC. They include 13th-century BC walls belonging to the Jebusite acropolis, fortifications and fragments of a palace attributed to David, and houses burnt in the Babylonian attack. About 100 m (330 ft) from the entrance to the acropolis

The Pool of Siloam, which stored the City of David's water supply

excavations is **Warren's Shaft**, named after Charles Warren, its 19th-century English discoverer. A sloping tunnel, accessed by spiral stairs, leads to the vertical shaft at the bottom of which is a pool fed by the Gihon Spring. The system was built by the Jebusites to ensure a water supply during sieges. Bring a flashlight to explore it. Nearby is their 18th-century BC city wall, identified by the large, uncut stone blocks used in its construction. It was built this far down the hill to bring the entrance to Warren's Shaft within the confines of the city.

In the 10th century BC a tunnel, later attributed to Solomon, was dug to take water from the Gihon Spring to fields in the Kidron Valley. In the face of Assyrian invasion in about 700 BC, King Hezekiah had a new tunnel built to bring the spring water right into the city, so concealing the source of the supply. **Hezekiah's Tunnel** ran 533 m (1,750 ft) from the spring to a large, new storage pool – the Pool of Siloam – in the south of the city. Not far from the Siloam end an inscription, carved by the engineer, describes the tunnel's construction. The pool is now smaller than it was originally and was rebuilt after the Romans sacked Jerusalem in AD 70 and burnt it "as far as Siloam", as told by contemporary historian Flavius Josephus.

Visitors can wade through the tunnel in thigh-high water from the Gihon Spring – wear shoes and bring a flashlight.

The beautifully painted interior of St Peter in Gallicantu

St Peter in Gallicantu ⓫

Malki Tsedek Rd. **Map** 2 D5. ⓒ (02) 673 1739. ⛙ 38. ⏰ 8:30am–5pm Mon–Sat. ⚿ ⛔

STANDING TO the east of Mount Zion, on the slopes overlooking the City of David *(see p111)* and the Kidron Valley, this church commemorates the traditional site of St Peter's reported denial of Christ which fulfilled the prophecy, "Before the cock crow twice, thou shalt deny me thrice" (Mark 14: 72). Built in 1931, the church has a modern appearance. In the crypt, however, are ancient caves where, it is said, Christ spent the night before being taken to Pontius Pilate. The remains of some Herodian architecture have been discovered under the church and, in the garden, there still exists part of a Hasmonean stairway, in use in Christ's time, which once connected the city with the Kidron Valley. Mosaics from a previous 5th–6th-century Byzantine church and monastery have also been unearthed.

Mount Zion ⓬

Map 1 C5. ⛙ 1, 2.

A SHORT WALK from Zion Gate is the hill synonymous with biblical Jerusalem and the Promised Land. Believed by many to be the site of King David's tomb and associated

with the final days of Christ, Mount Zion is revered by Jews, Muslims and Christians alike.

The hill is bounded to the east by the Kidron Valley, to the south and west by the Hinnom Valley and to the north by the city walls. This makes it seem like an island outside the confines of the Old City. This was not always the case, however, for on the Madaba mosaic map in Jordan *(see pp192–3)* it is shown inside the walls. It appears to have been excluded in 1542 when the walls were rebuilt. Legend has it that Suleyman the Magnificent's architects left it outside by mistake.

Christians began assembling here some time after Christ's death to worship in the Hall of the Last Supper and later at the stone where the Virgin Mary is said to have died. Now the site of the Church of the Dormition, this point marked the ceasefire border from 1949 to 1967 *(see p52).*

Church of the Dormition ⓭

Mount Zion. **Map** 1 C5. ⓒ (02) 671 9927. ⛙ 38, 20. ⏰ 9am–noon & 12:30–6pm Mon–Thu, 9am–noon & 2–6pm Fri, 10:30am–noon & 12:30–6pm Sun. ⚿

CROWNED BY a tall bell tower and a dome with four small corner turrets, the Neo-Romanesque Church of the Dormition dominates the Mount Zion hilltop. The large, airy, white-stone church stands on the site where the Virgin Mary is said to have fallen into an "eternal sleep". After Christ's death, according to Christian tradition, his mother went to live on Mount Zion until she herself died.

The hill soon became a holy site, available information suggesting that there may have been a church here as early as the 4th century AD. It is known with more certainty that around the 6th century a large basilica was built on the site which later fell into ruins. When the Crusaders came, they too erected a church with chapels devoted to the Dormition of the Virgin and the Last Supper.

The present-day church, which includes the Chapel of the Dormition and Dormition Abbey, was built in the early 20th century for Kaiser Wilhelm II and was inspired by the Carolingian cathedral in Aachen, Germany.

During the 1948 and 1967 wars the church was used as a strategic outpost by Israeli soldiers and was damaged in

The conical dome and bell tower of the Church of the Dormition

The Crusader-built Hall of the Last Supper, with fine Gothic details

the crossfire of several battles. The main part of the church boasts a fine mosaic floor featuring zodiac symbols and the names of saints and prophets. In the crypt is a wood and ivory sculpture of the "sleeping" Virgin, while the walls are adorned with images of women from the Old Testament, including Eve, Judith, Ruth and Esther. In the rooms on the mezzanine are some of the remains from the site's previous churches.

Hall of the Last Supper ⓴

Mount Zion. **Map** 1 C5.
◐ 8am–8pm (winter: 6pm) daily.

ON THE FIRST floor of a Gothic building – all that remains of the large church constructed by the Crusaders to commemorate Mary's Dormition and overshadowed slightly by the more recent Church of the Dormition – is the Hall of the Last Supper, or Coenaculum. Christian tradition maintains that it is on the site of Christ's last meal with his Disciples. The room is unadorned apart from the Gothic arches dividing it.

In the Middle Ages it became part of the adjacent Franciscan monastery, while in the 15th century it was turned into a mosque by the Turks, who added a mihrab and some stained-glass windows.

King David's Tomb ⓯

Mount Zion. **Map** 1 C5. ◖ (02) 671 9767. 🚌 1, 2. ◐ summer: 8am– 8pm Sat–Thu & hols, 8am–2pm Fri; winter: 8am–sunset Sun–Thu, 8am– 1pm Fri.

BENEATH THE Hall of the Last Supper, on the lower floor of the Crusader building, are some small chambers venerated as King David's Tomb. The main chamber is bare apart from a cenotaph covered by a drape. The site was first identified as David's tomb in the 11th century AD and in the 15th century was incorporated into a mosque by the Muslims,

who consider David one of the true prophets. In spite of recent doubts about the tomb's authenticity, it is one of the most revered Jewish holy sites. It was particularly so between 1948 and 1967, when the Old City was under Jordanian control. As the Western Wall was inaccessible to Jews, they came here to pray. Today the entrance hall is still used as a synagogue. From the 4th to the 15th centuries, the tomb was associated with Pentecost and the death of the Virgin, and, according to tradition, it was here that Christ washed his Disciples' feet after the Last Supper (John 13: 1–17).

Schindler's Tomb ⓰

Mount Zion. **Map** 1 C5. 🚌 1, 2.

STRAIGHT DOWN the hill from Zion Gate, the path forks left past the Chamber of the Holocaust, a small museum commemorating the thousands of Jewish communities wiped out by the Nazis. Across the road at the end of the path is a Christian cemetery. It is here that the grave of German-born Oskar Schindler is located.

Schindler was an industrialist who, during World War II, went out of his way to use Jewish prisoners as labourers in his factory. By doing this, he saved over 1,000 people from the death camps. He became a symbol of the fight against the Holocaust and before he died, in 1974, he asked to be buried in Jerusalem. The story of his courageous stand against the Nazis was told in Steven Spielberg's successful 1993 movie, *Schindler's List.*

Schindler's tomb in the Christian cemetery on Mount Zion

MODERN JERUSALEM

Y THE 1860s the Old City had become overcrowded, and the need for more space gave rise to a period of unrestricted building activity outside the walls. The earliest developments, such as Yemin Moshe, Nakhalat Shiva and Mea Shearim, were Jewish community projects or, like the Russian Compound, intended

Young Israelis in the lively district around Ben Yehuda Street

to cater for Holy Land pilgrims. The architecture of the new city became increasingly eclectic as colonial builders imported their own national styles. As a result, exotic features such as Muscovite domes and Florentine towers form the backdrop to the equally multi-cultural bustle on the streets of the modern city.

SIGHTS AT A GLANCE

Historic Districts
Ben Yehuda and
   Nakhalat Shiva **4**
Ha-Neviim Street **9**
Mea Shearim **11**
Russian Compound **8**

Holy Places
Italian Synagogue **5**
St Etienne Monastery **14**
St George's Cathedral **15**

Tombs
Garden Tomb **13**
Kings' Tombs **16**

Museums and Historic Buildings
American Colony Hotel **17**
Cinematheque **3**
Italian Hospital **10**
King David Hotel **2**
New City Hall **7**
Rockefeller Museum **18**
Ticho House **6**
YMCA **1**

Archaeological Sites
Solomon's Quarries **12**

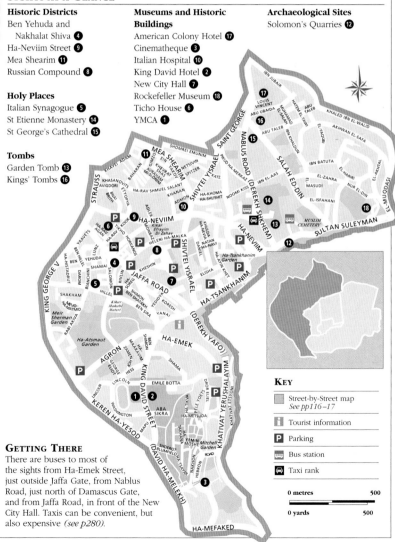

KEY

▨	Street-by-Street map *See pp116–17*
ℹ	Tourist information
P	Parking
🚌	Bus station
🚕	Taxi rank

0 metres	500
0 yards	500

GETTING THERE
There are buses to most of the sights from Ha-Emek Street, just outside Jaffa Gate, from Nablus Road, just north of Damascus Gate, and from Jaffa Road, in front of the New City Hall. Taxis can be convenient, but also expensive *(see p280)*.

◁ **The Bloomfield Gardens' Lion Fountain in the Yemin Moshe district**

Street-by-Street: Yemin Moshe

SIR MOSES MONTEFIORE, a rich British Jewish philanthropist was so shocked by the living conditions in the squalid Old City that he decided to improve the Jews' lot by building new homes outside the walls. The first project was Mishkenot Shaananim ("Dwellings of Tranquillity"), a communal block of 16 apartments, completed in 1860. Initially, people were afraid to move outside the security of the walls because of bandits, but by the end of the century a small community called Yemin Moshe had been established nearby and was thriving. From this core, the vast spread of modern Jerusalem has grown. Yemin Moshe survives as its beautifully renovated historic heart.

Public Sculptures
Outdoor sculptures, such as these buried cubes, are found all around Yemin Moshe.

Jaffa Road ↑

★ **YMCA**
Even if a room is beyond your budget, as one of Jerusalem's most elegant and beautiful buildings, both inside and out, the YMCA is well worth looking around ❶

ABA SIKRA

KING DAVID STREET (DAVID HA-MELEKH)

KING DAVID HOTEL

King David Hotel
Still the premier hotel in Jerusalem, and all Israel, the King David has been hosting royalty, politicians and international celebrities since it first opened its doors in the 1930s ❷

BLOOMFIELD

KING DAVID STREET (DAVID

KEY

– – – Suggested route

0 metres   100
0 yards   100

STAR SIGHTS

★ YMCA

★ Yemin Moshe

★ Montefiore's Windmill

Herod's Family Tomb
The splendour of this 1st-century BC tomb, discovered in 1892, suggests that it may be that of Herod's family. The king himself was supposedly buried at the Herodion (see p172).

★ **Yemin Moshe**
Built on the slope of the valley facing the Old City walls, these early, attractive Oriental-style houses are now some of the most sought-after and exclusive residences in all Jerusalem.

LOCATOR MAP
See Jerusalem Street Finder, map 1

Jaffa Gate

★ **Montefiore's Windmill**
Montefiore meant Mishkenot Shaananim to be self-sufficient, hence a windmill to grind the settlement's own flour. Unfortunately, there was rarely enough wind to turn the sails.

Mishkenot Shaananim
In the earliest days, lodging in this block had to be offered rent-free in order to attract tenants. Now the place serves as a government guest-house for artists and writers. Saul Bellow, Marc Chagall and Simone de Beauvoir have all been accommodated here.

Cinematheque
(see p118)

Bloomfield Gardens
Grassy parks fringe Yemin Moshe. Attractive in their own right, and dotted with ornament, such as the Lion Fountain (right), the parks also afford great views across the valley to the Old City.

YMCA **①**

24 King David St. **Map** 1 A4.
((02) 569 2692. 7, 8, 30, 38.
Tower 8am–6pm Mon–Sat.

BUILT IN 1926–33 by Arthur Loomis Harmon, who also created New York's Empire State Building, Jerusalem's YMCA *(see p233)* is one of the city's best-known landmarks. It consists of three sections – the central body, dominated by a bell tower offering extraordinary views of the city, and the two side wings. The stone and wrought-iron decorative elements on the outside of the building, including the 5-m (16.5-ft) bas-relief of one of the six-winged seraphim described in the Old Testament (Isaiah 6: 2–3), reflect a stylized form of Oriental Byzantine design, combined with elements of Romanesque and Islamic art.

Yet the exterior, splendid as it is, does not prepare the visitor for the fabulously elaborate decor on the inside. Here design elements from three different cultures are woven through with symbols from the three main monotheistic religions. In the concert hall, the dome's twelve windows represent the Twelve Tribes of Israel, the Twelve Disciples of Christ and the Twelve Followers of Muhammad, while depicted on the chandelier are the Cross, Crescent and the Star of David. The entire creation has a kind of Art Deco gloss, while the ethos of its eclectic design is clearly one of peace and tolerance between faiths and cultures.

The distinctive bell tower of Jerusalem's YMCA

King David Hotel **②**

23 King David St. **Map** 1 B4. **(** (02) 620 8888. 7, 8, 30, 38.

EYE-CATCHING not least for its pink stone walls and green windows, this impressive 1930s hotel *(see p234)* is a grandiose display of colonial architecture. It was designed by Swiss architect Emile Vogt for the Jewish-Egyptian Mosseri family.

Inside, the spacious lobbies and public areas, with their discreet period wooden furnishings, reflect a sense of splendour from an altogether different era. The richly ornamental style is achieved through a mixture of various

Inside the elegant lobby of the King David Hotel

ancient architectural and decorative elements, including Egyptian, Phoenician, Assyrian and Greek, as well as aspects of Islamic art. The hotel boasts an impressive list of former guests, including Winston Churchill and Haile Selassie, and for a long time, part of the British Mandate administration *(see p50)* was housed here. In 1946 it was the target of a bomb attack perpetrated by the Zionist paramilitary terrorist group Irgun, led by Menachem Begin *(see p51)*. It was rebuilt and the two top floors were added later.

Cinematheque **③**

11 Hebron Rd. **Map** 1 B5.
((02) 672 4131. 7, 8, 38, 99.

JUST SOUTH OF Yemin Moshe *(see pp116–17)* stands one of Jerusalem's most popular entertainment spots. This attractive cinema with its two screens specializes in international and arthouse films. Each year the centre hosts the Jerusalem Film Festival *(see p263)*. As well as possessing an interesting Israeli cinema archive, the centre also has a pleasant restaurant.

The Cinematheque is located in a group of redroofed houses which once formed part of the Shamah district. Built by Sephardic Jewish artisans in the early 20th century, it was among the first settlements to be established outside the walls of the Old City. The complex looks out over the Hinnom Valley, the lowest part of the city. In the Old Testament, the valley is described as a place of human sacrifice, where babies were burnt alive to honour Moloch,

The square-set form of the King David Hotel, the choice of many rich and famous visitors to Jerusalem

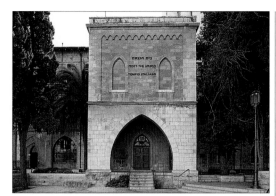

The Italian Synagogue and Museum of Italian-Jewish Art in a quiet square

the Canaanite god of fire (II Kings 23: 10). The Hinnom Valley is also known as Gehenna, from the Greek and Latin versions of its name, used in the New Testament, where the place became synonymous with Hell.

Ben Yehuda and Nakhalat Shiva ❹

Map 1 A3. 🚌 *20, 23, 27.*

One of the popular streetside cafés and restaurants in Ben Yehuda

A T THE HEART of modern Jerusalem are the pedestrianized precincts of Ben Yehuda Street and Nakhalat Shiva. They constitute one of the liveliest parts of the city, with shops, restaurants, street vendors and musicians coming together to create a rich and varied atmosphere. In the minds of local people, Ben Yehuda Street and Nakhalat Shiva are the embodiment of secular Jerusalem. The contrast with the Orthodox city, just a short distance to the north in Mea Shearim *(see p121)*, could not be more marked.

Ben Yehuda Street was built in the 1920s, and has since been the traditional meeting place for Jewish intellectuals, politicians and journalists.

South of Ben Yehuda Street is a series of narrow lanes, with low houses and connecting courtyards. These are collectively known as Nakhalat Shiva, meaning "the Domain of the Seven", which refers to the seven families who built them. Dating back to 1869, this area was the third Jewish residential quarter to appear outside the Old City walls. Despite being threatened with demolition on more than one occasion, the area was finally renovated in the 1980s. Today it is filled with shops, workshops, bars, restaurants and cafés and is invariably busy until the early hours.

Other streets in this locality also have much to interest the visitor. Buildings of varied architectural styles reflect the diverse cultural influences that have shaped the city.

Italian Synagogue ❺

27 Hillel St. **Map** 1 A3. 📞 *(02) 624 1610.* 🚌 *20, 23, 27.* 🕐 *9am–2pm Sun–Tue, 9am–5pm Wed, 9am–1pm Thu.* 🚫 *Jewish hols.* 📷

O RIGINALLY A GERMAN college constructed in the late 19th century, this building now houses an 18th-century synagogue from Conegliano Veneto, near Venice in Italy. In 1952, with no more Jews living there, the synagogue had fallen into disuse. It was decided to dismantle the interior and bring it here. It is arguably the most beautiful synagogue in Israel, and on Saturdays and Jewish holidays

the Italian-Jewish community worships here. The building also houses the Museum of Italian-Jewish Art, which boasts some fascinating items, including medieval ritual objects. On the lower floor is the Centre of Studies on Italian Judaism and a well-stocked library on the same subject.

Ticho House ❻

9 Ha-Rav Kook St. **Map** 1 A2.
📞 *(02) 624 5068.* 🚌 *1, 3.*
🕐 *10am–5pm Mon, Wed, Thu, Sun; 4–10pm Tue; 10am–2pm Fri.*
🚫 *Jewish hols.* 📷

B UILT IN THE 19th century as the luxurious residence of a wealthy Jerusalem family, this is one of the city's loveliest examples of an Arab mansion. Its large central drawing room is the focal point of both the architecture and the social life of the building. In the early 20th century the house was bought by Dr Abraham Ticho, a famous Jewish ophthalmologist who used to give the poor free treatment, irrespective of their ethnic origin or religion. Dr Ticho's Viennese wife, Anna, was an artist. By day the house was a clinic and by night it was the centre of Jerusalem's social and intellectual life.

Nowadays the house is administered by the Israel Museum *(see pp128–33)*, to which Anna left a collection of more than 2,000 watercolours and drawings. Some of these are exhibited here. The house also has a charming and very popular café overlooking a delightful garden.

View over the beautiful garden at the back of Ticho House

New City Hall ❼

Jaffa Rd. **Map** 1 B3. 📞 (02) 625 8844.
🚌 13, 18, 20, 23. 🕐 8:30am–4pm
Sun–Thu, 8:30am–noon Fri. 🖼

C OMPLETED IN 1993, the New
City Hall complex is sited
just outside the Old City walls,
where Jewish West Jerusalem
meets Arab East Jerusalem. Its
architecture displays an appropriate spirit of synthesis – the
complex includes ten renovated historical buildings, along
with two modern blocks that
draw heavily on historical
models (for example, the
banding of different coloured
stone echoes the Mameluke
buildings of the Old City).
   One of the renovated buildings, on Jaffa Road, is the old
City Hall. Its rounded façade
is still pocked with bullet holes
from when, between 1948 and
1967, Jerusalem was a divided
city (see p51), and this was a
frontline Israeli army post.

Russian Compound ❽

Kheshin St. **Map** 1 B3. 🚌 13, 18,
20, 23. **Underground Prisoners'
Museum 1918–48** 📞 (02) 623
3166. 🕐 8am–4pm Sun–Thu. 🖼

T HE RUSSIANS were some of
the first people to settle
outside the Old City in the
19th century (see p109).
The process began around
1860 when a few acres of
land were acquired a short
distance outside the city
walls. The Russians built a
virtually self-contained
compound to provide
lodgings for the city's
growing number of
Russian pilgrims, and
erected a cathedral
for services.

The New City Hall, seen through the palms of Safra Square

Consecrated in 1864, the
Cathedral of the Holy Trinity
is fashioned in an unmistak-
ably Muscovite style, with
eight drums topped by green
domes. Unfortunately, it is
closed to the public. Across
the plaza, under a pavement
grille, is what is known as
Herod's Column, a 12-m (40-ft)
stone pillar, which historians
believe was intended for the
Second Temple before it
cracked and was abandoned.
   These days the Russians own
only the cathedral, as many of
the other buildings belonging
to the compound were sold
off by the Soviet
Union in exchange
for shipments of
Israeli oranges.
   The building with
the crenellated
tower – the
grandest of the
former pilgrims'
hostels – is now
home to the Agriculture
Ministry. The street on which
it stands, Heleni ha-Malka,
is one of the city's
nightlife centres, filled
with bars and cafés.
The former women's
hostel, behind the
cathedral, now
houses the

**Royal lion above the
door, Ethiopian Church**

**Underground Prisoners'
Museum 1918–48**, which is
dedicated to Jewish resistance
fighters, some of whom were
jailed in this building during
the period of the British
Mandate (see pp50–51).

Ha-Neviim Street ❾

Map 1 B2. 🚌 27.

O NE OF THE OLDEST streets
outside the Old City,
Ha-Neviim (Street of the
Prophets) roughly marks the
dividing line between the
religious and
secular halves of
modern Jerusalem
(ultra-Orthodox
Mea Shearim lies
just to the north;
the drinking and
dining scene of
the Russian Com-
pound is to the
south). Once a prestigious
address, Ha-Neviim is lined
with some grand buildings. At
No. 58 is Thabor House, the
self-designed home of Conrad
Schick, a German who arrived
in the Holy Land a Protestant
missionary and became the
city's most renowned architect
of the late 19th century. The
house now belongs to the
Swedish Theological Institute,
but visitors can admire the
eccentric fortress-like main
gate. Someone will usually
answer the bell and admit the
curious into the courtyard to
admire the building's façade,
complete with embedded
archaeological finds.
   A few steps west at No. 64
is the house once occupied
by the Victorian painter

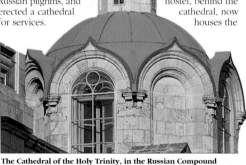

The Cathedral of the Holy Trinity, in the Russian Compound

William Holman Hunt *(see p31)*. It is now a private residence and closed to the public. A couple of minutes' walk to the north, along narrow, leafy Etyopya Street, is Ben Yehuda House, named after the man responsible for reviving popular usage of the Hebrew language. This was his residence in the early years of the 20th century.

A little further up the lane is the striking, round form of the Ethiopian Church, which sits in beautifully tended gardens. It was built between 1873 and 1911, and is modelled after churches in Ethiopia, with its sanctuary clearly separated from the main body of the church. Just five minutes' walk away, back on Ha-Neviim Street, the Ethiopians also have their consulate. It is notable for a vivid blue and gold mosaic on the façade depicting the Lion of Judah.

Italian Hospital ❿

Corner of Ha-Neviim and Shivtei Yisrael Sts. **Map** 1 B2. 🚌 *27.* ⬤ *to public.*

THE GRANDEST building of all on Ha-Neviim Street is the Italian Hospital. It was built just before World War I to underscore Italian presence in the Holy City, at a time when the colonial powers were using architecture to assert their influence and status. Designed by prolific architect Antonio Barluzzi, the hospital is clearly inspired by the Palazzo Vecchio in Florence. The building now houses the Ministry of Education.

The extravagant Italian Hospital

Mea Shearim, the heartland of Jerusalem's insular ultra-Orthodox community

Mea Shearim ⓫

Map 1 A1. 🚌 *1.*

POSSIBLY THE MOST unusual district in all Jerusalem, Mea Shearim is a perfectly preserved, living model of 18th-century Jewish Eastern Europe. It is a quarter inhabited exclusively by ultra-Orthodox Jews, where the influence of the outside world is kept to an absolute minimum. Dress is traditional in the extreme; many men wear black stockings and long black coats, and women keep their hair covered beneath a snood. The streets either side of main Mea Shearim Street are narrow alleyways, which squeeze between long, narrow two-storey dwellings, occasionally opening out into washing-strewn communal courtyards. The area is completely self-contained, with its own bakeries, markets, synagogues and, although no longer in use, its own huge cistern.

Mea Shearim was founded in the late 19th century and built in three stages, to a design by Conrad Schick, for Jews from Poland and Lithuania. Until well into this century the quarter was shut off from the rest of the city each night by six gates. The gates are gone but visitors should bear in mind that this is still a very insular community. Skirts should reach below the knee, and men must not wear shorts or T-shirts. Discretion is advised when taking photographs.

Northwest of Mea Shearim is the Bukharan Quarter, founded in the late 19th century by wealthy Central Asian Jews. Traces of its former grandeur remain in some elegant, if dilapidated, mansions.

ULTRA-ORTHODOX JEWS

The life of the ultra-Orthodox *(haredim)* is grounded in rigorous observance of Judaic law and study of the Torah. Their lifestyle involves an uncompromising rejection of modern life and all its trappings, which means no television, no cars and minimum intrusion by technology. The ultra-Orthodox live and dress strictly according to traditions practised in Eastern Europe several centuries ago. This lifestyle means that they segregate themselves from less observant Jews. More radical factions are opposed to the common use of Hebrew, the "Holy tongue", and instead speak Yiddish; some do not recognize the State of Israel or its laws, even refusing to pay taxes. They claim that there can be no true Jewish state until the coming of the Messiah.

Ultra-Orthodox Jews dressed in everyday attire

Solomon's Quarries ⓬

Sultan Suleyman St. **Map** 4 D1.
🚌 *23, 27.* ⏰ *9am–4pm Sun–Thu, 9am–2pm Fri.* 🏛

THIS IS AN ENORMOUS empty cave stretching under the Old City, with its entrance at the foot of the wall between Damascus and Herod's gates. Despite the popular name, historians are not convinced that the cave has any connection with Solomon, but it is likely that Herod took stone from here for his many building projects, including his modification of the Second Temple.

The quarry is also known as Zedekiah's cave, after the last king of Judaea who, legend has it, hid here during the Babylonian conquest of Jerusalem in 586 BC.

Garden Tomb ⓭

Conrad Schick St. **Map** 3 C1.
📞 *(02) 627 2742.* 🚌 *23, 27.*
⏰ *8:30am–noon & 2–5:30pm Mon–Sat.*

TOWARDS THE END of the 19th century the British general, Charles Gordon, of Khartoum fame, was visiting Jerusalem and started a dispute among archaeologists. He argued that this skull-shaped hill was the Golgotha referred to in the New Testament (Mark 15: 22) and that the real burial site of Jesus Christ was here and not at the Holy Sepulchre

Tourists visiting the ancient Garden Tomb in its attractive setting

(see pp88–91). Excavations carried out in 1883 did in fact unearth some ancient tombs, but further study found them to date back to the 9th–7th century BC, with an entirely different configuration from those in use in Christ's time. However, regardless of its authenticity, this place is well worth a visit if only for the lovely garden.

St Etienne Monastery ⓮

Nablus Rd. **Map** 1 C2. 📞 *(02) 626 4468.* 🚌 *23, 27.* ⏰ *9am–4pm Mon–Sat; ring the bell.*

THE NAME OF this site relates to the belief that in AD 439 Cyril of Alexandria interred the remains of St Stephen (St Etienne in French), the first Christian martyr, in a basilica built on this spot. The basilica was destroyed by the Persians in AD 614, and a subsequent 7th-century chapel on the same site was also destroyed, this time by the Crusaders holding Jerusalem, who feared Saladin would use it as a base for assaults on the city.

The present monastery was built between 1891 and 1901 by the French Dominicans. Its eclectic design includes an Oriental tower, Romanesque walls and Neo-Gothic flying buttresses. Within are remains of the mosaic floor of the original Byzantine church, as well as the Ecole Biblique, the Holy Land's first school of biblical archaeology.

The simple Neo-Romanesque chapel at St Etienne Monastery

St George's Cathedral ⓯

53 Nablus Rd. **Map** 1 C1. 📞 *(02) 628 3261.* 🚌 *23, 27.* ⏰ *10am–1pm Tue–Sat; ring the bell.*

THIS ARCHETYPAL Middle England church, with its pretty, cloistered courtyard and connotations of vicars, tweeds and cucumber sandwiches, stands in startling contrast to the chaotic Arab streets of its East Jerusalem neighbourhood.

The cathedral dates from 1910 and is named for the patron saint of England, who was actually a Palestinian conscript in the Roman army, executed in AD 303 for tearing up a copy of the emperor Diocletian's decree forbidding Christianity. He is supposedly buried at Lod (ancient Lydda), now better known as the site of Ben Gurion airport.

In World War I the cathedral was the local headquarters of the Turkish army, and the 1917 truce sanctioning British presence in Palestine was signed in the bishop's quarters.

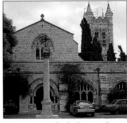

St George's Cathedral, part of Jerusalem's colonial heritage

Kings' Tombs 🔟

Salah ed-Din St. **Map** 1 C1. 🚌 *23, 27.* ⏰ *8am–5pm Mon–Sat.* 📷

DESPITE THE NAME, this single but elaborate tomb is thought to have been that of Queen Helena of Adiabene. In the 1st century AD she converted to Judaism and moved to Jerusalem from her kingdom in Mesopotamia. A small entrance leads down into a dimly lit maze of chambers with stone doors.

   Nearby is the 19th-century Orient House, a fine example of Islamic vernacular architecture. Visitors must observe from a distance as it is now the Jerusalem headquarters of the Palestinian Authority.

Well-worn steps leading to the deceptively named Kings' Tombs

American Colony Hotel 🔟

2 Louis Vincent St. **Map** 1 C1.
📞 *(02) 627 9777.* 🚌 *23.*

THIS ELEGANT hotel *(see p233)* built in 1865–76 has long been a favourite of diplomats and journalists. It started life as the home of a rich Turkish merchant. The name American Colony came about in the late 19th century when Anna and Horatio Spafford of Chicago bought the building and made it the centre of an American religious community dedicated to good works. When the community broke up in the early 20th century, a Baron Ustinov, related to the actor Peter Ustinov, suggested converting the building to accommodate pilgrims to the Holy Land. Soon after, it was turned into a beautiful hotel,

The Rockefeller Museum courtyard

which it remains today. If you cannot afford to stay here, it is definitely worth coming for lunch, taken out in the tree-shaded courtyard.

Rockefeller Museum 🔟

Sultan Suleyman St. **Map** 2 D2.
📞 *(02) 628 2251.* 🚌 *1,2.*
⏰ *10am–5pm Sun–Thu, 10am–2pm Fri & Sat.* 📷 ♿

THIS MUSEUM was made possible by a substantial financial gift made in 1927 by the American oil magnate John D Rockefeller. British

architect Austin Harrison designed the building along Neo-Gothic lines. It is vaguely reminiscent of the Alhambra in Spain and runs around a central courtyard. Constructed from the white stone typical of Jerusalem buildings, the Rockefeller has Byzantine- and Islamic-type decorative motifs. It was once one of the most important museums in the Middle East and the first to make a systematic collection of finds from the Holy Land. These days, it is a branch of the Israel Museum *(see pp128–33)*, but still houses a very impressive collection.

   Among its many remarkable objects are the stuccowork from Hisham's Palace in Jericho, beams from the Holy Sepulchre church and wooden panels from El-Aqsa mosque. Other exhibits worth seeing include a fascinating portrait modelled on an 8,000-year-old cranium discovered in Jericho; a lovely Bronze Age bull's head; a Canaanite vase in the shape of a human head; sculptures from the time of the Crusades; and Hellenistic and Roman objects found in Judaean desert caves. The museum also holds a number of the Dead Sea Scrolls *(see pp132–3)*.

The delightfully secluded courtyard of the American Colony Hotel

FURTHER AFIELD

SINCE THE CREATION of the state of Israel in 1948, the boundaries of Jerusalem have greatly expanded in all directions. The city has also been endowed with a great many significant new buildings. Two stand out as being of particular importance: the Israel Museum, a world-class institution that incorporates several collections of priceless treasures, including the famous Dead Sea Scrolls; and the Knesset, the seat of national government.

Another cornerstone in the psyche of Israeli society is Yad Vashem, the moving – and, in parts, harrowing – memorial complex that honours the more than six million Jews who died at the hands of the Nazis during the Holocaust. The site of this memorial is Mount Herzl, named after Theodor Herzl, the founding father of Zionism *(see p49)*. The grassy slopes here are also home to an extensive military cemetery, in which many figures of national importance are buried.

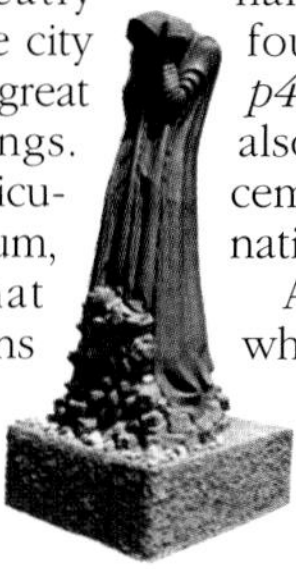

A memorial statue at Yad Vashem

As Jerusalem has expanded, what, not too long ago, were small, isolated villages are now virtually suburbs of the city. They have not, however, lost their character. Places such as Ein Kerem, nestled in the valley below Mount Herzl, and Abu Ghosh, further to the north-west, have a great deal of rural charm, as well as several attractive religious buildings linked with biblical events.

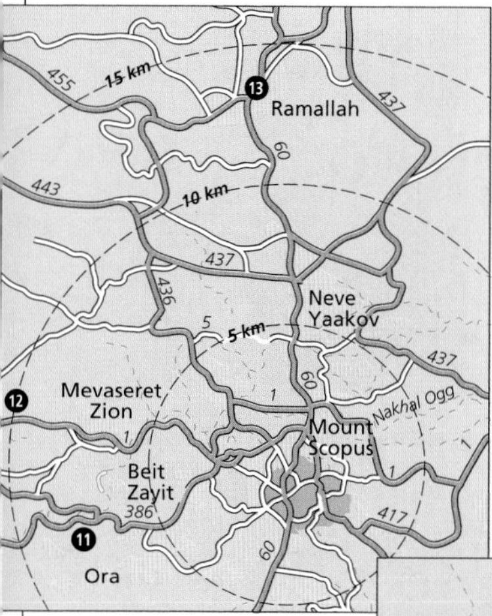

JERUSALEM AND ENVIRONS

KEY

- Main sightseeing area
- Built-up area
- Major road
- Minor road

0 kilometres 2

0 miles 2

SIGHTS AT A GLANCE

Museums
Bible Lands Museum 4
Israel Museum pp128–33 3
LA Mayer Museum of Islamic Art 1
Model of Ancient Jerusalem 8

Memorials
Yad Vashem 9

Holy Places
Monastery of the Cross 2

Modern Buildings
Hadassah Hospital Synagogue 11
Knesset 5
Supreme Court 6

Districts
Makhane Yehuda and Nakhlaot 7

Towns and Villages
Abu Ghosh 12
Ein Kerem 10
Ramallah 13

GREATER JERUSALEM

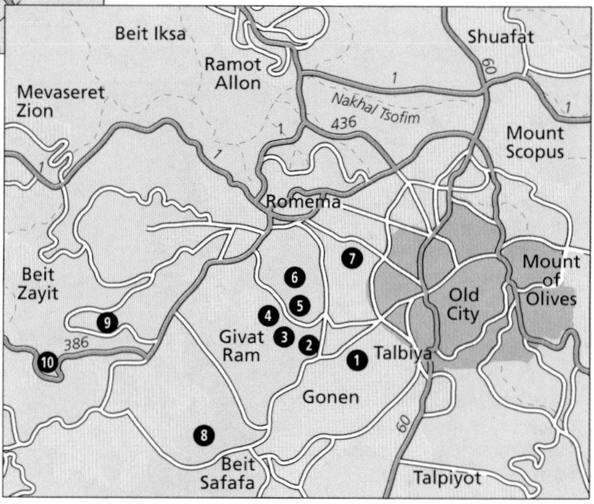

Crusader church complex at Abu Ghosh, 13 km (8 miles) west of Jerusalem

The refectory at the Monastery of the Cross

LA Mayer Museum of Islamic Art ❶

2 Ha-Palmakh St, Talbiya. 🄲 (02) 566 1291. 🚌 15. 🕐 10am–3pm Sun, Mon, Wed & Thu, 10am–6pm Tue, 10am–2pm Fri & Sat. 📷

WHILE THE CREAM of Islamic artifacts collected in the Holy Land are to be found in the Rockefeller Museum (see p123) and the Museum of Islamic Art on the Haram esh-Sharif (see p68), this modern, purpose-built museum offers a beautifully presented collection of pieces from the greater Islamic world. Especially attractive are the examples of Persian tiling and Indian Moghul miniatures, and there is a very informative section on Arabic calligraphy.

Monastery of the Cross ❷

Shalom St, Neve Granot. 🄲 (02) 679 0961. 🚌 18, 31, 32. 🕐 10am– 4:30pm Mon–Sat. 📷

STRANDED IN the middle of a large area of scrubland, ringed at its outer perimeters by main roads and modern buildings, this solitary Byzantine monastery has the look of a place that time forgot and urban planners ignored. Its high, buttressed walls emphasize still more its seclusion and reflect its once precarious position outside the Old City.

There was a church here in the 5th century, but it was destroyed by the Persians in 614. Part of its mosaic floor can still be seen on one side of the main altar in the present church. The monastery which exists today was built in the

11th century by monks from Mount Athos, with financial backing from King Bagrat of Georgia. According to tradition, it marks the spot where the tree grew that was used to make Christ's cross.

In the 13th century the Georgian poet Shota Rustaveli lived here and commissioned the frescoes in the main church. They were repainted in the 17th century respecting the original style.

By the 14th century the monastery had become the centre of Jerusalem's Georgian community and a major centre of Georgian culture in the region. Gradually, however, their standing declined and by 1685 the monastery had been taken over by the Greek Orthodox Patriarchate.

The church is largely in its original, 11th-century form, while many other parts of the complex have been altered or added to. The courtyard and the late Baroque bell tower display clear signs of 19th-century changes. In the late 1990s large-scale restoration was undertaken. The simple dome is one of the church's most beautiful features. Also remarkable are the frescoes, which show an unusual combination of Christian, pagan and worldly images. Visitors are permitted to wander freely around the complex. Particularly evocative of monastic life are the refectory on the upper floor and the kitchen.

Israel Museum ❸

See pp128–33.

Bible Lands Museum ❹

25 Avraham Granot St, Givat Ram. 🄲 (02) 561 1066. 🚌 9, 24. 🕐 9:30am–5:30pm Sun–Tue & Thu, 9:30am–9:30pm (Nov–Mar: 1:30– 9:30pm) Wed, 9:30am–2pm Fri & eves of Jewish hols, 11am–3pm Sat & Jewish hols. 📷

OPPOSITE THE Israel Museum is this rather unremarkable building which houses an outstanding collection of archaeological finds that reflect the different cultures of the Holy Land region in biblical times. The museum was inaugurated in 1992 with the private collection of Elie Borowski, a passionate scholar of ancient Middle Eastern civilizations. The collection features many finely crafted objects from ancient Egypt, Syria, Anatolia, Mesopotamia and Persia. Among these are a great number of artifacts that shed light on the culture of the Mesopotamian region in

Babylonian tablet, Bible Lands Museum

The Bible Lands Museum, covering the early history of the Middle East

The sculpted menorah near the entrance to the Knesset

the millennia before the Christian era. The many fascinating and unique objects include ancient inscriptions, jewellery, mosaics, seals, ivory carvings and scarabs.

The exhibits are displayed in a way that enables the visitor to build a clear and illuminating picture of the cultural context in which the biblical texts were written. The items are arranged according to both chronology and region. The result is a clear illustration of the way in which different cultures influenced each other and new societies evolved.

Knesset ❺

Rothschild St, Givat Ram. 🚍 (02) 675 3416. 🚌 9, 24, 99. ⏰ 8:30am–2pm Sun & Thu. 🎟 compulsory (ring in advance to book).

THE KNESSET (Assembly) is the seat of the Israeli Parliament. It takes its name from the Knesset ha-Gedola (Great Assembly) of 120 men that governed the political and civic life of Jews in the Second Temple period (see p40). The building, inaugurated in 1966, was designed by Joseph Klarwin. His design makes use of classical elements and is inspired by the Parthenon in Athens and various reconstructions of the Temple.

Opposite the entrance is a large, seven-branched menorah (candelabrum), symbol of the State of Israel. It is the work of British sculptor Benno

Elkan and was a gift from the British parliament. The relief work on its branches depicts crucial moments in Jewish history and is accompanied by biblical quotations. Nearby is a monument with an eternal flame, commemorating the dead of the Holocaust and Israel's wars (see pp51–3).

The reception area inside the Knesset was designed and decorated by the Russian-Jewish artist Marc Chagall (see p31). It is adorned with his mosaics and a triple tapestry which depicts the creation of the world, the exodus of the Israelites from Egypt, and the city of Jerusalem. The main chamber ends in a stone wall that is a very clear reference to the Western Wall (see p83).

The Supreme Court, one of the city's architectural highlights

Supreme Court ❻

Shaarei Mishpat St, Givat Ram. 🚍 (02) 675 9612. 🚌 9, 24, 99. ⏰ 10:30am–2:30pm Sun–Thu. 🎟 compulsory (ring in advance to book).

IN THE ABSENCE of a formal constitution, Israel's Supreme Court plays a pivotal role in the lives of ordinary citizens. Its significance is reflected in

the building's design – by Ram Karmi and Ada Karmi-Melamed – which manages to depict the concept of justice in architectural terms. The two copper pyramids on the roof are powerful symbols of the immutable nature of the principles of law. The long sweeping stairway seems to represent the accessibility of the law to ordinary people, and at the top it offers an all-embracing view of Jerusalem.

Motifs from the past, such as the Islamic elements in the inner courtyard and the Byzantine-era mosaic outside the entrance, recall the cultural and historical influences that have shaped contemporary Israel. They are given a modern context to link the past with the present and reflect the universality of justice.

Makhane Yehuda and Nakhlaot ❼

🚌 6, 13, 21.

THE DISTRICT of Makhane Yehuda, which means Field of Judah, was built in 1929 to house Jewish immigrant workers. It is famous for its vibrant and very colourful market, selling mainly foodstuffs. It is also home to a large number of popular local restaurants, which specialize in Middle Eastern salads and kebabs. To the south of Makhane Yehuda is the older district of Nakhlaot. This lively, warren-like jumble of low houses and narrow alleyways is fascinating to explore.

Displays of fruit and vegetables at the market in Makhane Yehuda

Israel Museum ❸

BUILT IN 1965 on a ridge overlooking West Jerusalem, the Israel Museum contains some of the country's finest pieces of art and archaeology. Its modular design, by Israeli architects A Mansfeld and D Gad, consists of a series of pavilions that climb the gentle slope, echoing the layout of traditional Arab villages. Inside, the collection includes entire synagogue interiors from Europe and India, the country's best Israeli art, an outstanding array of regional archaeology and the world-famous Dead Sea Scrolls.

Apple Core (1992), Claes Oldenburg

★ **Shrine of the Book**
This innovatively designed under-ground hall houses the Dead Sea Scrolls. It is the most visited part of the museum (see pp132–3).

★ **Beth Shean Mosaic**
This 6th-century mosaic floor, from a synagogue at Beth Shean (see p165), shows the Ark of the Covenant (see p19) flanked by two menorahs.

Ibex Sceptre
This copper sceptre deco-rated with ibex heads is part of a hoard of treasure found in the Judaean Desert. The workman-ship is remarkable for its era (late 5th millennium BC).

Open-air plaza

Anthropoid sarcophagi *(see p131)*

KEY TO FLOORPLAN
- ☐ Judaica and Jewish Ethnography
- ☐ Art collections
- ☐ Archaeology
- ☐ Temporary exhibitions
- ☐ Non-exhibition space

To Youth Wing

Café

Walkway from entrance pavilion

Billy Rose Art Garden
Woman Combing Her Hair (1914), by Ukrainian-born Alexander Archipenko, is one of the art garden's striking sculptures.

PLAN OF MUSEUM

KEY
- ☐ Entrance pavilion
- ☐ Main museum block
- ☐ Ruth Youth Wing
- ☐ Billy Rose Art Garden
- ☐ Shrine of the Book
- ☐ Temporary exhibitions

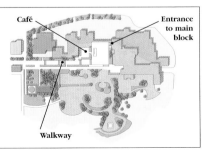

Café

Entrance to main block

Walkway

Red Blue Chair *(1918)*
The design collection includes this famous chair by Gerrit Rietveld. Like others in the Dutch De Stijl art movement, Rietveld used primary colours and simple geometric shapes.

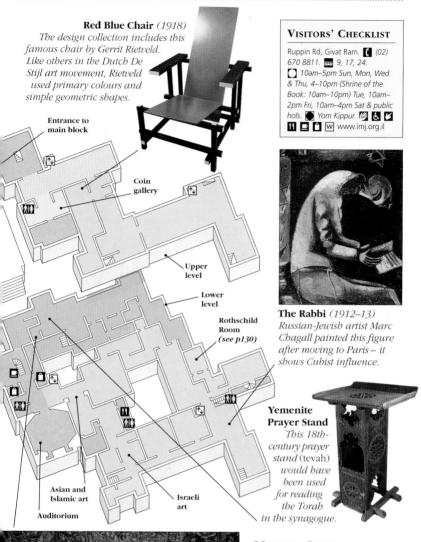

Entrance to main block

Coin gallery

Upper level

Lower level

Rothschild Room *(see p130)*

Asian and Islamic art

Auditorium

Israeli art

The Rabbi *(1912–13)*
Russian-Jewish artist Marc Chagall painted this figure after moving to Paris – it shows Cubist influence.

Yemenite Prayer Stand
This 18th-century prayer stand (tevah) would have been used for reading the Torah in the synagogue.

MUSEUM GUIDE
The main block is on two levels. The upper (entrance) level concentrates on contemporary art and design. The lower level displays Judaica, archaeology and the rest of the art collection. The complex also has a sculpture garden, a space for children's activities and the Shrine of the Book.

★ Horb Synagogue
This richly painted synagogue interior from Horb in Germany dates from 1735. The decoration includes flowers, animals and excerpts from traditional prayers.

STAR EXHIBITS

★ **Shrine of the Book**

★ **Beth Shean Mosaic**

★ **Horb Synagogue**

Exploring the Israel Museum

THANKS TO ITS WIDE VARIETY of sources, the collection is extraordinarily eclectic. Its core was inherited from the Bezalel School and Museum (Israel's first arts academy) and the Israel Department of Antiquities, and this has been supplemented by gifts, loans and acquisitions from around the globe. The biggest draw, though, for most visitors is the Shrine of the Book, which houses the Dead Sea Scrolls (see pp132–3).

Byzantine-era oil lamp

JUDAICA AND JEWISH ETHNOGRAPHY

JEWISH CULTURE is represented by two separate sections. The Judaica section, one of the largest of its kind in the world, displays objects connected with Jewish religious practice (see pp20–21). It spans the period from the Middle Ages to the present, and has exhibits from as far afield as Spain and China. Among the most precious objects are the medieval illuminated manuscripts. These include a 14th-century German *Haggadah* (the story read at Passover of the Israelites' liberation from Egypt) and the Rothschild Miscellany, a 15th-century collection of biblical, legal and other pieces.

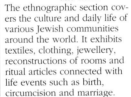

The Rothschild Miscellany

Elaborate silverwork on display includes *hadassim* (spiceboxes used during the ceremony of separation between the Sabbath and the start of the week) and the *rimonim* (pomegranates that decorate Torah scrolls in the synagogue). Another highlight is the large collection of *Hannukkiot* – the oil lamps that are lit for Hanukkah (see p37). There are also three beautiful, complete synagogue interiors, from Italy, Germany and India.

The ethnographic section covers the culture and daily life of various Jewish communities around the world. It exhibits textiles, clothing, jewellery, reconstructions of rooms and ritual articles connected with life events such as birth, circumcision and marriage.

Jeanne Hebuterne, Seated (1918), by Amedeo Modigliani

ART COLLECTIONS

THE MUSEUM'S various art collections cover a wide range of periods and artistic disciplines. In consecutive rooms visitors can take in Chinese porcelain, African figurines, Impressionist masterpieces and even an entire 18th-century French salon.

Rooms on the lower level house the modern art collection, which has international works from the 1890s to the 1960s. These include paintings by figures such as Gauguin, Cézanne, Chagall, Matisse and Modigliani. Twentieth-century sculpture is also represented,

The Rothschild Room, an 18th-century Parisian salon donated by Baron Edmond de Rothschild

both here and outdoors in the Billy Rose Art Garden (see p132). On the upper level, the rooms are devoted to design, architecture and contemporary art. The exhibits on this level are rotated regularly.

One of the largest collections of Israeli art in the country is exhibited in a series of rooms on both floors. It begins with paintings and drawings produced in the 19th century, at the beginning of Jewish resettlement (see p49). The 1920s and 30s are represented by figurative pieces by artists such as Reuven Rubin and Yitzhak Danziger. The contemporary Israeli art on display mirrors, and sometimes anticipates, tendencies seen elsewhere in the world.

Other lower-floor rooms are devoted to prints and drawings, photography, Old Master paintings (including a large work by Poussin depicting the sacking of the Second Temple; see p43), Islamic and East Asian art and the art of Africa, Oceania and the Americas.

Anthropoid sarcophagi, a highlight of the archaeology collection

ARCHAEOLOGY

THE ARCHAEOLOGY collection constitutes the largest section of the museum. Most pieces are on loan from the Israel Antiquities Authority and come from excavations carried out all over the country, which has the highest concentration of digs in the world. The digs cover a vast period of history – from as far back as 1.5 million BC – and have revealed artifacts from an impressive number of civilizations, from Palaeolithic flint

utensils, through Canaanite and Israelite figurines, to Byzantine mosaics and Islamic jewellery. The museum's collection represents most aspects of this cultural spectrum, and visitors will require at least two hours to fully appreciate the range of pieces on display.

The artifacts are arranged chronologically, starting in the gallery that leads from the main staircase. Objects to look out for in the first section (Palaeolithic to Chalcolithic periods, 1.5 million–3500 BC) include the jewellery and sculpted figures of the Natufian culture (10th–9th millennium BC), the 6,000-year-old, house-shaped ossuaries at the end of the first gallery and the elegant copperware of the so-called Judaean Desert Treasure (5th millennium BC). Highlights of the following rooms, the Canaanite Period (3500–1200 BC), are the sophisticated gold jewellery and, particularly, the anthropoid sarcophagi found in a cemetery at Deir el-Balah, in the Gaza Strip.

The Israelite Period (1200–586 BC) starts with the rise of the Israelites in the region and ends with the destruction of Solomon's Temple. In these rooms, look out for the beautiful Philistine pottery, the ivory pomegranate inscribed with ancient Hebrew (believed to be the only object ever found relating to worship in Solomon's Temple) and the priestly benediction written on a tiny silver amulet – the earliest known fragment of biblical text (7th century BC).

Mosaic from floor of 6th-century AD synagogue at Gaza, showing King David playing the lyre

Finds from the next 300 years are relatively scarce but the Hellenistic, Roman and Byzantine periods (332 BC–AD 636) offer fascinating objects, such as the sarcophagi and ossuaries from various Jewish catacombs, the bronze statue of the emperor Hadrian and the beautiful mosaics from Tsipori (Sepphoris), Kisufim, Gaza and Beth Shean.

In the last room are objects from neighbouring Middle Eastern and Mediterranean civilizations that had some bearing on the history of the Holy Land. The artifacts here include Egyptian cult and game objects, Assyrian and Babylonian reliefs, Greek vases and Roman jewellery.

Throughout the section are interesting models and reconstructions of some of the most important sites in this part of the world. The permanent exhibition is also flanked by temporary displays based on historical themes or particular archaeological sites.

JEWISH ART OF THE DIASPORA

During the many centuries of the Diaspora, Jews around the world directed their artistic talents primarily to ritual objects connected with the life cycle and synagogue liturgy. They produced fine examples of applied art, especially in the fields of gold- and silverware, other metalwork and manuscript decoration. Naturally, the motifs and techniques reflect the place and time in which the objects were produced, but many elements, both functional and iconographic, recur again and again. These recurring themes and local variations can be appreciated among the many exhibits in the museum's Judaica section.

18th-century silver spicebox from Germany

RUTH YOUTH WING

THIS SECTION of the museum is devoted to interactive art activities. The idea behind it was to introduce children to art and culture. The largest of its kind in the world, the centre has now extended its reach to adults. With ten classrooms, an auditorium, library, recycling workshop and exhibition space, it provides a stimulating environment for children and adults to learn about creative processes. There are regular "hands on" exhibitions, art courses and summer schemes for all ages, as well as tours for groups with special needs.

Children participating in creative activities in the Ruth Youth Wing

BILLY ROSE ART GARDEN

FOR MANY VISITORS, one of the highlights of the museum is the Billy Rose Art Garden, which occupies the western side of the museum grounds.

The garden was designed by the American sculptor Isamu Noguchi. It is an extraordinary combination of elements from local history and landscape, motifs from the traditional Zen garden and significant works of modern sculpture. It is laid out as a series of semi-circular terraces echoing those made for centuries by farmers in the Judaean Hills. Indigenous plants such as olive trees, cypresses and rosemary bushes are dotted around the garden.

Plans for the garden were resisted by ultra-Orthodox Jews before the museum opened. The modern collection donated by New York entre-preneur Billy Rose was thought offensive. However, the objec-tions were dismissed by Prime Minister David Ben Gurion.

Today, the garden offers an overview of sculpture through the 20th century. There are stunning early works by Rodin, Maillol, Picasso and Bourdelle. The curvaceous shapes in Henry Moore's pieces contrast with the angular composition of David Smith's *Cubi VI* (1963). Contemporary sculp-tures include James Turrell's intriguing installation with a large rectangular opening in the top for observing the sky, and Claes Oldenburg's "rotting" apple core, rich in symbolism and existential allusions.

SHRINE OF THE BOOK

BUILT TO HOUSE the Dead Sea Scrolls and other impor-tant artifacts, the intriguingly shaped Shrine of the Book has become a symbol of the whole museum. The unusual design, by American archi-tects F Kiesler and A Bartos, is inspired by the scrolls them-selves. The distinctive dome is intended to imitate the lids of the jars in which the scrolls were found. Near the entrance is a black granite wall. The contrast between the black of the wall and the white of the dome is a reference to the decisive battle between the Children of Darkness and the Children of Light, described in the scroll known as the War Scroll. This final confrontation between good and evil would, the authors believed, herald the coming of the Messiah.

Inside, a long, subtly lit passageway, designed to evoke the catacomb-like environ-ment in which the scrolls were found, has a permanent exhibition on life in Qumran at the time the scrolls were written. It leads into the main

Magdalena Abakonowicz's *Negev* (1987), Billy Rose Art Garden

chamber under the dome. The imposing showcase directly beneath the dome contains a facsimile of the Great Isaiah Scroll, the only biblical book that survived in its entirety. Its 66 chapters were written on several strips of parchment, which were then sewn togeth-er, making it more than 7 m (23 ft) long. One of the sur-rounding display cases contains part of the real scroll. Also on show are the Psalms Scroll, 28 columns of text consisting of psalms, hymns and a prose passage about the psalms; the War Scroll; the Manual of Discipline; the Temple Scroll; and the 10th-century Aleppo Codex – not one of the Dead Sea Scrolls, but one of the oldest copies of the Bible.

On the Shrine's lower level is a collection of 2nd-century AD articles, such as shoes, keys and baskets, found in the Cave of Letters, south of Ein Gedi *(see p177)*. The cave is named after letters discovered there that were written by Simon Bar-Kokhba during the Second Jewish Revolt *(see p41)*.

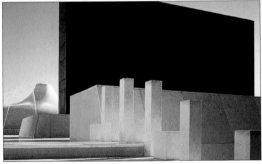

Symbolic clash of darkness and light at the Shrine of the Book entrance

The Dead Sea Scrolls

IN 1947, a Bedouin shepherd, in search of a lost goat near the Dead Sea, entered a cave and discovered jars containing seven ancient scrolls. Over the next two decades fragments of some 800 more were found in 11 caves. At the same time, archaeologists, looking for signs of habitation, uncovered the nearby settlement of Qumran *(see p171)*. The scrolls had been written in the Late Second Temple period, between the 3rd century BC and AD 68. Some contain the oldest existing versions of biblical scriptures. Others are tracts on history, daily life and the messianic predictions of a Hebrew sect generally identified with the separatist and monastic Essenes. Since the discovery of the scrolls, their interpretation, the identity and mission of their authors and the significance of nearby Qumran have been the subject of passionate academic and theological debate.

Jar in which scrolls were found

The Shrine of the Book is dominated by a dramatic display case, which contains a copy of the Great Isaiah Scroll. It was designed to look like the wooden rods around which the Torah scrolls are rolled for readings at synagogue services.

Inkwell found at Qumran

The reconstruction of thousands of scroll fragments is still being carried out by researchers hoping to unravel the mysteries surrounding the scrolls.

The parchment on which the scrolls were written was made from sheepskin. Inkwells found near a table at Qumran suggest a scriptorium – a room for copying manuscripts.

The Great Isaiah Scroll is the largest and best preserved of the scrolls. Written around 100 BC, it is 1,000 years older than the oldest biblical manuscript known before the finds at Qumran.

Qumran was excavated by Roland de Vaux, a French Dominican friar. He believed that the settlement was a communal retreat used by the Essenes.

Model of Ancient Jerusalem ❽

Holyland Hotel, Uziel St, Malkha.
📞 (02) 643 7777. 🚌 21, 21A.
🕐 8am–10pm (Fri & Sat: 6pm) daily.

IN THE GARDENS of the Holy-land Hotel, out in West Jerusalem, is this large-scale representation of the city as it was in AD 66, at the time of the Second Temple (see pp42–3). Measuring roughly 20 m (65 ft) across, the model is fantastically detailed and is constructed out of wholly natural materials such as stone, copper and wood, all of which would have been employed in the construction of the ancient city itself. It is continually updated to incorporate new archaeological discoveries.

Yad Vashem ❾

Mount Herzl. 📞 (02) 644 3400.
🚌 13, 21, 23, 27. 🕐 9am–5pm Sun–Thu, 9am–2pm Fri.

FOR MANY VISITORS to Israel a visit to Yad Vashem makes for the most moving experi-ence of their trip. Meaning "a name and a place" (from Isaiah 56: 5), it is an archive, research institute, museum and, above all, a monument to perpetuate the memory of the more than six million who died in the Nazi Holocaust.

Entrance to the site is along the Avenue of the Righteous Among Nations, which is lined with plaques bearing the names of Gentiles who helped Jews and, in so doing, put their own lives at risk. Some 16,000 people are recognized, including Oskar Schindler (see p113). The avenue leads to the Historical Museum, which, with its large collection of documents, photographs and personal effects, adds a harrowing first-person dimension to the horrors that began with the rise of the Nazis in 1933 and culminated in the death camps.

The Hall of Remembrance beside the museum is a stark, tomb-like chamber that bears the names of 21 of the main camps on flat, black, basalt slabs. At the centre of the vast chamber is a casket of ashes from the cremation ovens; above it is an eternal flame. The nearby Hall of Names is devoted to recording the names of all those Jews who perished, along with as much biographical detail as possible.

Altogether, more than 20 monu-ments occupy this hillside site, but perhaps the most harrowing of all is the Children's Memorial, a candle-lit cavern in which a looped tape recites the names of some of the estimated 1.5 million children exterminated by the Nazis.

Visitors to Yad Vashem are expected to dress appropriately; shorts and miniskirts are not acceptable.

Church of St John the Baptist, Ein Kerem

Janusz Korczak Memorial, Yad Vashem

Ein Kerem ❿

7 km (4 miles) W of central Jerusalem.
🚌 17, 184.

A PICTURESQUE VILLAGE, Ein Kerem ("the vineyard spring") has strong biblical associations. According to Christian tradition, John the Baptist was born and lived here. The village boasts several fine churches and monasteries connected with his life. Recognizable by its tall, thin tower, the Fran-ciscan **Church of St John the Baptist** dates from the 17th century, but is built over the ruins of earlier Byzantine and Crusader struc-tures. Steps inside the church lead down into a natu-ral cave, known as the Grotto of the Nativity of St John, which tradition connects with the birth of the Baptist.

The other church of note is the two-tiered **Church of the Visitation**, completed in 1955 to a design by Antonio Barluzzi, architect of the Dominus Flevit Chapel (see p109) and the Chapel of the Flagellation (see p62). It commemorates the Virgin Mary's visit to Elizabeth, then pregnant with John, an episode depicted on the church's mosaic façade. Within is a natural grotto, in front of which are the remains of Roman-era houses. According to tradition, the grotto is where Elizabeth hid

Memorial to the Victims in Camps, Yad Vashem

with her infant son to escape from the Massacre of the Innocents (the killing of all first-born sons, ordered by Herod). The courtyard walls are lined with tiled panels inscribed with the *Magnificat* (Luke 1: 46–55), Mary's hymn of thanks, in 42 languages.

At the bottom of the hill below the church is a small, abandoned mosque. Beside it surfaces the spring (popularly known as the Spring of the Virgin) from which the village takes its name.

One of the other pleasures of Ein Kerem is its tranquil, wooded, valley setting. This is best appreciated on a beautiful walk through the trees that starts beside the sculpture at the beginning of the access road to Yad Vashem.

Hadassah Hospital Synagogue ⓫

Ein Kerem. 【 (02) 677 6279.
🚌 19, 27. ◷ 8am–1:15pm & 2–3:45pm Sun–Thu, 8am– 12:30pm Fri. 🎫 🗗 🚫

A SPLENDID cycle of 12 stained-glass windows decorates the synagogue at the otherwise unremarkable Hadassah Hospital. The windows were created in 1960–61 by the Russian-Jewish artist Marc Chagall *(see p31)*, and installed the following year for the inauguration of the building. Each of the windows repre-sents one of the 12 tribes of Israel (Genesis 49). Tradition associates each of the tribes with a symbol, a precious stone and a social role, and these elements are all repre-sented in Chagall's imagery and choice of colour.

Several of the windows were damaged by shrapnel during the 1967 War *(see p52)* and had to be repaired by the artist. However, one of the windows (a green one) bears a small symbolic bullet hole in the lower half, deliberately left there as a testimony to the fighting.

Ramallah's bustling market, just east of the central square

Abu Ghosh ⓬

13 km (8 miles) W of central Jerusalem.
🚌 185, 186.

T HIS ARAB VILLAGE just north of the main Jerusalem-Tel Aviv highway was considered by the Crusaders to be Emmaus, where Christ made himself known to two disciples in the days following his Resurrection. The Crusaders endowed the place with one of the most beautiful Roman-esque buildings in the Holy Land. Known simply as the **Crusader Church**, it was built in the early 12th century by the Knights Hospitallers and stands almost complete in its original form. The 12th-century frescoes in the church are lovely but are unfortu-nately in a poor state of repair. The adjacent early 20th-century monastery belongs to French Olivetan Benedictine monks, who produce and sell pottery. Up on the hill above the village stands the

Church of Notre Dame de l'Arche de l'Alliance, built in 1924 over the remains of a 5th-century church, whose mosaics are still visible. It is said to occupy the site of the house of Abinadab, where the fabled Ark of the Covenant *(see p19)* rested for 20 years (1 Samuel 7: 1–2) until David took it to Jerusalem.

Ramallah ⓭

16 km (10 miles) N of central Jerusalem.
🚌 from Nablus Rd or service taxi from Damascus Gate. 🚕 daily.

I T POSSESSES no monuments or famed attractions, but for anyone interested in visiting a modern Palestinian town, then Ramallah is worth a look. Since the Arabs lost ground in Jerusalem in the 1967 War, Ramallah has developed as an alternative centre of Palestinian intellec-tual life and cultural heritage. Many of the ministries of the Palestinian Authority are located here, and nearby Bir Zeit University is the region's major Arab academic insti-tution. Ramallah also has several theatres and night-spots featuring Arabic music *(see pp260–63)*, and along Sharia Yafa (Jaffa Rd) there is a string of good, low-priced, open-air cafés and restau-rants, serving traditional Arab *meze* and full meals *(see p248)*.

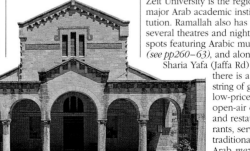

The modern Church of Notre Dame de l'Arche de l'Alliance, Abu Ghosh

JERUSALEM STREET FINDER

THE MAP REFERENCES that are given throughout the Jerusalem chapters of this guide refer to the maps on the following pages. References are also given in the listings for hotels *(see pp232–4)* and restaurants *(see pp246–8)*. Some of the many small streets and alleys may not be named on the maps. Many streets and monuments have two or even three names: one in Hebrew, one in Arabic and, occasionally, a commonly used English-language form,

too. What we call Damascus Gate is also known as Shaar Shkhem to Israelis and Bab el-Amud to Arabs. In this guide and on the following maps, where there is a sufficiently well-recognized English name, we have used it; otherwise, we have used the Arabic names for predominantly Arab areas (for example, the Muslim Quarter of the Old City) and Hebrew names for Jewish areas. Spellings in this guide may vary from those you see on street signs.

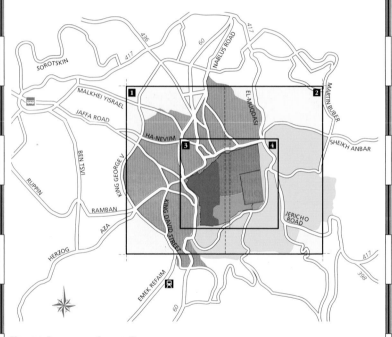

KEY TO JERUSALEM STREET FINDER

Major sight		◖ Mosque	
Other sight		···· Route of Via Dolorosa	
Other important building		IV Station of the Cross	
Bus station		Police station	
Train station		⊠ Post office	
Taxi rank		✚ Hospital with casualty unit	
P Parking		City wall	
Tourist information		→ One-way street	
Synagogue		Covered street	
Church		25» Street number	

SCALE OF MAP ABOVE
0 metres   1000
0 yards   1000

SCALE OF MAPS 1 – 2
0 metres   250
0 yards   250

SCALE OF MAPS 3 – 4
0 metres   100
0 yards   100

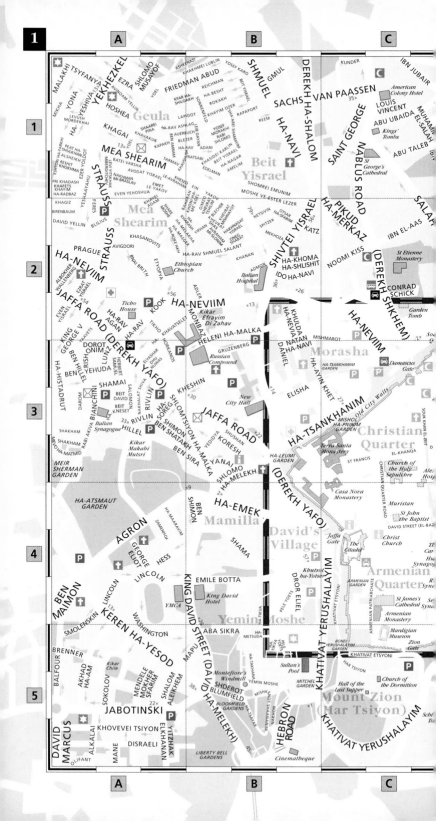

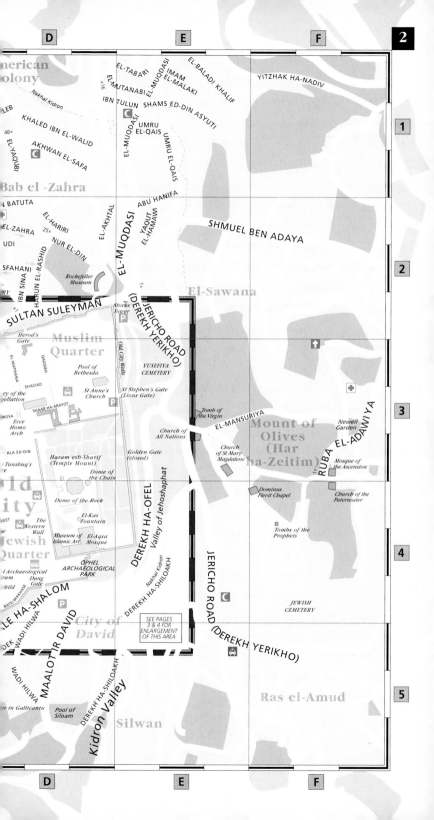

2

D **E** **F**

1

2

3

4

5

merican
olony

Nakhal Kidron

ELEB

EL-YAQUBI

46*

KHALED IBN EL-WALID

AKHWAN EL-SAFA

Bab el -Zahra

N BATUTA

EL-ZAHRA

UDI

SFAHANI

IBN SINA

HARUN EL-RASHID

NUR EL-DIN

EL-HARIRI

25*

EL-AKHTAL

EL-MUQDASI

EL-TABARI

EL-MUTANABI

IBN TULUN

EL-MUQDASI

UMRU
EL-QAIS

IMAM
EL-MALAKI

EL-BALADI KHALIF

SHAMS ED-DIN ASYUTI

UMRU EL-QAIS

ABU HANIFA

YAQUT
EL-HAMAWI

YITZHAK HA-NADIV

SHMUEL BEN ADAYA

*Rockefeller
Museum*

RY

EL-MUQDASI

SULTAN SULEYMAN

*Storks
Tower*

P

El-Sawana

JERICHO ROAD
(DEREKH YERIKHO)

*Herod's
Gate*

**Muslim
Quarter**

EL-MATHANA

QADISEH

SHADAD

*Pool of
Bethesda*

*St Anne's
Church*

ROSA

Ecce
Homo
Arch

SHAAR HA-ARAYOT

ALA ED-DIN

*Tunsbuq's
e*

Old City Walls

*YUSEFIYA
CEMETERY*

*St Stephen's Gate
(Lions Gate)*

P

*Tomb of
the Virgin*

EL-MANSURIYA

**Mount of
Olives
(Har
ha-Zeitim)**

*Newell
Garden*

RUBA EL-ADAWIYA

*Church
of All Nations*

*Church
of St Mary
Magdalene*

*Mosque of
the Ascension*

*Golden Gate
(closed)*

Ol d

*Haram esh-Sharif
(Temple Mount)*

*Dome of
the Chain*

*Dominus
Flevit Chapel*

*Church of the
Paternoster*

Ci ty

Dome of the Rock

DEREKH HA-OFEL

Valley of Jehoshaphat

*El-Kas
Fountain*

STREET

*The
Western
Wall*

**Jewish
Quarter**

*Museum of
Islamic Art*

*El-Aqsa
Mosque*

*Tombs of the
Prophets*

l Archaeological
um
child

*OPHEL
ARCHAEOLOGICAL
PARK*

*Dung
Gate*

JERICHO ROAD
(DEREKH YERIKHO)

LE HA-SHALOM

P

WADI HILWA

**City of
David**

MAALOT IR DAVID

DEK

WADI HILWA

Nakhal Kidron

DEREKH HA-SHILOAKH

SEE PAGES
3 & 4 FOR
ENLARGEMENT
OF THIS AREA

*JEWISH
CEMETERY*

Ras el-Amud

r in Gallicantu

*Pool of
Siloam*

DEREKH HA-SHILOAKH

Kidron Valley

Silwan

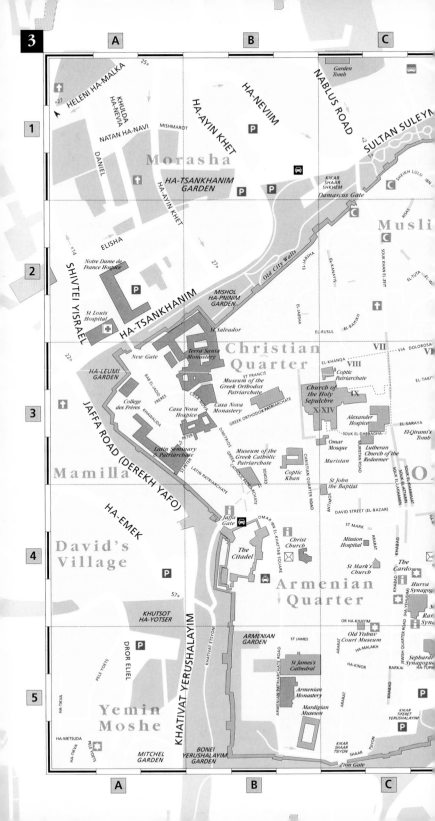

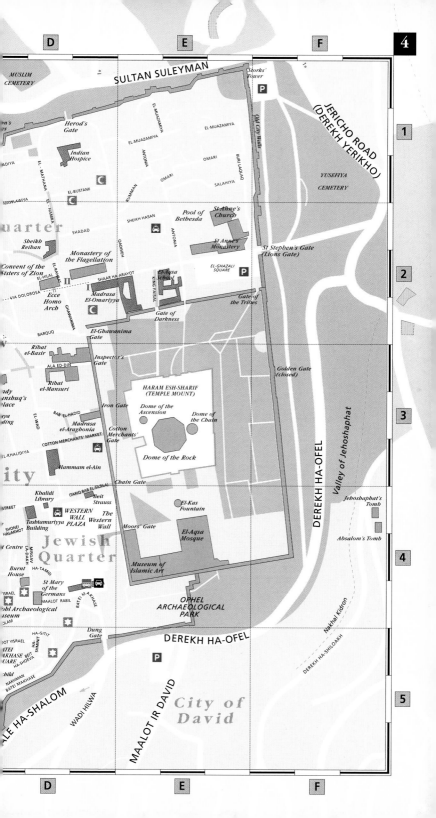

THE HOLY LAND
REGION BY
REGION

The Holy Land at a Glance

T HE HOLY LAND is rich in historical sights far beyond its
biblical associations. In Petra it has one of the most
unusual and magical ruined cities in the world, and the
Roman-era remains at sites such as Jerash in Jordan and
Beth Shean in northern Israel are similarly stunning. The
scenery that the visitor encounters while travelling can also
be dramatic, especially in the region of the Dead Sea
(a geographic marvel in itself) and in the Sinai peninsula.
Off the coast of Sinai, the Red Sea conceals underwater
scenery every bit as spectacular as that on dry land.

**Waterfront at Jaffa, a virtual suburb of Tel Aviv and a favourite
place for city-dwellers to dine at weekends**

**THE DEAD
SEA AND THE
NEGEV DESERT**
(See pp166–183)

**Beautiful sandstone cloisters at the Church of the
Nativity in Bethlehem**

**THE RED SEA
AND SINAI**
(See pp210–225)

**St Catherine's Monastery, Sinai, one of the world's
oldest continuously functioning monasteries**

◁ **Spectacular desert scenery at Wadi Rum in Western Jordan**

THE COAST
ND GALILEE
(See pp148–165)

WESTERN
JORDAN
(See pp184–209)

**View from the shore of the Sea of Galilee, rich in associations
with the miracles and teachings of Jesus Christ**

**The ruined main street of Jerash, the best-preserved
Roman city in the Holy Land**

**The mountaintop fortress of Masada on the Dead
Sea, the most visited site in Israel after Jerusalem**

**The incredible shaping of the landscape in
the carved rock façades of Petra**

| 0 kilometres | 50 |
| 0 miles | 50 |

THE COAST AND GALILEE

A FERTILE CORRIDOR *squeezed between the sea and the desert, this is the Promised Land of the Old Testament. The green hills and fresh waters of Galilee provided the setting for many episodes in the early life and ministry of Christ. Beside all its religious associations this is very much a secular paradise too, the heartland of modern Israel and a sun-drenched scenic magnet for tourists.*

The wealth of ancient sites along this stretch of coast bears witness to the fact that for centuries this has been an important land corridor connecting Africa, Europe and Asia. The great empires of ancient Egypt to the south and Assyria and Babylon to the east met here in trade and battle. Later, the Romans exploited this coast-line with the laying of a great highway, the Via Maris, and Herod built a magnificent port in Caesarea *(see p156),* one of the grandest and most important in the eastern Mediterranean. Ports such as this formed the nuclei of the Latin Kingdoms when the Crusaders came conquering in the Middle Ages. The Muslim Arabs eventually drove out the Christian knights but their legacy remains in some superb muscular architecture, especially at Acre, which retains one of the most charming old towns in the whole of the Holy Land.

When in the 19th century the first major waves of Jewish immigrants began arriving, it was on the fertile coastal plains and rolling hills of Galilee that they chose to settle. They planted wheat and cotton in the fields, orange groves and vineyards on the slopes, and cities overlooking the sea. The capital they founded, Tel Aviv, has become a vibrant centre of culture and commerce, while Haifa, attractively tumbling down Mount Carmel to the sea, is a thriving economic powerhouse. Inland Galilee remains rural and idyllic, equally pleasing to pilgrims on the trail of Christ and to seekers after relaxation and the picturesque.

The harbour at Acre, stronghold of the Crusaders and one of the Holy Land's best preserved old cities

◁ A vaulted street in Jaffa, an important ancient port now part of metropolitan Tel Aviv

Exploring the Coast and Galilee

Northern Israel is arguably the most attractive region in the Holy Land. The coast has long white sandy beaches, while Galilee is a landscape of rolling green hills, forested valleys and clear freshwater lakes. The Golan even has mountains that are capped with snow for part of each year. Places of interest include the hilltop Jewish holy town of Safed, Nazareth, traditionally held to be where Jesus spent his childhood, and many fine archaeological sites, including Crusader castles and Roman towns. With such a concentration of beauty spots and picturesque vistas, this is an area ideally explored by car.

Sights at a Glance

Herod the Great's port of Caesarea, now an impressive set of ruins beside the sea

Getting Around

Jerusalem and Tel Aviv are linked by a good motorway. By bus the journey takes under an hour with departures roughly every 15 minutes. Northbound services along the coastal highway from Tel Aviv to Caesarea and Haifa are only slightly less frequent. There is also a coastal railway line from Tel Aviv to Nahariya.

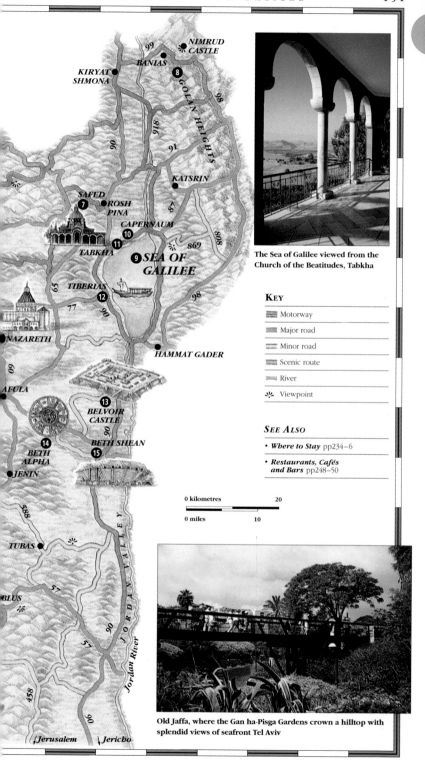

NIMRUD
CASTLE

99

BANIAS

KIRYAT
SHMONA

8

GOLAN HEIGHTS

98

918

90

91

KATSRIN

SAFED

7

ROSH
PINA

87

CAPERNAUM

10

808

TABKHA

11

869

9 SEA OF
GALILEE

TIBERIAS

65

98

12

77

90

NAZARETH

HAMMAT GADER

AFULA

BELVOIR
CASTLE

13

90

BETH
ALPHA

14

BETH SHEAN

15

JENIN

JORDAN VALLEY

588

TUBAS

57

BLUS

90

57

458

90

Jordan River

Jerusalem   Jericho

The Sea of Galilee viewed from the
Church of the Beatitudes, Tabkha

KEY

▨ Motorway

▨ Major road

▨ Minor road

▨ Scenic route

▨ River

☼ Viewpoint

SEE ALSO

• *Where to Stay* pp234–6

• *Restaurants, Cafés
and Bars* pp248–50

0 kilometres   20

0 miles   10

Old Jaffa, where the Gan ha-Pisga Gardens crown a hilltop with
splendid views of seafront Tel Aviv

Tel Aviv ❶

TEL AVIV REPRESENTS the modern face of the Jewish state – a brash, confident centre of commerce and contemporary culture. It is also a true Mediterranean resort city, with a long, sandy beach fringed by cafés, bars and shops. Away from the seafront are grand palm-lined avenues, with elegant buildings in International Modern and Art Deco styles. All this has been constructed since 1909, when the Jewish National Fund purchased land among the dunes north of the old Arab port of Jaffa *(see pp154–5)* on which to build a new city, to be called Tel Aviv (meaning Hill of the Spring).

Wall mosaic by Nahum Gutman, Shalom Tower

Exploring Tel Aviv
A white sand beach stretches right along the seafront of central Tel Aviv, backed by a long promenade, modern hotels and Miami-style condominiums. One of them, the huge, pink **Opera Towers**, with shops and restaurants at street level, is an easily recognizable landmark. The beach is crowded all summer with sun-seekers and swimmers and after dark with open-air concert- and disco-goers. Strong sea currents mean that you should swim only where you see white flags. Red flags mean that it is dangerous; black flags that it is forbidden.

Just north of the centre is a residential area of attractive, white, Bauhaus-style architecture and **Ben Gurion House**, the former home of Israel's first prime minister *(see p51)*.

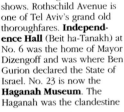

Fountain performance, Dizengoff Square

Rabin Square is named after Prime Minister Yitzhak Rabin, who was assassinated *(see p53)* outside City Hall on the square's northern side.

Dizengoff Street, the city's main shopping street, is named after Tel Aviv's first mayor. It is at its liveliest at its junction with Frishman Street. Further on, **Dizengoff Square** sports a drum-like fountain by Israeli artist Yaako Agam, which has water jets programmed to perform hourly light and music shows. Rothschild Avenue is one of Tel Aviv's grand old thoroughfares. **Independence Hall** (Beit ha-Tanakh) at No. 6 was the home of Mayor Dizengoff and was where Ben Gurion declared the State of Israel. No. 23 is now the **Haganah Museum**. The Haganah was the clandestine

pre-1948 military organization that afterwards became the Israeli army. At right angles to Rothschild Avenue is Sheinkin Street, filled with trendy cafés.

The maze of small streets in the **Yemenite Quarter** (Kerem ha-Temanim), the oldest part of town, contrasts sharply with the orderly layout of the rest of the city, but is now a fashionable area. Nakhalat Binyamin Street, with elegant, if slightly faded, Art Deco buildings, some with decorated tile panels, is full of boutiques and cafés and has a craft market on Tuesday afternoons and Fridays. The northern end of Ha-Carmel Street has a huge, daily market with side streets specializing in different food produce.

🏛 **Haganah Museum**
23 Rothschild Ave. ☎ *(03) 560 8624.*
○ *Sun – Thu.* ♿

The striking 1990s Opera Towers, with the modern centre of Tel Aviv stretching away behind the beach

🏛 Shalom Tower

Herzl Road. 【 *(03) 517 0991.*
○ *daily.*
In the centre of the oldest part
of the new city, this austere,
1960s office building was once,
at 140 m (460 ft) high, the
tallest structure in Israel, but it
is now surpassed by the radio
tower. There are shops on the
first and second floors and a
modest wax museum on the
third, but the main attraction
is the observation area on the
34th (top) floor. On a clear
day the view stretches from
the coast to Jerusalem.

🏛 Tel Aviv Museum of Art

27 Ha-Melekh Shaul Ave. 【 *(03) 696
1297.* ○ *Mon–Sat.*
The paintings here form Israel's
most important collection of
19th- and 20th-century art.
Artists represented include
Monet, Renoir, Van Gogh, Dalí,
Picasso, Chagall, Munch and
Pollock. Other works range
from 17th-century Flemish to
modern Israeli. A ticket covers
entrance to the Helena Ruben-
stein Pavilion, where contemporary art shows are held.

**Traditional olive press at the
Land of Israel Museum**

🏛 Land of Israel Museum

2 Haim Levanon, Ramat Aviv.
【 *(03) 641 5244.* ○ *daily.*
Built around the archaeological
site of Tel Quasile, where
excavations have revealed
layers of human habitation
dating back to 2000 BC, this
museum (the Eretz Yisrael
Museum) comprises 11 themed
pavilions. One of them has a
very fine collection of ancient
glass. Others are devoted to
ceramics, folklore, coins,
ancient crafts (with live demonstrations by artisans) and
temporary exhibitions, and
one is a planetarium. Together
they house the region's largest
collection of archaeological
and historical artifacts.

VISITORS' CHECKLIST

Road Map B3. 👥 *360,000.*
✈ *Ben Gurion, 22 km (14 miles)
SE.* 🚉 *Arlosoroff Station, Haifa
Rd, (03) 577 4000.* 🚌 *New
Central Bus Station, Levinsky St,
(03) 639 4444 (local buses), (03)
694 8888 (long-distance buses).*
ℹ *6th Floor, New Central Bus
Station, (03) 639 5660.* 🏖 *Beach
Festival (Jul & Aug).* 📅 *daily.*

🏛 Museum of the Jewish Diaspora

University Campus, Gate 2, Klausner St.
【 *(03) 646 2020.* ○ *Sun–Fri.*
It is well worth setting aside
several hours to visit this well-
presented museum (Beit ha-
Tefuzot). Instead of showing
historical artifacts, it uses
dioramas, models, videos and
interactive displays to illu-
strate aspects of Jewish life,
past and present, throughout
the world and the influence of
Jewish arts and literature on
other cultures. There is also a
collection of beautifully-made
scale models of synagogues
from many countries.

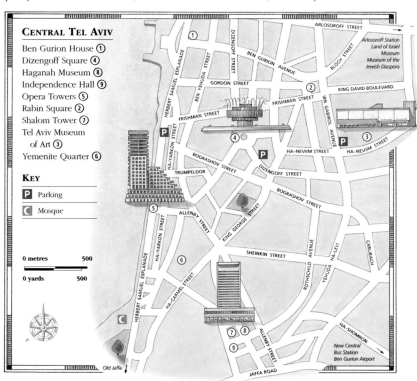

CENTRAL TEL AVIV

Ben Gurion House ①
Dizengoff Square ④
Haganah Museum ⑧
Independence Hall ⑨
Opera Towers ⑤
Rabin Square ②
Shalom Tower ⑦
Tel Aviv Museum
 of Art ③
Yemenite Quarter ⑥

KEY

P Parking

C Mosque

0 metres   500
0 yards   500

Street-by-Street: Old Jaffa

**Artists'
Quarter
mural**

Aⁿccording to the bible, Jaffa (then called Joppa) was founded in the wake of the great flood by Noah's son Japheth. Archaeologists have unearthed remains dating back to the 20th century BC, establishing Jaffa as one of the world's oldest ports. However, with the growth of Tel Aviv, Jaffa, which had flourished under the Ottomans, went into decline. Following Jewish victory in the 1948 War it was absorbed into the new city to the north. The core of the old town has since been revived as an attractive arts, crafts and dining centre.

The seafront of Old Jaffa, with its warehouses reborn as restaurants

Ha-Pisga open-air amphitheatre is used for concerts during the summer.

Archaeological Museum
Housed in an elegant 18th-century local government building, this museum holds finds from digs in the area.

To Clock Tower

The Mahmoudiya Mosque dates from 1812 and remains in use by the local Muslim community.

Base of 19th-century *sabil* (fountain)

MIFRAZ SHLOMO

Clock Tower
Built in 1901 to mark the 25th anniversary of the then Turkish sultan, the clock tower has since been heavily restored and now serves as a symbol of modern Jaffa.

Napoleonic cannons

HA~ALIYAH HA~SHNIYA

The Sea Mosque was the mosque of local fishermen.

0 metres		50
0 yards		50

KEY

– – – Suggested route

Gan ha-Pisga
Ha-Pisga garden lies on top of the ancient 'tel' (mound) of Jaffa. An observation area, marked by the curious Statue of Faith, offers good views across to Tel Aviv.

★ Artists' Quarter
A compact area of old Arab houses and narrow stone-flagged alleys, in recent times this has been transformed into residences, studios and galleries for artists and craftspeople.

Ha-Simta Theatre

MAZAL DAGIM

Ilana Goor Museum of Ethnic and Applied Art

Synagogue

The House of Simon the Tanner is traditionally held to be where the apostle Peter once stayed (Acts 9: 43).

★ Kedumim Square
Underneath the picturesque main square of Old Jaffa is the Visitors' Centre exhibiting exposed Roman-era remains.

St Michael's Church
Dating from the 19th century, this small Greek Orthodox church has recently been renovated.

L NATIV HA-MAZALOT

The Monastery of St Nicholas, built around 1667, still serves Jaffa's Armenian community.

Monastery of St Peter
Built in Latin American Baroque style, this Roman Catholic monastery and church was dedicated in 1891. It stands on a site formerly occupied by a Crusader citadel.

STAR SIGHTS
★ Artists' Quarter
★ Kedumim Square

The impressive Roman aqueduct at Caesarea

Caesarea ❷

Road map B2. 🚌 from Khadera.
ℹ️ *(06) 636 4453.*

A T THE HEIGHT of his power, in 29–22 BC, Herod the Great *(see pp41–3)* built a splendid city over the site of an ancient Phoenician port and dedicated it to Augustus Caesar, the Roman emperor. The splendour of this city is attested to by the lavish description of it by Flavius Josephus in his book *The Jewish War*. Until the many recent excavations, this had been seen by many scholars as wild exaggeration.

This period of prosperity lasted in Caesarea until AD 614, after which its history became more unstable. During the early 12th century and the Crusades, Caesarea again became an important city, and was used once more as a port. By the late 13th century however, it had been destroyed by the Mamelukes and was left to be reclaimed by the sand, with only a small

Arab village remaining. The importance of these great hidden ruins was not realized until the 1940s, and now Caesarea is one of Israel's major archaeological sites.

Most of the main sights lie in the **Caesarea National Park**. If entering from the south, you will first see the huge Roman theatre. Capable of seating 4,000 spectators, it has now been restored, and often hosts summer concerts. A short distance to the west, on a small coastal promontory, a group of half-submerged walls indicate the site of Herod's palace. To the right is a splendid view of the ruins

along the seashore. Further inland are the neglected ruins of one of the largest hippodromes in the Roman Empire. The massive stone remains give some idea of its former size. Nearby to the west are the restored columns of a Roman and Byzantine street.

On the coast by the inner harbour is the Crusader citadel, still surrounded by walls which date back to around AD 1250. Enclosing this whole area are the ruins of the much larger Crusader city walls, defended with four towers and a wide moat.

North of the ancient city is the extraordinary Roman aqueduct dating from the Herodian period. Extending for 17 km (11 miles), it carried water from the foothills of Mount Carmel to Caesarea. A short way to the south of the site, the **Caesarea Museum** has an interesting collection of artifacts found during excavations of the Roman city.

⛰️ **Caesarea National Park**
🎫 *(06) 636 1358.* ⭕ *daily.* ♿ ♿
🏛️ **Caesarea Museum**
Kibbutz Sdot Yam. 🎫 *(06) 636 4367.*
⭕ *daily.* ♿ ♿ ♿

RUINS OF CAESAREA

Byzantine street ④
Crusader citadel ⑤
Crusader wall ⑥
Herod's palace ②
Hippodrome ③
Roman aqueduct ⑦
Roman theatre ①

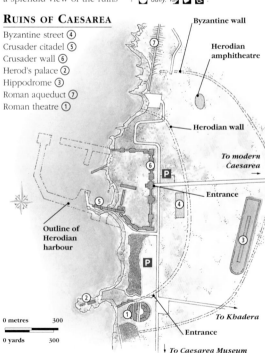

Byzantine wall

Herodian amphitheatre

Herodian wall

To modern Caesarea

Entrance

Outline of Herodian harbour

P

P

To Khadera

Entrance

0 metres   300

0 yards   300

↓ To Caesarea Museum

The magnificent ruins of the Roman theatre at Caesarea

Haifa and Mount Carmel ❸

T HE CITY OF HAIFA LIES on the Mediterranean coast at the foot of Mount Carmel. Israel's third largest city, it is a major industrial centre. Away from the busy port, steep wooded slopes rise up the mountain, providing quiet and attractive suburbs for the city's wealthy. A small trading port for most of its history, Haifa was conquered by the Crusaders in the early 12th century *(see pp46–7)*, and later fortified under Ottoman rule. It was not until the late 19th century that it became important as a refuge for Jewish immigrants. More recently, in 1918, Haifa was taken over by the British in the occupation of Palestine. They finally left from Haifa in 1948.

VISITORS' CHECKLIST

Road map *B2.* ▨ 290,000. ✈
▨ ▨ ▯ 48 Ben Gurion St,
(04) 853 5606.

The spectacular Baha'i Temple and gardens in Haifa

🏛 National Museum of Science and Technology
Old Technion, Balfour. **(** *(04) 862 8111.* ○ *Daily.* ▨ ▨
The former Technology Institute in the city centre is one of Haifa's most important buildings. Founded by German immigrants in the early 1900s, it was Israel's first institute of higher education. Renovated many times, the complex now houses the National Museum of Science and Technology, which has many interesting interactive exhibits, exploring the latest innovations in Israeli science.

🅒 Baha'i Temple and Gardens
Ha-Ziyonut St. **(** *(04) 835 8358.* ○ *daily (temple: am only).* ▨
On the edge of the city centre towards Central Carmel is Haifa's most striking landmark, the impressive golden-domed Baha'i Temple. Standing imperiously on the hillside, it is surrounded by a splendidly manicured park,

and is the headquarters of the Baha'i faith. Its followers believe that no religion has a monopoly on the truth, and aim to integrate the teachings of all holy men. The ornate temple houses the tomb of the Bab, the herald of Bahaulla. Bahaulla (1817–92) is the central figure of the Baha'i faith and is considered by his disciples to have been the most recent of God's messengers.

Central Carmel
South of the temple, Central Carmel spreads up the slopes of the mountain. A largely wealthy residential area, it manages to resist the onslaught of traffic and busy modern life. Its many parks, cafés, and stylish bars make it a relaxing detour.

Bat Galim
Northwest of Central Carmel is the popular coastal area of Bat Galim. Close to the city centre, its beach and busy seafront promenade have made it a favourite with tourists. For those wanting more extensive beaches, however, try the attractive Carmel Beach. This is 6 km (4 miles) to the south, away from the busy city.

⛪ Carmelite Monastery
Stella Maris St. **(** *(04) 833 7758.* ○ *daily.* ▨
On much of the upper slopes of Mount Carmel are wide stretches of vegetation, the remnants of an ancient forest. On these slopes, to the southwest of Bat Galim, is the Stella Maris Carmelite Monastery, which can be reached by cable car or on foot. Built in an area that for centuries was frequented by hermits, this was a place of worship where the Carmelite order was founded. The beautiful church here dates from the early 1800s.

⛪ Elijah's Cave
Stella Maris St. **(** *(04) 852 7430.* ○ *Sun–Fri (Fri: am only).* ▨
Below the monastery is Elijah's Cave, with its small altar, where Elijah is said to have lived and meditated before defeating the pagan prophets of Baal on Mount Carmel. Today it is a pilgrimage site for all three monotheistic religions.

Dome of the Stella Maris Carmelite Monastery

Acre

OUTSIDE OF JERUSALEM Acre (in Hebrew, Akko) has the most complete and charming old town in all of the Holy Land. Its origins date back to Canaanite times, but the form in which it survives today was set by the Arabs and their Crusader foes. After the Crusaders took Jerusalem in 1099, they seized Acre as their main port and lifeline back to Europe. Lost at one point to the Muslim armies under Saladin, it was regained by Richard I "the Lionheart". For most of the 13th century, with Jerusalem in the hands of the Muslims, Acre was the Crusaders' principal stronghold. As the Christian armies steadily lost ground, it was the last bastion to fall. Acre's fortunes were revived under a series of Ottoman governors, one of whom, Ahmed Pasha el-Jazzar, successfully defended the city against an invasion by Napoleon in 1799.

Khan el-Umdan clocktower

The harbour at Acre, in continuous use since Canaanite times

Exploring Acre

Crusader Acre was destroyed by the victorious Arab armies in 1291 and what can be seen today is largely an 18th-century Turkish town built on the site of the old. The heavy defensive **walls** are rebuildings of the original Crusader walls, fragments of which are still discernible. The tight, warren-like street pattern within the walls is interrupted by three great khans, or merchants' inns: the **Khan el-Umdan** (Khan of the Columns) with its distinctive clocktower; the **Khan el-Faranj** (Khan of the Franks or Foreigners); and the **Khan el-Shohada** (Khan of the Martyrs). While the khans date from the Ottoman era they echo the fact that in Crusader times Acre had autonomous quarters given over to the merchants of Italy and Provence. Such was the rivalry between these colonies that at one point open warfare erupted between the Venetians and Genoese, who

fought a sea battle off Acre in 1256. The khans are no longer in commercial use but Acre does have a lively **souk**, selling fruit and vegetables and household items – no tourist knick-knacks here. You'll also find plenty of fresh fish, which you can see being brought ashore at the town's picturesque harbour early each morning.

Mosque of El-Jazzar

El-Jazzar St. ☐ daily. ● during prayers.

Acre lay semi-derelict for more than 400 years after its destruction in 1291. Its rebirth came with the rule of the emir Dahr el-Amr and his successor, Ahmed Pasha el-Jazzar ("the Butcher"), both of whom governed the city for the Ottomans in the second half of the 18th century. El-Jazzar, in particular, was a prolific builder. Among his legacy is the attractive Turkish-style mosque (built 1781) that bears his name and continues to dominate the old town skyline. Its courtyard contains recycled columns from the Roman ruins of Caesarea and, at the centre, a small, elegant fountain used for ritual ablutions. Inside the mosque are the sarcophagi of El-Jazzar and his son, while underneath (and accessed from the courtyard cloisters) are the remains of a Crusader church that El-Jazzar had transformed into a cistern to collect rainwater.

Crusader City

El-Jazzar St. ☐ (04) 991 1764. ☐ daily (Fri: am only).

When the Ottoman governors rebuilt Acre they did so on top of the ruins of the Crusader city. The Crusader-era street level lies some 8 m (25 ft) below that of today. Part of it has been excavated revealing a subterranean wealth of well-preserved examples of 12th- and 13th-century streets and buildings. There are some amazingly

Acre's dominant landmark, the Turkish-style Mosque of el-Jazzar

Gothic-arched halls of the former Crusader city in Acre

grand Gothic knights' halls, each belonging to one of the nations represented in the crusading Order of the Knights Hospitallers: Auvergne, England, France, Germany, Provence and Spain. From the halls, a narrow passage leads to a large refectory with huge columns; in two corners you can still see carved lilies that may indicate building work done in the period of Louis VII of France, who arrived at Acre in 1148. One of Acre's

other well-known visitors was Marco Polo and it is quite possible that he dined in this very room. Below the refectory is a network of claustrophobic underground passageways that lead to an area known as El-Bosta (from the Arabic for "post office", which is what the Turks used this space for); it is divided by columns into six sections and was most probably the Crusaders' infirmary.

🏛 **Citadel**

Off Ha-Haganah St. 【 (04) 991 8264. ◯ Sun–Fri (Fri: am only). 🖼
Acre's Citadel was built by the Turks in the 18th century on top of Crusader foundations. During the British Mandate it served as a prison for Jewish activists and political prisoners, some of whom were executed in the gallows room. These events are commemorated in the Citadel's **Museum of Underground Prisoners**.

Fountain from the Hammam el-Pasha

🏛 **Municipal Museum**

Off El-Jazzar St. 【 (04) 991 1764.
◯ daily (Fri: am only). 🖼
This is not a museum as such, but a Turkish bathhouse dating to 1780 and the rule of El-Jazzar (hence the alternative name of Hammam el-Pasha, meaning "Bathhouse of the Governor"). It was in use until as recently as the 1940s and remains in an excellent state of repair. The floors and walls are composed of panels of different coloured marble, and the fountain in the "cold room" (where patrons would relax after bathing) retains most of its beautiful majolica decoration.

THE OLD CITY OF ACRE

Citadel ④
Crusader City ②
El-Jazzar's Wall ⑤
Khan el-Faranj ⑦
Khan el-Shohada ⑧
Khan el-Umdan ⑥
Lighthouse ⑩
Mosque of El-Jazzar ①
Municipal Museum
    (Hammam el-Pasha) ③
Souk ⑨

0 metres   50
0 yards   50

KEY

🅿 Parking
ℹ Tourist information
C Mosque
✝ Church

Aerial view of the ruined hilltop city of Megiddo

Megiddo ❺

Road map B2. Route 66, 35 km (22 miles) SE of Haifa. 🅲 *(06) 652 6815.* 🚌 *from Haifa & Tiberias.* ⭕ *8am–4pm (winter: 3pm) daily.* 🎫

THIS ANCIENT TOWN at the head of the Jezreel valley was the scene of so many battles that the Book of Revelation in the New Testament says that it is where the final battle between Good and Evil will take place at the end of the world. The biblical name of "Armageddon" derives from "Har Megedon", or mountain of Megiddo.

The settlement controlled the main communication routes between the East and the Mediterranean, and in the 3rd millennium BC it was already a fortified city. In 1468 BC its Canaanite fortress was destroyed by the troops of the Egyptian pharaoh Thutmose III, and became an Egyptian stronghold. Megiddo was subsequently conquered and again fortified, possibly by Solomon, and in the 8th century BC came under Assyrian rule, after which it fell slowly into decline.

Extensive excavation of the spectacular mound (or 'tel') has, over the years, revealed 20 successive settlements, each built over the other. The visible remains include defensive walls, a fortified gate, a temple, an enormous grain silo and the foundations of numerous buildings. On the eastern side of the 'tel' is an old reservoir, at the base of which a 60-m (66-yard) tunnel leads to a spring that lies outside the city walls. Visitors can go through the tunnel at the end of their tour of the site. From the tunnel exit there is a path leading back up to the main entrance, where there is a museum explaining the fascinating archaeology of Megiddo.

Nazareth ❻

Road map B2. 🏠 *60,000.* 🚌 ℹ️ *Casa Nova St, (06) 657 3003/0555.*

LYING ON THE RISE between the Jordan Valley and the Jezreel plain, Nazareth consists of two parts. The old town is inhabited by Christian

Mosaic of Joseph, Basilica of the Annunciation, Nazareth

and Muslim Palestinians, and contains all of the major sights. To the north is Nazareth Illit, a large Jewish district founded in 1957 by colonists as part of the plan to settle all Galilee.

Famous as the site of the Annunciation and the childhood of Jesus, Nazareth has had a colourful history. The village suffered at the hands of the Romans during the Jewish Revolt of AD 66 *(see p41)*, then flourished under the Byzantines, and later became an important Christian site with the Crusader conquest of the Holy Land in 1099. After the resurgence of Muslim power in the 12th and 13th centuries, Christians found it increasingly dangerous to visit. Improving relations by the 18th century eventually allowed the Franciscans to acquire the Basilica, and they have maintained a Christian presence here ever since. Today the town is a pilgrimage site, with its many Christian churches attracting large numbers of visitors. Recent restoration projects and modern hotel developments have helped Nazareth to cope with the crowds. Unfortunately though, such high levels of tourism have done little to preserve the city's magical atmosphere. The old town is still fascinating however, with much of its traditional architecture remaining. The souk, the heart of local life, is a maze of narrow alleys where you can find a wide range of unusual goods.

Built in 1969 over the ruins of the original Byzantine church, and the successive Crusader one, the **Basilica of the Annunciation** is the major focal point in Nazareth. A bold, modern church, its large dome towers over the town. The crypt includes the Cave of the Annunciation, where the angel Gabriel is said to have appeared to Mary. A peaceful garden leads past some ruins to **St Joseph's**, a small, intimate church, rebuilt in 1914 on what is thought to be the site of Joseph's home and workshop.

ENVIRONS: The main attraction of the ruined fortified town of **Tsipori** (Sepphoris), northwest of Nazareth, is its splendid 3rd-century AD mosaics. The hilltop site includes a Roman theatre that seated 5,000, the remains of a Crusader citadel and sections of the ancient water supply. Tsipori is also famous as being the supposed birthplace of the Virgin Mary. On **Mount Tabor**, 10 km (6 miles) east of Nazareth, is a beautiful basilica, built here in 1924 to commemorate the Transfiguration (Mark 9: 9–13). It lies within the ruins of a 12th-century Muslim fortress.

⋔ Tsipori
Route 79, 3 km (2 miles) NW of Nazareth. **【** (06) 656 8272. **◯** daily. ✍

Safed ❼

Road map C2. **⋔** 26,000. **▭**
ℹ Town Hall, (06) 692 7485.

THE HIGHEST TOWN in Israel, Safed is also one of the four holy cities of the Talmud, together with Jerusalem, Hebron and Tiberias. In the Middle Ages Safed became a popular meeting place for many groups of Sephardic Jews who had been driven out of Spain in the course of the Christian Reconquest. Religious schools were founded and many interpreters of the Kabbalah lived in the town. To this day Safed has remained an important centre of Jewish religious studies.

Safed covers a number of small hilltops, with its attractive old town centre located around the slopes of Gan ha-Metsuda, once the site of a Crusader citadel. The old quarters of the town centre are best explored on foot, via their narrow streets and steep stairways. The Synagogue Quarter has many interesting Kabbalist synagogues including those of Itzhak Luria, Itzhak Abuhav and Joseph Caro. The former Arab Quarter (which became Jewish in 1948) is now home to a large colony of artists and is known as the Artists' Quarter. In the narrow streets and alleys between the area's picturesque houses, artists display their paintings and sculptures. Many also use their own homes as galleries.

Banias Falls, Golan Heights

Golan Heights ❽

Road map C2. **▭** to Katsrin.
ℹ Central Shopping Mall, Katsrin, (06) 696 2885.

THIS REGION of long-running historical conflict has nevertheless got much to recommend it. A high fertile plateau, dominated by Mount Hermon, it borders Israel, Syria, Jordan and Lebanon. This unique geography, aside from making it strategically important, also makes it a spectacular place to visit, with incredible vistas all around.

A major source of the Jordan River, one of the most popular places to visit is **Banias**, 15 km (9 miles) east of Kiryat Shmona. Here a large spring cascades downstream to the attractive Banias Falls nearby. **Nimrud Castle**, a short way to the northeast, originates from biblical times, though it owes its present shape to the rule of the Mameluke sultan Baybars I (1260–77). Nine of the defensive towers remain, along with much of the outer wall, a keep, and the moat.

In the south of the Golan is the administrative capital of **Katsrin**. Founded as an Israeli settlement in 1974, the town itself is unremarkable, but is a good base for exploring the beautiful countryside around. This is ideal hiking country, and the spectacular **Yehudiya Reserve** to the south of Katsrin is well worth a visit.

⋔ Nimrud Castle
26 km (16 miles) E of Kiryat Shmona. **【** (050) 813 227. **◯** daily. ✍

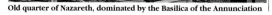

Old quarter of Nazareth, dominated by the Basilica of the Annunciation

Sea of Galilee 🄎

Statue of Saint Peter, Tiberias

ISRAEL'S CHIEF SOURCE OF WATER, the Sea of Galilee (Lake Tiberias/Kinneret) lies 212 metres (696 feet) below sea level and is fed and drained by the Jordan River. It is 21 km (13 miles) long, and 9 km (6 miles) wide, and since biblical times has been famous for its abundance of fish. Many of Jesus's disciples were fishermen here, and he did much of his preaching by its shores. Today, this beautiful area is one of Israel's most popular tourist centres, with a mix of fascinating historical and religious sites, and a varied selection of hotels and outdoor activities.

Speedboating on the Sea of Galilee, one of many water sports available

KEY

🚌	Major road
🚌	Minor road
⛴	Ferry
⛴	Excursion boat
🌊	Water sports
Ⓐ	Camping site
🏖	Beach
🔭	Viewpoint

Mount of the Beatitudes *(see p164)*   To Safed

Church of the Primacy of St Peter *(see p164)*   Caperna...

Church of the Multiplication of the Loaves and the Fishes *(see p164)*

Tabkha

Kibbutz Ginosar is home to a fishing boat from Jesus's time, found here in 1986 *(see p27)*.

Kibbutz Ginosar

Migdal

HAR ARBEL

Ⓐ

TIBERIAS

To Nazareth

Tiberias

The largest town on the Sea of Galilee, Tiberias is a popular resort with many hotels, bars and restaurants. The busy lakeside offers beaches and water sports.

The Hammat Tiberias Hot Springs have long been renowned for their curative properties, and are said to date from the time of Solomon.

HAR MENORIM

Poriya

Kibbut. Kinnere

Kibbutz Kinneret's cemetery, with great views of the sea, is resting place to many spiritual leaders of the Zionist movement.

Yardenet Baptism Site

The Jordan River has always been an important Christian site since Christ was supposedly baptized here. At Yardenet, large crowds of pilgrims gather to be baptized in the river themselves.

**A View of the
Sea of Galilee**
*This view is taken
from the hills above
the northeastern shore.*

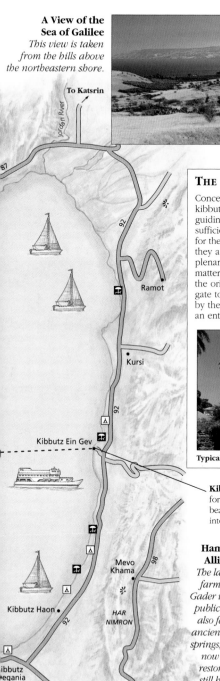

To Katsrin

Jordan River

87

92

Ramot

Kursi

92

Kibbutz Ein Gev

Kibbutz Haon

92

Mevo
Khama

98

HAR
NIMROD

ibbutz
egania

98

Beth Shean

Hammat
Gader

VISITORS' CHECKLIST

Road map C2. ▨ *from Tel Aviv
and Jerusalem.* ▮ *19 Habanim St,
Tiberias, (06) 672 5666.* ▨ *from
Tiberias to Kibbutz Ein Gev (daily in
summer), (06) 665 8008.* ▨ *Lido
Kinneret Sailing Co, Tiberias
(summer only), (06) 665 8008.*
▨ *Kibbutz Ein Gev Music Festival
(Apr), Galilee Song Festival (May).*

THE FIRST KIBBUTZ — DEGANIA

Conceived by Eastern European Jews, the first
kibbutz was founded at Degania in 1909. The
guiding ideals behind Israel's kibbutzim are self-
sufficiency and equality, with everyone working
for the common good. Rural farming communities,
they are highly productive, and hold their own
plenary meetings to decide on community
matters.There are now two kibbutzim here, with
the original called Degania Alef (A). By the main
gate to the kibbutz is a Syrian tank, stopped here
by the kibbutzniks when they famously defeated
an entire armoured column during the 1948 war.

Typical kibbutz house at Degania

Kibbutz Ein Gev is renowned
for its fish restaurants, good
beaches and its annual
international music festival.

**Hammat Gader
Alligator Farm**
*The large alligator
farm at Hammat
Gader is open to the
public. The town is
also famous for its
ancient Roman hot
springs, which have
now been largely
restored. You can
still bathe in their
relaxing waters.*

0 kilometres   4

0 miles   2

Capernaum ❿

Road map C2. Route 87, 12 km (7.5 miles) N of Tiberias. 🚌 from Tiberias. 📞 (06) 672 1059. ⬚ daily. 🖉

CAPERNAUM, on the northern shoreline of the Sea of Galilee, was an important Roman town and one of the focal points of Christ's teachings in Galilee. It was also home to a number of his Disciples, including Simon Peter. In Capernaum's fascinating archaeo-logical precinct there are surviving houses from the period, as well as a church, built over the ruins of what is said to have been **Simon Peter's house**. There are also the remains of a synagogue that has been dated to the 4th century AD.

Carved relief, Church of the Multiplication

Tabkha ⓫

Road map C2. Route 87, 10 km (6 miles) N of Tiberias. 🚌 from Tiberias to junction of routes 90 and 87.

JUST TO THE SOUTHWEST of Capernaum, Tabkha (Ein Sheva) is one of the most important sites of Christ's ministry in Galilee, where he did much of his preaching. Heading from the bus-stop, a short way along Route 87 you will come to the **Church of the Multiplication of the Loaves and the Fishes**. Built in the 1980s, it boasts the remains of a 5th-century Byzantine basilica and fragments of splendid mosaics. This original church was built over the supposed spot from which Christ fed 5,000 followers with five loaves and two fish.

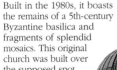

The modern Church of the Beatitudes near Tabkha

Nearby to the east, on the lakeside, is the **Church of the Primacy of Peter**. A black basalt Franciscan chapel, it is built on the site where Jesus Christ is said to have appeared to the Apostles after his Resurrection. The area has various other ruins, including a 4th-century chapel.

On top of the hill behind, known as the Mount of the Beatitudes, is the modern **Church of the Beatitudes**. The hill is so called, because it is thought that here, over-looking the lake, Christ gave his Sermon on the Mount. This famously began with his blessings or "beatitudes".

Tiberias ⓬

Road map C2. 🚶 29,000. 🚌 ℹ Archaeological Garden, Rehov ha-Banim, (06) 672 5666.

THE BUSY TOWN of Tiberias (Tverya) is the largest on the shores of the Sea of Galilee. It was founded during Roman times by Herod Antipas, who dedicated it to the Emperor Tiberius and moved the regional capital here from Tsipori. The town has been home to many notable scholars and rabbis, and became one of Israel's holy cities, along with Jerusalem, Hebron and Safed. The **Tomb of Maimonides**, the great medieval Jewish philosopher, can be found on Ben Zakki Street.

Today, Tiberias is a popular tourist centre, with an attractive lakeside setting and in an ideal location for exploring Galilee. The town has a lively

atmosphere, especially along the busy lakeside promenade. Just behind here is **St Peter's Church**, built originally by the Crusaders. The current church has a boat-shaped nave, reflecting St Peter's life as a fisherman.

Tiberias is also known for its curative hot springs, of which there are several to visit in the town. There are also some public beaches to the north of town, and the popular **Gai Beach Water Park** is 1 km (half a mile) to the south of Tiberias.

🌊 Gai Beach Water Park
Sederot Eliezer Kaplan. 📞 (06) 670 0700. ⬚ daily. ⬤ Nov–Mar. 🖉

Ruined arches at Belvoir Castle

Belvoir Castle ⓭

Road map C2. Off Route 90, 27 km (17 miles) S of Tiberias. 🚌 to Beth Shean, then taxi. 📞 (06) 658 1766. ⬚ daily. 🖉

THE RUINED Crusader fortress of Belvoir, in the Kokhav ha-Yarden nature reserve, offers incomparable views of the Jordan Valley. The impres-sive fortress is surrounded by two huge walls, the outer one pentagonal and the inner one square. Built by the Knights Hospitallers in 1168, Belvoir was besieged many times by Saladin. It capitulated only in 1191, after a four-year siege, with the Muslim leader sparing both the fortress and its defenders' lives, in recognition of their great courage. Belvoir was finally destroyed by troops from Damascus in the 13th century. The area around the fortress is dotted with modern sculpture.

Detail from 6th-century mosaic at Beth Alpha, showing signs of the zodiac

Beth Alpha ⑭

Road map C2. Off Route 71, 11 km (7 miles) W of Beth Shean. 🎫 (06) 653 2004. 🚌 ⬜ daily. 📷 ♿

THE REMNANTS of this 6th-century synagogue were discovered quite by chance in 1928 by colonists from the nearby Hefzi-Bah kibbutz. The ruined walls give an idea of the original basilica-shaped building, but the main interest is the magnificent mosaic floor, which has survived largely intact. The upper part of the floor depicts the Ark of the Covenant, with cherubs, lions and religious symbols. The large central patterns represent the zodiac and symbols of the seasons. These show the continuing importance of pagan beliefs at the time, and the need for Judaism to try to accommodate these. The lower part relates the story of Abraham and the sacrifice of his son Isaac.

Beth Shean ⑮

Road map C2. 🚶 17,000. 🚌 from Tiberias.

THE BEST-PRESERVED Roman-Byzantine town in Israel, Beth Shean lay on the old trade routes between Mesopotamia and the Mediterranean. First inhabited 5,000 years ago during the Canaanite era, it later became the main city in the region during the period of Egyptian occupation (see p39). Falling to the Philistines in the 11th century BC, it then became part of Solomon's kingdom. After the conquest of Alexander the Great it was renamed Scythopolis, and became a flourishing Hellenistic city. The Roman conquest in the 1st century BC saw Scythopolis further prosper as one of the ten city states of the Decapolis. It later retained its economic importance under the Byzantines, also becoming a major centre of Christianity. An economic collapse, then an earthquake in AD 749, eventually left only a small remaining Jewish community.

The archaeological sites at Beth Shean are in two areas. The main site comprises the Roman-Byzantine city, and the archaeological mound, or 'tel'. These are both within the Beth Shean National Park, 1 km (half a mile) north of the town. The jewel of this site is the Roman theatre, one of the best preserved in Israel, and once capable of seating 7,000. The old Byzantine baths have surviving mosaic and marble decoration, and tall columns from the ruined temples are equally impressive. The *tel* offers a good overview of the site, and consists of 16 or more superimposed towns. It is difficult however to understand the details of its complex archaeology.

The other site focuses on the ruined Roman amphitheatre, a short way to the south. Used for gladiatorial contests, it was connected to the main town by a paved street. Some of this street survives today, paved with huge blocks of basalt.

🏛 Beth Shean National Park
🎫 (06) 658 7189. ⬜ daily, (Fri: am only). 📷

Ruined colonnade along an old Byzantine street, Beth Shean

THE DEAD SEA AND THE NEGEV DESERT

I N THIS THE MOST ARID *and inhospitable region of the Holy Land, even the waters of its great lake are incapable of supporting life, hence the "Dead Sea". But in times past, the harsh remoteness of the hills and desert was prized by reclusive communities and rebels, and so the area is dotted with ancient ruins charged with biblical significance.*

Today, the Dead Sea is no longer so remote – just a 20-minute ride from Jerusalem on an air-conditioned bus. Tourists flock to its shores to test its incredibly buoyant waters. The lowest body of water in the world, it has such a high salt content it is impossible to sink. Its mineral-rich mud is also claimed to have therapeutic qualities and a string of lakeside spas do good business out of the black, sticky silt. Away from the water, high up on the rocky hillsides are the caves in which the Dead Sea Scrolls were discovered, while on a mountain top to the south is Herod the Great's fortress of Masada, one of the most stunning attractions in all Israel.

Where the Dead Sea ends, the Negev Desert begins. Here, the only signs of life, apart from the odd convoy of tourists exploring canyons and craters,

are a few groups of Bedouin *(see p225)* tenaciously clinging to traditional nomadic ways.

Over the centuries, there have been many attempts to cultivate the desert. More than 2,000 years ago, the Negev was the final stage for caravans on the spice and incense route from India and southern Arabia to the Mediterranean; the Nabataeans who controlled the route perfected irrigation and cultivation techniques and established flourishing cities, such as Ovdat *(see p182)*. More recently, Israel has initiated programmes for the economic development of the region in the form of desert kibbutzim.

In spite of this desire to tame the desert, more and more people these days come in search of all that remains wild and undeveloped. In this respect, the Negev still has much to offer.

The secluded retreat of St George's Monastery, hidden in a desert canyon near Jericho

◁ Masada on the Dead Sea, one time rebel fortress, now the most visited archaeological site in Israel

Exploring the Dead Sea and the Negev Desert

ALL THE SITES as far south as Masada can be visited in a series of day trips from Jerusalem. Heading south beyond Masada or Beersheba and into the Negev Desert is more of an undertaking. There are only two main routes through this vast wedge of sun-baked wilderness: along the border with Jordan on Route 90; or straight down the centre of the country via Ein Ovdat and Mitspe Ramon. This latter route is by far the more interesting.

The mountain-top fortress of Masada, conveniently visited as a day trip from Jerusalem

SIGHTS AT A GLANCE

Beersheba **9**
Bethlehem pp173–5 **7**
Ein Gedi **10**
Ein Ovdat **13**
Hebron **8**
Herodion **6**
Jericho **2**
Khai Bar Biblical Wildlife
  Reserve **16**
Makhtesh Ramon **15**
Mar Saba Monastery **5**
Masada pp180–81 **11**
Nebi Musa **3**
Ovdat **14**
Qumran **4**
Sodom **12**
St George's Monastery **1**
Timna National Park **17**

0 kilometres   25

0 miles   20

Map labels:

Tel Aviv
MEDITERRANEAN SEA
ASHDOD
3
ASHKELON
4
40
GAZA
25
4
232
222
10
211
BEERSHEBA **9**
EIN OVDAT **13**
OVDAT
MITSPE RAMO
171
MAKHT
N E
10

Ein Gedi, where waterfalls and greenery provide respite from the heat and dust

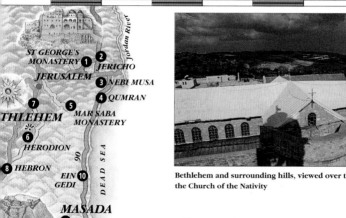

ST GEORGE'S
MONASTERY ①
② JERICHO
JERUSALEM
③ NEBI MUSA
④ QUMRAN
⑦ ⑤
MAR SABA
THLEHEM MONASTERY
⑥
HERODION
⑧ HEBRON
EIN ⑩
GEDI
MASADA
⑪
⑫ SODOM

⑯ KHAI BAR BIBLICAL
WILDLIFE RESERVE

TIMNA NATIONAL PARK
⑰

Bethlehem and surrounding hills, viewed over the roof of
the Church of the Nativity

GETTING AROUND

The easiest way of getting from Jerusalem to Jericho,
Bethlehem and Hebron is a shared taxi from Damascus
Gate *(see p280)*. From Bethlehem you can take a taxi
on to the Herodion or Mar Saba. For longer trips, the
Israeli bus company Egged serves all Dead Sea and
Negev locations *(see pp282–3)*. For those who only
want to visit the Negev Desert, there are direct flights
to Eilat with Arkia *(see pp278–9)*.

KEY

Motorway

Major road

Minor road

Scenic route

☆ Viewpoint

SEE ALSO

• *Where to Stay* pp236–7

• *Restaurants, Cafés and Bars* pp250–51

The volcano-like mound of the Herodion,
a 1st-century BC hilltop fortress

The waters of the Dead Sea, the most saline on earth and at their
saltiest at the southern end, where crystalline pools are formed

St George's Monastery **❶**

Road map C3. Route 1, 27 km
(17 miles) E of Jerusalem. **☎** (050)
259 949. **🚌** from Jerusalem.
◯ 8–11am & 3–5pm Sun–Fri,
8–11am Sat.

ONE OF THE FINEST HIKES in
the region is rewarded by
the spectacle of St George's
Monastery, an ancient retreat
hollowed out of the sheer
rock wall of a deep and
narrow gorge. The monastery
was founded in 480 around a
cluster of caves where,
according to tradition,
St Joachim learned from an
angel that Anne, his sterile
wife and mother-to-be of the
Virgin Mary, had conceived.

In 614 invading Persians
massacred the monks and
destroyed the monastery.
It was partially reoccupied by
the Crusaders in the Middle
Ages but only fully restored
at the end of the 19th
century. Some attractive 6th-
century mosaics remain, and
there is a Crusader-era church
with a shrine containing the
skulls of the martyred monks.

The monastery can be
reached in 20 minutes on foot
via a signposted track off the
main Jerusalem-Jericho road.
From the same starting point
energetic hikers can take a
more scenic path to the
monastery along the full
length of the Wadi Qelt gorge.

**St George's Monastery, built into
the cliff face of Wadi Qelt**

Jericho, regarded as perhaps the world's oldest city

Jericho **❷**

Road map C3. **👥** 17,000. **🚌** or
taxi from Jerusalem. **🏠** daily.
🎫 Jericho Festival (Feb).

CLAIMED TO BE the world's
oldest city and with rich
biblical associations, Jericho
lies just a few miles north of
the Dead Sea, 258 m (846 ft)
below sea level, in the middle
of the Judaean desert. It owes
its existence to the Ain es-
Sultan spring (the
biblical Elisha's
Spring), the same
one that, 10,000
years ago in the
late Mesolithic
period, attracted
a semi-nomadic
population of
hunter-gatherers
to first settle here.

**Islamic-era mosaic from
Hisham's Palace**

According to the
Bible, Jericho was the first
town captured by the
Israelites under the leadership
of Joshua. The Book of
Joshua tells how, in order to
possess the land promised to
them by God, the Israelites
brought down the city walls
with a tremendous shout and
a trumpet blast (Joshua 6).
During Roman times Mark
Antony made a gift of the
oasis town to Cleopatra of
Egypt, who, in turn, leased
the place to Herod the Great.
Being at a lower altitude than
Jerusalem, Jericho is notably
warmer, and Herod wintered
in a palace here (of which
nothing remains).

The Bible's New Testament
mentions several visits to
Jericho by Jesus, who healed
two blind men and lodged at

the home of the tax collector
Zacchaeus (Luke 19: 1-10).
Near the centre of town there
is still the centuries-old
sycamore tree up which
Zacchaeus was said to have
climbed in order to see Jesus.

Repeated Bedouin raids led
to the decline of Jericho
around the 12th century, and
it wasn't until the 1920s that
the town's former irrigation
network was restored and the
area was brought to bloom
again. After the 1948
War, the town took
in more than
70,000
Palestinian
refugees. The
camps have
since emptied,
and under the
administration of
the Palestinian
National Authority
Jericho is now a centre of
local tourism thanks to a
recently opened casino – a
huge crowd puller, given that
gambling is outlawed on
Israeli territory.

More cerebral attractions
include **Tel Jericho** (also
known as Tell es-Sultan), the
sun-baked earthen mound
that represents something like
10,000 years of continuous
settlement. Most striking of
all is a large stone tower with
great thick walls that dates
back as far as 7,000 BC.

A cable car service connects
Tell es-Sultan with the Greek
Orthodox **Monastery of the
Temptation** 2 km (1 mile) to
the north. Like St George's in
Wadi Qelt, this holy retreat
has a spectacular location,
perched high up on a cliff

face. The views from its terraces are breathtaking. The monastery dates back to the 12th century and is supposedly built around the grotto where the Devil appeared to tempt Jesus away from his 40-day fast (Matthew 4: 1–11).

Hisham's Palace (Qasr Hisham) is an early Islamic hunting lodge built in AD 724 for the Omayyad caliph Hisham. It lies in ruins, destroyed centuries ago by an earthquake, but it is worth a visit if only for a gorgeous floor mosaic depicting a lion hunting gazelles grazing under a broad leafy tree.

♈ **Tel Jericho**
◯ *daily.* 🏞 ☑
♈ **Monastery of the Temptation**
☎ *(02) 232 2827.* ◯ *Mon–Sat.* ♿
♈ **Hisham's Palace**
☎ *(02) 232 2522.* ◯ *daily.* 🏞

Nebi Musa ❸

Road map C4. Route 1, 10 km (6 miles) S of Jericho. 🚌 *to Jericho, then taxi.* ♿

Aᴌᴛʜᴏᴜɢʜ ᴛʜᴇ ᴄʟᴀɪᴍ is heavily disputed, Muslims revere the desert monastery of Nebi Musa as the burial place of Moses. There has been a mosque on the site since 1269, built under the patronage of the Mameluke emir Baybars. In 1490 a two-storey hospice was added to accommodate visiting

Nebi Musa, regarded by Muslims as the burial place of Moses

pilgrims. However, the attractive whitewashed structures of the present day date from around 1820 and the days of Ottoman rule. The disputed cenotaph of Moses, covered with a traditional Islamic green drape, occupies the spartan, domed tomb chamber of the mosque.

Although the five-day festival of feasting and prayer that used to occur here each year now no longer happens, many Muslims still desire to be laid to rest in the large cemetery that covers the hills around the complex.

Qumran ❹

Road map C4. Route 90, 20 km (12 miles) S of Jericho. ☎ *(02) 994 2235.* 🚌 *from Jerusalem.* ◯ *8am–5pm (winter: 4pm) daily.* 🏞 ♿

Qᴜᴍʀᴀɴ ɪꜱ ᴋɴᴏᴡɴ chiefly as the place where the Dead Sea Scrolls were discovered. From 150 BC to

AD 68 this remote site was the home of a radically ascetic and reclusive community, often identified with the Essenes. According to their school of thought, the arrival of the Jewish Messiah was imminent, and they prepared for this event with fasting and purification through ritual ablutions. These activities were rudely brought to a halt through conflict with the Romans.

The Essenes largely vanished from history until 1947 when a Bedouin shepherd boy looking for a lost goat happened upon a cave full of jars. These jars were found to contain a precious hoard of 190 linen-wrapped scrolls that, thanks to the dry desert climate, had been preserved for 2,000 years. Following much study by academics some of the scrolls are now on view in a purpose-built hall at the Israel Museum (*see pp132–3).*

Visitors to Qumran watch a short film on the Essenes and view a small exhibition on the community before being directed to the archaeological site at the foot of the cliffs. Signs indicate the probable uses of different areas of the vaguely defined remains.

From the site you can see the caves above where the scrolls were found. It is possible to scramble up to the caves for a fine view, but you need to allow about two hours; you should also carry a plentiful supply of water.

Caves at Qumran, where the hot, dry, desert climate helped to preserve the Dead Sea Scrolls

The gorge-top monastery of Mar Saba near Bethlehem

Mar Saba Monastery ❺

Road map C4. Off Route 398, 17 km (11 miles) E of Bethlehem. ☎ *(02) 277 3135.* ▣ *Bethlehem, then taxi.* ◯ *8am–5pm daily. Ring bell. No women allowed.*

LOCATED OUT IN THE WILDS of the Judaean desert, Mar Saba is one of the dozens of retreats built in this area from the 5th century on by hermits seeking an austere life of solitude and prayer. This particular monastery was founded in 482 by St Saba, a monk whose preachings were said to have impressed the Byzantine emperor Justinian. Despite a massacre of the monks by the Persians in the 7th century, the monastery survived to bloom in the 8th and 9th centuries, when its thick defensive walls housed some 5,000 devotees.

Although only a handful of monks now live in Mar Saba, it remains a functioning desert monastery. As seen today, topped by bright blue domes, the complex largely dates to 1834, when it was rebuilt following a major earthquake.

An ornate canopy in the monastery's main church shelters the remains of St Saba, which were returned to the Holy Land only in 1965 having being carried off by the Crusaders and kept in Venice for seven centuries. The church walls are hung with icons and a lurid fresco depicting Judgment Day.

Unfortunately, women are not allowed to enter the monastery, but the views from a neighbouring tower (which women are permitted to climb) of Mar Saba itself are alone worth the trouble and expense of a visit.

Herodion ❻

Road map B4. Route 356, 12 km (7 miles) SE of Bethlehem. ☎ *(050) 505 007.* ▣ *Bethlehem, then taxi.* ◯ *8am–5pm (Tue: 4pm) daily.* ▣ ▣ *on Sat but call ahead.* ♿

DOMINATING THE DESERT landscape south of Bethlehem is the volcano-like mound of the Herodion, named for Herod the Great. He had this circular structure built in 24–15 BC as a fortified palace for entertaining, and as a memorial to his defeat of the Hasmoneans. It was long thought this might also have been his mausoleum, but despite extensive excavations no tomb has been found.

During the Second Revolt in AD 132–5 the Herodion became the headquarters of the Jewish leader Bar-Kokhba. In expectation of a Roman attack, the rebels turned its cisterns into a network of escape tunnels.

Around the 5th century, early Christians occupied the site as a monastery and added cells and a chapel, where you can still see carved Christian symbols. Also clearly identifiable are a massive round tower and three semicircular ones, ruins of the palace baths, the *triclinium* (dining room) and fragments of columns and mosaics, all dating from Herod's time.

At the foot of the mound are the remains of the Lower Herodion, with the dry imprint of a large pool that, in Herod's day, served as a reservoir and centrepiece for ornamental gardens.

The hilltop Herodion with sweeping views of the landscape

Bethlehem **7**

PERCHED ON A HILL at the edge of the Judaean desert, Bethlehem is in biblical tradition the childhood home of David, who was named king here as he tended his father's sheep. It is also the birthplace of Jesus Christ and a major site of pilgrimage since the construction of the Church of the Nativity in the 4th century AD. The town flourished until Crusader times, but the following centuries witnessed a great reduction in population, reversed only after the 1948 war with the arrival of thousands of Palestinian refugees.

VISITORS' CHECKLIST

Road map B3. 36,000. Hebron Road. Manger Square, (02) 274 1581. daily. Almond Blossom Festival (Feb), Olive Harvest (Oct), Midnight Mass (24 Dec).

The church spires and towers of Bethlehem, birthplace of Jesus Christ

Exploring Bethlehem

Since 1995 Bethlehem has been under the control of the Palestinian National Authority, which has initiated a programme of economic recovery and tourism. Despite the huge number of pilgrims and chaotic urban growth, Bethlehem has retained a certain amount of fascination, especially in the central area around Manger Square and in the souk just to the west. The souvenir shops are filled with kitsch religious objects but also sell fine carved olive-wood crib scenes that local craftsmen have produced for centuries. No visitor should miss the ancient Church of the Nativity (see pp174–5) on Manger Square, and the town's other main sights also deserve attention.

St Catherine's Church

Manger Square. (02) 274 2425. daily.
Connected to the Church of the Nativity, St Catherine's faces a heavily-restored, Crusader-period cloister (see p174). The church was built by Franciscans in the 1880s on the site of a 12th-century Augustinian monastery, which had replaced a 5th-century monastery

associated with St Jerome. On the right side of St Catherine's nave, stairs descend to the grottoes of the Holy Innocents, St Joseph and St Jerome, which connect (via a locked door) to the Grotto of the Nativity. These were used as burial places by Christians as early as the 1st century AD and contain the tombs of St Jerome and his follower St Paula.

The Milk Grotto

Milk Grotto Street. (02) 274 2425. daily.
This serene grotto only a few minutes' walk from Manger Square is considered sacred because tradition has it that the Holy Family took refuge here during the Massacre of the

Innocents, before their flight into Egypt. While Mary was suckling Jesus, a drop of milk fell to the ground, turning it white. Both Christians and Muslims believe scrapings from the stones in the grotto boost the quantity of a mother's milk and enhance fertility.

Old Bethlehem Folklore Museum

Paul VI Street. Mon–Sat (Thu: am only).
In an old Palestinian house the Arab Women's Union has mounted this small but interesting museum. One room is given over to the embroidery typical of Palestinian women's dress and to silver jewellery, which normally represented a family's fortune. The diwan (living room) is furnished with rugs, old photographs, musical instruments, braziers and oil lamps. The simple kitchen contains old copper kitchenware and a bread oven. Examples of the traditional embroidery are on sale at the entrance.

Rachel's Tomb

Hebron Road. Sun–Fri (Fri: am only).
On the road to Jerusalem, just before the border checkpoint between Palestinian territory and Israel, is the tomb of Rachel, Jacob's wife and the mother of two of his twelve sons. It resembles a small fort, protected by soldiers and barbed wire. The site, which is sacred to Jews and Muslims alike, was built around 1620 by the Ottomans and restructured in 1860 by Moses Montefiore (see p49). Inside, the tomb itself is covered by a velvet drape. It is visited by Jewish women who come here to pray for children.

The Virgin Mary and Child, a maternal relationship celebrated at the Milk Grotto

Church of the Nativity

Plaza in front of the Church of the Nativity, with the plain façade in the distance

THE FIRST EVIDENCE of a cave here being venerated as Christ's birthplace is in the writings of St Justin Martyr around AD 160. In 326, the Roman emperor Constantine ordered a church to be built and in about 530 it was rebuilt by Justinian. The Crusaders later redecorated the interior, but much of the marble was looted in Ottoman times. In 1852 shared custody of the church was granted to the Roman Catholic, Armenian and Greek Orthodox churches, the Greeks caring for the Grotto of the Nativity.

Statue of Mary

Stairs to main church

★ **Grotto of the Nativity**
The grotto is the church's focal point. A silver star is set in the floor over the spot where Christ is said to have been born.

St Catherine's Church (see p173)

Altar of the Adoration of the Magi (Manger Altar)

Nave
The wide nave survives intact from Justinian's time, although the roof is 15th-century, with 19th-century restorations. Fragments of high-quality mosaics decorate the walls.

Other grottoes, reached by these steps, contain the supposed tomb and study of St Jerome (see p173).

Statue of St Jerome

Cloister of St Catherine's Church
Incorporating columns and capitals from the 12th-century Augustinian monastery that previously stood here, this attractive, peaceful cloister was rebuilt in Crusader style in 1948.

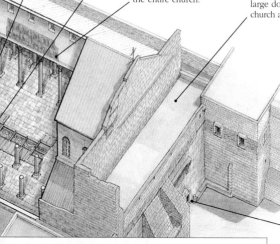

Painted Columns
Thirty of the nave's 44 columns carry Crusader paintings of saints, and the Virgin and Child, although age and lighting conditions make them hard to see. The columns are of polished, pink limestone, most of them reused from the original 4th-century basilica.

★ Mosaic Floor
Trap doors in the present floor, here and to the left of the altar, reveal sections of mosaic floor surviving from the 4th-century basilica.

Wall mosaics, made in the 1160s, once decorated the entire church.

The narthex was originally a single, long porch with three large doors leading into the church and three onto the street.

★ Door of Humility
The Crusader doorway, marked by a pointed arch, was reduced to the present tiny size in the Ottoman period to prevent carts being driven in by looters. A massive lintel above the arch indicates the door's even larger original size.

St Jerome Writing (c.1604) by Caravaggio

ST JEROME
Born at Stribo (not far from Venice), St Jerome (c.342–420) was one of the most learned scholars of the early Christian Church. He travelled widely and, in 386, settled in Bethlehem, where he founded a monastery. Here, he completed a new version of the Bible *(see p22)*, inspired by the pope's suggestion that a single book should replace the many differing texts in circulation. His great work later became known as the Vulgate. Tradition places the saint's study and tomb next to the Grotto of the Nativity.

STAR FEATURES

★ Grotto of the Nativity

★ Mosaic Floor

★ Door of Humility

The Tomb of the Patriarchs, also known as the Mosque of Machpelah, Hebron

Hebron **8**

Road map B4. 👥 120,000. 🚌
🚕 daily.

NESTLED AMONG gentle hills 40 km (25 miles) south of Jerusalem, Hebron is one of the most densely populated towns in the West Bank. Its market is the centre of activity for the surrounding villages, but the town's fame rests on its handcrafted glass-making, which began in the Middle Ages and for centuries has been managed by a single family.

This coloured glassware can be found for sale in another of Hebron's major attractions, its medieval Arab souk, which contains some imposing Crusader-era vaulted passageways. The souk is currently the object of a large-scale urban renewal and restoration programme, which has already won international recognition.

However, Hebron is a town undermined by troublesome political tensions. It is divided into two zones: the greater area is governed by the Palestinian Authority, but the town centre is occupied by Jewish settlers. Large numbers of Israeli soldiers maintain a constant peace-keeping presence. Friction between the two communities began in the early 20th century. In 1929 there was a pogrom in which the Arabs massacred Hebron's centuries-old Jewish community. After the Six Day War of 1967 the centre of town was resettled by militant Jewish colonists, who occupied the properties of those who had been killed or forced to leave in 1929. Tension with the Palestinian inhabitants continues to erupt into occasional violence. For your personal safety, ask about the situation before making a trip to Hebron, which in any case should be by taxi in order to avoid having a rented car with an Israeli licence plate.

Hebron is regarded as a sacred place by the Jewish, Christian and Muslim religions alike; it was here they believe that Abraham buried his wife Sarah, in the Cave of Machpelah, purchased from the Hittite Ephron (Genesis 23). The cave then became his own tomb and later that of his descendants Isaac and Jacob.

Around 20 BC Herod the Great sealed the cave and built a great hall over it. Under Byzantine rule the structure was turned into a church. After the Arab conquest of 638 the church became a mosque. The in-vading Crusaders attempted to reclaim the site for Christ-ianity and built much of the present-day construction, but it was completed by Saladin as a mosque. In the 13th century the Mameluke emir Baybars forbade non-Muslims from entering the building, which until that time had been open to all regardless of their religion.

After the 1967 war the mosque remained Muslim, but access was granted to Jews as well. Today, the complex, known as the **Tomb of the Patriarchs** (Haram al-Khalil in Arabic), or Mosque of Machpelah, is divided into a Jewish synagogue and a Muslim mosque, each with its own entrance. It remains a bone of contention between the faiths; in 1994 Jewish colonist Baruch Goldstein entered the mosque and killed 29 Muslim worshippers.

🄲 ✿ Tomb of the Patriarchs
🄲 (02) 227 992. ◯ 8am–4pm Sun–Thu except during prayer times.

Beersheba **9**

Road map B4. 👥 141,000. 🚌
ℹ️ 1 Hebron Rd, Beer Abraham, (07) 623 4613. 🚕 Bedouin market Thu.

THE SO-CALLED CAPITAL of the Negev is a city that has grown rapidly and chaotically. In the Old Testament it is famous as the place where Abraham made a pact with the Philistine Abimelech for the use of a well for his animals (Genesis 21: 25–33).

Bedouin selling sheep at Beersheba's Thursday market

Beersheba means "well of the covenant". For centuries it remained little more than a Bedouin well until the Turks transformed the site into an administrative centre (which was the object of a valiant cavalry charge by the Australians in World War I).

After the Israelis captured Beersheba in 1948, it rapidly filled with Russian Jewish immigrants to become the country's fourth largest city.

There is an attractive grouping of an Ottoman-era mosque and Governor's House in the town centre, but the most interesting thing about Beersheba is the Bedouin market. This is held on the edge of town every Thursday from dawn and attracts hundreds of nomads. Besides the livestock and everyday objects bought by the locals, visitors can also buy traditional Bedouin handicrafts such as jewellery and copperwork.

Just outside town is **Tel Beersheba**, a city founded at the end of the 11th century BC and fortified around the time of Solomon. It was destroyed in the 9th century by the Egyptians but was rebuilt, remaining a bulwark of the southern frontier of Judaea until 700 BC, when it was razed to the ground by the Assyrians. Remains include a 10th-century BC city gate and a Roman fortress. There is also a museum of Bedouin life.

Ein Gedi, the most convenient Dead Sea beach for visitors from Jerusalem

Tel Beersheba
6 km (4 miles) NE of Beersheba.
(07) 646 7286. daily.

Ein Gedi ⓾

Road map C4. Route 90, 56 km (35 miles) S of Jericho. from Jerusalem.

THIS LOCALITY on the shores of the Dead Sea, whose name means "spring of the kid", is famous as a lush oasis in an otherwise barren landscape. Several springs

Trail sign at Ein Gedi

provide plentiful water to support a luxuriant mix of tropical and desert vegetation. Ein Gedi is mentioned in the Bible for its beauty (Song of Songs: 1–14) and as a refuge of David who was fleeing from King Saul (I Samuel: 24).

Protected as **Ein Gedi National Park**, the oasis is a haven for desert wildlife. Visitors can often spot ibexes and rock hyraxes, which look like large rodents, while the more remote areas are the abode of the desert leopard. Two gorges, belonging to the Nakhal David and Nakhal Arugot rivers, are at the core of the park and these are crossed by a network of paths. The shortest

walking tour takes about an hour and ends at the spectacular Shulamit falls. A short way from the park entrance are the ruins of a 5th-century BC synagogue with mosaics and inscriptions in Hebrew and Aramaic.

Ein Gedi is also a popular spot with Dead Sea bathers, with a beach 1 km (half a mile) south of the national park, which has public showers, necessary to wash off the lake's salty residue. For a more luxurious experience, the **Ein Gedi Health Spa**, a further 3 km (2 miles) to the south, has hot sulphur baths and private access to the Dead Sea.

Ein Gedi National Park
(07) 658 4285. daily.
Ein Gedi Health Spa
(07) 659 4813. daily.

THE MINERAL WATERS OF THE DEAD SEA

The Dead Sea (which is actually a lake, not a sea) lies at the lowest point of the 6,000-km (4,000-mile) Great Rift Valley that runs from southern Turkey to East Africa. At 411 m (1,348 ft) below sea level, it is also the lowest point on earth. The water is so mineral-laden that it is around 26

percent solid, heavy with magnesium, bromine and iodine. The therapeutic qualities of the water and its mud have been touted since ancient times, and spas and sanatoriums are dotted along the western shore. However, the Dead Sea is endangered; its water level has gone down 12 m (40 ft) since the beginning of the 20th century because its main source, the Jordan River, has been over-exploited for irrigation purposes.

The blinding white salt terrain of the Dead Sea's southern shores ▷

Masada ⑪

THIS ISOLATED MOUNTAIN-TOP FORTRESS about 440 m (1,300 ft) above the banks of the Dead Sea was fortified as early as the 1st or 2nd century BC and then enlarged and reinforced by Herod the Great, who added two luxurious palace complexes. On Herod's death the fortress passed into Roman hands but it was captured in AD 66 during the First Revolt by Jews of the Zealot sect. After the Romans had crushed the rebels in Jerusalem, Masada remained the last Jewish stronghold. Held by less than 1,000 defenders, it was under Roman siege for over two years before the walls were breached in AD 73.

Cable Car
The cable car operates daily between 8am and 4pm; otherwise it is a strenuous 45–60-minute climb up the twisting Snake Path.

Upper terrace

Snake Path

Storerooms

Middle terrace

Lower terrace

★ Hanging Palace
Part of the large Northern Palace complex, the Hanging Palace was Herod's private residence. It was built on three levels; the middle terrace had a circular hall used for entertaining, the lower had a bathhouse.

Calidarium
Masada's hot baths are one of the best preserved parts of the fortress. The columns remain on which the original floor was raised to allow hot air to circulate underneath and heat the room.

The Water Gate
is at the head of a winding path to reservoirs below.

STAR FEATURES

★ **Hanging Palace**

★ **Western Palace**

Synagogue
Possibly built by Herod, this synagogue is thought to be the oldest in the world. The stone seats were added by the Zealots.

Cistern
At the foot of the mountain Herod built dams and canals that collected the seasonal rainwater to fill cisterns on the northeast side of the fortress. This water was then carried by donkey to the cisterns on top of the rock, such as this one in the southern part of the plateau.

Southern Citadel

Columbarium
This is a small building with niches for funerary urns; it is thought the urns held the ashes of non-Jewish members of Herod's court.

Western Wall

West Gate

The Roman ramp is now the western entrance to the site.

★ Western Palace
Used for receptions and the accommodation of Herod's guests, the Western Palace was richly decorated with mosaic floors and frescoes adorning the walls.

THE ROMAN SIEGE OF MASADA (AD 70–73)

According to a 1st-century account by historian Flavius Josephus, the Roman legions laying siege to Masada numbered about 10,000 men. To prevent the Jewish rebels from escaping, the Romans surrounded the mountain with a ring of eight camps, linked by walls; an arrangement that can still be seen today. To make their attack, the Romans built a huge earthen ramp up the mountainside. Once this was finished, a tower was constructed against the walls. From the shelter of this tower the Romans set to work with a battering ram. The defenders hastily erected an inner defensive wall, but this proved little obstacle and Masada fell when it was breached. Rather than submit to the Romans the Jews inside chose to commit mass suicide. Josephus relates how each man was responsible for killing his own family. "Masada shall not fall again" is a swearing-in oath of the modern Israeli army.

Roman catapult missiles

Remains of one of the Roman base camps viewed from the fortress top

A typically barren Dead Sea
landscape near Sodom

Sodom ⓬

Road map C4. Route 90, 50 km (31 miles) S of Ein Gedi. ▯ (07) 658 4161. 🚌 from Jerusalem.

BIBLICAL TRADITION holds that the city of Sodom lay on the southern shore of the Dead Sea (Genesis 19). Its sinful inhabitants, along with those of neighbouring Gomorrah, angered God, and he destroyed the cities with "brimstone and fire". Archaeologists now favour Bab ed-Dhra in Jordan as the likely site but the name Sodom remains attached to a spot on the Israeli side of the Dead Sea. There is nothing to visit but nearby are the two spas of Ein Bokek and Neve Zohar, famous for their therapeutic centres, and a public beach with showers.

Inland and 9 km (6 miles) south of Neve Zohar is Mount Sodom, a mountain composed largely of rock salt. A well-marked path goes up to the top, from where you can enjoy incomparable views of the Dead Sea and the Moab mountains in Jordan. You can also go up by car: take the dirt road that heads west off route 90 just north of the unattractive Dead Sea Works plant. Another sign-posted scenic hiking route leads to what is known as the Flour Cave. The cave gets its name from the white crumbly chalk coating that covers the interior and the clothing of all who visit.

Ein Ovdat ⓭

Road map B5. Route 40, 52 km (32 miles) S of Beersheba. ▯ (07) 655 5684. 🚌 from Jerusalem. 🕐 summer: 8am–4pm (3pm Fri & hol eves); winter: 8am–3pm (2pm Fri & hol eves) daily. 🌿

AT EIN OVDAT a white-walled gorge gouged 200 m (656 ft) deep into the desert floor shades two icy-cold pools. The larger of the pools is fed by a waterfall with its source in the rock face high above. Archaeologists have found traces of human presence in this area that date back perhaps 35,000 years, suggesting that the springs were known in antiquity.

A well-marked trail through the gorge begins at a roadside viewpoint 2 km (1 mile) south of the turn-off for Kibbutz Sde Boker. During the hike, which takes at least a couple of hours, you may see eagles on the wing or glimpse gazelles on the cliff tops above. The trail ends with a set of rough rock-cut steps ascending the cliffs; the views from these back down the gorge are spectacular. From the clifftop a path leads to a roadside car park 7 km (4 miles) south of the viewpoint.

Ovdat ⓮

Road map B5. Route 40, 60 km (37 miles) S of Beersheba. ▯ (07) 655 0954. 🚌 from Jerusalem. 🕐 summer: 8am–4pm (3pm Fri & hol eves); winter: 8am–3pm (2pm Fri & hol eves) daily. 🌿

LOCATED ON A FLAT hilltop, the ancient town of Ovdat was built by the Nabataeans in the 2nd century BC as a stopover on the trade route between Egypt and Asia Minor. It continued to prosper under the Byzantines, and most of what you see today dates from the 4th or 5th century, including the remains of houses, baths and two churches. The smaller of these has its original apse and bishop's throne; a white line divides the original and reconstructed parts. The views across the desert are

Spring-fed pool at Ein Ovdat in the shade of canyon walls

Partially reconstructed Byzantine-era ruins at Ovdat

excellent. Below the hill you can make out evidence of the network of dams built by the Nabataeans to channel rain-water towards the dry land, enabling them to plant vine-yards and fruit orchards. Ovdat was abandoned after the Persian invasion of 620. The Visitors' Centre has an exhibition of archaeological finds from the ancient site.

Makhtesh Ramon 15

Road map B5. Route 40, 80 km (50 miles) S of Beersheba. from Beersheba. **Visitors' Centre** (07) 658 8691. 8am–5pm (Fri & hols: 4pm) Sun–Fri.

MAKHTESH RAMON is Israel's most spectacular natural phenomenon: a crater 40 km (25 miles) long, 9 km (5 miles) wide, with a depth of 300 m (1,300 ft). It is the largest of three craters in the Negev Desert, which scientists believe were formed more than half a million years ago by a combination of tectonic movement and erosion.

Traffic between Beersheba and Eilat has to cross Makhtesh Ramon, negotiating switchback roads that wind down to the crater floor and back up again. Nabataean caravans also travelled this way between Petra and Ovdat, and the ruins of an ancient caravanserai stand at the centre of the depression.

On the crater's rim is the town of Mitspe Ramon, the main base for exploring this part of the desert. The town's

Visitors' Centre has exhibits on the geology of the great crater and its flora and fauna. It also has hiking maps – but make sure to take plenty of water if you go trekking here. In Mitspe Ramon you can also arrange to tour the crater by camel or jeep.

A caracal, one of the biblical species nurtured at Khai Bar

Khai Bar Biblical Wildlife Reserve 16

Road map B6. Route 90, 35 km (22 miles) N of Eilat. (07) 637 3057. from Eilat. 8:30am–5pm (Fri & Sat: 4pm) Mon–Sat. Obligatory with departures every hour.

KHAI BAR WAS FOUNDED with the aim of reintroducing some of the creatures named in the Bible, which have since

vanished from the Negev. Most of the animals roam freely, safari-park style, in a 40-sq km (15-sq mile) territory in the Arava Valley. Visits can be made only by jeep in the company of a ranger guide. Native species in the reserve (not all of which receive biblical mention) include scimitar-horned oryxes, wild Somali donkeys, ostriches and the addax antelope with their curved horns. A Predator Centre houses wildcats, caracals (desert lynxes), foxes, leopards and hyenas in spacious enclosures.

Timna National Park 17

Road map B6. Route 90, 30 km (19 miles) N of Eilat. (07) 635 6215. from Eilat. 7:30am–sunset daily.

ANCIENT REMAINS indicate working mines at Timna as far back as 3000 BC, and the Egyptians were mining copper here around 1500 BC. They left two temples dedicated to the goddess Hathor, protectress of mines. A hieroglyphic inscription mentions pharaoh Rameses III offering a sacrifice to Hathor. The mines continued to be worked under the Nabataeans and Romans before being abandoned. With the added attraction of some curious mushroom-shaped rock formations created by wind erosion, the area has been preserved as a national park. An underground passage gives access to the ancient mines, and you can see Egyptian graffiti representing ibexes and hunters armed with bows and arrows.

Modern sculptures set in the natural splendour of Makhtesh Ramon

WESTERN JORDAN

WHILE MOST VISITORS *to Jordan come for the sole purpose of seeing the magnificent rock-cut city of Petra, many depart with their most treasured experiences being encounters with the gracious and hospitable locals. Beside these two attractions, the western part of the country has a great many fascinating archaeological sites from prehistoric, Roman, Byzantine and Crusader times.*

Only partitioned off from Palestine in 1923 and made fully independent in 1946, the nation of Jordan has a maturity that belies its youth. That the kingdom is viewed as an anchor in the often turbulent sea of Middle Eastern politics is due, in large part, to the efforts of the late King Hussein (1953–99) who worked solidly to establish and maintain peace in the region. The extreme warmth and friendliness of the population is an expression of the stability Hussein secured for his country. Day-to-day patterns of life in Jordan are also shaped by a relaxed and tolerant interpretation of Islam. Tourists who have just visited neighbouring Israel may well appreciate the laissez-faire nature of the Jordanian people.

Although Jordan has an area of about 92,000 sq km (36,000 sq miles),

around nine-tenths of this is desert. Consequently, the population of approximately three million is concentrated in the northwest on a plateau above the Jordan Valley. Watered by the Jordan River and surrounded by mountains, this little pocket enjoys a lush greenhouse-like climate and is entirely devoted to agriculture. But south of Amman the fertile plains abruptly end and give way to the vast stony desert that extends all the way down to the Red Sea. Largely shunned by the local populace, this is the region that visitors come to see. This is where you find the craggy sandstone landscapes out of which Petra was carved. Further south is Wadi Rum with its great cinemascope sandy oceans that provided a dramatic backdrop for the exploits of Lawrence of Arabia.

Perfectly suited to the Jordanian terrain, the camel, pictured here at Mount Nebo

◁ **The Treasury at Petra, arguably the single most spectacular sight in the whole Middle East**

Exploring Western Jordan

THOUGH POSSESSING FEW SITES itself, Jordan's modern capital, Amman, makes a very comfortable base from which to explore the northwest of the country. The Arab fortress at Ajlun, the Roman ruins at Jerash, the Byzantine mosaics of Madaba, and further mosaics along with splendid views at Mount Nebo, are all within an hour's drive. If you can spare the time and secure the use of a car (self-drive or a taxi hired by the day), then Amman is certainly worth a couple of days. The Crusader castles of Kerak and Shobak are perhaps best visited while heading south, en route to the site that truly epitomizes the magic of the region, Petra. While it is possible to see the major attractions in just one day, Petra more than repays repeated visits: multiple-day passes are available. Accommodation is easy to find in the neighbouring town of Wadi Musa. Be sure also to leave enough time for the surreal rockscapes of Wadi Rum, full of hidden oases and evidence of prehistoric civilizations.

The impressive stone sweep of the colonnaded Oval Plaza at Jerash

SIGHTS AT A GLANCE

Ajlun **2**
Amman **4**
Jerash **3**
Kerak **7**
Madaba pp192–3 **6**
Mount Nebo **5**
Petra pp196–207 **9**
Shobak **8**
Umm Qais **1**
Wadi Rum pp208–9 **10**

GETTING AROUND

Most major tourist destinations can be reached by good, modern roads. There are two main routes south – take the King's Highway (Route 49) for Mount Nebo, Madaba, Kerak and Shobak, and the Desert Highway (Routes 15 and 53) to head directly to Petra and Wadi Rum. It is possible to fly between Amman and Aqaba and an inexpensive bus service connects all areas of the country. For many people, however, coach tours are the most comfortable way to get about.

SEE ALSO

- *Where to Stay* pp237–8

- *Restaurants, Cafés and Bars* p251

Wadi Rum, where sandstone mountains rise sheer from the desert floor

Aqaba

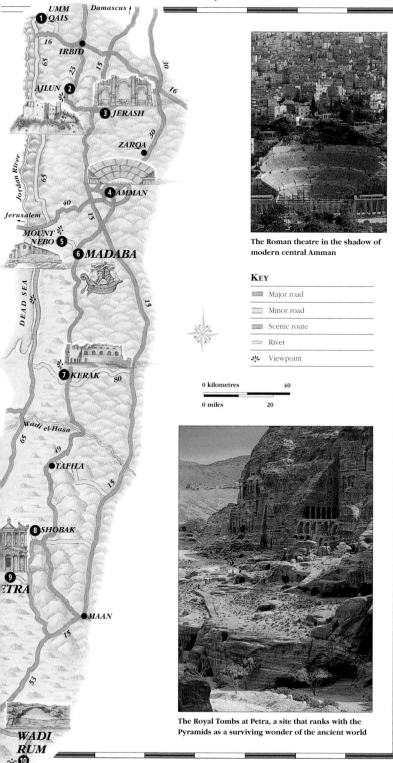

1 UMM QAIS

Damascus

Damascus

16

IRBID

65 23 15 30

AJLUN **2**

16

3 **JERASH**

30

ZARQA

Jordan River

65

4 **AMMAN**

40

Jerusalem

15

MOUNT NEBO **5**

6 **MADABA**

DEAD SEA

15

7 **KERAK**

80

Wadi el-Hasa

65

49

TAFLA

15

8 **SHOBAK**

9

ETRA

MAAN

15

53

WADI RUM

10

The Roman theatre in the shadow of
modern central Amman

KEY

▦	Major road
▦	Minor road
▦	Scenic route
~	River
☀	Viewpoint

0 kilometres   40

0 miles   20

The Royal Tombs at Petra, a site that ranks with the
Pyramids as a surviving wonder of the ancient world

Umm Qais ❶

Road map C2. 100 km (62 miles) NW of Amman. ⏰ *7am – sunset daily.* 🚻

UMM QAIS is the site of the ancient Graeco-Roman city of Gadara. The ruins lie in lush hill country overlooking the Golan Heights and the Sea of Galilee. The city is well known from the Bible for Jesus's miracle of the Gadarene Swine, when he cast out demons into pigs (Matthew 8: 28–34). Since 1974, archaeologists have uncovered many impressive Roman remains, including a colonnaded street, a theatre and a mausoleum.

Ajlun ❷

Road map C3. 50 km (31 miles) W of Amman. ℹ️ (02) 642 0115. **Fortress** ⏰ *9am – 5pm daily.* 🚻

THE MARKET TOWN of Ajlun is dominated by the fortress of **Qalat ar-Rabad**, a superb example of Arab military engineering. Built in 1184–5, partly in response to Crusader incursions in the region, it was later used by the Ottomans up until the 18th century. At a height of more than 1,200 m (4,000 ft), it offers fantastic views over the Jordan Valley.

ENVIRONS: About 30 km (19 miles) northwest of Ajlun is **Pella**. Water, fertile land and, later, its location on two major trade routes were drawing settlers here well before 3000 BC. Its Roman-Byzantine ruins are today's attraction, particularly the colonnaded atrium.

The Arab fortress at Ajlun, built to stem the Crusaders' advance

View of Jerash's Cardo, Agora (market place) and unusual Oval Plaza

Jerash ❸

Road map C3. 50 km (31 miles) N of Amman. 🚌 *from Amman.* 🚗 (02) 635 0082. ⏰ *7:30am – 5pm (Nov – Mar: 4:30pm) daily.* 🎭 *Arts Festival (late Jul – early Aug).* 🚗 (06) 567 5199.

EXCAVATIONS OF JERASH, known as Gerasa in Classical times, began in the 1920s, bringing to light one of the best preserved and most original Roman cities in the Middle East. It was during the Hellenistic period of the 3rd century BC that Jerash became an urban centre and a member of the loose federation of Greek cities known as the Decapolis *(see p40).* From the 1st century BC Jerash drew considerable prestige from the semi-independent status it was given within the Roman province of Syria. It also prospered greatly as a result of its position on the incense and spice trade route from the Arabian Peninsula to Syria and the Mediterranean. Jerash lost its autonomy under Trajan, but his annexation of the Nabataean capital Petra *(see pp196–207)* in AD 106

Detail of floor mosaic in St George's Church

brought the city even more wealth. By AD 130 ancient Gerasa was at its zenith. Having become a favourite city of Hadrian *(see p41),* it flourished both economically and socially. After a period of decline in the 3rd century, it enjoyed a renaissance as a Christian city under the Byzantines, notably in the reign of Justinian (AD 527–65). The Muslims took over the city in 635, and it was badly damaged by a series of earthquakes in the 8th century. The final blow to the city was dealt by Baldwin II of Jerusalem in 1112 during the Crusades *(see pp46–7).* The city is reached through **Hadrian's Arch**, built in honour of the Roman emperor. Alongside is the **Hippodrome**, where Gerasa's chariot races and other sporting events took place, and a little way down the track is the **South Gate**, part of the 4th-century AD city wall. To its left, and on a prominent rise is first the **Temple of Zeus**, and then the **South Theatre**, which nowadays is used as a venue for the Jerash Festival *(see p35).* The most unusual feature of the Roman city is the **Oval Plaza** (1st century AD) which, with its asymmetrical shape, is a unique monument from the Roman world. The plaza, 80 m by 90 m (262 ft by 295 ft), is enclosed by 160 Ionic columns. Beneath its stone paving runs a complex drainage system. From here, going north, is the **Cardo**, a spectacular paved street about 600 m (660 yards) long, which was lined with the city's major buildings, shops and residences. Chariot tracks are clearly visible in the stones. To the left lies the **Agora**, the city's main food market, which had a central fountain. At the Tetrapylon (crossroads) the Cardo meets a second major street, the **South Decumanus**, which runs east–west. Further along on the left side of

Temple of Zeus (2nd century AD)

the Cardo is the 2nd-century **Nymphaeum**, a lavish public fountain. One of its basins has a touching design of four fish kissing. Nearby is the impressive **Temple of Artemis**, the patron goddess of the city in Greek and Roman times.

Close to the Temple are the remains of a number of Byzantine churches. The largest is usually referred to as the **Cathedral**. There is also a complex of three churches, dedicated to **SS Cosmas and Damian, St John the Baptist** and **St George**, which dates back to AD 526–33 and has fine mosaic floors. Further along the Cardo, to the right, is the **Propylaeum Church** with the remains of an ornate plaza in front, while next to it are the ruins of an **Omayyad Mosque**. Beyond lie the unexcavated **West Baths**, which preserve a splendid domed ceiling. At the **North Tetrapylon**, once marked by a dome resting on four arches, the road to the left leads to the small **North Theatre**.

Allow at least half a day to see the ruins and round off the tour by visiting the **Museum**, which has exhibits of carved sarcophagi, statuary and coins.

Byzantine city wall

Entrance

Visitors' Centre and restaurant

Modern town

Museum

South Gate

Irbid

Amman

0 metres   200
0 yards   200

KEY TO THE RUINS OF JERASH

Agora ⑦
Cardo ⑥
Cathedral ⑨
Hadrian's Arch ①
Hippodrome ②
North Tetrapylon ⑯
North Theatre ⑰
Nymphaeum ⑫
Omayyad Mosque ⑭

Oval Plaza ⑤
Propylaeum Church ⑬
SS Cosmas and Damian, St John the Baptist and St George ⑩
South Decumanus ⑧
South Theatre ④
Temple of Artemis ⑪
Temple of Zeus ③
West Baths ⑮

The reconstructed South Gate, the 4th-century AD entrance to Jerash

Amman's Roman Theatre, completed during the reign of Emperor Marcus Aurelius

Amman ❹

Road map C3. ♞ *1,500,000.* ⬦
🚌 🛈 *Ministry of Tourism, Midan al-Malik Talal (Third Circle),* (06) 464 2311.

Essentially a modern city built of locally-quarried stone, Amman began to grow in the early 1920s when Emir Abdullah made it the capital of Trans-Jordan.

Its history, however, goes back many millennia. The settlement mentioned in the Bible as Rabbath Ammon was the capital of the Ammonites, who for centuries fought the Israelites before falling under the yoke of the Assyrians. Then, after a period of domination by the Nabataeans *(see p203),* the city became a great trade centre in the Roman era and was renamed Philadelphia. It continued to prosper under the Omayyads after the Arab conquest in 635, but decline set in during the mid-8th century and Amman remained a backwater right through the Ottoman era *(see pp48–9).*

Today, Amman is a lively, modern city, the result of rapid development in the second half of the 20th century following the massive dispersal of the Palestinians after the wars with Israel *(see pp52–3).* The historic centre is at the foot of the Citadel. Here you will find the El-Hussein Mosque, built in 1932, surrounded by the city's souk and the ruins of Roman Philadelphia. The **Roman Theatre**, with a seating capacity of about 6,000, dates from

around AD 170. The vaults below it are occupied by the **Folklore Museum** and the **Jordanian Museum of Popular Traditions**. The latter has a good display of traditional costume, Bedouin jewellery and mosaics rescued from sites such as Jerash *(see pp188–9)* and Madaba *(see pp192–3).*

The **Citadel (El-Qala)**, on the hill facing the theatre, can be reached by a very steep climb up Shabsugh Street. It is a good vantage point from which to view the hills and valleys of Jordan's capital. At the top are the ruins of a Roman temple dedicated to Hercules, built at the same time as the theatre, and the

Amman's 1932 El-Hussein Mosque, built on the site of a 7th-century Omayyad mosque

Archaeological Museum of Jordan, which has an outstanding collection of material. Starting from the Neolithic era, this gives an exhaustive picture of human activity in Jordan up to the Byzantine period and includes Nabataean artifacts from Petra *(see pp196–207)* and a collection of Dead Sea scrolls.

Not far from the museum is the **Omayyad Palace (El-Qasr)** completed around AD 750. The enormous complex incorporates a whole, colonnaded Roman street and is thought to have comprised administrative offices as well as the residence of Amman's local governor.

Among the broad avenues of the modern city are the large, blue-domed **El-Malek Abdullah Mosque**, built in 1990, and the **Royal Cultural Centre**, which hosts exhibitions and cultural events.

⋔ Roman Theatre
El-Hashimi St. ⬯ *daily.*
🏛 Folklore Museum
Al-Hashimi St. 🕻 *(06) 465 1742.* ⬯ *daily.* ⬨
🏛 Jordanian Museum of Popular Traditions
El-Hashimi St. 🕻 *(06) 465 1760.* ⬯ *Wed–Mon.* ⬨
🏛 Archaeological Museum of Jordan
Jebel el-Qala. 🕻 *(06) 463 8795.* ⬯ *daily.* ⬨
🏛 Royal Cultural Centre
Queen Alia St. 🕻 *(06) 566 1026.* ⬯ *daily.*

Mount Nebo ❺

Road map C3. 10 km (6 miles) NW of Madaba. 🚌 *from Madaba then a 4-km (2.5-mile) walk, or taxi from Madaba.*

Detail of a mosaic from the Memorial Church of Moses on Mount Nebo

THIS MOUNTAIN RISES at the end of the long chain skirting the Dead Sea, and offers spectacular views of the Jordan River and Dead Sea 1,000 m (3,300 ft) below. It was from here that Moses saw the Promised Land just before he died (Deuteronomy 34: 1–5).

In the 4th century a sanctuary, mentioned by the pilgrim nun Egeria *(see p30)*, was built on Mount Nebo (Fasaliyyeh in Arabic) to honour Moses, probably over the remains of a more ancient construction. During the Byzantine period, the church was transformed into a fine basilica with a sacristy and new baptistry. Monastic buildings were added later.

Since 1933, reconstruction work has been carried out on the church, now known as the **Memorial Church of Moses**. Mosaics inside include a remarkable example in the Old Baptistry depicting animals, farmers and hunters surrounded by geometric decoration. A Greek inscription dates it to 531. Next to the New Baptistry, a mosaic cross from the original church stands on a modern altar. Outside, the foundations of the monastery can be seen.

Madaba ❻

See pp192–3.

Kerak ❼

Road map C4. 🏛 19,000. 🚌 ❗ *El-Mujamma Street, (03) 351 150.*

THE TOWN OF KERAK, on top of a hill with a sheer drop on three sides, is dominated by a magnificent Crusader citadel. Kerak was an important city (and for a time the capital) of the Biblical kingdom of Moab. For this reason, the **castle** is also sometimes known as Krak des Moabites.

It was built in 1142 by the Frankish lord of Oultrejourdain, Payen le Bouteiller, to whom the territory had been ceded by King Baldwin II of Jerusalem in 1126. It was the pearl in the chain of fortifications that ran between Jerusalem and Aqaba, and replaced Shobak as the centre of Oultrejourdain. Under Reynald de Châtillon it resisted assaults by Saladin's troops in 1183 and 1184, but finally fell after a siege in 1188.

Arab repairs and additions in white limestone contrast with the Crusader parts built in dark, volcanic tufa. The impressive upper courtyard, containing a much-damaged Crusader chapel, provides an exceptional viewpoint. Steps lead down to vast, dimly-lit, vaulted rooms and corridors below ground. The lower courtyard gives access to a small **Archaeological Museum** displaying locally excavated artifacts.

⋔ Castle
El-Mujamma St. ◯ *daily.*
🏛 Archaeological Museum
▮ *(03) 351 149.* ◯ *Wed–Mon.* ◪

Shobak ❽

Road map C5. 60 km (37 miles) S of Tafila. ▮ *(03) 215 6020.* 🚌 *to Shobak village, then taxi.* ◯ *daily.*

SHOBAK, ISOLATED on a rocky, conical hill in rough, barren surroundings at 1,300 m (4,265 ft) above sea level, is perhaps the most impressively sited castle in Jordan. It was called Krak de Montréal, or Mons Regalis, and was the first outpost (1115) built beyond the Jordan River by King Baldwin I of Jerusalem to guard the road from Egypt to Damascus. It resisted many sieges until 1189, when it fell to Saladin's troops.

The towers and walls are well preserved and decorated with carved inscriptions dating from 14th-century Mameluke renovations, but the inside is ruinous. Near the gatehouse, a well with over 350 dangerously slippery, spiral, rock-cut steps descends to a spring.

The impressive and well-preserved Crusader fortress at Kerak

Madaba ❻

Road map C4. 🏛 75,000.
🚌 from Amman. 🏛 Hussein bin
Ali St, (08) 543 376.

ACCORDING to the Old
Testament the Moabite
city of Madaba was one of
those conquered by the
tribes of Israel. After
changing hands several
times it flourished under
Roman dominion and by
the 4th century AD it had
become an important centre
of Christianity with its own
bishop. The town weathered
invasions by the Persians
and Muslims and declined
under the Mamelukes and
was completely abandoned
during the 16th century. It
was not reoccupied until
the late 19th century.

The main attraction is the
fabulous mosaic map housed
in **St George's Church** in
the town centre, but there
is also an **Archaeological
Park** encompassing the
remains of several more
6th-century churches,
all with impressive
mosaics, including one
depicting scenes from
the legend of Adonis
and Aphrodite. The **Church
of the Apostles** on the
southern edge of town has
a mosaic depicting the sea
goddess Thetis surrounded
by fish and sea monsters.

🏛 **St George's Church**
⏰ 8:30am (10:30am Fri &
Sun)–6pm daily. 🈂
🏛 **Archaeological Park**
⏰ daily. 🈂

St George's Church, also known
as the Church of the Map

The Madaba Mosaic Map

IN THE LATE 19TH CENTURY clashes
with the Muslim community led to
a group of Christians from Kerak
voluntarily moving to the long-
uninhabited site of ancient
Madaba. They were permitted to
build new churches only on the
sites of old ones. In 1884, while clearing such
a site, the mosaic map was uncovered. It was
incorporated into the new St George's Church but
was badly damaged in the process. It wasn't until
ten years later that scholars recognized the great
historic value of the mosaic, which was probably
made during the reign of the Emperor Justinian
(AD 527–65).

**Mosaic gazelle
from the map**

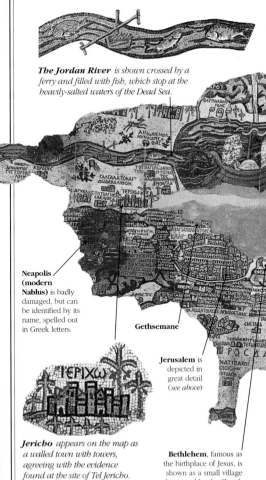

The Jordan River *is shown crossed by a
ferry and filled with fish, which stop at the
heavily-salted waters of the Dead Sea.*

**Neapolis
(modern
Nablus)** is badly
damaged, but can
be identified by its
name, spelled out
in Greek letters.

Gethsemane

Jerusalem is
depicted in
great detail
(*see above*)

Jericho *appears on the map as
a walled town with towers,
agreeing with the evidence
found at the site of Tel Jericho.*

Bethlehem, famous as
the birthplace of Jesus, is
shown as a small village
dominated by the Church
of the Nativity.

The Madaba map, visited by up to a thousand visitors a day

JERUSALEM AS DEPICTED ON THE MAP

In the 6th century, Jerusalem was still essentially the Roman city of Aelia Capitolina with its walls and gates, and the main streets of the Cardo Maximus and the Decumanus. Identifiable landmarks include Damascus Gate and the Church of the Holy Sepulchre, as well as the long-vanished Nea Basilica *(see p80)* and Damascus Gate column.

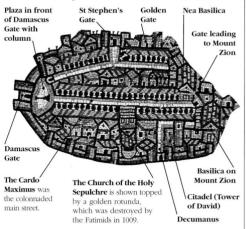

Plaza in front of Damascus Gate with column

St Stephen's Gate

Golden Gate

Nea Basilica

Gate leading to Mount Zion

Damascus Gate

The Cardo Maximus was the colonnaded main street.

The Church of the Holy Sepulchre is shown topped by a golden rotunda, which was destroyed by the Fatimids in 1009.

Basilica on Mount Zion

Citadel (Tower of David)

Decumanus

Kerak sits on top of a high mountain.

Mamshit was a Nabataean city in the Negev Desert

The Mountains of Sinai separate the desert to the north from the Nile Delta.

The Dead Sea is shown with two boats carrying salt and grain. The sailors have been hacked out, probably by iconoclasts who objected to the representation of living beings in art.

Ashdod, an ancient port on the Mediterranean, remains an important deep-water harbour.

Beersheba, although existing only in part, can be identified by the text – and by its accurate location in the western Negev Desert.

Pelusium in Sinai was an important Byzantine-era city; it has long since disappeared.

The Nile is depicted as flowing east-west rather than the reality, which is from south to north.

WHAT THE MAP SHOWS

The map is oriented east–west rather than north–south, with Palestine on the left and Egypt's Nile Delta on the extreme right. The cities and villages are located remarkably accurately for the time, and they are represented in plan form, corresponding to a large degree to modern cartography.

Gaza was a major port in ancient times with trade links to Egypt and Africa and, by its comparatively large size, the map accords it great importance.

Petra 9

PETRA IS ONE OF THE WORLD'S most impressive and atmospheric archaeological sites. Its marvellously preserved rock-hewn tombs and temples once encircled a thriving metropolis. There has been human settlement here since prehistoric times, but before the Nabataeans (see p203) came, Petra was just another desert watering hole. Between the 3rd century BC and the 1st century AD, they built a superb city and made it the centre of a vast trading empire. In AD 106 Petra was annexed by Rome. Christianity arrived in the 4th century, the Muslims in the 7th and the Crusaders briefly in the 12th. Thereafter Petra lay forgotten until 1812 when rediscovered by JL Burckhardt (see p198).

The City of Petra
The city's main street leads to the Temenos Gate, entrance to the sacred precinct of Qasr el-Bint, Petra's most important temple (see pp204–5).

★ **The Monastery**
The imposing façade of the Monastery, or El-Deir, is 47 m (154 ft) wide and 40 m (131 ft) high. This magnificent Nabataean temple may later have served as a church (see pp206–7).

Map labels

- Lion Triclinium (see p206)
- Modern Museum (see p204)
- Little Petra (see p207)
- JEBEL UMM ZAYTUNA
- JEBEL EL-DEIR
- WADI ABU ULLAYQA
- WADI EL-MATAHA
- WADI EL-SIYYAGH
- Old Museum (see p204)
- El-Habis Crusader fortress (see p204)
- Qasr el-Bint (see p204)
- WADI MUSA
- Outer Siq
- JEBEL EL-QURAY
- WADI EL-FARASA
- JEBEL ATTUF
- High Place of Sacrifice (see pp206–7)
- WADI EL-THUGHRA
- WADI UMM RATTAM
- Aaron's Tomb (see p207)

VISITING PETRA

- It is worth spending more than a day here. There are passes for 1–4 days.
- Cars allowed up to ticket gate but not beyond.
- Horses may be hired to take you the 900 m (half a mile) to Siq entrance.
- Two-seater horse-drawn carts go from the ticket office to the Treasury. From there Petra can be covered on foot or camel.
- Basic food and drinking water available in Petra.
- Wear sunhat and high-factor sunscreen.
- Avoid wandering off main walk routes without guide and water supply.

The Theatre
Carved into the mountainside by the Nabataeans, probably in the 1st century AD, this theatre follows the standard Roman design of the time. It was large enough to seat up to 7,000 people (see p201).

◁ **The Monastery, one of Petra's most breathtaking monuments**

★ **The Royal Tombs**
These monumental façades sculpted into the mountain at the eastern end of the Petra basin create an awe-inspiring panorama when viewed from a distance (see pp202–3).

VISITORS' CHECKLIST

Road map C5. Wadi Musa, 260 km (160 miles) S of Amman. to Wadi Musa from Amman, Aqaba. ☐ 6:30am–sunset daily. passes sold for 1, 2, 3 or 4 days. Ask at the Visitors' Centre. Petra Visitors' Centre, (03) 215 6020 (7am–sunset daily). Do not photograph Bedouin without their permission. **Museum** ☐ 8am–3:30pm daily.

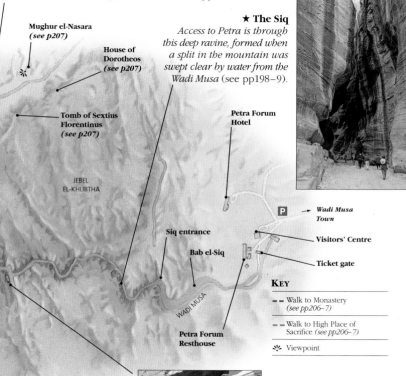

Mughur el-Nasara
(see p207)

House of
Dorotheos
(see p207)

Tomb of Sextius
Florentinus
(see p207)

JEBEL
EL-KHUBTHA

★ **The Siq**
Access to Petra is through this deep ravine, formed when a split in the mountain was swept clear by water from the Wadi Musa (see pp198–9).

Petra Forum
Hotel

Wadi Musa
Town

Siq entrance

Bab el-Siq

Visitors' Centre

Ticket gate

KEY

– – Walk to Monastery
(see pp206–7)

– – Walk to High Place of
Sacrifice *(see p206–7)*

☆ Viewpoint

Petra Forum
Resthouse

WADI MUSA

0 metres   500

0 yards   500

STAR SIGHTS

★ **The Siq**

★ **The Treasury**

★ **The Royal Tombs**

★ **The Monastery**

★ **The Treasury**
The best-known of all Petra's magnificent temples, deliberately positioned at the end of the Siq for maximum impact, the 1st-century BC Treasury takes its name from Bedouin folklore. They believed that the Khasneh el-Faroun (Treasury of the Pharaoh) was the magical creation of a great wizard who had deposited treasure in its urn (see p200).

The Siq: the Ancient Entrance to Petra

To REACH THE SIQ, the narrow gorge that leads into Petra, you must first walk 900 m (half a mile) along the wide valley known as the Bab el-Siq. This prelude to Petra has many tantalizing examples of the Nabataeans' appetite for sculpting monuments out of mountainsides. The entrance to the Siq is marked by the remains of a monumental arch. It is the start of a gallery of intriguing insights into the Nabataeans' past. These include water channels cut into the rock, Nabataean graffiti, carved niches with worn outlines of ancient deities, Nabataean paving stones, and eerie flights of steps leading nowhere. As the Siq descends, it closes in and at its deepest, darkest point unexpectedly opens out on Petra's most thrilling monument – the Treasury *(see pp200–1)*.

Djinn Blocks
In Arab folklore these carved blocks, of which Petra has 26, house djinn *(spirits). They may have been tower tombs.*

Obelisk Tomb and Bab el-Siq Triclinium
Two rock-cut tombs on the way to the Siq stand one above the other. They seem to be one complex but are, in fact, separate. The upper, probably earlier, Obelisk Tomb shows Egyptian inspiration. The lower structure, known as the Bab el-Siq Triclinium (funerary dining chamber), is a superb illustration of the Nabataean Classical style (see p201).

A votive niche, to one side of the remains of the monumental arch supports, was reached by steps.

FROM THE TICKET GATE, THROUGH THE SIQ, TO THE TREASURY

It is about 1.5 km (nearly one mile) from the ticket gate to the end of the Siq. The route follows the course of a wadi which runs through the Siq and into the city. As the Siq descends, almost imperceptibly, it becomes deeper and narrower. At its narrowest point, the walls are only one metre apart.

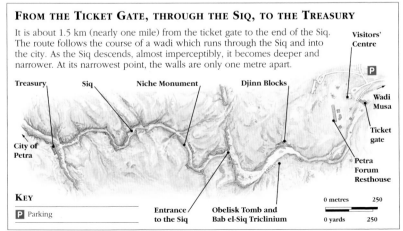

Treasury   Siq   Niche Monument   Djinn Blocks

Visitors' Centre

P

Wadi Musa

Ticket gate

City of Petra

Petra Forum Resthouse

KEY

P Parking

Entrance to the Siq

Obelisk Tomb and Bab el-Siq Triclinium

0 metres   250

0 yards   250

Nabataean Pavements
The Siq was probably paved by the Nabataeans in the 1st century AD. Substantial stretches of this paving can still be seen. Next to the most extensive stretch is the Niche Monument (see below).

Water Channels
Water Channels
The water channels were part of a sophisticated system of water conservation and flood prevention devised by the Nabataeans.

The Niche Monument
Carved into a free-standing rock, a quarter of the way along the Siq, is a small Classical shrine. Within the niche are two Djinn blocks, one of which has eyes and a nose.

The remains of the supports of the monumental arch consist of a carved niche flanked by pilasters.

Entrance to the Siq
In ancient times, the Siq was entered via a monumental arch. It fell in 1896, leaving only traces of its supporting structures.

JOHANN LUDWIG BURCKHARDT

Burckhardt in the disguise he assumed to enter Petra

In 1812, after lying hidden for more than 500 years to all except local Arabs, Petra was rediscovered by an explorer called Johann Ludwig Burckhardt. The son of a Swiss colonel in the French army, he was an outstanding student with a thirst for adventure. In 1809 he was contracted by a London-based association to explore the "interior parts of Africa". Three years later, after intense study of Islam and Arabic, he disguised himself as a Muslim scholar, took the name Ibrahim ibn Abdullah and set out for Egypt. On his way through Jordan, however, he was lured by tales of a lost city in the mountains. To get there, he had to persuade a guide to take him. Using the pretence that he wanted to offer a sacrifice to the Prophet Aaron, he became the first modern Westerner to enter Petra.

View of the Treasury
The first breathtaking glimpse of the Treasury is when its pink-hued, finely chiselled façade suddenly appears through a chink in the dark, narrow walls of the Siq. It is a moment filled with powerful contrasts.

From the Treasury to the Theatre

SET DEEP IN THE ROCK and protected by the valley walls, the magnificent 1st-century BC Treasury creates a formidable first impression of Petra. As its design had no precedent in the city, it is thought that architects from the Hellenistic Near East were brought in to create it. From the Treasury the path leads into the Outer Siq, lined on both sides with tombs of all sizes, some half buried by risen ground levels. At the end of the Outer Siq, in the midst of this great necropolis, is the Classical Theatre. Started by the Nabataeans and possibly added to by the Romans, it was a project requiring advanced engineering skills.

Treasury Tholos
The central figure may be the Petran fertility goddess El-Uzza. Bullet marks in the tholos and urn have been made over the years by Bedouin attempting to release hidden treasure.

The Outer Siq
From the Treasury to the Theatre tombs display a range of intermediate design styles. One, freestanding, uniquely combines Classical features with a crowstep used as a battlement.

Eagle, Nabataean male deity symbol

"Attic" burial chambers were a device to protect the dead from animals and tomb robbers.

The vertical footholds may have been to aid the sculptors.

Mounted figures of Castor and Pollux, sons of Zeus, flank the portico.

The single-divide crowstep was a design devised by the Nabataeans to complement the Classical cornice.

THE OUTER SIQ
The artwork above shows some of the major constructions on the left-hand side of the Outer Siq as you walk from the Treasury to the Theatre. In reality, of course, the route bends and twists and on both the left and right sides are a great number of other tombs and features of architectural interest that could not be included.

Treasury Interior
A colossal doorway dominates the outer court (left) and leads to an inner chamber of 12 sq m (14 sq yards). At the back of the chamber is a sanctuary with an ablution basin, suggesting that the Treasury was in fact a temple.

THE ARCHITECTURE OF PETRA

The Nabataeans were adventurous architects, inspired by other cultures but always creating a distinctive look. The multiple crowstep can be seen as a design of the first settlers, whereas complex Nabataean Classical buildings reflect a later, cosmopolitan Petra. However, the dating of façades is very difficult, as many examples of the simple "early" style appear to have been built during the Classical period or even later.

Multiple crowstep

This early design, *seen in the Streets of Façades, was probably Assyrian-inspired. Fragments of the once brightly painted plaster pediments have been found.*

Slot for primitive plaster pediment

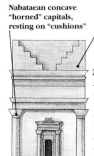

Nabataean concave "horned" capitals, resting on "cushions"

Single-divide crowstep, lending height

Stacked look, favoured by Nabataeans

Hellenistic broken pediment

This intermediate style, *seen frequently in Petra, replaced multiple crowsteps with a huge single-divide crowstep, adding Classical cornices and pillars and Hellenistic doorways. This style continued well into the 1st century AD.*

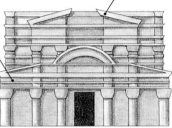

Nabataean Classical *designs, such as the Bab el-Siq Triclinium (above), are complex, possibly experimental fusions of Classical and native styles.*

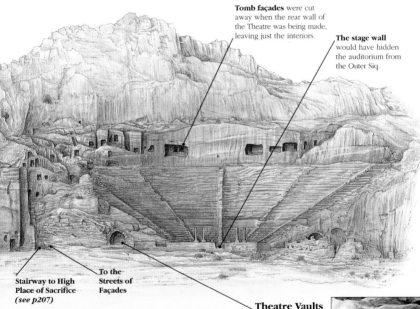

Tomb façades were cut away when the rear wall of the Theatre was being made, leaving just the interiors.

The stage wall would have hidden the auditorium from the Outer Siq.

Stairway to High Place of Sacrifice (see p207)

To the Streets of Façades

Theatre Vaults

For access there were tunnels either side of the stage. Inside (right) these were dressed with painted plaster or marble.

Streets of Façades

Carved on four levels, these tightly packed tombs may include some of Petra's oldest façades. Most are crowned with multiple crowsteps.

The Royal Tombs

CARVED INTO THE BASE of El-Khubtha mountain, a short detour to the right at the point where the Outer Siq opens out on to Petra's central plain, are the Urn, Corinthian and Palace Tombs. They are collectively known as the Royal Tombs, their monumental size suggesting they were built for wealthy or important people, possibly Petran kings or queens. These tombs and their neighbours are also remarkable for the vivid striations of colour rippling through their sandstone walls, an effect heightened in the warm glow of the late afternoon sun. Particularly striking are the Silk Tomb and the ceiling inside the Urn Tomb.

Panoramic view of the Royal Tombs from the direction of the ruined city

Palace Tomb
The largest of all the Royal Tombs, the Palace Tomb had a grandiose façade on five levels which was taller than the rock into which it was carved. The upper levels, since collapsed, had to be built up using large blocks of stone.

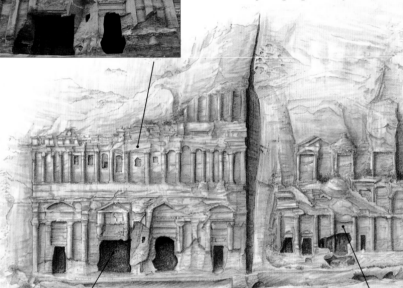

Of the four inner chambers, only the middle two connect.

Corinthian Tomb
There is no doubt that this was an important tomb in its day, but its design has baffled archaeologists because of its lack of symmetry. The doorways, each in a different style, are a clear illustration of this.

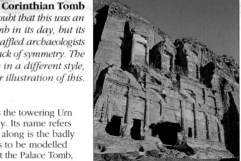

THE ROYAL TOMBS

First in the sequence of Royal Tombs is the towering Urn Tomb *(far right)*, reached by a stairway. Its name refers to a relatively tiny urn on top. Further along is the badly eroded Corinthian Tomb, which seems to be modelled largely on the Treasury, and beyond that the Palace Tomb, thought to be based on Nero's Golden House in Rome.

THE NABATAEANS

The Nabataeans were a people whose original homeland lay in north-eastern Arabia and who migrated westward in the 6th century BC, settling eventually in Petra. As merchants and entrepreneurs, they grasped the lucrative potential of Petra's position on the spice and incense trade routes from East Asia and Arabia to the Mediterranean. By the 1st century BC they had made Petra the centre of a rich and powerful kingdom extending from Damascus in the north to Leuke Kome in the south and had built a city large enough to support 20–30,000 people. Key to their success was their ability to control and conserve water. Conduits and the remains of terracotta piping can be seen along the walls of the Outer Siq – part of an elaborate system for channelling water around the city. The Romans felt threatened by their achievements and took over the city in AD 106. Although the Nabataeans ceased to be an identifiable political group, Petra continued to thrive culturally for a time. In the end the transfer of trade from land to sea and two devastating earthquakes in the 4th and 8th centuries AD brought about the city's demise.

Sculpted head, possibly of a priest

Greek (left) and Nabataean pottery vessels found at Petra

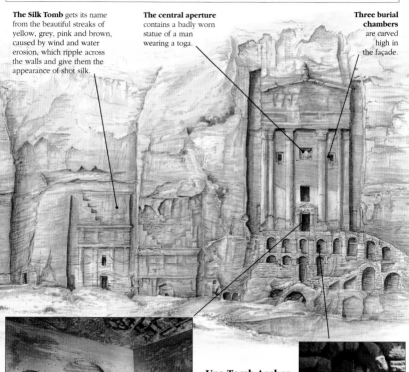

The Silk Tomb gets its name from the beautiful streaks of yellow, grey, pink and brown, caused by wind and water erosion, which ripple across the walls and give them the appearance of shot silk.

The central aperture contains a badly worn statue of a man wearing a toga.

Three burial chambers are carved high in the façade.

Urn Tomb Interior
In AD 447 the Urn Tomb was turned into a church and two of the four recesses in the back wall were combined to make an apse. A Greek inscription records the consecration.

Urn Tomb Arches
Two levels of arches support the large terrace in front of the Urn Tomb. Their appearance earned them a place in Bedouin folklore as sinister dungeons underneath a law court.

The City of Petra

JUST PAST THE THEATRE, the Outer Siq opens out into a wide plain. The ruins of the city of Petra are in the middle of this vast basin and the path alongside the Wadi Musa leads down to the site. Today, fragmented remains of the main street and a few nearby buildings are almost all that is left of the great city that once filled the valley. The grand Roman-style Cardo would have been Petra's main artery, fringed with markets and leading to the city's most sacred temple, the Qasr el-Bint. This building, like all the important buildings around the Cardo, would have been lavishly decorated. Traces of ornate plasterwork and marble veneer can still be seen on its walls and steps.

View of the ancient city of Petra from a point just past the Theatre

The Monastery
(see p206)

Little Petra
(see p207)

WADI ABU ULLAYQA

Modern Museum
Among the exhibits are a marble basin with lioness handles found in Petra Church and a small carved plaque of the Nabataean goddess al-Uzza (left) *found in the Great Temple.*

EL-HABIS RISE

Altar

The Old Museum is in a rock-cut tomb, built, unusually for Petra, with windows. It houses a collection of statuary.

Small temple

This small fortress was built by the Crusaders. While they were here they also used the Qasr el-Bint as a stable.

Aaron's Tomb
(see p207)

Qasr el-Bint el-Faroun
The name "Palace of the Pharaoh's Daughter" was a colourful invention of Bedouin mythology. The 1st-century BC building was probably Petra's main temple, the huge slab of stone at the foot of the steps being an altar to the sun god Dushara, chief deity of the Nabataean pantheon.

Temenos Gate
The imposing entrance to the sacred precinct of Qasr el-Bint had freestanding columns in front of its three massive, possibly metal-clad wooden doors. It probably dates from after the Roman annexation. The carvings of animal deities on its capitals are a Nabataean slant on an otherwise Classical design.

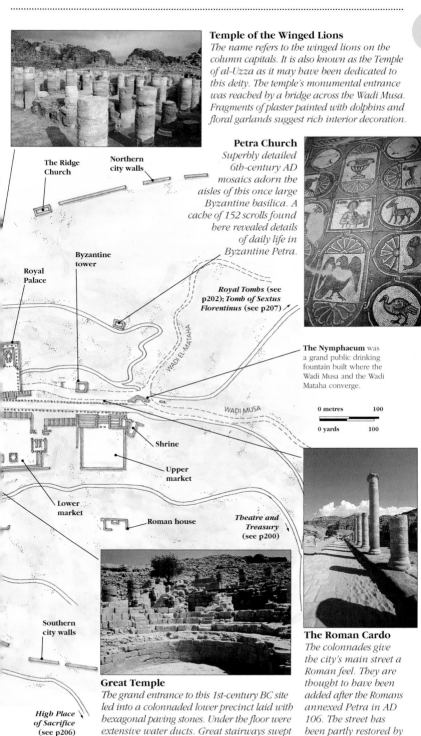

Temple of the Winged Lions
The name refers to the winged lions on the column capitals. It is also known as the Temple of al-Uzza as it may have been dedicated to this deity. The temple's monumental entrance was reached by a bridge across the Wadi Musa. Fragments of plaster painted with dolphins and floral garlands suggest rich interior decoration.

Petra Church
Superbly detailed 6th-century AD mosaics adorn the aisles of this once large Byzantine basilica. A cache of 152 scrolls found here revealed details of daily life in Byzantine Petra.

The Ridge Church

Northern city walls

Byzantine tower

Royal Palace

Royal Tombs (see p202); Tomb of Sextus Florentinus (see p207)

WADI EL-MATAHA

The Nymphaeum was a grand public drinking fountain built where the Wadi Musa and the Wadi Mataha converge.

WADI MUSA

Shrine

Upper market

Lower market

Roman house

Theatre and Treasury (see p200)

0 metres   100
0 yards   100

Southern city walls

High Place of Sacrifice (see p206)

Great Temple
The grand entrance to this 1st-century BC site led into a colonnaded lower precinct laid with hexagonal paving stones. Under the floor were extensive water ducts. Great stairways swept up to a 600-seat auditorium, of uncertain function. The decor was red and white stucco.

The Roman Cardo
The colonnades give the city's main street a Roman feel. They are thought to have been added after the Romans annexed Petra in AD 106. The street has been partly restored by Jordan's Department of Antiquities.

Other Sites Around Petra

MANY OF PETRA'S most famous sights can be visited in half a day. However, having come so far, it would be a pity not to explore more of this unique capital of a vanished civilization. A full day is enough to do the basic route from the ticket gate to the ancient city (see p204), taking in the Royal Tombs (see p202), and to include a walk to either the Monastery or the High Place of Sacrifice. Two days will enable you to do the basic route, both excursions and leave you with time to explore the area around the Tomb of Sextius Florentinus. Of the more distant sights, Little Petra can be visited in a day, while two days should be allowed for Aaron's Tomb.

High Place of Sacrifice: the round altar with the main altar behind

Façade of the Lion Triclinium

Walk to the Monastery

Just beyond the Qasr el-Bint (see p204) a path crosses the Wadi Musa. It leads past the Forum Restaurant to the start of an arduous but thoroughly worthwhile climb to one of Petra's most awe-inspiring and best-preserved monuments – the Monastery. The path, which cuts through the wadi, is paved in parts and features more than 800 rock-cut steps. The afternoon, when the sun is not directly in front, is the best time to do this walk.

A short detour off the main route, indicated by a Department of Antiquities signpost, leads to the **Lion Triclinium**. This monument, with the peculiar keyhole effect in the façade, caused by erosion, has blurred leonine representations of the goddess al-Uzza guarding its entrance. Its largely Classical façade has unusually ornate Nabataean features, such as "horned" capitals with floral scrollwork. After this, the path to the Monastery rises steeply. There are occasional flights of steps through the winding and narrowing gorge,

and several interesting carved monuments along the way. Finally, the path slips between two boulders, and drops on to a wide, once-colonnaded, rock-cut terrace. Immediately to the right is the **Monastery**, Petra's most colossal temple, dedicated to the deified king, Obodas 1, who died in 86 BC. Although it resembles the Treasury (see p200), it was never as ornate, even when statues adorned its niches. Its simple, powerful architecture, thought to date from the 1st century AD, is seen by many as the quintessential Nabataean Classical design (see p201). The interior has one large chamber with an arch-topped niche where the altar stood. It came to be known as the Monastery because of the many Christian crosses carved on its walls.

The Monastery's massive tholos crowned with an urn resting on Nabataean "horned" capitals

Walk to the High Place of Sacrifice

Midway between the Treasury and the Theatre, a rock-cut stairway, marked at the start by several djinn blocks (see p198), leads to the top of Jebel Attuf mountain. It is here, at 1,035 m (3,000 ft), that one of the best preserved of Petra's many places of sacrifice is located. The ascent, while gradual, requires stamina and a good head for heights, and is best attempted in the early morning. The first part of the summit is a large terrace with two 6-m (20-ft) stone obelisks, possibly fertility symbols. The second, reached by a north-wards scramble past the ruins of a small Nabataean building, is another plateau. Here, just beyond a rock-cut cistern, is the **High Place of Sacrifice**. In the centre of a large courtyard is a low offering table. Steps at the far end lead up to the main altar, which has a rectangular indentation in the top. The adjacent round altar has a basin with a carved channel, quite possibly for draining the blood of animal and human sacrifices. The nearby cisterns may have been used for ritual ablutions.

The path winding down the other side of Jebel Attuf into the Wadi Farasa valley is a spectacular stepped descent, sometimes with sheer drops. The first thing you see, carved into the rock face, is the **Lion Monument**, representing the goddess al-Uzza. It was originally a fountain, perhaps for pilgrims to the High Place, with water pouring from the lion's mouth. Water channels and the shape of the lion's head and legs can still be seen.

Thereafter, the path becomes a series of steps leading to the delightfully secluded **Garden Triclinium**. The tomb takes its name from the surrounding greenery. On top of the tomb is a large cistern. Further along, to the left, is the **Tomb of the Roman Soldier**, so called because of the remains

Beautifully carved interior of the Triclinium, unusual for Petra

in one of the façade niches of a figure wearing the uniform of a high-ranking Roman officer. Although Classical, the façade has Nabataean "horned" capitals on top of the pillars. Opposite is the façadeless **Triclinium**, thought have been part of the Roman Soldier Tomb complex. It has the only carved interior in Petra and its niches, fluted half columns and cornice are spectacularly enhanced by the amazing bands of colour running through the walls and ceiling.

Further down the track is the relatively plain **Broken Pediment Tomb**, named after its most striking feature. Nearby is the elegant **Renaissance Tomb**, with the three urns above its arched entrance. Similar in style to the Tomb of Sextius Florentinus, it may date from the same period. Past this point the Wadi Farasa widens and the descent ends in the main valley, not far from the Qasr el-Bint (*see p204*).

Aaron's Tomb

This site is venerated by Muslims, Christians and Jews as the place where Moses's brother Aaron was buried. The white dome of the shrine can be seen from the High Place of Sacrifice, which may be a close enough viewing for most people. The journey there involves a three-hour ride on horseback and a hard three-hour climb to the top of Petra's highest peak – Jebel Haroun. For those determined to go, a guide and adequate supplies are essential.

Tomb of Sextius Florentinus

Beyond the Palace Tomb (*see p202*), along a track skirting the cliff, stands the **Tomb of Sextius Florentinus**. Despite its badly eroded north-facing façade, the beautiful and unusual details of its design are clearly visible. Above its entrance is a Latin inscription listing the positions held by Florentinus up to his last post as Governor of Arabia in AD 127. Further north is the **Carmine Façade** with its vivid striations of red, blue and grey. Continuing alongside the Wadi Mataha brings you to a rock-cut complex known as the **House of Dorotheos** because of two Greek inscriptions found here. On the other side of the wadi is a cluster of homes and tombs known as

The lonely mountaintop shrine of Aaron's Tomb, Petra's holiest place

Mughar el-Nasara, including the fine **Tomb with Armour**. Local Christians were probably responsible for the many crosses etched into the walls.

Little Petra

This northern suburb of Petra, Siq el-Berid, has come to be known as Little Petra because it is like a miniature version of the main city. Situated 8 km (5 miles) north of Wadi Musa town, it is most easily reached by taxi. The journey on foot, north along the Wadi Abu Ullayqa, which starts just past the Qasr el-Bint, is hard, but rewarding. A guide is essential.

Detail from ceiling of the Painted House

Little Petra seems to have been a largely residential settlement, as relatively few tombs have been discovered here. It may well have been where Petra's wealthy merchants had their homes. Just outside its Siq-like entrance, which was once controlled by a gate, are a large cistern and a Classical temple. The gorge, shorter than the one leading into Petra, contains a simple temple. As you emerge from the quiet of the gorge into the town, the incredible profusion of façades is overwhelming, with houses, temples and cisterns carved into every exposed rock face. Flights of steps shoot off in all directions, evoking images of a bustling urban centre. One of Little Petra's main attractions is the **Painted House** with its plaster ceiling and walls delightfully decorated with flowers, vines, bunches of grapes, Eros with his bow and Pan playing his pipes.

Tomb of Sextius Florentinus, Roman governor of the province of Arabia

Wadi Rum ❿

THE DESERT LANDSCAPE of Wadi Rum is one of the most awe-inspiring sights in the entire Middle East. Huge ochre-coloured rock pinnacles, weathered into bulbous, outlandish shapes, rise up 600 m (2,000 ft) from the flat valley floors, like islands in a sea of red sand. Hundreds of hiking and climbing routes wind their way up and around the many peaks. This area was once on a major trade route, and evidence of settlement here includes ruins of a temple built by the Nabataeans (see p203) and carvings and inscriptions left by the later Thamud people. Today the region is still inhabited by semi-nomadic Bedouin tribes.

Thamudic rock graffiti

Aqaba
Petra

JEBEL HUBEIRA

JEBEL LEYYAH

WADI LEYYAH

WADI RUM

JEBEL RUM

Rum

JEB UM E

WADI RUMMAN

Nabataean Temple

Abu Aina campsite

JEBEL QATTAR

Aqaba

★ **Lawrence's Spring**
Not far from Rum village, this tranquil spring was described by TE Lawrence as "a paradise just 5 feet square". A Nabataean-built water channel can be seen nearby.

Rum Village
The main settlement is a rapidly growing Bedouin village. The Rest House on the outskirts offers spartan accommodation and simple meals.

Khazali Canyon
This steep defile is dotted with Thamudic inscriptions. It is possible to scramble 200 m into the canyon, starting on a ledge on the right-hand side.

0 kilometres   4

0 miles   2

STAR FEATURES

★ **Lawrence's Spring**

★ **Jebel Umm Fruth Rock Bridge**

KEY

═ Road

━ Walk

━ Hike/scramble

━ Four-wheel-drive/camel track

Rock Map at Jebel Amud
In a cave 20 km (12 miles) north-east of Rum is a rock marked with indentations and lines. It is thought by some to be a topographical map of the area, dating from around 3000 BC.

Seven Pillars of Wisdom
This spectacular peak, also known as Jebel Makhras, is named after TE Lawrence's famous book, not, as is often suggested, vice versa. Wadi Siq Makhras, just to the south, provides hiking access to Wadi Umm Ishrin and beyond.

Jebel Barrah
This large outcrop, seen here at its northern end, flanks beautiful Barrah Canyon, which is a stunning hike best negotiated from the south.

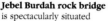
Jebel Burdah rock bridge
is spectacularly situated and can be reached via a moderately difficult climb.

TE LAWRENCE (1888–1935)

Lawrence of Arabia, the most famous British hero of World War I, earned his nickname for his exploits fighting alongside the Arab tribes that revolted against Turkish rule in 1915. Sent to Mecca in 1916 to liaise with leaders of the revolt, he then led many Arab guerrilla operations in the desert, including attacks on the Hejaz Railway, some launched from Wadi Rum. He also took part in the capture of Aqaba and the advance on Damascus. *The Seven Pillars of Wisdom*, his account of the Arab Revolt, contains lyrical descriptions of the dramatic scenery around Wadi Rum.

★ Jebel Umm Fruth Rock Bridge
This dramatic natural phenomenon is one of several rock bridges in the area. It rises straight from the desert floor and can be climbed and crossed without difficulty.

(Map labels)
Diseh
Jebel Amud
Diseh
JEBEL UMM ANFUS
JEBEL RASHRAASHA
JEBEL BARRAH
EL YYEH
BARRAH CANYON
JEBEL ABU JUDAYDA
KHOR AL AJRAM
JEBEL BURDAH

THE RED SEA AND SINAI

O NCE COVETED BY EGYPT'S PHARAOHS *for its reserves of turquoise, copper and gold, Sinai is now equally prized by tourists for its white, palm-fringed sands and the limpid waters of the Red Sea, rich with marine life. Its close association with key episodes from the Old Testament also makes the Sinai's mountainous interior an area of deep religious significance for Jews, Muslims and Christians alike.*

The Sinai Peninsula forms a triangle between the gulfs of Aqaba and Suez, two finger-like extremities of the Red Sea. Although the whole of Sinai is Egyptian territory, Israel and Jordan also have small stretches of Red Sea coast at Eilat and Aqaba, respectively.

The word "Sinai" probably derives from "Sin", the moon god worshipped in Egypt under the pharaohs. But the region is better known through the Bible as the "great and terrible wilderness" negotiated by Moses and his people in their epic 40-year journey from Egypt to the Promised Land. It's here that God supposedly first spoke to Moses through the medium of a burning bush and here, on Mount Sinai, that Moses received the Ten Commandments. The peninsula has been crossed by countless armies, including most recently that of the Israelis, who held the region from 1967 to 1982 when it was returned to Egypt under the terms of the Camp David peace treaty. In the years since then tourism has boomed as southern Sinai and the peninsula's eastern coast have been developed with all-inclusive resorts, such as Sharm el-Sheikh. But the wilderness is far from tamed. Inland Sinai remains virtually uninhabited with barren mountains sheltering hidden oases such as Feiran, with its thousands of date palms. More dramatic still are the underwater landscapes of the Red Sea, where vast coral reefs provide a home for more than 1,000 species of marine life, making for one of the world's richest dive sites.

Divers filming at Eilat's Dolphin Reef

◁ **Central Sinai inland of Nuweiba, dramatic but accessible only by four-wheel-drive or camel**

Exploring the Red Sea and Sinai

M OST VISITORS head for where the mountains and desert meet the clear cool waters of the Red Sea; specifically, Eilat, Aqaba and, most picturesque of all, the Sinai peninsula's east coast. Its string of modern resorts, while uninteresting in themselves, are set against a backdrop of extraordinary natural beauty. Nuweiba, Dahab, Naama Bay and Sharm el-Sheikh are the largest and most well-developed tourism centres, but there are many smaller, more private beach retreats. St Catherine's Monastery can be visited as a day trip.

SIGHTS AT A GLANCE

Aqaba ❶
Dahab ❹
Eilat ❷
Feiran Oasis ❽
Nuweiba ❸
Ras Muhammad
  National Park ❻
Sharm el-Sheikh ❺
St Catherine's
  Monastery
  pp222–5 ❼

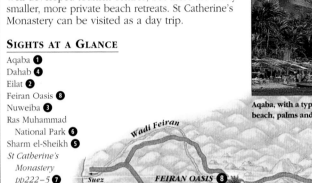

Aqaba, with a typical Red Sea scene of beach, palms and looming mountains

Suez

Wadi Feiran

FEIRAN OASIS ❽

ST. CATHERINE'S MONASTERY
❼
● *MOUNT SINAI*

EL-TUR ●

Gulf of Suez

St Catherine's Monastery, an ancient walled retreat in the Sinai Desert

GETTING AROUND

The coastal roads are good and the main resorts can be reached by car. Travelling in the Sinai interior is trickier, especially as foreigners are not permitted to stray off the main roads. Organized hikes or camel trips are perhaps the best options for those wanting to explore the desert. Buses serve coastal locations, as well as some places in the interior such as St Catherine's Monastery. Israeli and Jordanian visas and Sinai passes can be obtained at the borders *(see p266).*

SI
EL-SH

RAS MUHAMMAD NATIONAL PARK

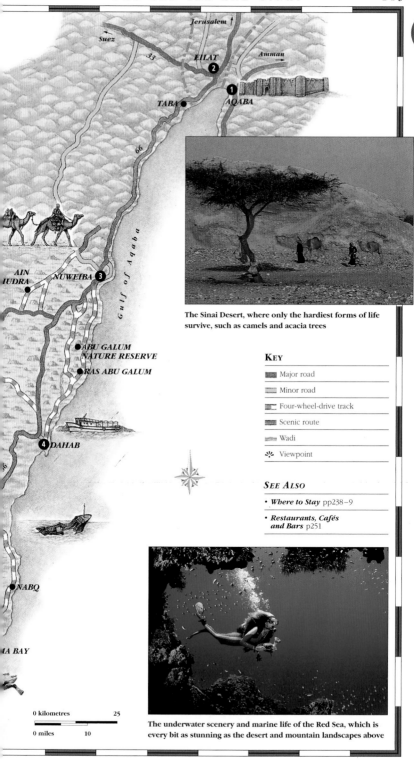

Jerusalem

Suez

33

EILAT ❷

Amman

TABA ●

AQABA ❶

66

AIN
IUDRA ●

NUWEIBA ❸

Gulf of Aqaba

● ABU GALUM
NATURE RESERVE

● RAS ABU GALUM

❹ DAHAB

● NABQ

A BAY

The Sinai Desert, where only the hardiest forms of life
survive, such as camels and acacia trees

KEY

▬ Major road

▬ Minor road

▬ Four-wheel-drive track

▬ Scenic route

▬ Wadi

☆ Viewpoint

SEE ALSO

• *Where to Stay* pp238–9

• *Restaurants, Cafés
  and Bars* p251

0 kilometres   25

0 miles   10

The underwater scenery and marine life of the Red Sea, which is
every bit as stunning as the desert and mountain landscapes above

Ruins of the old fortified Islamic town of Ayla, in modern Aqaba

Aqaba ❶

Road map: B7. 👥 *62,000.* ✈ 🚌
ℹ *Al Koornish St (next to the Fort),*
(03) 201 3731.

THE ONLY Jordanian outlet to the sea, Aqaba is a very important commercial port town. The relentless stream of heavy trucks going to and coming from Amman along the Desert Highway is clear evidence of this.

Southofthe town however, away from the busy port, the crystal clear waters are home to fabulous coral reefs. These are the main reason for Aqaba's popularity with visitors, as they offer some of the best scuba diving in the world. Closer to the shore, many other types of water sports also help to provide escape from the extreme summer heat. Large sandy beaches stretch out along the coast, bounded by modern hotels, and the steep mountains behind form a spectacular natural backdrop.

Aqaba's long and glorious past also provides it with some notable archaeological sites to visit. It is thought to be close to the site of biblical Ezion-Geber, the large port which is said to have been built by King Solomon. Its existence has, however, yet to be proved.

The town's deep freshwater springs ensured

Sign to Aqaba Aquarium

that Aqaba became a popular caravan stop for merchants travelling between Egypt, the Mediterranean coast and Arabia. By the 2nd century BC, the now prosperous town had fallen under the control of the Nabataeans *(see p203).* Such prosperity saw it conquered by the Romans in AD 106, and later the Muslims

in AD 630. Under Muslim control, Aqaba became an important stage on the pilgrimage to Mecca, and the Muslims built the fortified town of **Ayla** nearby to the north. After suffering a major earthquake in 748, the town was rebuilt, and thrived with an increasing sea trade. Following another earthquake in 1068 however, and then the Crusader conquests of the 12th century, the city was finally abandoned. You can visit the ruins at the Ayla digs, next to the coastal Corniche road. Much of the foundations of walls, towers and a series of buildings still remain. The **Archaeological Museum**, next to the tourist office, features material from the digs, as well as illustrating the history of Aqaba.

The other main archaeological site in Aqaba is the **Mameluke Fort**, set between the palm trees on La Côte Verte. Built in the 16th century, its portal now bears the coat-of-arms of the Hashemites, placed there after Lawrence of Arabia's troops conquered the port during World War I. The fort also served as a caravanserai for hundreds of years, and some restored rooms pay testament to this more peaceful role.

By going west past the industrial port and just beyond the ferry passenger terminal you will come to the small Aqaba Marine Science Station **Aquarium**. This contains a collection of the most important species of the varied flora and fauna in the Gulf of Aqaba, including moray eels and deadly stonefish. It also displays information on the campaign to protect the Red Sea.

⚓ **Mameluke Fort**
La Côte Verte. 【 *(03) 201 3731.*
◯ *daily.* 📷 ⭣
🏛 **Archaeological Museum**
Al Koornish St (next to Fort). 【 *(03)*
201 3731. ◯ *Wed–Mon.* 📷 ⭣
🐟 **Aquarium**
South Coast (near ferry terminal).
【 *(03) 201 5144.* ◯ *daily.* 📷 ⭣

Sailing boats anchored in the Gulf of Aqaba

Eilat ❷

Road map: B7. 🏛 50,000. ✈ 🚌
ℹ Central Park, Ha Arava Rd.
(07) 637 2111.

LYING AT THE END of the Gulf of Aqaba, on a stretch of Israel's 12 km (7 mile) long southern coast, Eilat is the only Israeli town on the Red Sea. The town is filled with hotels and tourist villages, and is a centre for diving and trips into the desert. Eilat is similar in many ways to Aqaba, which faces it from 6 km (4 miles) away on the other side of the Gulf. Along with an equally stunning location, Eilat also shares a similar history to Aqaba, due to their close proximity. Now separated by political boundaries however, it is Eilat that has prospered the most. With the United Nations partition of Palestine in 1947, Israel was ceded this small stretch of coastline, and Eilat has since developed rapidly, both as a port and as a popular holiday resort, with excellent tourist facilities.

The bottom of the Red Sea is the main attraction here. If you don't want to dive to admire this multicoloured

Coral Island, south of Eilat in the Gulf of Aqaba.

ecosystem, there are glass-bottomed boats as well as the 'Yellow Submarine'. This large 23 m (75 ft) long submersible leaves from Coral World, and cruises out over the reef, descending to a depth of around 60 m (200 ft).

The large **Coral World Underwater Observatory** is an oceanographic complex where you can get a close-up view of the marvellous marine life here. It contains 25 tanks with more than 500 species of fish, sponges, corals and invertebrates. The most interesting displays are those with the larger creatures such as sharks and sea turtles. The main spectacle though is

at the underwater observatory itself, which is some 6 m (20 ft) underwater and gives a spectacular live view of the local marine life through its large glass windows.

Divers and expert swimmers will be delighted at **Dolphin Reef**, where small groups led by an instructor can actually swim with the dolphins and observe their behaviour as they play, swim and hunt.

The salt marshes just north of Eilat are the feeding grounds of many species of migratory birds travelling between Africa and Eurasia every spring and autumn. The **International Birdwatching Centre**, at Kibbutz Eilot, has an interpretation centre, and organizes guided birdwatching tours. In season, the skies are filled with thousands of storks, flamingos and herons, as well as eagles, hawks and buzzards.

By boat you can go to the fabulous reefs off **Coral Island** (or Pharaoh's Island), which lies just across the Egyptian border. Regular trips are run for divers, but those wishing to land and visit the 12th-century Crusader fortress that dominates the island will need to find a tour that can arrange a group visa.

🏊 **Coral World Underwater Observatory**
Coral Beach. 📞 (07) 636 4200.
🕐 daily (Yellow Submarine: Mon–Sat).
📷 ♿
🏊 **Dolphin Reef**
Southern Beach. 📞 (07) 637 5935.
🕐 daily. 📷 ♿
🏊 **International Birdwatching Centre**
Kibbutz Eilot, 2 km (1 mile) N of Eilat.
📞 (07) 633 5339. 🕐 Oct–Jun:
Sun–Thu (am only). 📷 ♿ 🅿

The Coral World Underwater Observatory, Eilat

The Coral Reefs of the Red Sea

THE CORAL REEF is one of the richest ecosystems on earth. Visitors to the Red Sea cannot but marvel at the contrast between the barren, almost lifeless desert and the explosion of marine life on the coastal reefs. The waters are so clear that even from the surface you can appreciate the huge diversity of species inhabiting the reefs. Scuba divers can use the facilities of the many diving centres along the coast *(see pp276–7)*. Remember that a reef is an extremely fragile and threatened environment and divers should look but not touch.

View of lagoon and the shallow waters covering the reef-top

The edge of the reef is the best place for snorkellers to appreciate its wealth of marine life.

The lagoon teems with small colourful fish, including the fry of species found on the reef beyond.

Moray eel, emerging from its reef-wall lair

The clown fish protects itself from the sea anemone's stinging tentacles with a layer of mucus, using its host as a refuge from predators and for laying its eggs.

School of flag basslets, a very common species in the Red Sea

Manta rays are harmless plankton-eaters. Growing up to 6 m (20 ft) across, they are most common in open water or where there are strong currents.

Alcyonarians, brightly coloured soft corals

CORALS, THE ARCHITECTS OF THE REEF

Corals are animals, colonies of polyps, which require very precise conditions of water temperature and sunlight to grow. They take many forms – from hard rock-like corals, such as *Acropora* species, to the horny gorgonians which project from the reef into the current to feed on micro-organisms, to various soft corals. Most reefs are built over many thousands of years from the skeletons of hard corals.

Gorgonians filtering the water for plankton

An *Acropora* growing in still, shallow water

Feathery red plume of Klunzinger's soft coral

The sea fan is a horny coral, whose polyps emerge at nights to feed.

Jacks are usually seen in large schools in open water, but large solitary individuals will visit the reef.

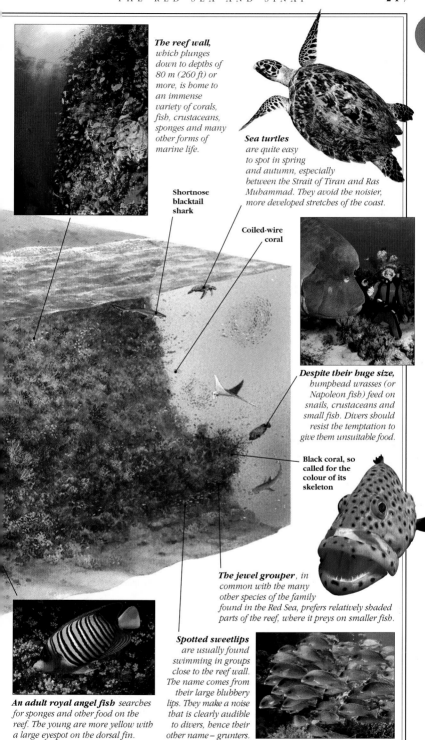

The reef wall, which plunges down to depths of 80 m (260 ft) or more, is home to an immense variety of corals, fish, crustaceans, sponges and many other forms of marine life.

Sea turtles are quite easy to spot in spring and autumn, especially between the Strait of Tiran and Ras Muhammad. They avoid the noisier, more developed stretches of the coast.

Shortnose blacktail shark

Coiled-wire coral

Despite their huge size, humphead wrasses (or Napoleon fish) feed on snails, crustaceans and small fish. Divers should resist the temptation to give them unsuitable food.

Black coral, so called for the colour of its skeleton

The jewel grouper, in common with the many other species of the family found in the Red Sea, prefers relatively shaded parts of the reef, where it preys on smaller fish.

An adult royal angel fish searches for sponges and other food on the reef. The young are more yellow with a large eyespot on the dorsal fin.

Spotted sweetlips are usually found swimming in groups close to the reef wall. The name comes from their large blubbery lips. They make a noise that is clearly audible to divers, hence their other name – grunters.

Carvings on the Haggar Maktub (Rock of Inscriptions), in the desert near Nuweiba

Nuweiba ❸

Road map F6. 🚌
🚢 *from Aqaba (Jordan).*

NUWEIBA LIES midway along the Gulf of Aqaba at the side of a promontory and consists of two distinct districts. To the south is the luxuriant Nuweiba Muzeina oasis, which for centuries was a port for travellers and pilgrims going to Mecca. It now has many hotels and tourist villages. To the north is Nuweiba el-Tarabin, named after the Bedouin tribe that lives in the village. Here you can see the ruins of the large **Tarabin fortress**. Built in the 16th century by the Mameluke sultan Ashraf el-Ghouri, it was designed to protect those coming to the city-port and also to defend Sinai from the Turks. Inside the fortress is a spring, which is an invaluable source of water for the locals. The Nuweiba area is rich in beaches and diving areas, along with much of the Gulf Coast. Some of the most interesting diving, however, is towards the Israeli border at **Pharaoh's Island** (or Coral Island, *see p215*). There are regular boat trips from Nuweiba to the island, which as well as its reefs also has an impressive Crusader fortress.

ENVIRONS: Nuweiba is perhaps most useful as a convenient starting point for trips to the interior. One of the most fascinating is to the

Coloured Canyon, a narrow sculpted gorge created by water erosion. Its vertical sandstone walls have taken on many hues of yellow, red and ochre due to the slow process of oxidation of the ferrous minerals in the rocks. The canyon opening can be reached by car from the Ain Furtaga oasis, about 15 km (9 miles) from Nuweiba on the road west. Here, follow the Wadi Nekheil track, passable in an ordinary car, for 12 km (7 miles) and at the junction turn left. After about 1 km (half a mile) you will need to leave your car and proceed on foot into the canyon.

Another fascinating trip uses a jeep track from Ain Furtaga through the immense Wadi Ghazala to **Wadi Khudra.** Midway along the track you will come to the Ain Khudra oasis, a lovely patch of palms and tamarisks seemingly wedged between the high red walls of the canyon. A short way south of here, take the walking trail up to the panoramic observation point, which offers fantastic views across the whole area. If you continue a little further along the trail you will come to the solitary Haggar Maktub (Rock of Inscriptions). Since the Nabataean period, pilgrims of all faiths going to Sinai have left graffiti carved into the face of the rock.

Heading south from Nuweiba Muzeina along the coast is another worthwhile trip. Following the jeep track

along the seaside will lead you to the **Abu Galum Nature Reserve**. A maze of narrow wadis penetrates the interior, with an abundance of plants and wildlife, such as foxes, ibexes and hyraxes. The beach at Ras Abu Galum is completely deserted except for a few Bedouin fishermen.

Dahab ❹

Road map F6. 🚌

IN ARABIC the word *dahab* means 'gold', and the name derives from the sand on the beautiful beaches at El-Qura and Ghazala. The crown of palm trees, the beaches and the light blue sea make this one of the most popular localities in Sinai. It has

Bedouin enjoying the shade with his camel, outside Nuweiba

grown up around the old Bedouin village of Assalah, which still survives today. The many camping sites, simple hotels and restaurants attract a colourful array of independent travellers who lend a cosmopolitan air to the town. Most visit for the world-class diving sites around Dahab. Among the most famous and dangerous are the 'Canyon' and the 'Blue Hole'. Almost entirely surrounded by reef, the Blue Hole drops to a depth of 80 m (260 ft) only a few metres off the shore. Although many sites are for expert scuba divers only, there are still plenty of others suitable for beginners or snorkellers.

Raccoon butterflyfish with diver, off coast of Dahab, Gulf of Aqaba

Sharm el-Sheikh ⑤

Road map E7. 🛬 🚌 🛈 *Tourist Office, Sharm el-Sheikh, (062) 600 170.*

UNTIL RELATIVELY recently, the most famous tourist seaside resort in Sinai was only a military airport. Situated on the western side of the Strait of Tiran, Sharm el-Sheikh became famous when Egyptian president Nasser decided to block Israeli access to the Red Sea, thus provoking the 1967 war. Under Israeli occupation of Sinai, the first hotels were built and began to attract tourists, especially expert scuba divers. The Sharm el-Sheikh bay is still a military port, but the sports-craft port in nearby Sharm el-Maiya bay has hotels, shops and small restaurants. A few kilometres to the north though is **Naama Bay**, a long beach with a host of luxury resorts and diving centres. For those wanting to stay above water, tourists are taken in glass-bottomed boats to observe the magnificent multicoloured world of the coral reef from above. For others, there are diving-centre boats that will take snorkellers as well as scuba divers and allow you to make fascinating drift dives in the open sea. Here, in the Strait of Tiran, you can observe manta rays, sharks, tuna, dolphins and, occasionally, sea turtles.

Another spectacular sight is the long reef under the cliffs to the west of the **Ras Umm Sidd** lighthouse. Reachable from land, here you can admire a forest of gorgonians, huge Napoleon fish and, sometimes, barracuda.

ENVIRONS: A 29-km (18-mile) journey by jeep along the coast road north of Sharm el-Sheikh brings you to the 600-sq km (232-sq mile) **Nabq National Park**. This coastal park on the edge of the desert boasts crystal-clear lagoons and the most northerly mangrove forest in the world, which extends for 4 km (2.5 miles) along the shoreline. The hardy mangroves are able to live in salt water, making this an extremely important environment, linking land to sea. It is used as a feeding ground by migratory birds, including storks, herons and many species of birds of prey. You can also spot desert foxes, gazelles, ibexes and hyraxes.

Gazelle at watering hole, Ras Muhammad National Park

Ras Muhammad National Park ⑥

Road map E7. 20 km (12.5 miles) S of Sharm el-Sheikh. 🛬 🚌 *to Sharm el-Sheikh, then taxi.* 🔆 *daily.* 🖭 🎫

ON THE SOUTHERN TIP of the Sinai peninsula, where the waters of the Gulf of Suez and the Gulf of Aqaba converge, is a park instituted in 1983 to protect the incredibly varied coastal and marine environment. It includes extensive coral reefs, a lagoon, mangroves and a rugged desert coastline, and there is a series of well-marked trails leading to the most interesting spots. Among the most beautiful of these is the Ras Muhammad headland, the southernmost point in Sinai. Formed from fossilized corals, the headland is surrounded by beautiful reefs. The diving sites are very varied, with both reefs and wrecks to explore. There are also long, sandy beaches and a fascinating Shark Observatory.

Entrance to Ras Muhammad National Park

Diver exploring coral reef in the Red Sea, surrounded by glittering shoal of sweeper fish ▷

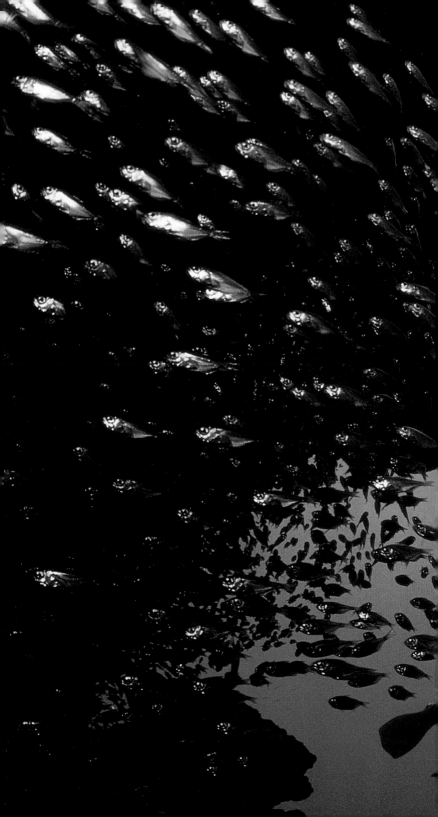

St Catherine's Monastery **7**

A COMMUNITY OF GREEK ORTHODOX MONKS has lived here, in the shadow of Mount Sinai, almost uninterruptedly since the monastery was founded in AD 527 by Byzantine emperor Justinian. It replaced a chapel built in 337 by St Helena, mother of Emperor Constantine, at the place where tradition says that Moses saw the Burning Bush. The monastery was named after St Catherine only in the 9th or 10th century, after monks claimed to have found her body on nearby Mount Catherine.

Library
The collection of priceless early Christian manuscripts is second only to that in the Vatican Library in Rome.

★ Icon Collection
Most of the monastery's 2,000 icons, such as this one of St Theodosia, are kept here, in the Icon Gallery. A selection is always on public view in the Basilica.

The Walls of Justinian, built in the first half of the 6th century, are part of the complex's original structure.

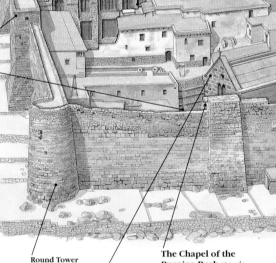

The Burning Bush
This spiny evergreen is said to be from the same stock as the bush from which Moses heard God's voice, instructing him to lead his people out of Egypt to the Promised Land.

Round Tower

The Chapel of the Burning Bush stands where it is claimed the miraculous bush seen by Moses originally grew.

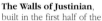

★ Basilica of the Transfiguration
This magnificently decorated church owes its name to the 6th-century Mosaic of the Transfiguration in the apse. It can be glimpsed behind the gilded iconostasis that dates from the early 17th century.

STAR FEATURES

★ **Basilica of the Transfiguration**

★ **Icon Collection**

Bell Tower

This was built in 1871. The nine bells were donated by Tsar Alexander II of Russia and are nowadays rung only on major religious festivals.

The Mosque was created in 1106 by converting a chapel originally dedicated to St Basil.

VISITORS' CHECKLIST

Road map E6. Sinai, 90 km (56 miles) W of Dahab and Nuweiba. ✈ 10 km (6 miles) NE of monastery. 🚌 from Taba, Nuweiba or Dahab to St Catherine's Village (El-Milga), then taxi 3.5 km (2 miles). Petrol available at monastery. ◯ 9am–noon Sun–Thu. ● Greek Orthodox hols. ☎ (062) 470 343. Admission free, but offerings welcome.

Monks' quarters

St Stephen's Well

Dispensary

Guest house

Monastery Gardens

In the orchard lies the cemetery, from which the monks' bones are periodically exhumed and transferred to the nearby Charnel House.

To Charnel House

The elevated entrance, reached by a pulley system, used to be the only access.

The underground cistern was dug to store fresh water from the monastery's springs.

Visitors' entrance

Well of Moses

One of the monastery's main water sources, this is also known as the Well of Jethro, as Moses is said to have met his future wife, Jethro's daughter, here.

St Catherine of Alexandria

St Catherine is one of the most popular of early Christian female saints. Her legend, not recorded before the 10th century, recounts that she was a virgin of noble birth, martyred in Alexandria in the early 4th century. After being tortured on a spiked wheel (hence the Catherine wheel), she was beheaded. Her body was then transported by angels to Sinai, where it was found, uncorrupted, some six centuries later by the local monks.

Detail from icon showing angels setting down the body of St Catherine in Sinai

Exploring St Catherine's Monastery

FORTIFIED BY MASSIVE CURTAIN WALLS, the monastery lies at the head of Wadi el-Deir (Valley of the Monastery), surrounded by high, red granite mountains. It is inhabited by about 20 Greek Orthodox monks, who follow the rule of St Basil, and the only buildings normally open to visitors are the Basilica and the Charnel House. Despite this and the constant crowds of pilgrims and tourists, the remote location in the heart of Sinai and spectacular, rugged scenery are awe-inspiring. For the reasonably fit, there are well-marked paths to the top of Mount Sinai and other nearby peaks.

Coptic Cross in monastery wall

Rock steps leading to the Gate of Confession on Mount Sinai near St Catherine's Monastery

Inside the monastery

Entry nowadays is through a small postern in the curtain wall, whose impressive thickness varies from 1.8–2.7 m (6–9 ft). Some sections of wall survive from the monastery's origins in the 6th century, but large-scale rebuilding took place in the 14th century, after an earthquake, and in 1800, on Napoleon's orders.

The monastery's Basilica was built in AD 527 with three aisles in typical Byzantine style. Eleventh-century, carved wooden doors open into the narthex (porch), where some of the monastery's splendid icons, all painted on wood, are displayed. The collection is exceptional for its size and quality, and because it contains the only examples of Byzantine

painting to have survived the Iconoclast era (726–843). Among them are a *St Peter* (5th–6th century), a *Christ in Majesty* (7th century), both in encaustic painting, and the *Ladder of Paradise* (7th century).

Carved cedar doors, made in the 6th century, lead into the central nave, which contains 12 columns topped by grey granite capitals and hung with icons showing the saints of the months of the year. The marble floor and coffered ceiling are 18th century. The iconostasis, dating from 1612, is by a Cretan monk, Jeremiah the Sinaite. The large figures represent Christ, the Virgin Mary and Saints Michael, Nicholas, Catherine and John the Baptist.

Behind it can be glimpsed the exceptionally beautiful 6th-century Mosaic of the Transfiguration decorating the roof of the apse. It shows Christ surrounded by Elijah, Moses and the Disciples John, Peter and James. In the apse, (often closed), on the right, is a marble coffin containing the remains of St Catherine.

The Chapel of the Burning Bush, behind the apse and also usually closed to the public, is the holiest part of the monastery. It was built on the site where God is thought to have appeared to Moses for the first time (Exodus 3: 2–4). Tradition says that the bush itself (*see p222*) was moved outside when the chapel was built.

The library has over 3,000 manuscripts in Greek, Coptic, Syriac, Arabic, Georgian, Armenian and Old Slavonic. The oldest is the 5th-century *Codex Syriacus*, one of the earliest existing copies of the Gospels.

St Catherine's has, uniquely for a Christian monastery, a mosque within its walls. It was built for the Bedouin who worked in the monastery and also as a way of avoiding attacks by the Muslims.

Outside the walls

In the gardens (*see p223*) are the monks' cemetery and the Chapel of St Triphonius. The latter's crypt holds the Charnel House containing the bones of deceased monks. The robed skeleton is that of Stephanos, a 6th-century guardian of the path to Mount Sinai.

Moses receiving the tablets inscribed with the Ten Commandments from God, 6th-century wall painting, St Catherine's Monastery

Chapel of the Holy Trinity on the summit of Mount Sinai

ENVIRONS: According to tradition, **Mount Sinai** (Gebel Musa, the Mountain of Moses) is the Biblical Mount Horeb, where Moses spent 40 days and received the Ten Commandments (Exodus 24). Two paths climb to the 2,286-m (7,500-ft) summit from behind the monastery, both requiring three hours' walking. The route said to have been taken by Moses is the most tiring as it consists of 3,700 rock steps cut by the monks and called the Steps of Repentance. There are several votive sites along it: **Moses' Spring**, which gushes from a small cave; a chapel of the Virgin Mary; the **Gate of Confession**, where a monk once heard pilgrims' confessions; and **St Stephen's Gate**.

A cypress-shaded plain, 700 steps below the summit, is the so-called Amphitheatre of the Seventy Elders of Israel, where those who accompanied Moses stopped, leaving him to go to the top alone. It is also called Elijah's Hollow, as Elijah is said to have heard the voice of God here. It contains **St Stephen's Chapel** and is where people spending the night on the mountain are asked to sleep. This is also where the second, longer but easier, path joins the first. Camels can be hired to this point, but the final 700 steps have to be done on foot.

On the summit is the small **Chapel of the Holy Trinity** (often closed). It was built in 1934 on the ruins of a 4th–5th-century church and is said to be where God spoke to Moses from a fiery cloud. Inside, frescoes represent the life of Moses. Nearby is a small,

12th-century mosque and the cave where Moses spent the 40 days. The summit offers grandiose views – on clear days as far as the Gulf of Aqaba – but is often crowded. If you join the many who go up to see the sunrise or sunset, take a flashlight and warm clothes. The paths are well marked.

Other lonelier, longer hikes in the region include one to the top of **Mount Catherine** (Gebel Katarina), Egypt's highest peak. Angels supposedly transported St Catherine of Alexandria's body here, away from her torturers' wheel.

Where the Nuweiba–Feiran road meets the St Catherine's road, a dirt road leads 6 km (4 miles) to the **Blue Desert**. Here, in 1980–81, large rocks over an area of 15 sq km (6 sq miles), were painted blue, to symbolize peace, by Belgian artist Jean Verame, with Egyptian president Sadat's approval.

Feiran Oasis ❽

Road map E6. Sinai, 60 km (37 miles) W of St Catherine's Monastery.

THIS IS THE LARGEST and most fertile oasis in Sinai, verdant with date palms, tamarisks and cereal fields. Just south of the Bedouin village of adobe houses is a small, modern convent built with stone from the Byzantine bishop's palace which formerly stood here.

The oasis was the earliest Christian site in Sinai. Many chapels already existed here when, in 451, it became the seat of a bishopric. This governed St Catherine's Monastery until the 7th century, when Feiran's bishop was deposed for heresy and the city fell into ruin. Excavations have revealed its fortified walls, several churches and many other buildings. Feiran is said to be the place where Joshua defeated the Amalekites (Exodus 17).

Shaded gardens surrounding the convent in the Feiran Oasis

THE BEDOUIN OF THE SINAI PENINSULA

In Arabic the word *bedu* means "desert dwellers" and refers specifically to the nomadic tribes that live in Saudi Arabia, the Negev and Sinai. For centuries the Bedouin have lived in close contact with nature, depending for their livelihood on the breeding of sheep, goats and camels. Those in Sinai descend from the peoples who arrived from the Arabian Peninsula from the 14th to the 17th century. The last 20 years of the 20th century have seen a drastic change in their customs and traditions. Today, about 25,000 Bedouin live in Sinai. Many are still nomadic livestock breeders, while others live in permanent camps in wood and corrugated-iron dwellings, making their living as guides, desert tour operators, or by working in large hotels on the coast.

TRAVELLERS' NEEDS

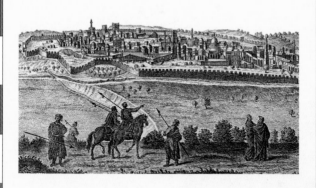

WHERE TO STAY 228-239
RESTAURANTS, CAFÉS AND BARS 240-251
SHOPS AND MARKETS 252-259
ENTERTAINMENT IN
THE HOLY LAND 260-263

WHERE TO STAY

JERUSALEM OFFERS an impressive range of accommodation: from the luxury of the King David and the American Colony hotels, to the plain but welcoming hospices of the various Christian communities, which cater for pilgrims and tourists alike. You will find even more varied accommodation in the rest of the Holy Land. Across Israel, kibbutz hotels offer moderately priced accommodation with good facilities and attractive country settings. Field schools are located near many of the country's nature reserves, and have cheaper, more basic rooms. By the Dead Sea there are many hotels and health resorts, while by the Red Sea and along the Sinai coast, large tourist villages offer water sports and diving. Those who want to cater for themselves will also find many options at a range of prices, from rented villas and apartments to the many excellent youth hostels and camp sites. The listings on pages 232–9 give full details on a selection of accommodation to suit every budget.

Doorman at the King David Hotel

The towering Sheraton Hotel, Tel Aviv

GRADING AND FACILITIES

AT LEAST for the moment, there is no official hotel grading system in Israel, although hotels in Jordan do have their own rating system, with the best (4–5 stars) being comparable to a standard international hotel. Most of the Israeli hotels lie within the medium to high price range, with excellent levels of service and amenities. Rooms are normally equipped with air-conditioning, televisions and minibars, with other facilities often including fitness centres, pools, and business suites. Most hotels also have bars and restaurants, as well as a dining area where a large buffet-style breakfast is served.

For disabled travellers, many hotels have wheelchair access, and bathrooms and other facilities which have been specially adapted. The largest hotels in the Jewish areas are also equipped to satisfy the needs of practising Jews. These are classed as kosher hotels, and they observe the main Jewish religious laws, especially those concerning the Shabbat and *Kashrut*. Many have synagogues and automatic lifts which can be used during the Shabbat rest.

Larger hotels and tourist villages, such as those by the Red Sea, offer private beaches, scuba diving and a range of water sports; while the Dead Sea hotels, often more akin to health resorts, are ideal for those in need of pampering, with their therapeutic hot spas.

PRICES

COMPARED TO Western standards, hotel prices in Israel and Jordan are usually rather high, although the same level of accommodation and service will cost you significantly less in Sinai. Hotel rates fluctuate widely, depending on the season and the various Christian, Muslim and Jewish holidays, so make sure to verify the price before booking. The price of a room almost always includes breakfast, but not other extras. In Israel the room price also includes local taxes, although you can avoid the 17 per cent VAT by paying in foreign currency or on credit card. US dollars, especially, are taken almost everywhere, and all major credit cards are accepted.

In Jordan and Sinai the situation is slightly different. In the large hotels and tourist villages in Sinai all costs over and above the basic room price are subject to double taxation if paid together with the final bill, or on credit card. You can avoid this by paying in cash at the time. Also, listed room rates in Sinai and Jordan exclude tax, which can be as much as 23 per cent, so make sure that you know the final cost. Credit cards are accepted in both Sinai and Jordan, but when using cash, note, that while most major currency is taken in Sinai, you can only use dinars in Jordan.

BOOKING A HOTEL

DURING CERTAIN PERIODS of the year, such as Christmas and Easter, or during Jewish holidays – Passover, Rosh ha-Shanah, Yom Kippur, Sukkoth and Hannukah *(see pp34–7)* – finding accommodation can be a real problem, especially in Jerusalem. In Israel as a whole, you may also have difficulty finding a room during the hottest months of

◁ **Diners at a restaurant overlooking the harbour at Old Jaffa**

A reception room at the luxurious American Colony Hotel, Jerusalem

July and August, as this is the busiest time of year, with many Israelis also taking their own holidays.

It is, therefore, always wise to book well in advance, and the **Israel Hotel Association**, the **Kibbutz Hotel Chain**, field schools, youth hostels and some local bed-and-breakfast associations all have centralized booking services, which are often accessible via the internet and e-mail. The same also applies to many independent hotels and guest houses. If you do need to make arrangements yourself over the phone, most hotel staff can speak good English.

KIBBUTZ HOTELS

T HESE HOTELS were first established as a source of supplementary income for the largely agricultural kibbutzim, and are completely separate from the very basic type of accommodation offered to those on kibbutz working holidays *(see p277)*. Located mostly in the country, they are ideally placed for visitors wanting a relaxing country break or a base near some of the region's archaeological attractions. Here again there is no grading system: accommodation ranges from very plain lodgings on working kibbutzim, offering bed and breakfast, to more comfortable (albeit informal) hotel complexes with restaurants, swimming pools and other facilities. Most of the hotels are members of the **Kibbutz Hotel Chain** (KHC), the largest hotel group in Israel. As well as providing accommodation, they also organize package tours, adventure breaks, organized nature tours and fly-drive holidays. These can often be good options, as, owing to their often remote locations, many kibbutz hotels are not served by public transport, and may only be convenient if travelling by car.

Kibbutz hotels are very popular among the Israelis for their own vacations, especially during the Jewish holidays and in July and August. It is consequently difficult to find accommodation during these times, unless you book well in advance. Prices usually range between NIS 200–700 for a double room and breakfast, depending on the type of kibbutz and the season.

SELF-CATERING

I N JERUSALEM and throughout the rest of Israel you can find a wide selection of property to rent, from smart city apartments to luxury country homes. The cost can vary considerably, depending on the type of property you require, but if you are a large family or party, then it can often work out very reasonably when compared to the same length of stay in a hotel. One of the biggest agents dealing with rented holiday homes in Israel is **Homtel**.

CHRISTIAN HOSPICES AND GUEST HOUSES

T HIS TYPE of accommodation, mainly in Jerusalem and near the holy sites, is a popular and inexpensive alternative to hotels. Clean and unashamedly basic, they are often centrally located, and for many are an ideal place to stay for a few nights. You don't have to be a practising Christian to lodge at the Christian hospices, but at times the house rules can be quite strict (you must leave the room early in the morning and the doors are locked at 10–11pm). For unmarried couples it may also be difficult to find a double room. Many guest houses have over the years become bona fide hotels, with their own special charm and character. In this case, prices are slightly higher, although they are still good value when compared to the large hotels.

Enjoying the view of Jerusalem's Old City from the terrace at the King David Hotel

Youth Hostels

For those on a tight budget youth hostels are ideal, and often the cheapest places to stay in Israel. They have no age limits either, so you will find a mixture of people staying at them, from young backpackers to many older travellers. There are plenty of hostels to choose from, with around 32 **Israel Youth Hostel Association (IYHA)** hostels, affiliated to Hostelling International, as well as a large number of independent ones. In Sinai and Jordan there are no proper hostels with an official national association, but there are many cheap hotels and dormitories which serve the same purpose.

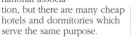

A direction sign to a hostel in the Old City, Jerusalem

Hostels in Israel are located in the major tourist areas – Jerusalem, Tel Aviv, Eilat and Galilee – and throughout the rest of the country. Most offer single, double, and family rooms as well as the more usual dormitories, with prices starting between NIS 40 and NIS 120 per person. Israeli hostels are generally modern, with basic facilities and clean, simple accommodation. The price includes linen, and in the IYHA hostels it also includes breakfast, which you are required to pay for. In the

independent hostels you can pay for the room only, and be entirely self-catering.

If you plan to stay at IYHA hostels for any length of time, you may want to pay for membership. While this is not compulsory, it does entitle you to preferential rates, and may be more cost-effective.

As well as providing basic accommodation, the IYHA also offers package tours. A range of different itineraries includes full dinner, bed-and-breakfast at a choice of hostels, and passes for public transport and national parks. They also organize fly-drive packages, which can be a cheap and easy way of seeing the country if you want to follow your own, more flexible, holiday schedule.

Field Schools

There are 24 Field Study Centres in Israel, run by the **Society for the Protection of Nature in Israel (SPNI)**. These are located in the vicinity of some of Israel's major natural reserves, and were established as a way of promoting a better understanding of the country's natural environment and history through organized educational holidays, lecture programmes

and summer schools. This is still their main focus, and their varied selection of organized holidays revolves around the region's diverse history, archaeology, geology, flora and fauna.

If you would prefer to visit these areas on your own, these centres will also often offer accommodation at a daily rate. The rooms are simple but clean, and all include a private bathroom and air-conditioning. They mostly sleep between four and six people, although some double rooms are also available. If you are paying on a room-only basis, the cost is generally less than NIS 190 per person, although prices for the organized holidays can vary significantly depending on the type of itinerary. Booking in advance is obligatory, and the SPNI's centralized booking office can also reserve rooms at some of the kibbutz hotels located in the natural reserves and parks.

Resort Hotels

Many visitors to the Holy Land go simply to relax and to enjoy the fabulous weather, golden beaches and warm clear waters. Concentrated along the Mediterranean coast, and by the Red Sea, numerous modern hotels, and holiday villages, offer a huge range of holiday facilities.

Holiday-makers relaxing on one of the beautiful beaches at Eilat, on the Red Sea coast

Sunbathing by the Dead Sea

Along the Mediterranean coast, resort hotels cater for sun-worshippers and water sports enthusiasts. Their extensive beaches and many recreational facilities mean that you could easily spend your entire holiday here. For those who want to make excursions, though, many of the prominent sites, including the major cities of Jerusalem and Tel Aviv, are only a short journey away.

By the Red Sea, scuba diving is the main attraction for many visitors, as it offers some of the best in the world. Many hotels run scuba diving courses for beginners, and arrange boat trips out to the best dive sites. There are also excellent beaches and other water sports to choose from.

Away from the coast, Sinai has some fascinating desert areas, and hotels run Jeep trips to the interior. The Red Sea is, however, very isolated from the rest of Israel, and not an ideal base for those also wanting to explore outside of Sinai.

The resorts around the Dead Sea are quite different to others in the Holy Land, and are ideal for those needing to unwind. They are mainly health resorts, taking advantage of their location next to the steaming, mineral-rich waters of the Dead Sea. Their unique facilities include revitalizing hot spas, and a range of elaborate health treatments using the famous local mud.

CAMPING

THERE ARE CAMPSITES across Israel for those wanting to spend time under canvas and visit more remote places. Details can be obtained from the **Society for the Protection of Nature in Israel (SPNI)** or from tourist information offices. Prices start from NIS 12 per person, increasing at sites with better facilities. These may include launderettes,

electricity points, shops, bars and swimming pools. Some places will also hire out tents or trailer homes.

Campsites in Jordan and Sinai are much less common, with fewer facilities. They are found only in some of the more popular national parks and at some Red Sea resorts.

In Israel, camping rough is also quite common, but choose a secluded public area and leave the site tidy if you want to avoid problems. Places such as the West Bank and Gaza Strip are totally no-go areas, as are all military and border zones. If in doubt, check first. Also be very aware of your possessions and personal safety, especially if in a remote area and alone. Make sure that you have protection against mosquitoes, and check thoroughly for other unwanted guests, such as scorpions.

Camping in the woods near the Sea of Galilee

DIRECTORY

BOOKING A HOTEL

Israel Hotel Association
29 Hamered Street,
PO Box 50066,
Tel Aviv, Israel.
((03) 517 0131.
FAX (03) 510 0197.
@ infotel@israelhotels.
org.il
W www.Israelhotels.org.il

KIBBUTZ HOTELS

Kibbutz Hotel Chain (KHC)
1 Smolanskin Street,
PO Box 3193,
Tel Aviv, Israel 61031.
((03) 524 6161.

FAX (03) 527 8088.
@ yael@kibbutz.co.il
W www.kibbutz.co.il

SELF CATERING

Good Morning Jerusalem
9 Coresh Street,
PO Box 966,
Jerusalem, Israel.
((02) 623 3459.
FAX (02) 625 9330.
@ gmjer@netvision.net.il
W www.accommodation.
co.il

Homtel
Home Association of
Jerusalem,
PO Box 7547,
Jerusalem,
Israel 91074.
((02) 645 2198.
W www.bnb.co.il

CHRISTIAN HOSPICES AND GUEST HOUSES

Christian Information Centre
Jaffa Gate
(opposite David Tower).
((02) 627 2692.
FAX (02) 628 6417.

YOUTH HOSTELS

Israeli Youth Hostel Association (IYHA)
Jerusalem International
Convention Centre,
PO Box 6001, Jerusalem,
Israel 91060.
((02) 655 8400.
FAX (02) 655 8432.
@ iyhytb@iyha.org.il
W www.youth-hostels.
org.il

FIELD SCHOOLS

Society for the Protection of Nature in Israel (SPNI)
13 Heleni Hamalka St,
Jerusalem,
Israel.
((02) 624 4605 (shop),
(02) 625 7682 (office).
W www.spni.org.il

CAMPING

Society for the Protection of Nature in Israel (SPNI)
4 Hasfela St,
Tel Aviv,
Israel 66183.
((03) 638 8674.

Choosing a Hotel

THE HOTELS IN THIS GUIDE have been selected across a wide price range for the excellence of their facilities, location or character. Many have a highly recommended restaurant. The chart below first lists hotels in Jerusalem by area, followed by a selection in the rest of the Holy Land. The price ranges are given in US dollars. For more details on restaurants, see pages 246–51.

	NUMBER OF ROOMS	CREDIT CARDS	PRIVATE PARKING	SWIMMING POOL	RESTAURANT
JERUSALEM					
MUSLIM QUARTER: *Our Lady of Zion* $$ Ecce Homo Convent, 41 Via Dolorosa. **Map** 4 D2. **C** *(02) 627 7293.* **FAX** *628 2224.* **@** *eccehomo@inter.net.il* In a superb location, this hospice has clean, simple rooms and a magnificent view of the Old City from the roof. Doors locked at 11pm.	28				●
CHRISTIAN AND ARMENIAN QUARTERS: *Casa Nova* $ Casa Nova Street. **Map** 3 B3. **C** *(02) 627 1441.* **FAX** *626 4370.* This simple Christian hospice maintains a high quality of cleanliness and comfort. Its location and the good value for money it offers make it popular with Catholic groups, so book well in advance. Doors locked at 11pm.	89				
CHRISTIAN AND ARMENIAN QUARTERS: *Maronite Monastery Hospice* $ Omar Ibn el-Khattab Sq. **Map** 3 B4. **C** *(02) 628 2158.* **FAX** *627 2821.* This hospice occupies one of the most beautifully-kept buildings in the area. Rooms are very clean and well-maintained and the restaurant is good. As it is small and very popular, book in advance. Doors locked at 10:30pm.	22				●
CHRISTIAN AND ARMENIAN QUARTERS: *Christ Church Guest House* $$$ Omar ibn el-Khattab Square, Jaffa Gate. **Map** 3 B4. **C** *(02) 628 2999.* **FAX** *627 7730.* **@** *christch@netvision.net.il* Recently renovated, this is one of the oldest Christian hospices in Jerusalem. Rooms are small, plain and comfortable. Good range of services. Very popular, so book well in advance.	32	■			●
MOUNT OF OLIVES AND MOUNT ZION: *Mount of Olives* $$ 53 Mount of Olives Rd. **Map** 2 F3. **C** *(02) 628 4877.* **FAX** *626 4427.* **@** *info@mtolives.com* Close to the Mosque of the Ascension, this family-run hotel is clean and quiet. Eleven of the rooms and the one suite have panoramic views.	61	■			●
MOUNT OF OLIVES AND MOUNT ZION: *Jerusalem Panorama* $$$ Ras el-Amud St, Hill of Gethsemane. **C** *(02) 627 2277.* **FAX** *627 3699.* **@** *jenorama@netvision.net.il* Although the area is not well served by public transport, this hotel offers good service and facilities for the price. Fine views, but rooms overlooking the street can be noisy.	74	■	●		●
MOUNT OF OLIVES AND MOUNT ZION: *Seven Arches* $$$ Main Road, Mount of Olives. **Map** 2 F4. **C** *(02) 626 7777.* **FAX** *627 1319.* **@** *svnarch@trendline.co.il* A large, modern hotel *(see p107)* with its location on the summit of the Mount of Olives providing spectacular views. Rooms are comfortable and the service courteous.	197	■	●		●
MODERN JERUSALEM: *A Little House in the Colony* $$ 4a Lloyd George St, German Colony. **C** *(02) 563 7641.* **FAX** *563 7645.* **@** *melonit@netvision.net.il* Once a Templar hospice, this quiet, comfortable little hotel, set among greenery, is a 10-minute walk from the Old City.	19	■	●		
MODERN JERUSALEM: *El-Zahra* $$ El-Zahra St. **Map** 2 D2. **C** *(02) 628 2447.* **FAX** *628 2418.* **@** *reservation@netours.com* This small, family-run hotel in a quiet alleyway is known for its friendly atmosphere and service. Good value for money.	14	■			●
MODERN JERUSALEM: *St Andrew's Scottish Hospice* $$ 1 David Remez St, off King David St. **C** *(02) 673 2401.* **FAX** *673 1711.* This hospice has a comfortable reading room and large, simple bedrooms, though those facing Hebron Road can be noisy. The breakfast is superb. Early booking is essential.	19	■	●		

Price categories are per night for two people occupying a standard double room, with tax, breakfast and service included:
$ under US $50
$$ US $50–100
$$$ US $100–175
$$$$ US $175–250
$$$$$ over US $250.

CREDIT CARDS
Major credit cards accepted (American Express, MasterCard, Visa, Diners Club).

PARKING
Attended car park provided at the hotel or very close by.

SWIMMING POOL
Private swimming pool for hotel guests.

RESTAURANT
Good restaurant, open to non-residents.

Hotel		Number of Rooms	Credit Cards	Parking	Swimming Pool	Restaurant
MODERN JERUSALEM: *Jerusalem Hotel* Nablus Rd, PO Box 19130. Map 1 C2. & FAX (02) 628 3282. @ raed@jrshotel.com An old, converted, Arab house with spacious rooms, which are all differently decorated in traditional style. The service cannot be bettered. Excellent business facilities and a good restaurant. Book well in advance.	$$$	14	■			●
MODERN JERUSALEM: *Notre Dame* 1 Ha-Tsankhanim Rd. Map 1 B3. (02) 627 9111. FAX 627 1995. Built in 1904, this hospice is part of a Vatican ecumenical and cultural centre. Very comfortable and good value. Book well in advance.	$$$	150		●		●
MODERN JERUSALEM: *Ritz* 8 Ibn Khaldun St. Map 1 C1. (02) 627 3233. FAX 628 6768. This recently renovated hotel offers all comforts and extremely courteous service. One of the few in east Jerusalem with a fitness centre.	$$$	102	■	●		●
MODERN JERUSALEM: *YMCA Three Arches* 24 King David St. Map 1 A4. (02) 569 2692. FAX 623 5192. @ y3arches@netvision.net.il The only hotel in Jerusalem run jointly by Jews, Christians and Muslims. Large rooms. Good service and sports facilities. *(See also p118.)*	$$$	56	■	●	●	●
MODERN JERUSALEM: *Dan Panorama Jerusalem* 39 Keren ha-Yesod St. Map 1 A5. (02) 569 5695. FAX 623 2411. @ panoramajlm@danhotels.com In a convenient location, with comprehensive facilities and attentive service, this hotel makes a good choice if you are not looking for character or views.	$$$$	292	■	●	●	●
MODERN JERUSALEM: *Hyatt Regency* 32 Lekhi St. (02) 533 1234. FAX 581 5947. @ hyatt@jer.co.il A pleasant, modern hotel with a wide range of services and superb sports facilities. Many of the upper rooms have fine views.	$$$$	503	■	●	●	●
MODERN JERUSALEM: *Mount Zion* 17 Hebron Rd. (02) 568 9555. FAX 673 1425. @ hotel@mountzion.co.il Built in 1882 as a hospital, this hotel has comfortable, well-furnished rooms, if lacking in character. Some have views of the Judaean Desert, Old City and Hinnom Valley. First-rate fitness centre.	$$$$	142	■	●	●	●
MODERN JERUSALEM: *St. George* 8 Salah ed-Din St. Map 1 C1. (02) 627 7232. FAX 628 2575. In the heart of the New City's Arab quarter, this hotel is well located, but lacks character. Rooms on Salah ed-Din Street can be noisy.	$$$$	140	■	●		●
MODERN JERUSALEM: *Addar Suite Hotel* 53 Nablus Rd. Map 1 C1. (02) 626 3111. FAX 626 0791. This hotel faces the American Colony. Each suite has two phone lines, satellite TV, video and CD player. Rooms are large.	$$$$$	21	■	●		
MODERN JERUSALEM: *American Colony* 2 Louis Vincent St. Map 1 C2. (02) 627 9777. FAX 627 9779. @ reserv@amcol.co.il The most historic and atmospheric hotel in Jerusalem. It consists of a complex of buildings with rooms of differing sizes and styles. The restaurant is excellent. *(See also p123.)*	$$$$$	84	■	●	■	●
MODERN JERUSALEM: *Jerusalem Hilton* 7 King David St. Map 1 B4. (02) 621 1111. FAX 621 1000. @ jrshitw@netvision.net.il Opened in 1997, this hotel offers excellent service and facilities. Many rooms have views of the Judaean Desert. Very expensive.	$$$$$	380	■	●	■	●

For key to symbols see back flap

<table>
<tr><td>

Price categories are per night for two people occupying a standard double room, with tax, breakfast and service included:
$ under US $50
$$ US $50–100
$$$ US $ 100–175
$$$$ US $175–250
$$$$$ over US $250.

CREDIT CARDS
Major credit cards accepted (American Express, MasterCard, Visa, Diners Club).

PARKING
Attended car park provided at the hotel or very close by.

SWIMMING POOL
Private swimming pool for hotel guests.

RESTAURANT
Good restaurant open to non-residents.
</td></tr>
</table>

	NUMBER OF ROOMS	CREDIT CARDS	PARKING	SWIMMING POOL	RESTAURANT

MODERN JERUSALEM: *King David* $$$$$
23 King David St. **Map** 1 B4. (02) 620 8888. **FAX** 620 8882.
@ danhtls@danhotels.co.il
The most prestigious hotel in the western part of the city, popular with Israeli government guests and used for state ceremonies. Large garden and pool. High standard of decor and facilities.

| 237 | ■ | ● | ■ | ● |

FURTHER AFIELD: *Laromme* $$$$$
3 Jabotinsky St. (02) 675 6667. **FAX** 675 6777. @ managmnt@laromme-hotel.co.il
Built in the 1980s, this hotel is conveniently central. The rooms are rather small, but well-appointed and pleasant. The upper rooms face east and have good views. Efficient service.

| 294 | ■ | ● | ● | ● |

FURTHER AFIELD: *Mount Scopus* $$
10 Nablus Rd. (02) 582 8891. **FAX** 582 8825. @ mountscopus@netvision.net.il
In a very attractive Arab residential area, this hotel has large, comfortable rooms, but the street is noisy in the early morning.

| 65 | ■ | ● | | ● |

FURTHER AFIELD: *Neve Museum-Rabin* $$
1 Avigad St. (02) 678 0101. **FAX** 679 6566. @ rabin@iyha.org.il
One of the newest, most modern hotels in Jerusalem. It is quiet, comfortable and close to the Israel Museum, bus stops and taxi ranks.

| 77 | ■ | ● | | ● |

FURTHER AFIELD: *Notre Dame de Sion Guesthouse* $$
23 Ha-Oren St, Ein Kerem. (02) 641 5738. **FAX** 643 7739. @ sionek@netvision.net.il
This peaceful, stone-built hospice outside the town (10 minutes' drive from the centre) has simple, spacious rooms and a large garden. Book early.

| 26 | ■ | | | |

FURTHER AFIELD: *Ambassador* $$$
Nablus Rd, Sheikh Jarah. (02) 582 8515. **FAX** 582 8202.
In a lovely location, this comfortable, recently renovated hotel is known for its good service and peaceful atmosphere. However, the area is not well served by public transport.

| 122 | ■ | ● | | ● |

FURTHER AFIELD: *Kibbutz Ramat Rachel* $$$
Ramat Rachel. (02) 670 2555. **FAX** 673 3155. @ resv@ramatrachel.co.il
A quiet and comfortable hotel, with an excellent gym and swimming pool (heated in winter). Ten minutes' drive from the Old City and Bethlehem. Rooms on the ground floor open directly onto lawns.

| 164 | ■ | ● | ■ | ● |

THE COAST AND GALILEE

AYELET HA-SHACHAR: *Kibbutz Ayelet ha-Shachar* $$$
Road map C2. (06) 693 2611. **FAX** 693 4777. @ atlashot@netvision.net.il
This simple kibbutz, 17 km (11 miles) NE of Safed, lies at the foot of Mount Hermon. Popular with tour groups so book in advance.

| 144 | ■ | ● | ■ | ● |

CAESAREA: *Dan Caesarea* $$$$
Road map B2. (06) 626 9111. **FAX** 626 9122.
Surrounded by one of the most beautiful parks on the coast, this quiet hotel is next to the only 18-hole golf course in Israel, and a 5-minute drive to the sea and the ruins of Caesarea.

| 114 | ■ | ● | ■ | ● |

CARMEL FOREST: *Carmel Forest Spa Resort* $$$$$
Road map B2. (04) 830 7888. **FAX** 832 3988.
More state-of-the-art health club than hotel, this spa near Caesarea only accepts guests over 16 years old. Book massages and other treatments when booking rooms. No smoking or mobile phones.

| 126 | ■ | ● | ■ | ● |

KFAR PEKIIN: *Peki'in Youth Hostel and Family Guesthouse* $$
Road map C2. (04) 957 4111. **FAX** 957 4116.
A modern, well-appointed hostel in a village in the hills close to Safed. Activities help guests understand local Druze life and culture.

| 50 | ■ | ● | | ● |

NAHSHOLIM: *Nahsholim Seaside Resort* ⓈⓈ 88
Nahsholim. **Road map** B2. ☎ *(06) 639 9533.* FAX *639 7614.*
@ hotel@nahsholim.org.il
A tourist village with simple, comfortable houses, good facilities for children and safe swimming at the private beach. Close to Caesarea. Book very early for stays in July and August. 🔲 🔲 🔲 🔲 🔲 ✿

NAZARETH: *Casa Nova Nazareth* Ⓢ 67
Casa Nova St. **Road map** B2. ☎ *(06) 645 6660.* FAX *657 9630.*
The traditional lodging place for Catholic pilgrims in Lower Galilee, this hospice is run by Franciscan friars. It is clean, simple and cosy, and has recently been renovated. Book well in advance. 🔲 🔲

NAZARETH: *Nazareth Marriott* ⓈⓈⓈ 260
Nazareth Ilit. **Road map** B2. ☎ *(06) 602 8235.* FAX *602 8222.*
@ nazareth.marriott@heihotels.com
An American-style, modern hotel, known for its good facilities, efficient service and great location rather than for its character. 🔲 🔲 🔲 🔲

ROSH PINA: *Auberge Shulamit* ⓈⓈⓈ 4
Road map C2. ☎ *(06) 693 1494.* FAX *693 1495.*
This old house, in one of the oldest Jewish settlements in Galilee, is decorated with exquisite taste and attention to detail. The breakfasts are superb. Weekends are booked up months in advance, so do likewise. 🔲

ROSH PINA: *Mitspe Hayamin* ⓈⓈⓈⓈ 84
Road map C2. ☎ *(06) 699 9666.* FAX *699 9555.*
In the hills east of Safed, this hotel offers all sorts of relaxation techniques for body and mind. A great place to unwind. The restaurant features home-grown organic produce. Book rooms and massages together. 🔲 🔲 🔲 🔲

SAFED: *Ruth Rimonim Inn* ⓈⓈⓈⓈ 78
Howard Johnson Plaza, Artists Colony. **Road map** C2. ☎ *(06) 699 4666.*
FAX *692 0456.* @ smichael@ildc.co.il
In the heart of Safed, a group of old houses has been renovated and transformed into one of Galilee's most attractive hotels. 🔲 🔲 🔲 🔲 ✿

SEA OF GALILEE: *Scottish Guesthouse* ⓈⓈ 46
1 Gdud Barak St, Tiberias. **Road map** C2. ☎ *(06) 672 3769.* FAX *679 0145.*
@ scottie@rannet.com
Full of character, this former hospital has fine views and a lovely garden. An oasis of peace in the town centre. Book ahead for weekends. 🔲 🔲 🔲

SEA OF GALILEE: *YMCA* ⓈⓈ 13
Gdud Barak St, N of Tiberias. **Road map** C2. ☎ *(06) 672 0685.* FAX *672 5943*
A lovely building with character in a prime, lakeside location. Good amenities. The rooms facing the lake are the best. Book in advance. 🔲 🔲

SEA OF GALILEE: *Kibbutz Nof Ginosar* ⓈⓈⓈ 174
Ginosar. **Road map** C2. ☎ *(06) 670 0300.* FAX *679 2170.*
@ ginosar@netvision.net.il �W www.ginosar.co.il
On the lakeside with a fine beach, this is one of the best possible choices for a stay by the Sea of Galilee. Rooms are simple, pleasant and comfortable. Busy on summer weekends. A little pricey. 🔲 🔲 🔲 🔲 🔲 🔲 ✡

SEA OF GALILEE: *Vered ha-Galil Guesthouse* ⓈⓈ 18
Korazim. **Road map** C2. ☎ *(06) 693 5785.* FAX *693 4964.*
@ vered@veredhagalil.co.il
A quiet, family-run hotel consisting of individual stone houses with verandas or terraces. It has a simple, but very good restaurant, a swimming pool and a riding school. Pony-trekking available. 🔲 🔲 🔲

SHLOMI: *Shlomit Hostel & Guesthouse* ⓈⓈ 100
Road map B2. ☎ *(04) 980 8975.* FAX *980 9163.*
Modern, comfortable, clean and quiet, for those on a limited budget this unpretentious hostel makes a good base from which to explore the coast, 6 km (4 miles) away, and Galilee. 🔲 🔲 ✿

TEL AVIV: *Dortel Savoy* ⓈⓈ 30
5 Geula St. **Road map** B3. ☎ *(03) 510 2939.* FAX *510 2866.*
In the heart of the district with the liveliest nightlife, this hotel near the beach consists solely of suites. Some rooms have a sea view. Good value for money. 🔲 🔲 🔲 🔲

Price categories are per night for two people occupying a standard double room, with tax, breakfast and service included:
$ under US $50
$$ US $50–100
$$$ US $ 100–175
$$$$ US $175–250
$$$$$ over US $250.

CREDIT CARDS
Major credit cards accepted (American Express, MasterCard, Visa, Diners Club).

PARKING
Attended car park provided at the hotel or very close by.

SWIMMING POOL
Private swimming pool for hotel guests.

RESTAURANT
Good restaurant open to non-residents.

	NUMBER OF ROOMS	CREDIT CARDS	PARKING	SWIMMING POOL	RESTAURANT
TEL AVIV: *Alexander* $$$$ — 3 Havakook St. Road map B3. (03) 546 2222. FAX 546 9346. alexanho@netvision.net.il — In the city centre very close to the beach, this quiet hotel consists solely of suites. Less expensive than neighbouring skyscraper hotels.	48	●	●		●
TEL AVIV: *Metropolitan* $$$$ — 11–15 Trumpeldor St. Road map B3. (03) 519 2727. FAX 517 2626. reserve@metrotlv.co.il www.hotelmetropolitan.co.il — Close to the most picturesque areas of the city, this comfortable hotel offers courteous service. Upper rooms have sea views.	227	●	●	●	●
TEL AVIV: *Dan Panorama* $$$$$ — 10 Kaufmann St. Road map B3. (03) 519 0190. FAX 517 1777. panoramatelaviv@danhotels.com — This modern, international hotel faces the sea in the picturesque southern part of the city. It has a good swimming pool.	490	●		●	●
TEL AVIV: *Radisson Moriah Palace* $$$$$ — 155 Ha-Yarkon St. Road map B3. (03) 521 6666. FAX 527 1065. radisson-moriah-il@ibm.net — This comfortable, well-appointed, international-class hotel lies near Tel Aviv's marina within five minutes' drive of the city centre. The facilities are excellent.	355	●	●	●	●
TEL AVIV: *Sheraton* $$$$$ — 115 Ha-Yarkon St. Road map B3. (03) 521 1111. FAX 523 3322. shtelviv@netvision.net.il www.sheraton-telaviv.com — In the centre of the city, this is a high-rise, luxury hotel. Many rooms have fine views.	345	●	●	●	●
TEL AVIV: *Tel Aviv Hilton* $$$$$ — Independence Park. Road map B3. (03) 520 2222. FAX 527 2711. — This is the most luxurious of all the seafront hotels, offering the best facilities and with panoramic views from its upper floors.	581	●	●	●	●
YEHIAM: *Kibbutz Yehiam* $$ — Road map B2. (04) 985 6057. FAX 985 6085. betteva@yechiam.org.il www.camon.co.il/yechiam — In the hills 23 km (14 miles) NE of Acre, this kibbutz hotel is built among the ruins of a Crusader castle. The standard rooms are simple; the new ones have more style. Very quiet. Book well in advance.	52	●	●	●	●

THE DEAD SEA AND THE NEGEV DESERT

	NUMBER OF ROOMS	CREDIT CARDS	PARKING	SWIMMING POOL	RESTAURANT
EIN GEDI: *Ein Gedi Hostel* $ — Road map C4. (07) 658 4445. FAX 658 4165. — Recently renovated and spartan but comfortable, this hostel makes a good base for exploring the Dead Sea and the Ein Gedi nature reserve. Guests benefit from reduced rates at Ein Gedi Health Spa.	50	●	●		●
EIN GEDI: *Ein Gedi Guest House* $$ — Road map C4. (07) 659 4222. FAX 658 4328. eg@kibbutz.co.il — Overlooking the Dead Sea and Ein Gedi oasis, this kibbutz has small, comfortable rooms, but the restaurant is no more than adequate. The price includes a shuttle bus and entry to Ein Gedi Health Spa.	120	●	●	●	●
JERICHO: *Jericho Resort Village* $$$ — PO Box 162. Road map C3. (02) 232 1255. FAX 232 2189. reservation@jericho-resort.com — Lying just outside the town on the road leading up the Jordan Valley, this is a recently-built complex of apartments and spacious bungalows overlooking a pool. Good restaurants and bars.	106	●	●	●	●

MITSPE RAMON: *Ramon Inn*   ⑤⑤⑤   96
1 Ein Akev St. **Road map** B5. ☏ *(07) 658 8822.* ℻ *658 8151.*
@ ramonmgr@isrotel.co.il
Built at the town's highest point, this comfortable hotel is ideally situated
for touring the Negev Desert. No lifts, but upper rooms look out over the
Ramon crater. Good Middle Eastern restaurant. ▤ ✿

NEVE ZOHAR: *Nirvana*   ⑤⑤⑤⑤   388
Hamei Zohar, N of Neve Zohar. **Road map** C4. ☏ *(07) 668 9444.*
℻ *658 4345.*
This huge luxury resort hotel on the Dead Sea has pools, spas and tennis
courts, as well its own cinema and nightclub. ▤ 24 🛏 🏃 ♿ ⬆ 🚗 ✿

NEVE ZOHAR: *Sheraton Moriah Plaza*   ⑤⑤⑤⑤   220
Hamei Zohar. **Road map** C4. ☏ *(07) 659 1591.* ℻ *658 4238.*
Near to *Nirvana*, this is the other big hotel in the area. Along with many
similar facilities, it has the largest private beach in the resort and all the
rooms have views over the Dead Sea. ▤ 24 🛏 🏃 ♿ ⬆ 🚗 ✿

QUMRAN: *Kibbutz Almog Holiday Village*   ⑤⑤   81
Kikar ha-Yarden, Almog. **Road map** C3. ☏ *(02) 994 5201.* ℻ *994 2447.*
Set in green and peaceful surroundings, this kibbutz is halfway between
Jericho and the Dead Sea. Guests get reduced rates at Qumran *(see p171)*,
the Ein Fashka oasis and all the area's beaches. ▤ 🏃 ♿ ✿

QUMRAN: *Kibbutz Kalya*   ⑤⑤   64
Kikar ha-Yarden, Almog. **Road map** C3. ☏ *(02) 994 2833.* ℻ *994 2710.*
Another peaceful kibbutz next to Kibbutz Almog and with the same
facilities. Individual rooms and family suites available. ▤ 🏃 ♿

WESTERN JORDAN

AJLUN: *Al Rabad Castle*   ⑤⑤   32
Road map C3. ☏ *(02) 642 0202.* ℻ *(06) 463 0414.*
Set among pine trees, this clean, simple hotel offers very courteous service.
The restaurant is very good and attractively located. Good value for money.
▤ 24 🛏 ♿ ⬆

AMMAN: *Hisham*   ⑤⑤   23
Abufirs St, Jabal Amman. **Road map** C3. ☏ *(06) 464 4028.* ℻ *464 7540.*
@ hishamhotel@net.com.jo Ⓦ www.hishamhotel.com
Peaceful and discreet, this small hotel is in a good location and offers both
good service and good value for money. ▤ 24 🛏 🏃 ♿ ⬆

AMMAN: *Torino*   ⑤⑤   15
Summet St, Sweifiyeh. **Road map** C3. ☏ *(06) 586 3052.* ℻ *586 3051.*
@ torino@torino-hotel.com
This hotel, much favoured by business visitors, consists of mini-
apartments. Efficient, courteous service. ▤ 24 🏃 ⬆

AMMAN: *Le Meridien Amman*   ⑤⑤⑤   300
Queen Noor St, Shmeisani. **Road map** C3. ☏ *(06) 569 6511.*
℻ *567 4621.* @ meridien@go.com.jo
A lavish, but rather uninspiring hotel towards the edge of the city centre.
Good general facilities. ▤ 24 🛏 🏃 ♿ ⬆

AMMAN: *Intercontinental*   ⑤⑤⑤⑤   475
Al Kulliyah al-Islamiya, Jabal Amman. **Road map** C3.
☏ *(06) 464 1361.* ℻ *461 5833.*
The premier venue for top-level congresses, this international-class hotel has
large, well appointed rooms and good sports facilities. There is a popular
café and an excellent bookshop in the lobby. ▤ 24 🛏 🏃 ♿ ⬆

MADABA: *LuLu's Pension*   ⑤   13
POB 14. **Road map** C4. ☏ *(08) 543 678.* ℻ *547 617.* @ yasirsh@yahoo.com
Small, clean and welcoming, this hotel is barely 10 minutes' walk from
the town centre and Madaba's famous mosaics.

PETRA: *Petra Forum Resthouse*   ⑤⑤   225
Wadi Musa. **Road map** C5. ☏ *(03) 215 6011.* ℻ *215 6977.*
Next to Petra's ticket gate, this hotel is reasonably comfortable, if a little
plain. The Nabataean tomb in the courtyard has been converted into a bar
and there is a great view over the mountains from the pool. ▤ 🛏 ♿ ⬆

For key to symbols see back flap

Price categories are per night for two people occupying a standard double room, with tax, breakfast and service included: $ under US $50 $$ US $50–100 $$$ US $ 100–175 $$$$ US $175–250 $$$$$ over US $250.	CREDIT CARDS Major credit cards accepted (American Express, MasterCard, Visa, Diners Club). PARKING Attended car park provided at the hotel or very close by. SWIMMING POOL Private swimming pool for hotel guests. RESTAURANT Good restaurant open to non-residents.	NUMBER OF ROOMS	CREDIT CARDS	PARKING	SWIMMING POOL	RESTAURANT
PETRA: *Petra Palace* $$ Wadi Musa. **Road map** C5. ((03) 215 6723. FAX 215 6724. @ ppwnwm@go.com.jo The cheapest of the hotels near the entrance to Petra, it is comfortable and simple with friendly service.	83	■	●	■	●
PETRA: *Mövenpick* $$$$ POB 214, 718101 Wadi Musa. **Road map** C5. ((03) 215 7111. FAX 215 7112. @ petra@moevenpick.ch An ultra-modern hotel in a prime position with a panoramic view of Petra's rocks. Comprehensive range of facilities.	183	■	●	■	●
PETRA: *Taybet Zaman* $$$$ Taybet Zaman. **Road map** C5. ((03) 215 0111. FAX 215 0101. @ petramph@go.com.jo Perched on a mountain ridge 14 km (8 miles) from Petra, this fascinating hotel is a renovated Bedouin village. Its studied simplicity is luxurious and the service is excellent. Magnificent sunset views.	105	■	●	■	●
SWEIMEH: *Mövenpick* $$$$ POB 815538, 11180 Amman. **Road map** C4. ((05) 325 2020. FAX 325 2030. @ dseezamp@mp.go.com.jo A luxury, village-style resort with health and beauty spas. Located on the Dead Sea, 45 km (28 miles) southwest of Amman.	225	■	●	■	●

THE RED SEA AND SINAI

	NUMBER OF ROOMS	CREDIT CARDS	PARKING	SWIMMING POOL	RESTAURANT
AQABA: *Aqua Marina I* $$ King Hussein St. **Road map** F5. ((03) 201 6250. FAX 203 2630. @ aquama@go.com.jo Of the three Aqua Marina hotels in Aqaba, this is the only one on the beach. It has superb sports facilities.	64	■	●	■	●
AQABA: *Coral Beach* $$$ Corniche St. **Road map** F5. ((03) 201 3523. FAX 201 3614. A quiet, reasonably comfortable hotel, next to the Royal Palace and right on the seashore.	100	■	●	■	●
DAHAB: *Nesma Resort Hotel & Diving Centre* $$ Dahab. **Road map** F6. ((062) 640 320. FAX 640 321. A group of domed houses with plain, but light and spacious rooms. There is a good restaurant, a magnificent pool and excellent diving facilities.	33	■	●	■	●
DAHAB: *Novotel Dahab* $$ Dahab. **Road map** F6. ((062) 640 301. FAX 640 304. This hotel lies on an attractive beach that is sheltered from sandstorms. Rooms are quiet, well-appointed and clean. Those with a sea view are better, but more expensive. There is an attractive pool. Very good value for money.	141	■	●	■	●
DAHAB: *Hilton Dahab* $$$ Dahab. **Road map** F6. ((062) 640 310. FAX 640 424. The Hilton has a fine position on a lagoon, a large, well-kept garden, elegant rooms and excellent sports facilities.	114	■	●	■	●
EILAT: *Eilat Hostel* $$ Mitzraim St. **Road map** F5. ((07) 637 0088. FAX 637 5835. A modern, clean, efficient hostel in the town centre, facing the sea.	100	■	●		●
EILAT: *Reef* $$$ Coral Beach. **Road map** F5. ((07) 636 4444. FAX 636 4488. A cosy, family-run hotel on the beach. Stunning sunset views. Good value, but the pool-side rooms are noisy until the evening.	79	■	●	■	●

EILAT: *Ambassador Hotel* $$$$
Coral Beach. **Road map** F5. ☎ *(07) 638 2222.* FAX *638 2200.*
@ info@ambassador.co.il
Well located near the coral reef reserve, 4 km (2 miles) from the town
centre, this hotel is clean and good value. No views. 🔲 🛗 🏃 ➶

40

EILAT: *Orchid* $$$$
Coral Beach. **Road map** F5. ☎ *(07) 636 0360.* FAX *637 5323.*
@ orchid@netvision.net.il W www.orchid.netvision.co.il
A curious, Thai-style holiday village on a mountain ridge away from the
bustle of the northern beach around Eilat. It has spacious rooms and a good
restaurant. Well located for exploring the coral reef. 🔲 24 🛗 🏃 ➶

137

EILAT: *Eilat Princess* $$$$$
Coral Beach. **Road map** F5. ☎ *(07) 636 5555.* FAX *637 6333.*
@ princess@isdn.net.il
Eilat's best hotel, but not the most expensive, is somewhat isolated at the
end of a wadi near the Egyptian border. Impeccable service. The beach is
small, but is within the coral reef reserve. 🔲 24 🛗 🏃 ♿ 🔼 🚲 ✿

420

NUWEIBA: *Nuweiba Hilton Coral Resort* $$$
Nuweiba. **Road map** F6. ☎ *(062) 520 320.* FAX *520 327.*
A quiet, well-appointed hotel/seaside village with courteous, efficient
service. The beach is attractive and the hotel has good sports facilities.
🔲 24 🛗 🏃 ♿ 🔼 🚲 ➶

200

ST CATHERINE'S MONASTERY: *El Wadi el-Muquddus* $$
Sinai. **Road map** E6. ☎ *(062) 470 225.*
The cleanest and best-managed of the hotels and hospices at St
Catherine's – the only one where the accommodation is worth the price.

75

SHARM EL-SHEIKH: *Umbarak Sharks Bay* $
Sharks Bay. **Road map** E7. ☎ *(062) 600 942.* FAX *600 944.*
@ umbi@sinainet.com.eg
Umbarak consists of a small village with chalets on the beach and on the
hill, as well as hotel rooms. Scuba divers are drawn to one of the most
peaceful locations on the Sinai coast. Very good value. 🚲 ➶

75

SHARM EL-SHEIKH: *Novotel Sharm el-Sheikh* $$$
Sharm el-Sheikh. **Road map** E7. ☎ *(062) 600 172.* FAX *600 193.*
The hotel's best feature is its isolated situation close to the Ras Muhammad
National Park. Good facilities and service. 🔲 24 🛗 🏃 ♿ 🔼 🚲 ➶

152

SHARM EL-SHEIKH: *Coral Bay* $$$$
Tiger Bay, Sheikh Coast. **Road map** E7. ☎ *(062) 601 610.* FAX *600 843.*
A self-contained city of white houses and well-kept gardens on a beautiful
part of the coast. The entire bay is at the disposal of hotel guests, and has
one of the best diving centres in Sinai. 🔲 24 🛗 🏃 ♿ 🔼 🚲 ➶

750

SHARM EL-SHEIKH: *Sonesta Sharm El Sheikh* $$$$
Naama Bay. **Road map** E7. ☎ *(062) 600 725.* FAX *600 733.*
The Sonesta's beach may not be very large, but it is still the most peaceful
at Naama Bay. Built in "Moorish" style, the hotel has fine pools and offers
cordial, efficient service. 🔲 24 🛗 🏃 ♿ 🚲

329

TABA: *Basata* $
44 km (27 miles) S of Taba. **Road map** F5. ☎ & FAX *(062) 500 481.*
In Arabic *basata* means "simplicity", and this cluster of straw huts on a
lovely, isolated beach lives up to its name. Its guiding principle is respect
for the environment and all the vegetarian food is organic. They also serve
good fish. Bicycles, flippers, snorkels and masks can be hired. 🏃 ♿ 🚲

20

TABA: *Salah ed-Deen Village* $$
4 km (2 miles) S of Taba. **Road map** F5. ☎ *(062) 530 340.* FAX *530 343.*
In a small bay in front of a Crusader castle, the village is simply, but
tastefully, built out of stone. Polite service and a relaxing atmosphere.
🔲 24 🏃 ♿ 🚲

114

TABA: *Hilton Taba* $$$
Taba. **Road map** F5. ☎ *(07) 632 6222.* FAX *632 6660.*
A luxury hotel with excellent facilities just across the border from
Israel. The rooms on the upper floors have a sea view, but the best
accommodation is in the Nelson Village cottages, which face the beach.
🔲 24 🛗 🏃 ♿ 🔼 🚲 ➶

410

For key to symbols see back flap

RESTAURANTS, CAFÉS AND BARS

MIDDLE EASTERN FOOD is often overshadowed by other more glamorous world cuisine, and as such, the Holy Land has been seen by many as a gastronomic desert. Often simple and unpretentious, the food is, however, usually tasty and substantial *(see pp242–3)*. A constantly changing restaurant culture reflects the huge interest in food in the Holy Land, and many restaurants are of a very high standard, offering a wide range of Middle Eastern food sure to excite even the most sceptical palate.

Vendor selling the iced drink *tamahindi*

Aside from the native cuisine, there are many other restaurants offering more international food, reflecting the broad ethnic mix of the Holy Land. You can find South American, Chinese, Indonesian, Italian and French food, along with the ever popular American fast food. There are also many busy and informal cafés, which offer a cheaper, more limited menu. For a quick snack, street food revolves around the *shawarma* and *falafel* stalls, which can be found almost everywhere.

OPENING HOURS

IN JERUSALEM and Tel Aviv especially, you will see people eating at all hours of the day, seated outside at cafés and restaurants or walking along the street with a pitta or *boureka*. In the evening though, people tend to eat late, and spend a long time over their meals. Eating is a big social and family event, with children accepted in many restaurants. Most dining is *al fresco*, and restaurants often stay open until after midnight, especially in the big cities and during the summer. However, restaurants are not always open all week, especially the Jewish ones. These always close for Shabbat (sundown on Friday until after sundown on Saturday), as well as for Yom Kippur, Shavuot,

and the first and last day of Sukkoth and Passover. In addition, throughout Israel, all Jewish-owned restaurants, whether kosher or not, are closed on Holocaust Day and Remembrance Day *(see p34)*.

TYPES OF RESTAURANT

FOOD IS A MAJOR part of Middle Eastern life, and there is a huge range of places to eat, from the trendy and expensive city restaurants of Jerusalem and Tel Aviv to the countless cheaper cafés and take-aways. With no fixed cuisine of its own, Israeli food is a melting pot of flavours, reflecting the cultural mix of the nation and adopting influences from the Middle East, the Mediterranean, and Eastern Europe. The main Israeli food is that of the Jews,

Dining outside in the spectacular setting of Petra *(see pp196–207)*

largely the Oriental (Middle Eastern) and Ashkenazi (eastern European) communities. Their food is as distinctly different as their origins. Oriental dishes revolve mainly around grilled meats and fish, stuffed vegetables, and a range of *meze*. The Ashkenazi specialities are spicy stews,

Barmen serving coffee at the popular Cinematheque bar in Yemin Moshe, Jerusalem *(see p118)*

The attractive Mamma Mia restaurant in Jerusalem *(see p247)*

such as goulash, fish balls and large, stuffed pancakes, known as *blintzes*.

Other major ethnic groups have also brought their own unique and unusual dishes. Armenian favourites include spicy meat stews and sausages, while the Yemenis are famous for their *malawach* – large, flaky-pastry pancakes, stuffed with a variety of fillings.

Aside from Israeli fare, you can also find restaurants serving more international food, including French and Italian (which tend to be very expensive), and Chinese, Thai and Korean. There are also the usual fast-food chains. Such a selection of restaurants is far more limited if travelling in Jordan or Sinai, however, as most are found in the hotels. Café culture in Israel is huge, and if you are after something cheaper and less substantial, then cafés offer salads, pizzas, club sandwiches and simple pasta dishes that will provide a tasty light meal. Cafés are also great places to sit and soak up the local atmosphere, and join in with Israeli life.

KOSHER RESTAURANTS

THE JEWISH dietary laws of *Kashrut* (literally, fitness), determine many of the eating habits in the Holy Land. To the outsider these can prove very confusing, as you will find that all types of restaurant can be kosher, not just the Jewish ones. This is especially true in Jerusalem, and the more Orthodox parts of the country. In the rest of

Israel, however, more secular Jews do not always adhere to dietary laws, and it poses less of a problem to the visitor.

What these laws mean in practice is that meat considered impure (such as pork, rabbit and horse meat), as well as certain types of seafood (anything without scales and fins), cannot be eaten at all. Animals that are permitted for consumption have to be slaughtered according to Jewish religious practice and cleansed of all traces of blood before cooking. Furthermore, during Passover a kosher restaurant cannot even serve any leavened food, such as bread or pastries.

The major complications of these laws revolve around the fact that meat and dairy produce can never be eaten together in the same meal. Dishes are consequently based on either one or the other, with many of the resulting problems deftly overcome through the use of a range of dairy substitutes.

VEGETARIAN FOOD

AS A VEGETARIAN visiting the Holy Land, your dining options are surprisingly varied. Kosher restaurants serve all types of dairy-only food, such as creamy pasta and yogurt-based dishes, as well as many potato dishes and salads.

Secular restaurants also have a large number of vegetarian options. Much of the cuisine is based around pulses, which are found in anything from houmous to hearty bean stews. Roasted and stuffed vegetables also feature widely, along with a variety of savoury pastries. For a quick vegetarian snack, the *falafel* is hard to beat.

SERVICE, PAYING AND TIPS

THE SERVICE in Israeli cafés and restaurants is not the most attentive and efficient that you will ever encounter. Low wages do nothing to improve the situation, and most waiting staff rely almost entirely on their tips. Service is not generally included on the bill, a fact often well highlighted, and you should expect to tip around 10–15 per cent, depending on the type of establishment.

Throughout Israel credit cards are widely accepted, and most of the restaurants listed in this guide accept all the major types. In the Sinai and Jordan, on the other hand, there is much more of a cash culture, and it is advisable to pay for food using the local currency. If you do choose to pay by credit card you are likely to incur significant extra taxes and charges.

Harbourside restaurant below the old city walls of Acre *(see pp158–9)*

What to Eat in Jerusalem and the Holy Land

Falafel sandwich

THE REGIONAL CUISINE is richly varied, reflecting the diverse origins of the people that have settled here. The predominant flavours and textures are those of the Middle East, with the ubiquitous *falafel* and *shawarma* of the eastern Mediterranean supplemented by dishes from Arab countries as far afield as Yemen and Morocco. Unsurprisingly, you will also encounter bagels, blintzes (filled pancakes) and other Jewish specialities, such as *cholent*, the meat and potato stew prepared for Shabbat.

STARTERS

A meal typically begins with a large selection of starters (*salatim* in Hebrew, *meze* in Arabic) laid out on the table to be shared by all. The food is scooped up with hot, fresh bread. Sometimes the *meze* can constitute a meal in themselves. Most *meze* are vegetarian.

Moroccan cigars *have recently become popular, especially in Jewish restaurants. Minced (ground) meat with lots of black pepper is rolled in thin pastry and fried.*

Tahini *is sesame seed paste, often with parsley, oil, lemon and garlic.*

Tabuleh *is a mixture of bulgur wheat with finely-chopped mint, parsley, spring onion, tomato and cucumber seasoned with oil and lemon.*

Houmous *is chickpea paste with olive oil, garlic and lemon. Common garnishes include whole chickpeas, pine nuts and, occasionally, minced meat.*

Kibbe *are croquettes made of bulgur wheat (burghul or cracked wheat) with meat, onions and pine nuts.*

Pickled vegetables *such as carrots, peppers, cauliflower, cabbage, beetroot and chillies make for a tangy cold dish.*

Peppers

Cabbage

Carrots   Peppers

Peppers and aubergines (eggplant) *are roasted with chopped tomatoes, onions, garlic and chillies.*

STUFFED VEGETABLES

Stuffed courgettes

Stuffed vine leaves

This is a favourite way of preparing a great many vegetables. Some variations can require much time and effort, and the more unusual the "surprise" of the stuffing, the more the result is appreciated. Of the more common dishes, aubergines (eggplant), courgettes (zucchini), pumpkins, carrots, and cabbage and vine leaves are stuffed with minced (ground) meat, herbs and rice, or rice alone, and then baked.

SOUP

In a full meal, soup always follows the starters. Most soups contain vegetables and dried pulses and are very rich in both nutritional value and taste. Many are traditionally cooked for very long periods, blending the flavours and giving them a thick, creamy consistency.

Kibbe soup *contains stewed kibbe, either with or without meat, in a vegetable broth.*

Bean soup *is made with a variety of beans cooked with tomatoes, onions, oil and herbs.*

MAIN DISHES

Meat is usually lamb or chicken, sometimes beef, but never pork. It may be roasted, griddled or grilled (broiled), but is very often cooked on a spit giving it a smoky taste. As with the *meze*, meat dishes are usually ordered for the table to be shared by all.

Lamb or mutton chops *are grilled (broiled) and served with parsley, a dash of lemon and a selection of vegetables.*

Jerusalem mixed grill *is a local speciality of chicken livers, hearts, lights and other offal, sizzled on a griddle with spices and lots of sliced onion, and served in a pitta.*

Shashlik and kebab *are, respectively, pieces of meat and spiced ground meat grilled (broiled) on a skewer.*

Chicken livers *are very popular. They are usually cooked on a griddle and eaten with fried onions.*

Mussakhan *is a Palestinian dish consisting of chicken roasted with almonds, onions and sumac (a red spice) on round pitta bread.*

DESSERTS AND FRUIT

Meals often end with a platter of fruit. The great climatic variations in the region mean that there is a wide variety of locally-grown, fresh fruit all year round including figs, dates, grapes, pomegranates, citrus fruits, mangos and melons. The common alternative to fruit is to choose from a vast range of sweet, sticky pastries filled with chopped pistachios or other nuts, dripping with syrup or honey.

Baklava *consists of layers of paper-thin pastry filled with ground pistachio nuts and almonds soaked in honey or syrup.*

Pomegranates

Konafa *is made of pistachios in a crisp coating of fine pastry threads.*

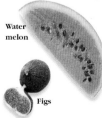

Water melon

Figs

STREET SNACKS AND BREADS

Baking Arab pitta in a clay oven

Falafel (deep-fried balls of mashed chickpeas) and *shawarma* (pressed lamb or turkey grilled on a huge spit) are sold from take-away restaurants on virtually every street. They are stuffed into a pitta bread along with mounds of salad. Many other types of bread are available from bakeries including bagels (unfilled and filled), *challah*, a sweet Jewish, plaited bread made for Shabbat and holy days, and a large, pancake-thin version of pitta called *pitta iraquit* in Hebrew. *Bourekas* are filo pastry filled with *kachkavel* (salty goats' cheese), potato and spinach and then baked.

Falafel on *pitta iraquit*

Bourekas

What to Drink in Jerusalem and the Holy Land

Tea with fresh mint leaves

JEWS AND ARABS ALIKE adore coffee but have different ways of making it. It will be offered to you at any hour of the day or night. Teas of many kinds and herbal infusions are also popular. However, the hot, very dry climate makes water of the utmost importance. It is advisable to carry a bottle of it with you at all times and drink some before you feel thirsty to avoid dehydration. Israel now produces a lot of wine of medium to high quality, but it tends to be expensive. Beer is available in all the areas covered in this guide, but neither the Israelis nor the Arabs consume large quantities, preferring to go to cafés or coffeeshops for socializing.

Enjoying outdoor café life on traffic-free Lunz Street in Jerusalem

WATER AND SOFT DRINKS

IN THE ENTIRE AREA described in this guide, bottled mineral water is readily available everywhere. Although tap water throughout Israel is safe to drink, it is more advisable to drink bottled water because it tastes better, especially in the Red Sea area, where tap water is so heavily chlorinated that it is unpalatable. Always make sure that the bottle is sealed when you buy water.

Bottled fruit juice is also popular, but remember that even juices that are sold as "natural" are really long-life juices produced on an industrial scale. Fruit juices freshly squeezed in front of you, especially citrus and pomegranate, are very good. All non-alcoholic beverages except for freshly-squeezed juice are almost always served very cold and with a lot of ice (which may be made of heavily chlorinated water), so if you don't want your drinks this way, remember to say so when ordering.

Bottled water

BEERS AND SPIRITS

MANY RESTAURANTS and cafés have draught beer, most of which is locally produced. The main Israeli beers are Maccabee, a slightly bitter, light lager, and Goldstar, which is reminiscent of British ale with a dash of malt. Taybeeh, similar to light, south German beer, is found in the Palestinian regions, East Jerusalem and some Israeli bars. Carlsberg is produced in Israel and Heineken in Jordan, both under licence, while most other major European brands are imported, especially into Israel.

Spirits are less widely available, but are always sold in hotel bars throughout the region. The commonest is arak, the typical Mediterranean distillate of anise.

Goldstar beer   **Arak**

COFFEE AND TEA

IN JEWISH AREAS, coffee and tea are drunk in European- or American-style cafés. The most widely available type of coffee is filter coffee, which is always served for breakfast in hotels. Many places also offer espresso coffee, but it is almost always rather weak. For a real espresso, you must ask for a *katzar* (strong coffee). What is called cappuccino almost always has a huge amount of whipped cream added to it. Tea is almost invariably served in tea-bag form, and caffeine-free herbal tea (*zmachim*) is becoming increasingly popular.

Tea and coffee in Arab areas are drunk in coffee-houses (*qahwa*), which serve nothing else – except sometimes traditional water pipes (*nargileh*) to accompany the drink. Arabic coffee (also called *qahwa*) is

strong and aromatic because of the spices, in particular the cardamom, added to it. It is served in tiny cups holding only a few sips. If you do not specify little or no sugar, it always arrives heavily sweetened. To avoid a gritty texture, allow the sediment to settle in the cup first. Arabic tea (*shai*) is more aromatic and stronger than Western-style tea and is also drunk without milk and with a lot of sugar. In restaurants it is often served after a meal with fresh mint leaves (*naana*).

In Arab coffeehouses, if you want Western-style tea, ask for *shai-Libton*; in Arab or Jewish establishments, for Western-style coffee ask for *nes* (short for Nescafé).

Elaborate Arabic coffee set

WINE

Although the middle east was the home of grape cultivation and wine-making, the first two modern wineries in the Holy Land were founded in the mid-19th century. They belonged to Baron Rothschild (at Zikhron Yaakov, not far from Caesarea) and the Salesian fathers (at Cremisan, near Bethlehem). The Salesian estate is still operating. For years it was the only producer of good, dry white wine, but its standards were later matched by the Latrun Trappist monks' winery, which has French vines and uses French wine-making techniques.

An Israeli Chardonnay

The number of vineyards then increased steadily and wine quality has improved dramatically since the early 1980s. The main wine areas are now: Golan and Upper Galilee at around 500 m (1,640 ft) above sea level, with ideal volcanic soil; Lower Galilee, the Jezreel Valley, the Mount Carmel region and Sharon, which are lower and more humid; Samson, the coastal plain south of Tel Aviv; and the hills of Judaea, which have poorer terrain and are very dry. A number of experimental vineyards in the Negev Desert are now in production.

The largest producers are the Carmel Winery, based in Zikhron Yaakov, whose Mizrachi "Private" series is especially good, and the Golan Heights Winery, based in Katsrin, whose main labels are Golan, Yarden, Gamla and Tishbi. Wines from small producers such as Kibbutz Tsora can be excellent.

Jordanian and Egyptian wines are very poor value for their price and, in both countries, imported wine is prohibitively expensive.

Israeli white wines, especially the Chardonnays and Sauvignon Blancs, are generally very enjoyable: often aromatic, sometimes fruity, smooth and full-bodied. Many of the reasonably-priced whites are produced by the Golan Heights Winery.

WINE-GROWING REGIONS OF ISRAEL

KEY

- Golan, Galilee and the Jezreel Valley
- Mt Carmel and Sharon
- Samson
- Judaean Hills
- Negev Experimental Areas

Israeli red wines are also good, but, with some notable exceptions, tend either to lack body or to be slightly heavy. The grapes most commonly used are Carignan, Cabernet Sauvignon and Merlot, with many wines being a blend of the last two. Among the wines now produced by a growing number of small-scale, specialist wine makers are the fine Cabernets produced by Castel, and the Margalit reds.

| Yarden white | Gamla Chardonnay | Tishbi Muscat | Carmel Mizrachi | Margalit red | Kibbutz Tsora |

Choosing a Restaurant

THE RESTAURANTS IN THIS GUIDE have been selected across a wide range of price categories for their value, good food, atmosphere and interesting location. The chart highlights some of the factors which may influence your choice. Restaurants are listed by region, starting with Jerusalem. For Jerusalem map references, see the Street Finder on pages 140–143.

	Price	Credit Cards	Outside Dining	Vegetarian Cuisine	International Cuisine	Good Wine List
JERUSALEM						
MUSLIM QUARTER: *Abu Shukri* 63 El-Wad Rd, corner of Via Dolorosa. **Map** 4 D2. **(** *(02) 627 1538.* This small, simple restaurant serves excellent houmous, *tahini* and freshly baked bread, as well as many other dishes. Very reasonable prices.	$		●	▪		
JEWISH QUARTER: *Quarter Café* Tiferet Yisrael. **Map** 4 D4. **(** *(02) 628 7770.* People stop here for the view rather than for the quality of the food. Close to the Western Wall, it is a handy spot in which to have a drink and a snack while exploring the Old City. ✡	$			▪		
MODERN JERUSALEM: *Falafel* 7 Shlomo Musayof St. **Map** 1 A1. This is a fast-food kiosk in the ultra-Orthodox Mea Shearim district, between a greengrocer's and a Talmudic School. It has no real name, but serves some of the best *falafel* in Israel. Well worth stopping if you are passing.	$			▪		
MODERN JERUSALEM: *Miznom Musa* 30 Jaffa Rd. **Map** 1 B3. Another hole-in-the-wall kiosk, opposite the main post office, where what are perhaps the best *bourekas* in town are served.	$			▪		
MODERN JERUSALEM: *Te Enim* 21 Emek Refaim. **(** *(02) 563 0048.* This small, pleasant place is the best vegetarian restaurant in the city. The menu combines the tastes of many cuisines, including Middle Eastern, Mediterranean, Japanese, Mexican and Indian. Generous portions. ♁ ✡	$	▪		▪		
MODERN JERUSALEM: *Agas ve Tapuach BaKikar* 6 Safra Sq, Russian Compound. **Map** 1 B3. **(** *(02) 623 0280.* In the Russian Compound, near the Old City, this Italian restaurant serves good, home-made pasta dishes and salads. ♁ ✡	$$	▪	●	▪	●	
MODERN JERUSALEM: *Barood* 31 Jaffa Rd. **Map** 1 B3 **(** *(02) 625 9081.* Set in an attractive courtyard, the Barood is tastefully furnished, with background jazz enhancing the mood. The menu is based around the interesting cuisine of the Sephardic (Spanish) Jews. ♿	$$	▪				
MODERN JERUSALEM: *Cacao* 11 Hebron Rd. **Map** 1 B5. **(** *(02) 671 0632.* A haunt of artists, intellectuals and students, inside the Cinematheque. Mediterranean cooking and pleasant, lively surroundings. ♁	$$		●	▪	●	
MODERN JERUSALEM: *Eucaliptus* 4 Safra Sq, Russian Compound. **Map** 1 B3. **(** *(02) 624 4331.* In an old building in the Russian Compound, this is one of the most appealing restaurants in Jerusalem. The food is traditional Middle Eastern and, while often quite simple and rustic, it incorporates the best regional produce and is beautifully prepared. ♿ ♁ ✡	$$	▪	●	▪		
MODERN JERUSALEM: *Gilly's* 33 Hillel St. **Map** 1 A3. **(** *(02) 625 5955.* This simple, unpretentious and popular restaurant is ideal for meat-eaters. The beef and pork in particular are very good and the portions substantial. Prices are very reasonable. ♿	$$	▪				
MODERN JERUSALEM: *HaChaverim shel Sergio* 34 Agrippas St. **(** *(02) 625 5665.* An Italian restaurant near the Makhane Yehuda market. Excellent pizza and antipasti. Ask for the special dishes of the day. ♁ ✡	$$				▪	●

Price categories are for a three-course meal per person, including a half bottle of house wine, tax and service.

⑤ Under US $15
⑤⑤ US $15 – 30
⑤⑤⑤ US $30 – 60
⑤⑤⑤⑤ Over US $60

CREDIT CARDS
Major credit cards accepted (including: American Express, Eurocard, MasterCard, Visa, Diners Club).
OUTSIDE DINING
Garden, courtyard or terrace with outside tables.
VEGETARIAN CUISINE
A good selection of vegetarian dishes available.
INTERNATIONAL CUISINE
Foreign restaurant, or menu offering international dishes.
GOOD WINE LIST
Extensive list of good wines, both regional and international.

	CREDIT CARDS	OUTSIDE DINING	VEGETARIAN CUISINE	INTERNATIONAL CUISINE	GOOD WINE LIST
MODERN JERUSALEM: *Ha Shipudia* ⑤⑤ 6 Ha-Shikma St. ((02) 625 4036. In the heart of the Makhane Yehuda market, this pleasant restaurant serves a range of excellent local dishes, including soups, stuffed vegetables and grilled meats. Good value and attentive service. 🏃 ✡	■		■		
MODERN JERUSALEM: *Kan Zaman* ⑤⑤ 14 Nablus Rd. **Map** 1 C2. ((02) 628 3282. This is the restaurant of the Jerusalem Hotel, and the vaulted ceilings and décor create a typically Arab atmosphere. Palestinian-Arab cuisine is carefully prepared and live Arab music is played at the weekends. 🏃		●	■		
MODERN JERUSALEM: *Le Tsriff* ⑤⑤ 5 Horkanos St. **Map** 1 A3. ((02) 624 2478. This simple restaurant offers informal but efficient service and good rustic food, such as pies and meat dishes. Desserts are also very good. 🏃 ♿	■	●	■		■
MODERN JERUSALEM: *Mamma Mia* ⑤⑤ 38 King George V St. **Map** 1 A3. ((02) 624 8080. One of the first authentic Italian restaurants in town, this attractive establishment excels at light, tasty sauces for its home-made pasta. 🏃 ✡	■	●	■	●	
MODERN JERUSALEM: *Pasha* ⑤⑤ 13 Shimon Ha-Tsadik St. ((02) 582 5162. There is a lively, informal atmosphere here, with efficient service and good Lebanese-Arab cuisine. Try the house specialities. 🏃	■	●	■		
MODERN JERUSALEM: *Philadelphia* ⑤⑤ 9 El-Zahra St. **Map** 2 D2. ((02) 628 9770. Highly recommended for those wanting genuine Palestinian-Arab cooking; the stuffed vegetables and spit-roasted meats are excellent.			■		
MODERN JERUSALEM: *Arabesque* ⑤⑤⑤ American Colony Hotel, 2 Louis Vincent St. **Map** 1 C2. ((02) 627 9777. The Arabesque features various specialities of Palestinian-Arab cuisine, as well as international dishes. The *meze* are excellent, as are the meat and fish.	■	●		●	
MODERN JERUSALEM: *Dalia Renau Bistro* ⑤⑤⑤ 10 Agrippas St. ((02) 625 7647. This small, pleasant restaurant offers an interesting selection of French dishes, including hearty country pies and tempting desserts. ♿	■		■	●	
MODERN JERUSALEM: *Darna* ⑤⑤⑤ 3 Horkanos St. **Map** 1 A3. ((02) 624 5406. Excellent Moroccan cuisine and a good atmosphere. Appetizers, soups and *meze* are very good and the portions substantial. ✡	■	●	■		
MODERN JERUSALEM: *Fink's* ⑤⑤⑤ 13 King George V St. **Map** 1 A3. ((02) 623 4523. This small, old-fashioned establishment is renowned both for its food and its drinks. Fare is eastern European, the goulash being particularly memorable. The choice of house cocktails is staggering.	■			●	■
MODERN JERUSALEM: *Sakura* ⑤⑤⑤ 31 Jaffa Rd. **Map** 1 B3. ((02) 623 5464. Small and simple and in a lovely courtyard, this Japanese restaurant serves excellent sushi, using only the best and freshest fish. ♿	■			●	
MODERN JERUSALEM: *Taverna* ⑤⑤⑤ 2 Naomi St. ((02) 671 9796. A classy, contemporary restaurant, the Taverna also has a superb outlook over southeast Jerusalem, to the Moab mountains in the distance. Food is Mediterranean in style and the desserts are particularly good. ♿ ✡	■				■

For key to symbols see back flap

<table>
<tr><td colspan="2">

Price categories are for a three-course meal per person, including a half bottle of house wine, tax and service.

$ Under US $15
$$ US $15 – 30
$$$ US $30 – 60
$$$$ Over US $60

</td><td>

CREDIT CARDS
Major credit cards accepted (including: American Express, Eurocard, MasterCard, Visa, Diners Club).

OUTSIDE DINING
Garden, courtyard or terrace with outside tables.

VEGETARIAN CUISINE
A good selection of vegetarian dishes available.

INTERNATIONAL CUISINE
Foreign restaurant, or menu offering international dishes.

GOOD WINE LIST
Extensive list of good wines, both regional and international.

</td></tr>
</table>

	CREDIT CARDS	OUTSIDE DINING	VEGETARIAN CUISINE	INTERNATIONAL CUISINE	GOOD WINE LIST
MODERN JERUSALEM: *Arcadia* $$$$ 10 Agrippas St. ((02) 624 9138. Considered by many to be one of the best restaurants in Jerusalem, the simple but elegant Arcadia specializes in creative *nouvelle cuisine*, with excellent meat and fish dishes and sumptuous desserts. &	■	●		●	■
MODERN JERUSALEM: *Mishkenot Sha'ananim* $$$$ Yemin Moshe St. **Map** 1 B5. ((02) 624 1042. With fabulous views over the Old City, this restaurant offers excellent food combining French and Middle Eastern influences. It is not strictly kosher, but all meat is kosher and dairy products are not used.	■	●			■
MODERN JERUSALEM: *Ocean* $$$$ 7 Rivlin St. **Map** 1 A3. ((02) 624 7501. This restaurant, in a fascinating old building in the Nakhalat Shiva district, specializes in fish and has an imaginative, Provençal-style menu. The fresh vegetables are also beautifully prepared with aromatic herbs and garlic. &	■		■	●	■
FURTHER AFIELD: *Abu Shukri* $ Main road, Abu Ghosh. ((02) 533 4963. In the village of Abu Ghosh, near the top of the hill, this restaurant has splendid views over the valley below. It is lively and informal, the service and food are both good and the prices very reasonable. & 🏃		●	■		
FURTHER AFIELD: *Angelo* $$ Main road, Ramallah. ((02) 295 6408. This first-floor restaurant serves fine pizzas from its wood-burning oven, as well as many tasty Middle Eastern dishes.	■		■		
FURTHER AFIELD: *Bardauni* $$ Jaffa St, Ramallah. ((02) 295 1410. The best restaurant in Ramallah. The Palestinian-Arab cooking here is very good, with superb *mussakhan* and delicious *meze*. & 🏃	■		■		
FURTHER AFIELD: *HaMitbach Shel Rama* $$ Nataf, near Abu Ghosh. ((02) 570 0954. Located on a hill terrace with spectacular views. Only local ingredients are used and food is cooked in an Arab stone oven. *Meze*, salads and mutton are all excellent, as is the bread. 🏃 & ● *winter.*	■	●	■		■

THE COAST AND GALILEE

ACRE: *Galileo* $$ Pisan Port. **Road map** B2. ((04) 991 4620. Situated on the old city walls, with views across the Crusader harbour. The excellent fish and spit-roasted meats are the best choices here. 🏃 &	■	●			
BETH SHEAN: *Herb Farm on Mount Gilboa* $$ On Route 667, Mount Gilboa. **Road map** C2. ((06) 653 1093. On the attractive slopes of Mount Gilboa, this restaurant has some amazing views overlooking the Jezreel Valley and is a great place in which to enjoy a meal at sunset. Try the salads and goat's cheese dishes. 🏃	■	●	■		
CAESAREA: *Pundak HaTzalbanim* $$$ Caesarea National Park. **Road map** B2. ((06) 636 1679. Restaurant set on the coast, with views of the ancient port. The simply baked or fried fish is the thing to have here. 🏃 &	■	●			
GOLAN HEIGHTS: *Dag'Al HaDan* $$ Route 99, W of Kiryat Shmona, near Kibbutz Ha-Goshrim & Dan River. **Road map** C1. ((06) 695 0225. A busy fish restaurant with pleasant outside dining, a good atmosphere and courteous service. The local salmon is very good. & 🏃	■	●	■		

HAIFA: *Felafel HaZkenim*   ⓢ
18 Ha-Wadi, Wadi Nisnas. **Road map** B2. 🎧 *(04) 851 4959.*
This restaurant faces *Felafel Michel* across the road. Both establishments
claim to serve the best *falafel* in town, and it would be hard to choose
between them. The *tahini* and houmous are delicious, and the range
of accompaniments is bewildering.

HAIFA: *Felafel Michel*   ⓢ
21 Ha-Wadi, Wadi Nisnas. **Road map** B2. 🎧 *(04) 851 7054.*
Opposite *Felafel HaZkenim (see above),* and just as good.

HAIFA: *Chaim Zimbonia Vegetarian Restaurant*   ⓢⓢ
30 Herzl St. **Road map** B2.
This busy Ashkenazi Jewish restaurant in the city centre serves simple,
but delicious, vegetarian food, as well as some good fish dishes. ✡

NAZARETH: *Diana*   ⓢⓢ
114 Paulus VI Rd. **Road map** C2. 🎧 *(06) 657 2919.*
One of the oldest restaurants in Nazareth, this is something of a local
institution. Try the delicious lamb kebabs and salads. 🏃 ♿

ROSH PINA: *Auberge Shulamit*   ⓢⓢⓢ
David Shuv St. **Road map** C2. 🎧 *(06) 693 1485.*
A top-class restaurant, with great attention paid to detail. The meat and
smoked fish is delicious, and other dishes adopt a Provençal or Italian
flavour. Great views over the valley below. Book well in advance. 🏃 ♿

SEA OF GALILEE: *Ein Camonim*   ⓢ
Amiad Junction, SE of Safed. **Road map** C2. 🎧 *(06) 698 9680.*
A rustic restaurant, located in a barn, where seating is on benches and the
menu is a set price. The simply cooked, fresh, local vegetables and home-
made goat's cheeses are excellent. 🏃 ♿

SEA OF GALILEE: *Vered HaGalil*   ⓢⓢ
Vered ha-Galil, SE of Safed. **Road map** C2. 🎧 *(06) 693 5785.*
In the heart of a farm holiday centre, this restaurant is set in an attractive
stone building. It offers excellent grilled specialities and baked fish,
good salads and great desserts. 🏃 ♿

SEA OF GALILEE: *Dikla*   ⓢⓢⓢ
Beth Gavriel, Zemach area S of Sea of Galilee. **Road map** C2.
🎧 *(06) 670 9302.*
A part of the Beth Gavriel cultural centre and situated in a beautiful spot
overlooking the Sea of Galilee, this restaurant is worth visiting for the
location alone. The food is not quite as remarkable as the setting. 🏃 ♿

SEA OF GALILEE: *Ein Gev Fish Restaurant*   ⓢⓢⓢ
Ein Gev. **Road map** C2. 🎧 *(06) 665 8036.*
Located on a river, this large, rather utilitarian fish restaurant offers
the local St Peter's fish as the house speciality. Main courses are quite
expensive; the starters are better value. 🏃

TEL AVIV: *Barbunia*   ⓢⓢ
192 Ben Yehuda St. **Road map** B3. 🎧 *(03) 524 0961.*
A simple, immaculate restaurant which serves excellent fried
fish at very reasonable prices. Fast, efficient service. ♿

TEL AVIV: *Bebale*   ⓢⓢ
42 Montefiori St. **Road map** B3. 🎧 *(03) 560 2228.*
At this small, simple restaurant, the attraction is the traditional, hearty,
eastern European Jewish country fare. Meat stews and pies are the order
of the day – a unique and substantial gastronomic experience. ♿

TEL AVIV: *Bix*   ⓢⓢ
14 Eliezer Peri St, Tel Aviv Marina. **Road map** B3. 🎧 *(03) 527 2456.*
Located at the marina, with attractive views of the sea and harbour,
this is a very pleasant place to dine on fish and shellfish on summer
evenings. The grilled specialities are highly recommended. 🏃 ♿

TEL AVIV: *Pronto*   ⓢⓢ
26 Nachmani. **Road map** B3. 🎧 *(03) 566 0915.*
The Israeli chef here trained in Italy, and the food reflects it. The innovative
pasta dishes are excellent, as are the meat dishes and the Tuscan
bruschetta. The atmosphere is friendly and the service good. 🏃 ♿

Price categories are for a three-course meal per person, including a half bottle of house wine, tax and service.

$ Under US $15
$$ US $15 – 30
$$$ US $30 – 60
$$$$ Over US $60

CREDIT CARDS
Major credit cards accepted (including: American Express, Eurocard, MasterCard, Visa, Diners Club).

OUTSIDE DINING
Garden, courtyard or terrace with outside tables.

VEGETARIAN CUISINE
A good selection of vegetarian dishes available.

INTERNATIONAL CUISINE
Foreign restaurant, or menu offering international dishes.

GOOD WINE LIST
Extensive list of good wines, both regional and international.

	CREDIT CARDS	OUTSIDE DINING	VEGETARIAN CUISINE	INTERNATIONAL CUISINE	GOOD WINE LIST
TEL AVIV: Bellini $$$ 6 Yekhieli St. **Road map** B3. (03) 517 8486. This restaurant lies in one of Tel Aviv's most picturesque quarters, near the delightful Suzanne Dellal Square. The food is Mediterranean in style, with good gnocchi and delicious aubergine dishes.	■	●	■	●	■
TEL AVIV: Blue $$$ Tel Baruch Beach. **Road map** B3. (03) 699 6620. Located at a private beach, Blue offers superb views with huge windows on three sides. The grilled fish is excellent and the service discreet.	■	●	■		■
TEL AVIV: Margaret Tayar $$$ 8 Retsif ha-Aliya ha-Shniya St. **Road map** B3. (03) 682 4741. Located by the clock tower in the heart of Jaffa, this restaurant serves outstanding fish-based dishes from Libya and Tunisia, including a piquant fish couscous and excellent starters. The food is good value for money.		●			
TEL AVIV: Taboon $$$ Jaffa Port. **Road map** B3. (03) 681 1176. Most of the tables here are outside, along the docks. The speciality is fish marinated in oil, herbs and garlic and cooked in a *taboon* (clay oven). The *meze* are particularly unusual.	■	●	■		
TEL AVIV: Golden Apple $$$$ 40 Montefiori St. **Road map** B3. (03) 566 0931. Run by one of Israel's top chefs and food authors, the Golden Apple is a gastronomic haven, with creative menus strongly influenced by Italian and French *nouvelle cuisine*. The fixed-price lunch offers excellent value.	■			●	■
TEL AVIV: Kapot Tmarim $$$$ 60 Akhad ha-Am St. **Road map** B3. (03) 566 3166. In the middle of the financial district, this classy restaurant offers a unique combination of French *nouvelle cuisine* and traditional Middle Eastern dishes. Book well in advance.	■			●	■
TEL AVIV: Keren $$$$ 12 Eilat St. **Road map** B3. (03) 681 6565. Located in a tastefully restored, old, wooden house, the Keren serves high-class *nouvelle cuisine* in the smart dining room above the first-floor cocktail lounge. Excellent service, but pricey. Book well in advance.	■			●	■
TEL AVIV: Mul Yam $$$$ Yordey Hasira St, Tel Aviv Port. **Road map** B3. (03) 546 9920. One of the best restaurants in the Middle East, specializing in seafood. Try the fresh anchovy salad and cuttlefish pasta with lobster. Prices can vary widely between fixed-price menus and à la carte.	■			●	■
### THE DEAD SEA AND THE NEGEV DESERT					
BETHLEHEM: Abu Kassara $ In front of the main church, Beth Jala, N of Bethlehem. **Road map** B3. A small, simple and cheap place which has no name sign. The chicken dishes, especially the grilled ones, are delicious, as are the *meze*.			■		
BETHLEHEM: Dolphin $$ Al Mahd St. **Road map** B3. (02) 274 3432. A typical, unassuming restaurant, not far from Manger Square, featuring good, fresh fish and tasty *meze*. The service is fast.			■		
BETHLEHEM: Everest $$ Main street in Beth Jala, N of Bethlehem. **Road map** B3. (02) 274 2604. Although obviously a tourist restaurant, located at the highest point of Beth Jala, the food is good and the views wonderful.		●	■		

JERICHO: *Al Rawada* $$
Rouda Park. **Road map** C3. (02) 232 2555.
This attractive restaurant is hidden in a garden of citrus and palm trees, so ask on the main street for directions. The starters, meat dishes and freshly-squeezed lemon drink are excellent. Attentive service.

JERICHO: *Ibrahim* $$
Ein es-Sultan. **Road map** C3. (02) 232 3252.
A tourist restaurant on the main street, this is an agreeable place with reasonable food, although slightly pricey.

WESTERN JORDAN

AMMAN: *Romero* $$
Hassinnen St, opposite Inter-Continental Hotel. **Road map** C3. (06) 464 4227.
A very pleasant restaurant offering courteous service and good food. The garden is delightful in the summer.

AMMAN: *Al Bustan* $$$
Jordan University St, near Times Newspaper. **Road map** C3. (06) 566 1246.
A typical Lebanese restaurant with fast and attentive service, a wide choice of *meze* and some good Arab desserts.

AMMAN: *Bukhara* $$$
Al Kulliyah al Islamiya, Jabal Amman. **Road map** C3. (06) 464 1361.
This Indian restaurant at the Inter-Continental Hotel offers largely Kashmiri cuisine and has a pleasant, relaxed atmosphere.

MADABA: *Dana* $
Al Nuhza St. **Road map** C4. (02) 740 9603.
At this simple Arab restaurant, the *meze* are good and fresh, and the spit-roasted meats very tasty. Extremely reasonable prices.

PETRA: *Al Iwan* $$
Wadi Musa. **Road map** C5. (03) 215 7111.
This is the Oriental restaurant of the Mövenpick Hotel. Impeccable service and a cultured and intimate atmosphere.

PETRA: *Sahtayn* $$
Taybet Zaman. **Road map** C5. (03) 215 0111.
The Bedouin décor here is simple, but cosy. Bedouin food is the speciality, with the roast mutton being particularly delicious.

THE RED SEA AND SINAI

EILAT: *Chopia* $$$
Orchid Hotel, Coral Beach. **Road map** B7. (07) 636 0360.
In a building shipped from Thailand and reassembled inside the hotel, this restaurant has great sea views. Tasty food, but a limited lunch menu.

EILAT: *La Brasserie* $$$
King Shlomo Hotel, North Beach. **Road map** B7. (07) 636 3444.
A great place for those who like American-style steaks and cutlets. The goose liver and stewed veal are also very good.

EILAT: *Oak Room* $$$
Princess Hotel, Taba Beach. **Road map** B7. (07) 636 5555.
This restaurant offers a great variety of choice meats. The mouth-watering steaks are cooked to perfection.

EILAT: *The Last Refuge* $$$
Coral Beach. **Road map** B7. (07) 637 3627.
A boat anchored in a small inlet, this floating restaurant has some outside dining on deck. Good seafood, especially the calamari and cuttlefish.

SHARM EL-SHEIKH: *El Fanar* $$
Near the lighthouse, Ras Umm Sid. **Road map** E7.
In a building inspired by Bedouin tents on a promontory jutting into the Red Sea. Fish is central to the menu, but there are also good pizzas and pasta.

TABA: *Casa Taba* $$$$
Hilton Hotel, Taba. **Road map** B7. (07) 632 6222.
An elegant and classy seaside restaurant, with attractive outside dining. The food is Italian in style and the seafood is excellent, especially the calamari and crayfish. Service is very good, if a little relaxed.

For key to symbols see back flap

SHOPS AND MARKETS

WHEN IT COMES to shopping, the main attraction in Jerusalem is undoubtedly the souks, or bazaars, of the Old City. In comparison with the great bazaars of Istanbul or Cairo, Jerusalem's souks can seem small and overly touristy, but they still reward exploration (see pp256–7). The streets of the Old City away from the souks are also dotted with interesting small shops, handicraft centres, workshops and boutiques. Most other towns and cities throughout the Holy Land also have souks, with particularly good ones

Armenian ceramic tile

in Acre, Amman, Hebron and Nazareth. Anybody intending shopping in the souks must become acquainted with the art of bargaining. In contrast to the traditional nature of the souk, bigger centres such as Jerusalem, Tel Aviv and Amman, all possess modern shopping districts, as well as large American-style malls, filled with familiar brand names from the West.

In Jordan, the major tourist sites such as Petra, Jerash and Madaba have small clusters of tourist-oriented shops where, sometimes, you can find local handicrafts and products of interest.

Fruit and vegetable stall in the souk at Ramallah

OPENING HOURS

IN JERUSALEM there are no strictly-defined opening hours; it depends on the individual proprietor. In general, however, except for food shops, which open quite early, business activity begins at roughly 9am. Some shops close from 1 to 4pm, but most remain open all day until around 7pm. The Old City's souks don't really get going until perhaps 10am and they close around sunset. Many shops and stalls in the souks are closed all day Sunday, as many of the shopowners are Christian, although others are Muslim and they stay closed on Friday instead. During the holy month of Ramadan, Muslim-owned shops close 30 minutes to one hour before sunset. All Jewish-owned businesses in Jerusalem and throughout Israel close from

Friday afternoon to sunset on Saturday for Shabbat. These shops are also closed during Jewish holidays (see pp34–7).

In Jordan the working day is usually divided into two shifts of 9am to 1pm and 4 to 7pm, but there are a great many exceptions to this rule.

HOW TO PAY

MAJOR CREDIT CARDS, such as Visa, American Express and MasterCard, are accepted in almost all shops throughout Israel; travellers' cheques are not. In Jordan and Sinai credit cards are much less widely accepted and, in most places, you will have to pay in cash. It is usual to pay in the local currency (in Jordan and Sinai use of any other currency is illegal), but in Israel, if you are making a large purchase, it is possible to get a discount by paying in US dollars. This

is because transactions made in a foreign currency are not subject to Israeli VAT.

VAT EXEMPTIONS

A WIDE RANGE of goods in Israel is subject to a Value Added Tax (Mam in Hebrew) of 17 per cent. Tourists are entitled to a refund on this for any purchases amounting to over 400 shekels (around US$40). Make sure the shop you buy from has a VAT (or tax) refund sign displayed. You need to ask the sales assistant for a special invoice showing the VAT paid in both dollars and shekels. This is then presented at the VAT counter at the airport at the time of your departure. You must have the purchases with you to cross-check against the invoice. Queues at this counter can be very long, so get there with time to spare.

Examining the wares at an Old City souvenir shop

Malkha Kanyon Mall in Malkha, Jerusalem

DEPARTMENT STORES AND SHOPPING MALLS

ISRAEL HAS a rapidly growing number of large shopping centres and US-style out-of-town malls. Both are filled with standard mall-type outlets that sell everything from greetings cards to electronics items, most of which are imported from Europe and the United States. The largest mall in Jerusalem, and in fact the country, is the **Malkha Kanyon Mall** out in the Malkha suburb of West Jerusalem, close to the new Teddy Stadium. In central Jerusalem, **City Tower** is a multi-storey shopping centre at the corner of Jaffa Road and King George V Street. Tel Aviv's largest mall is the **Ramat Gan** in the eastern suburb of the same name. More centrally located malls in Tel Aviv include the **Dizengoff Centre** on Dizengoff Street and the **Gan ha-Ir Shopping Centre** just north of Rabin Square. As well as extensive shopping opportunities, these malls are always full of good, moderately-priced restaurants, snack bars and cafés. Given that they are air-conditioned, they can be great places for pedestrians to escape from the often stifling heat outside.

BUYING ANTIQUES

IN JORDAN and Sinai it is forbidden to export any antique or archaeological find. The border authorities are extremely thorough in their checks in this regard. On the other hand, in Jerusalem and Israel you may buy antiques and objects from excavations but to take them out of the country you must obtain a free permit from the **Israeli Antiquities Authority** *(see p255)*. You must keep this document with the antiquity at all times and show it upon request.

Only certain shops are officially authorized to deal in objects of this kind, and if you buy from a non-accredited source there is a chance that you may be buying looted goods. **Zadok**, in West Jerusalem, is an authorized specialist and it often has items for sale garnered from recent digs. **Baidun** is one of the better known of a great many antiquities dealers along the Via Dolorosa (there is a whole clutch them on the stretch between El-Wad Road and the Monastery of the Flagellation); it occasionally has pieces dating back as far as the Canaanite era. The **Via Dolorosa Rest House**, in addition to antiques, always has a good selection of lovely high-quality Russian icons.

Be aware that the counter-feiting of antiquities is rife in Israel, especially of Roman and Byzantine-era coins and ancient glassware, so it is a good idea to get specialist advice before buying.

HOW TO BARGAIN

Buying and selling in the Middle East is traditionally a highly ritualized affair, in which bargaining is far more than just haggling for a cheap price. The aim of the exercise is to establish a fair price that both vendor and buyer are happy with. As part of the process, a shopowner may well invite you to have a cup of tea or coffee and may literally turn the place upside down to show you something; you should not feel obliged to buy because of this; it is common sales practice and all part of the ritual.

Bargaining, by the way, is not socially acceptable in city-centre shops, but it is unavoidable in the souks if you don't wish to pay greatly over the odds.

The way to go about it is that once you identify an article that interests you, especially an expensive one, be brave enough to offer half the price quoted by the shopowner. Don't be put off by any feigned indignation on the part of the shopkeeper and only raise your next offer by a small amount. Through offer and counter-offer you should

Haggling over the price – time-consuming but essential to avoid paying over the odds

arrive at a mutually agreeable price. If you don't reach a price you think is fair then simply say thank you and leave. Making to walk away often has the effect of bringing the price plummeting down.

In theory, no one gets cheated because you, the buyer, have set the price yourself; it follows that you are happy with what you have agreed to pay, and the shopkeeper will certainly never sell at a loss.

Where to Shop in Jerusalem and the Holy Land

JERUSALEM'S SOUKS are the first place to look for many of the items produced in this region. The wares here range from T-shirts and printed scarves to religious icons and archaeological artifacts. Jaffa Road is the main commercial centre, while Mea Shearim is the place to look for Judaica. Arts and crafts products can be found in the galleries along King David Street and around Yemin Moshe. Tel Aviv's Nakhalat Binyamin area is a good source of unusual jewellery and is especially worth visiting for the twice-weekly craft market.

![Jewish menorahs for sale in the Old City]

Jewish menorahs for sale in the Old City

RELIGIOUS ARTICLES

FOR CHRISTIAN religious items there are any number of shops along David Street and in the Muristan area of the Old City's Christian Quarter. However, prices are generally lower in Bethlehem, which is where many of these items are made. One place worth visiting here is the **Holy Land Arts Museum** on Milk Grotto Street (it has another shop on Manger Square), which spe-cializes in wooden objects with mother-of-pearl inlay, and inlaid metalwork (damascene).

For Jewish religious articles, try **Ot Ezra** and **Chabad**, both on the Cardo in the Jewish Quarter of the Old City. If you want works in silver, either old or modern, **Zadok** on King David Street is the best place to look. It also specializes in Yemenite filigree.

CERAMICS

THE ARMENIANS produce beautifully coloured ceramics. The attractive street-name plaques you see around the Old City are all Armenian

work. There are two large workshops worth visiting on Armenian Patriarchate Street: one is near the Armenian Convent, the other is opposite the entrance to St James's Cathedral. Another good sales studio is **Jerusalem Pottery** on the Via Dolorosa near the 6th Station of the Cross. East Jerusalem's **Palestinian Pottery**, on Nablus Road opposite the US Consulate, is also worth a look.

ARAB TEXTILES AND RUGS

THE SHOPS and market in the centre of Ramallah are a good place to look for densely embroidered Palestinian textiles. Cushions and bags made from Bedouin textiles are found in most souvenir shops in Israel. Prices vary little, but for Bedouin rugs, you would do better to buy in Jordan. One recommended place is **Madaba Oriental Gifts** in Madaba, opposite the

Church of St George. Two shops in Wadi Musa, close to the entrance to Petra, also have a decent selection.

JEWELLERY

SOME OF THE REGION'S most distinctive jewellery is made by the Bedouin. It is sold at the street markets of Nakhalat Binyamin in Tel Aviv, in Jaffa and at the Thursday market in Beersheba. To make your own necklaces, there are several shops in the Old City's souks that sell all kinds of beads, notably at the corner of David and Aftimos streets. For Jewish and modern Middle Eastern jewellery, including amulets and lucky charms, go to **Sheshet** in West Jerusalem.

FINE ART

FOR PAINTINGS, posters and prints by Israeli artists, visit **Arts and Crafts Lane** (Khutsot ha-Yotser), an arcade of noth-ing but galleries and ateliers just outside the Old City, south of Jaffa Gate. A scattering of more exclusive and expensive galleries can be found along nearby King David Street.

The **Artists' House** is a small sales gallery attached to the Bezalel Art School and has much more interesting work than the purely commercial galleries.

WINE

IF YOU are interested in purchasing some of the many first-rate Israeli wines *(see p245)*, visit **Gafen**. It is the only wine shop in Israel that gives its customers invoices for VAT refunds.

Craftsman hand-knotting the fringe of a rug

HEBRON GLASSWARE

THE FIRST THREE shops on the left-hand side of David Street, going from Jaffa Gate, have the best selection of glassware. However, much lower prices are offered in the souk at Hebron. At Madaba in Jordan, **Madaba Oriental Gifts** has a good range of Hebron glassware, often at prices even lower than those in Hebron.

COSMETICS

THE ARAB TOWN of Nablus is famed for its olive-oil soap, available at almost any East Jerusalem grocer's and in the souks, especially on Khan el-Zeit Street. In Galilee it is sold in many of the souvenir shops, particularly in Nazareth, but at higher prices. The reputed health-giving properties of the Dead Sea are exploited in the cosmetic products made by the two companies, Ahava and Mineral. These are sold

Water pipes, or nargilehs

at all well-stocked pharmacies and at the Duty-Free Shop at Ben Gurion airport. When visiting the Dead Sea, you can buy directly from the **Ahava Factory**, north of Ein Gedi. It is open daily, but closes at 2pm on Fridays.

SOUVENIRS

ONE OF THE MOST popular of Holy Land souvenirs is a Jerusalem Candle (sold everywhere, not just in the Holy City), which is spherical, comes in a variety of sizes and is beautifully coloured and patterned. Sandals, bags and belts are good articles to buy in Jerusalem, and many Muristan and Christian Quarter shops specialize in leatherwork. Copperware is also a good buy, notably coffeepots and trays, often etched with arabesque patterns. A more exotic souvenir is a nargileh, or Arab water pipe. All sorts of olive-wood items are

Making sand-filled bottles, Jordan's most prevalent souvenir

sold in the gift shops on David Street and Christian Quarter Road and in Bethlehem.

For a very different sort of souvenir, an extensive range of recordings of modern and traditional Jewish music can be found at **Tower Records**.

Decorative bottles filled with coloured sand are popular Jordanian souvenirs, especially at Wadi Rum and Petra.

DIRECTORY

SHOPPING MALLS

City Tower
Corner of Jaffa Rd & King George V St, Jerusalem.

Dizengoff Centre
Dizengoff St, Tel Aviv.
(03) 525 1249.

Gan ha-Ir Shopping Centre
71 Ibn Gabirol St, Tel Aviv.
(03) 527 9111.

Malkha Kanyon Mall
Malkha, West Jerusalem.
(02) 679 1333.

Ramat Gan Mall
Ramat Gan,
Tel Aviv.
(03) 570 3105.

ANTIQUES

Israeli Antiquities Authority
Tel Aviv.
(03) 642 4680.

Rockefeller Museum,
Jerusalem.
(02) 620 4690.

Baidun
6th Station of the Cross,
Via Dolorosa, Jerusalem.
(02) 628 2937.

Via Dolorosa Rest House
40 Via Dolorosa,
Jerusalem.
(02) 628 6838.

Zadok
21 King David St,
Jerusalem.
(02) 625 1973.

RELIGIOUS ARTICLES

Chabad
Cardo, Jerusalem.
(02) 627 2217.

Holy Land Arts Museum
Milk Grotto St,
Bethlehem.
(02) 274 4819.

Ot Ezra
8 Cardo,
Jerusalem.
(02) 628 8166.

CERAMICS

Jerusalem Pottery
6th Station of the Cross,
Via Dolorosa,
Jerusalem.

Palestinian Pottery
14 Nablus Rd,
East Jerusalem.

ARAB TEXTILES AND RUGS

Madaba Oriental Gifts
Madaba,
Jordan.

JEWELLERY

Sheshet
34 Emek Refaim St,
Jerusalem.
(02) 654 4857.

FINE ARTS

Arts and Crafts Lane
Mamilla, Jerusalem.

Artists' House
12 Shmuel ha-Nagid St,
Jerusalem.
(02) 625 3653.

WINE

Gafen
42 Emek Refaim St,
Jerusalem.
(02) 561 9617.

COSMETICS

Ahava Factory
Kibbutz Mitspe Shalem,
Route 90, Dead Sea.
(02) 994 5100.

SOUVENIRS

Tower Records
19 Hillel St, Jerusalem.
(02) 624 2002.
1 Allenby St, Tel Aviv.
(03) 517 4044.

Jerusalem's Old City Markets

Jewish skullcaps

THE STREETS in the Muslim and Christian quarters of the Old City form a single large market-place, or souk. However, in the traditional Middle Eastern manner, different areas specialize in specific types of wares. So whereas the stalls of David Street sell little but souvenirs to visiting tourists, the small grocers and bakeries just inside Damascus Gate are frequented on a daily basis by Arab locals. Such areas may not offer much for the visitor to buy, but the aromas and atmosphere amply reward any time spent here.

Damascus Gate Market
Small traders selling home-grown fruit and vegetables, or snacks such as sweet breads and roasted sweetcorn gather every morning on the plaza outside Damascus Gate (see p64).

MODERN JERUSALEM

Muristan
Leather is a speciality of the shops in the Muristan, in the form of bags, belts and purses. Prices are usually not cheap but hard bargaining can bring them down (see p94).

THE CHRISTIAN AND ARMENIAN QUARTERS

Christian Quarter Road
The mainstays of this street are religious souvenirs and richly coloured Palestinian rugs, cushion covers and scarves (see p95).

0 metres   250

0 yards   250

David Street Market
Almost entirely devoted to tourist trinkets, this is where to buy everything from carved olive-wood Nativity scenes to Dome of the Rock paperweights.

Souk Khan el-Zeit
This is a busy shopping street full of bakeries, their windows crammed with sweets and pastries. There are many small grocers and restaurants, which, as the street progresses south, give way to clothes and shoe shops.

El-Wad Road
El-Wad has all kinds of shops, including one that sells nothing but eggs. However, brass-and copperware in the form of trays and coffeepots are a speciality.

THE MUSLIM QUARTER

THE MOUNT OF OLIVES AND MOUNT ZION

Via Dolorosa
Many shops along the Via Dolorosa specialize in small religious items such as rosaries. There are also good shops selling Armenian ceramics (see p62).

THE JEWISH QUARTER

Central Souk
Shops and stalls, some of which are housed in Crusader-era vaulting, sell fruit and vegetables, and other assorted foodstuffs (see p64).

The Cardo
The Cardo is a prime place for Judaica, such as elaborate menorahs, and also for more unusual gifts, including prints and other items of fine art (see p78).

What to Buy in Jerusalem and the Holy Land

Fish pendants

V ISITORS ON THE LOOKOUT for unusual souvenirs, or the products of different cultures and ages, will certainly find something to their liking in Jerusalem, either in the souks and alleyways of the Old City, or in particular districts of the modern city. Some artifacts, such as pottery, brass and silver objects, Bedouin textiles and Arab jewellery, are sold throughout the Holy Land. However, in Jerusalem you will find an especially wide range of Jewish religious articles (while other places concentrate on Christian or Muslim items), and Armenian pottery.

Copper goblets

Firjan **with spirit stove**

Blue Hebron Glass
Most of this attractive glass, in shades of light blue and turquoise, is made to imitate Roman and Phoenician vessels. Some modern designs and full dinner services are also produced.

Copper- and Brassware
Copper plates, jugs, pots, trays and goblets, all usually engraved, are found everywhere. So, too, are traditional firjan (coffee pots) and large platters made of beaten brass.

Armenian Ceramics
The best-known decorative pottery is produced by the Armenian community, which has had a presence in Jerusalem since the 4th century (see pp102–3). It is characterized by the abundant use of blue and yellow, and of floral motifs. The designs are usually intricate and painted on a white ground.

Silver and Pewter Jewellery
The Yemenite tradition of silver filigree work has been extensively adopted by religious and secular jewellers in the Holy Land. Look out also for attractive, modern pewter jewellery set with semi-precious stones, as well as traditional blue glass-eye and khamsa (hand-shaped) lucky charms, popular with Arabs and Jews alike.

Olive-wood Objects
Crucifixes, rosaries, Nativity scenes and figures of Christ, the Virgin Mary and the saints carved in hard, light-coloured and attractively-grained olive wood make evocative souvenirs. The best come from the Bethlehem area.

Blue glass-eye pendants

Modern brooch

Silver *khamsa*

Olive-wood sculpture

Jewish Liturgical Articles

These often beautifully-made objects include the kippah (male skullcap), tallit (pure wool prayer shawl), kiddush (blessing) cup, besamim (spice-holder), mezuzah (prayer container hung at front doors) and shofar (ram's horn blown for Yom Kippur).

Kippah and tallit

Shofar

Silver mezuzah

Silver besamim

Rugs and Fabrics

Robust and vividly coloured Bedouin rugs, cushions and bags made from the cloth formerly used as Bedouin saddle covers, and traditional, finely embroidered Palestinian dresses are popular buys.

Bedouin cushion covers

Bedouin fabrics

Palestinian fabrics

Ancient Household Articles and Coins

Reputable dealers in finds from archaeological sites will often have attractive basalt, earthenware and stone kitchen vessels, small terracotta amphorae and Roman and Phoenician glassware. Coins from many historical periods are fairly plentiful, but beware of fakes.

Beauty Products from the Dead Sea and Nablus

A vast range of creams, soap, salts and Dead Sea mud, using the mineral properties of the unique Dead Sea salt, is sold to alleviate skin conditions. Nablus soap, which has olive oil and less than two per cent caustic soda as its only ingredients, is cheap, fragrant and long-lasting, and is good for use in dry climates.

Nablus soap

Dead Sea lotions

Local Delicacies

Specialist shops stocked with large sacks of nuts, dried fruits, pulses and dried vegetables are fascinating places to explore. They often sell spices, too. All these products make good buys as they are easy to carry, and keep well at home.

Dried apricots

Chickpeas

Mulberries

Almonds

Pistachio nuts

Dried red peppers and aubergines

ENTERTAINMENT IN THE HOLY LAND

Entrance, Performing Arts Centre, Tel Aviv

FOR A RELATIVELY small city, Jerusalem offers a wide range of high-quality entertainment, especially in the fields of music and cinema. It enjoys several months of dynamic artistic and cultural activity a year, although the number of concerts and events decreases before and after the Christmas season. Spring, summer and the period between Christmas and Epiphany mark the height of the various national and international cultural events and festivals. However, the Holy City is only 60 km (37 miles) from Tel Aviv, one of the most lively and interesting cities for entertainment and culture in the entire eastern Mediterranean, so an hour's drive will allow you to find nightlife and culture to suit your tastes every day of the year.

Lively nightlife at a café-bar on Salomon Street in Jerusalem

INFORMATION

THE JERUSALEM POST and the English-language edition of *Ha-Aretz*, both of which are available throughout Israel, carry daily entertainment listings. Both also have extensive cultural supplements on Fridays with detailed listings of events for the week to come. Tourist offices also have abundant events magazines.

In Jordan look out for the *Jordan Times* or visit **books@cafe** in Amman, an internet café-cum-bookshop, whose notice boards provide the best way of finding out what's on in the capital.

BUYING TICKETS

ALMOST ALL concert halls, theatres and cinemas in Israel have credit-card booking lines. There are also ticket agencies, such as **Klaim** and **Bimot** in Jerusalem and **LeAn** and **Hadran** in Tel Aviv.

CLASSICAL MUSIC

THE JERUSALEM Symphony Orchestra is highly rated internationally. The concert season runs from November to early July, with performances held at the Henry Crown Auditorium, part of the **Jerusalem Sherover Theatre** complex. The Israel Philharmonic, one of the world's most prestigious orchestras, is based in Tel Aviv at the **Performing Arts Centre**. However, it also holds about one concert a month in Jerusalem at the **Binyanei ha-Uma Conference Centre**.

In the village of Ein Kerem *(see p134)* near Jerusalem, young musicians give free recitals of chamber music every Friday at noon from October to May at the Fountain of the Virgin in the **Targ Centre**. There are also similar free concerts at the Henry Crown Auditorium of the Jerusalem Sherover Theatre on Wednesday and Thursday afternoons. During the annual **Festival of Israel** held each May there are numerous special music performances *(see p35)*.

OPERA

TEL AVIV'S Performing Arts Centre is home to the **New Israeli Opera**, a world-class company, which puts on four or five new productions a year. The centre also hosts visiting productions from Europe and America.

ROCK, JAZZ AND BLUES

THERE IS A LIMITED local scene in both Tel Aviv and Jerusalem. In Tel Aviv, Sheinkin Street and Nakhalat Binyamin are the areas to explore: **Camelot**, **Lola** and **Logos**, in particular, all have live music. In Jerusalem, several of the bars on or around Heleni ha-Malka Street, near the Russian Compound in the New City, play host to jazz and funk bands at the weekends, while **Mike's Place** on nearby Mounbaz Street has rock and blues every night of the week. The undisputed jazz centre in Jerusalem is the

Classical street musician

Pargod Theatre, near Makhane Yehuda market. **Zionist Confederation House**, five minutes' walk from the King David Hotel, often hosts excellent jazz, fusion and Middle Eastern music concerts.

Visiting international artists occasionally play outdoor venues such as the Sultan's Pool in Jerusalem, or the Roman Theatre in Caesarea *(see p156)* – the *Jerusalem Post* has notice of these events.

In Amman, weekly concerts of very varied music are put on by books@cafe.

Tel Aviv's Suzanne Dellal Centre, renowned for excellence in modern dance

BARS, CLUBS AND DISCOS

IN TEL AVIV, the main cluster of bars is along the northern end of Allenby Street, on Sheinkin Street and in the Nakhalat Binyamin district. There are also plenty of good late-night spots around the Cinematheque on Ha-Arbaa Street. Perhaps the most fascinating and singular disco is **Ha-Hamman**, a strikingly beautiful, converted Turkish bathhouse in Jaffa.

In Jerusalem, nightlife is centred on the Russian Compound area of the New City and in the bar-filled alleys of neighbouring Nakhalat Shiva. The larger clubs are in the industrial area of Talpiot, south of the city centre.

In Amman, there are plenty of bars and clubs in the uptown neighbourhoods such as Abdoun and Shmeisani;

one of the most popular places is the **Irish Pub** in the basement of the Dove Hotel. Nightlife in Sinai is concentrated at the five-star hotels.

ARABIC AND JEWISH MUSIC

OCCASIONAL performances of Arabic traditional music are held at the **El-Qawati Theatre** in East Jerusalem and at the **El-Kasaba Theatre** in Ramallah. The *oud* (Arabic lute) concerts held on Friday and Saturday evenings at the **Kan Zaman** restaurant *(see p247)* are also quite good. Curiously, some of the best Arabic (as well as Jewish) traditional music groups often perform in programmes organized by the Zionist Confederation House in Jerusalem.

Fans of traditional Jewish music should try to time their visit to coincide with the **Klezmer Music Festival** held in July and August in Safed.

DANCE

THE INTERNATIONALLY-known Bat Sheva company is the mainstay of modern Israeli dance. There are no classical ballet companies in Israel, but contemporary dance is very much alive here. The focal point of dance activity is the

Spontaneous outdoor dancing in Safra Square in Jerusalem

Suzanne Dellal Centre, a superb, old Ottoman building at the heart of the historic, southern Tel Aviv district of Neve Zedek, which has recently benefited from extensive architectural renewal. In Jerusalem, dance can often be seen at the Centre for Performing Arts in the Jerusalem Sherover Theatre complex, while Jewish and Arabic folk dancing performances take place on Monday, Thursday and Saturday evenings in the **YMCA** auditorium.

In Jordan, there are two well-established national folkloric groups. Both dance at the **Royal Cultural Centre** and, occasionally, at the Roman Theatre, both in Amman *(see p190)*. Folkloric dance also features quite heavily at the **Jerash Festival** *(see p35)*.

Dining, drinking and dancing al fresco in Atarim Square, Tel Aviv

Creative advertising for Cinematheque Film Festival

THEATRE

PLAYS IN ISRAEL are almost always performed in Hebrew (or, less commonly, Arabic), although some of the bigger theatres such as Tel Aviv's **Habima Theatre** and **Cameri Theatre** and Jerusalem's Sherover Theatre have headphones providing simultaneous English-language translation for selected performances. Productions, in all cases, range from revivals of the classics of world drama (both old and modern) to first-run stagings of new Israeli plays. The **Khan Theatre** in Jerusalem deserves mention, both for being an unusual venue (a converted Turkish merchants' inn) and for its often adventurous and experimental programming.

Arabic theatre in the Holy Land has its home in the El-Qawati and the El-Kasaba theatres, two small institutions that act as repositories of Palestinian tradition.

There are several theatre festivals throughout the year in Israel (see pp34–7), the most exciting of which is the **Acre Fringe Theatre Festival**, which stages some performances in the city's subterranean Crusader halls.

CINEMA

FOREIGN FILMS shown in Israel are not dubbed, but carry Hebrew subtitles. Cinemas are plentiful, especially in Tel Aviv, where complexes such as the **Rav-Or 1–5** are modern, comfortable and air-conditioned. They tend to screen first-run Hollywood fare. The **Cinematheques**, of which there is one in Jerusalem and one in Tel Aviv, specialize in art-house

and independent films, as well as holding themed seasons and retrospectives. The Jerusalem Cinematheque hosts an annual **Film Festival** (see p35) in July.

Few of the cinemas in Jordan screen anything other than overdubbed B-movies, although the showpiece **Galleria** in Amman does show recent releases in English with Arabic subtitles.

SPECTATOR SPORTS

FOOTBALL IS by far the most popular sport throughout the Holy Land. Two teams from Jerusalem play in Israel's premier league, Beitar and Ha-Poel, and matches take place in the new **Teddy Stadium** at Malkha in West Jerusalem.

Basketball is the next most popular sport. The Jerusalem team, Ha-Poel, plays in the Sports Arena near the Teddy Stadium, while the Maccabee team from Tel Aviv plays at the **Yad Eliahu Arena** just off the Ayalon highway.

SWIMMING

ALMOST ALL THE LARGE hotels have outdoor swimming pools; the YMCA in Jerusalem also has an indoor pool. You can also swim all year round

at the **Jerusalem Swimming Pool**, in the German Colony district. The sea is warm enough at the Red Sea resorts for year-round swimming, but too cool in winter at Tel Aviv.

CHILDREN

IN WEST JERUSALEM, the **Tisch Biblical Zoo** has vast enclosures amid greenery, with lakes, streams and waterfalls. Here visitors can observe all the animals that the Bible mentions as living in the Holy Land and others as well. The tropical aviary is outstanding. Children can ride around the zoo on a small train. There is a similar sort of park just north of Eilat in the **Khai Bar Biblical Wildlife Reserve** (see p183).

The **Bloomfield Science Museum** is a real hands-on place, acquainting children with science via lots of interactive displays. It is great fun for adults, too.

Exhibit, Bloomfield Science Museum

In Jerusalem's Liberty Bell (Ha-Paamon) Gardens, an old railway carriage acts as a summer **Puppet Theatre**. It is also one of the venues for an International Puppet Theatre Festival (see page 35).

In Tel Aviv, the **Ramat Gan Safari Zoo** makes a good outing for children. On the shores of the Dead Sea, just south of Jericho, **Attraktsion** is a large aquatic amusement park with water slides and splash pools. However, it is only open from April to October.

Tel Aviv's beach, starting to attract swimmers in early spring

DIRECTORY

INFORMATION

books@cafe
Mango St, Jebel Amman,
Amman, Jordan.
(*(06) 465 0457.*

BUYING TICKETS

Bimot
8 Shamai St, Jerusalem.
(*(02) 624 0896.*

Hadran
90 Ibn Gabirol Ave,
Tel Aviv.
(*(03) 527 9797.*

Klaim
12 Shamai St, Jerusalem.
(*(02) 625 6869.*

LeAn
101 Dizengoff St,
Tel Aviv.
(*(03) 524 7373.*

CLASSICAL MUSIC

**Binyanei ha-Uma
Conference
Centre**
1 Shazar Boulevard,
Jerusalem.
(*(02) 655 8558.*

Festival of Israel
PO Box 4409, Jerusalem.
(*(02) 561 1438.*

**Jerusalem
Sherover Theatre**
20 Markus St, Jerusalem.
(*(02) 560 5755.*

**Performing Arts
Centre**
19 Shaul Ha-Melekh St,
Tel Aviv.
(*(03) 692 7710.*

Targ Centre
Ein Kerem, near
Jerusalem.
(*(02) 641 4250.*

OPERA

New Israeli Opera
Performing Arts Centre,
19 Shaul Ha-Melekh St,
Tel Aviv.
(*(03) 692 7777.*

ROCK, JAZZ AND BLUES

Camelot
16 Shalom Aleichem St,
Tel Aviv.
(*(03) 528 5222.*

Logos
8 Ha-Shomer St,
Tel Aviv.
(*(03) 510 0913.*

Lola
54 Allenby St,
Tel Aviv.

Mike's Place
Horkanos St, Jerusalem.

Pargod Theatre
94 Bezalel St, Jerusalem.
(*(02) 623 1765.*

**Zionist
Confederation
House**
12 Emile Botta St,
Jerusalem.
(*(02) 624 5206.*

BARS, CLUBS AND DISCOS

Ha-Hammam
10 Mifraz Shlomo St,
Jaffa.
(*(03) 518 0126.*

Irish Pub
Dove Hotel, Qurtubah St,
Amman, Jordan.
(*(06) 569 7683.*

ARABIC AND JEWISH MUSIC

El-Kasaba Theatre
Abu Ubaida St,
East Jerusalem.
(*(02) 626 4052.*
*Moves to Ramallah in
the year 2000.*

El-Qawati Theatre
2 Abu Ubaida St,
East Jerusalem.
(*(02) 628 0957.*

Kan Zaman
Nablus Road,
East Jerusalem.
(*(02) 628 3282.*

KLezmer Music Festival
Safed Tourist Information
Centre.
(*(06) 692 7485.*

DANCE

Jerash Festival
Jerash Festival Office,
Amman, Jordan.
(*(06) 567 5199.*

**Royal Cultural
Centre**
Interior Circle, Shmeisani,
Amman.
(*(06) 566 1026.*

**Suzanne Dellal
Centre**
5 Yehieli St, Neve Zedek,
Tel Aviv.
(*(03) 510 5656.*

YMCA
King David St, Jerusalem.
(*(02) 569 2692.*

THEATRE

**Acre Fringe
Theatre Festival**
Acre Tourist Information
Centre.
(*(04) 991 1764.*

Cameri Theatre
101 Dizengoff St, Tel Aviv.
(*(03) 523 3335.*

Habima Theatre
Habima Square, Tel Aviv.
(*(03) 526 6666.*

Khan Theatre
2 David Remez Square,
Jerusalem.
(*(02) 671 8281.*

CINEMA

Galleria
Abdoun Circle,
Amman, Jordan.
(*(06) 461 8275.*

**Jerusalem
Cinematheque**
Hebron Rd, Jerusalem.
(*(02) 672 4131.*

Jerusalem Film Festival
(*(02) 672 4131.*

Rav-Or 1–5
Opera Towers, 1 Allenby
St, Tel Aviv.
(*(03) 510 2674.*

**Tel Aviv
Cinematheque**
2 Sprinzhak St, Tel Aviv.
(*(03) 691 7181.*

SPECTATOR SPORTS

Teddy Stadium
Agudat Sport Beitar,
Malkha, West Jerusalem.
(*(02) 678 8320.*

Yad Eliahu Arena
51 Yigal Allon St, Tel Aviv.
(*(03) 537 6376.*

SWIMMING

**Jerusalem
Swimming Pool**
43 Emek Refaim St.
(*(02) 563 2092.*

CHILDREN

Attraktsion
Kalia Beach, Dead Sea.
(*(02) 994 2391.*

**Bloomfield Science
Museum**
Givat Ram,
West Jerusalem.
(*(02) 561 8128.*

**Khai Bar Biblical
Wildlife Reserve**
Yotvata, Arava.
(*(07) 637 6018.*

Puppet Theatre
Liberty Bell Gardens,
King David St, Jerusalem.
(*(02) 561 8514.*

**Ramat Gan Safari
Zoo**
Ramat Gan, Tel Aviv.
(*(03) 674 4981.*

Tisch Biblical Zoo
Malkha, West Jerusalem.
(*(02) 675 0111.*

SURVIVAL
GUIDE

PRACTICAL INFORMATION

THE AREA covered by this guide is not very large, but because it includes the territory of three nations (Israel, Jordan and Egypt), as well as the Autonomous Palestinian Territories, getting about from one place to another is not always straightforward. The political situation in this part of the world changes frequently (although, thankfully, the tendency in recent years has been for changes for the better), and before embarking on a trip that involves any crossing of borders, you should make sure that there have been no significant changes to the international agreements between these countries. Israel, Jordan and Egypt all have their own tourist organizations, which have offices abroad *(see p269)*.

Israeli tourist board logo

CROSSING BORDERS

PEACE AGREEMENTS of recent years have made it possible to travel overland between Israel and Egypt, and between Israel and Jordan. There are two commonly used crossings between Jordan and Israel (plus a third, less convenient crossing near Beth Shean).

The King Hussein Bridge (also known as the Allenby Bridge) is 16 km (10 miles) east of Jericho. From East Jerusalem (opposite Damascus Gate) you can take a taxi or minibus to the border then, once across, pick up transportation on to Amman. There are hefty Israeli exit and Jordanian entry taxes to pay. The crossing is open 8am–noon Sunday–Thursday and 8am–3pm Friday and Saturday. A second border crossing point exists at Wadi Arava 4 km (2 miles) from Eilat and 10 km (6 miles) from Aqaba. Its opening hours are the same as the King Hussein Bridge. Again, the most convenient way to cross is to use public transport.

To enter Sinai you can take the ferry or catamaran from Aqaba in Jordan to Nuweiba.

Both depart once a day, and you can get your Sinai Permit on board. You can also cross overland using public transport from Eilat in Israel to Taba. Allow plenty of time if crossing any of these borders, as there are strict security measures in place and crossing often takes one or two hours.

VISAS FOR ISRAEL

YOU MUST HAVE a passport that is valid for at least six months to enter Israel. Citizens of European nations, as well as those from North America, Australia and New Zealand, do not, however, need a visa. Citizens of most Arab, Asian, African and South American countries do need visas, and must obtain them in advance from an Israeli consulate in their home country. The visa is usually valid for up to a three-month stay, but can be extended. You can also obtain a "volunteer visa" (valid for 6–12 months) that allows you to work temporarily in a kibbutz *(see p277)*.

An Israeli visa in your passport will bar you from entering some Arab countries, notably Syria and Lebanon, but not Egypt or Jordan. You can avoid this by asking at the airport that the visa be stamped on a separate piece of paper. Other than at the Allenby Bridge crossing, this cannot be done at the land borders.

At present there are no special formalities for visitors crossing the borders between Israel and the Palestinian territories. There may be security checks by Israeli or Palestinian police, though, who will ask to see your passport.

Entry card for Israel, and visa required to enter Jordan

VISAS FOR JORDAN

TOURISTS ARRIVING in Jordan must have a passport valid for at least six months, and also a visa. If you are arriving at Queen Alia international airport you can obtain a one-month tourist visa upon arrival. The price of this can vary dramatically depending on your nationality.

If you are entering Jordan by land then you must have already obtained your visa in advance, as the border posts do not issue them (the only exception to this being the Wadi Arava border crossing). Visas can otherwise be issued either by the Jordanian consulate or embassy in your home country, or by those in Tel Aviv or Cairo.

Israeli soldiers checking cars coming from the Palestinian Autonomous Territories

◁ **Bedouin tents in the mountainous wilderness of Wadi Rum**

VISAS FOR EGYPT

IF YOU ARE entering Sinai from Israel, you can obtain a special Sinai Permit that allows you to stay for up to 14 days; this is obtained at the border and is free. Bear in mind, however, that the Sinai Permit cannot be changed into a full visa. Neither can a full visa for Egypt be obtained at the border. If you plan to visit other parts of Egypt beyond Sinai, you must obtain a visa in advance from an Egyptian consulate or embassy in your home country, or else in Amman, Aqaba, Tel Aviv or Eilat.

Israeli road signs

DUTY-FREE ARTICLES AND CUSTOMS

THE DUTY-FREE allowance in all three countries is 200 cigarettes or 200 grams of tobacco, a litre of spirits and two bottles of wine. Valuable electrical objects such as computers and video cameras will be entered in passports by customs officers to prevent their resale in the country.

LANGUAGE

ENGLISH IS VERY MUCH a second language in Israel, where many immigrants do not speak Hebrew. All signs are bilingual and it is rare to meet someone who doesn't understand any English at all. The story is very different in Palestinian areas and in Jordan, however, but Arabs will make every effort to communicate with foreigners, even if it means resorting to sign language. In areas frequented by tourists it is easier to find English speakers, although attempts to speak Arabic will always be welcomed. Away from the main tourist circuit it can be much harder to get your message across without some rudimentary grasp of the language.

ETIQUETTE

ISRAELI SOCIETY, on the whole, is not that different from the West. There are exceptions; in ultra-Orthodox areas such as Jerusalem's Mea Shearim and parts of the Galilee town of Safed, behaviour and dress should definitely err on the side of conservatism. This is also the case in Arab areas, both in the Palestinian Autonomous Territories and in Jordan. Arab women usually cover their arms, legs and sometimes their heads in public, and men do not wear shorts. Visitors are not always expected to cover up in the same way, but you must be suitably clothed when visiting certain public places and any of the holy sites *(see p268).*

Intimate physical contact with a person of the opposite sex in public is also taboo in Arab society; Arabic couples are rarely seen kissing, embracing or even holding hands.

Arab women in customary dress, outside the Dome of the Rock, Jerusalem

Tips for Tourists

Israeli tourist office sign

TOURISM IN JERUSALEM and the Holy Land is considerable, given the region's major historical and religious importance, as well as its great natural beauty. As such, most towns are well adapted for visitors, with good public facilities and helpful tourist offices. Major sites are open long hours for much of the week, and also have good facilities as well as useful educational material. Some sites, however, are well off the beaten track, and difficult to reach using public transport. If visiting desert areas, make sure you arrive early, to avoid the extreme afternoon heat.

Free brochures available from tourist sites

Free tourist office brochure

TOURIST INFORMATION

AS WELL AS providing useful information in the form of free brochures and maps, Israeli tourist offices are usually able to help with other matters, such as finding accommodation and arranging transport. In smaller towns, or at archaeological sites, the tourist offices are of more limited use, and information is usually confined to the immediate area. The Autonomous Palestinian Territories are also in the process of organizing a network of information bureaux, but for the present, their sole office is in Bethlehem.

In Jordan the only tourist information offices are in the main tourist destinations such as Amman, Petra and Jerash, while in Sinai there are no tourist information offices at all. All three countries have international tourist bureaux, however, which you can use before you leave. The national airline offices can also often help with travel information.

ENTRANCE FEES

MOST OF THE HISTORIC and archaeological sites in Jerusalem and the Holy Land have some kind of admission charge, although some smaller churches and mosques have no fixed fee at all. In these cases a small donation is customary. Prices are generally very reasonable, with most minor sites in Israel charging only a few shekels. Larger places may charge slightly more, with the most expensive site to visit by far being Petra.

In Israel you can purchase a 14-day Green Card for around NIS 160, that gives free access to all sites under the control of the Nature and National Parks Protection Authority. These are mainly natural and more minor archaeological sites, but if you are planning to spend some time sightseeing in Israel, this may be a good investment.

OPENING HOURS

BECAUSE of the many religious holidays (*see pp34–7*) celebrated in the region (Jewish, Muslim and Christian), opening hours for the many tourist sites and historic monuments can vary greatly. As a general rule, however, sites in Israel are usually open daily, except for Friday, when they keep more restricted hours, and Saturday, when they are closed altogether. Christian sites, other than the churches, are open on Saturdays but closed on Sundays.

In Jordan the main sites (including Petra and Jerash) are open daily, but other, smaller sites, including many of the museums, are closed on Tuesdays. From around October to March (considered the winter season), most sites in the Holy Land close an hour earlier than usual.

WHAT TO WEAR AT SACRED SITES

WHEN VISITING holy sites such as churches, synagogues and mosques, it is essential that you dress appropriately. This means that your arms and legs must be fully covered; shorts or short skirts and sleeveless tops are not acceptable. At certain

Visitors removing footwear before entering The Dome of the Rock, Jerusalem

places cloaks are provided to cover up visitors who are deemed to be immodestly dressed. Shoes must be removed before entering a mosque, and at some Jewish holy sites, such as the Western Wall, heads must also be covered. In such cases a *kippah* (skullcap) is provided free of charge.

TIME

THE TIME in Israel, Jordan and Egypt is two hours ahead of Greenwich Mean Time (GMT), and seven hours ahead of Eastern Standard Time (EST). All three countries have daylight saving time which lasts from approximately March to September.

DISABLED VISITORS

ISRAEL IS VERY AWARE of the needs of disabled visitors, and many hotels and modern museums are adapted for disabled use. **MILBAT** is a useful advisory centre on such matters, while **JDC-Israel** is also able to advise on suitable hotel accommodation and site accessibility. The **Yad Sarah Organization** lends out wheelchairs and other useful aids free of charge. Jordan and Sinai make no real provision for the disabled, and as most sites are surrounded by rough terrain, visiting these areas can be very problematic.

Student ISIC identity card

STUDENT INFORMATION

IN ISRAEL, the presentation of a recognized student card, such as an International Student Identity Card (ISIC), will get the holder a ten per cent discount on bus fares, as well as discounts on most museum and site admissions. The **Israel Student Tourist Association (ISSTA)** can arrange cheap flights and accommodation, and provide information on student discounts, as well as arranging its own package holidays. There are no student discounts offered in Jordan, but Egypt offers a 50 per cent concession on most site admissions.

WCs

PUBLIC TOILETS are easily found throughout Israel, and are of the standard type found in the West. In Jordan they are much less common and a lot more rudimentary, but still usually clean, as they are tended by caretakers. In Sinai public toilets do not exist at all. It is always wise to have a supply of paper with you, as

Sign for public toilets

this is often not provided. All paper should be disposed of using the bins provided, and not put down the toilet, as the local plumbing cannot cope.

ELECTRICAL ADAPTORS

THE ELECTRIC CURRENT in Israel, Jordan and Sinai is 220V. Plugs in Israel are round-pronged and three-pinned, whereas in Jordan and Sinai they are round-pronged and two-pinned. Adaptors should be bought prior to departure.

Two-pin plug adaptor for use in Jordan and Sinai

CONVERSION CHART

Imperial to Metric
1 inch = 2.54 centimetres
1 foot = 30 centimetres
1 mile = 1.6 kilometres
1 ounce = 28 grams
1 pound = 454 grams
1 pint = 0.6 litres
1 gallon = 4.6 litres

Metric to Imperial
1 centimetre = 0.4 inches
1 metre = 3 feet, 3 inches
1 kilometre = 0.6 miles
1 gram = 0.04 ounces
1 kilogram = 2.2 pounds
1 litre = 1.8 pints

Security and Health

Israel and the Middle East suffer from a bad press when it comes to security. However, despite the occasional alarming headline, Israel and its neighbouring territories of Jordan and Sinai are perfectly safe for tourists. Visitors rarely encounter crime, and there are next to no hazards in the form of dangerous animals, or endemic diseases. Political unrest does from time to time result in acts of terrorism or rioting, but this hardly ever affects visitors. With the present ongoing attempts to reach peace between Israel and the Palestinians, even these infrequent incidents of violence may, hopefully, soon be a thing of the past.

Israeli Defence Force soldiers at Damascus Gate

Law and Order

Israel, Jordan and Sinai all have special tourist police to deal with any complaints or problems visitors may encounter. These police mostly speak English, and are posted at most major sites and at tourist resorts. They wear identifying armbands. The Jordanians have a special form of tourist police, active in the Wadi Rum area, known as the Desert Patrol. These officials are easily identified by their smart khaki uniforms, their distinctive red-and-white checked headdress and by the fact that they often ride camels.

Normal Israeli police wear navy blue uniforms and peaked caps. Also part of the police force are the border guards, who wear a military style uniform and a green beret. They operate mainly in the Israeli-controlled areas of the West Bank. The Palestinians also have their own security forces, who come in a multitude of guises.

Visitors will notice a preponderance of military personnel on the streets in Jerusalem and Israel. Every citizen must

perform military service in the Israeli Defence Force (IDF) as soon as they reach the age of 18. The term of service is three years for men and 18 months for women. Men serve for an additional 30 days a year until the age of 35. Consequently, you will see armed soldiers around all the time, particularly at bus stations, as they are usually on the way to or from their bases.

Personal Safety

On arrival at Ben Gurion Airport, you will almost immediately experience just how tight security is in Israel. During your stay, you may be subject to security checks on

A member of the Desert Patrol, Wadi Rum, Jordan

entering hotels, cinemas and shopping complexes, so it is wise always to carry some identification, preferably your passport. But as far as the visitor is concerned, terrorism is not a major worry. Tourists have never been the target of terrorists and most attacks have occurred well away from all tourist sites. Naturally, you have to be alert when in the streets, and also keep an eye on the local news. Among the "sensitive" areas are East Jerusalem and West Bank towns such as Hebron and Ramallah. In times of unrest you should definitely give such places a wide berth. Should you be unlucky enough to encounter a disturbance in the streets, the wisest course of action is to move away from

Israeli policeman

the scene quickly, and make it completely clear that you are a foreign tourist.

Stories of theft, mugging and other similar opportunistic crimes are rare in the Holy Land. Crime is not the problem here that it is in many other parts of the world. As a rule, all areas are considered safe for visitors, unless the visitor is an unaccompanied woman. Lone females are frequently subjected to unwanted verbal pestering and harrassment from local males, both Israeli and Arab. This problem is particularly acute in Jerusalem's Old City and its surrounding areas, such as the Mount of Olives and Mount Zion. Incidences of rape have even been reported, and so our advice to women must be that they should not walk alone in unpeopled areas or in the Old City after dark.

Personal Property

On the whole Israelis and Arabs are very honest people. Arabs, especially, will go to great lengths to return lost property. If you lose anything it is always worth going to the last place the item was seen, or going to the tourist police. On occasion, unpleasant experiences do happen. To minimize the risk of this, do not leave valuable objects inside a car or in full view in your hotel room. Leave your valuables in the hotel safe or at the reception desk. The fact that credit cards are accepted almost everywhere is a good reason not to carry a lot of cash with you. In case of theft, remember to make a report to the police and to ask for a copy of the report, which you will then have to present to your insurance company when you make your claim.

Security considerations mean that you should not leave luggage or packages unattended (especially in airports and bus stations), as they might cause alarm or trigger a reaction on the part of the security forces.

HEALTH PRECAUTIONS

MEDICAL CARE in Jerusalem and the Holy Land is costly, making it inadvisable to travel without some form of medical insurance. The policy should at least cover the cost of a flight home.

No specific vaccinations are legally required before entering Israel, Jordan or Sinai, but doctors may advise inoculation against hepatitis A (spread through contaminated food or water), hepatitis B, tetanus and also typhoid.

There are no particular endemic diseases in the Middle East, but the hot climate necessitates that you take certain precautions, at least until you are used to the change in diet. It is advisable to drink mineral water (which is sold everywhere) and not use ice in your drinks. Avoid raw vegetables or food that has obviously been left standing for some time since it was cooked, and peel fruit. Continually

A small pharmacy in Jerusalem

drinking large quantities of liquids is essential: the lack of humidity in the air causes rapid dehydration, even though you may not be aware of it. Other than this, the most frequent problems are intestinal. A change of diet often upsets the stomach. It is recommended that you should always carry diarrhoea pills. If the upset continues then consult a doctor or pharmacist for more powerful medication.

Mosquitoes can sometimes be a nuisance, but there is no threat of malaria. Bring repellent lotion or spray from your own country – although, if you forget, it is easy to find in any pharmacy. If you go diving in the Red Sea, you need to be careful of sharp corals and be aware of which species of fish are poisonous and are to be avoided.

Pharmacy sign in Israel

PHARMACIES

GOOD PHARMACIES are easy to find throughout both Israel and Jordan. However, if you need a particular medicine, it is

Magen David Adom ambulance

still advisable to travel with your own supplies and keep a note of the product and its composition so that, if worst comes to worst, a pharmacist will be able to find a local equivalent. In Israel, the *Jerusalem Post* lists the names and addresses of pharmacies that stay open late and during Shabbat and holidays.

MEDICAL TREATMENT

IN AN EMERGENCY in Israel, you can call 101 to request an ambulance or to ask about the nearest casualty department. Alternatively, contact the local branch of the **Magen David Adom** (Israel's equivalent of the Red Cross), or call its countrywide toll-free number.

In Jordan, if you need a doctor, call into a pharmacy and ask for a recommendation or call your embassy. In Sinai, most large hotels have a resident doctor. For divers, there is a special **Hyperbaric Medical Centre** in Sharm el-Sheikh equipped with a recompression chamber.

DIRECTORY

EMERGENCY NUMBERS

In Israel
Ambulance
[101.
Magen David Adom
[(02) 652 3133 (Jerusalem).
[(03) 546 0111 (Tel Aviv).
[(04) 851 2233 (Haifa).
[1 800 700 101 (toll-free – countrywide).
Police and General Enquiries
[100.

In Jordan
Ambulance
[191.
Police
[193.
Tourist Police
[196.

In Sinai
Ambulance
[123.
Hyperbaric Medical Centre
[(012) 333 1325 (24 hr).
[(012) 212 4292 (24 hr).
Police
[122.

Banking and Currency

Mizrahi bank logo

EXCHANGING AND OBTAINING money pose no problems in Israel and the Holy Land. Cash and traveller's cheques can be exchanged at banks, exchange offices and in many hotels. Credit cards are widely accepted and can be used to obtain funds. The only issues to be aware of are the greatly varying levels of commission charged on transactions, and the limited opening hours of banks.

Official money exchange office

BANKS

BANKS IN ISRAEL, Jordan and Sinai will exchange all major European currencies, but the most welcome currency of all is the US dollar. ATMs (automatic cash dispensers) linked into international banking networks, such as Cirrus or Plus, are widespread in Israel. You will find them in the foyers of most banks. These machines are less common in Jordan and Sinai, and found only in Amman, Petra and Sharm el-Sheikh. Some banks in Israel also have automatic currency exchange machines, which are accessible 24 hours a day. The drawback is that these machines usually charge a high transaction fee combined with a very poor rate of exchange.

Automatic currency exchange machine

Jerusalem's banking district is centred on Zion Square, at the bottom of Ben Yehuda Street in the New City. Banks are generally open from 8:30am to 12:30pm, reopening for another hour or two from around 4pm (but not on Wednesdays or Fridays). They are shut on Saturdays. In Jordan

ATM machine at an Israeli bank

and Sinai banking hours are similar to Israel, except that they are closed on Fridays, not on Saturdays.

EXCHANGE OFFICES

THE BANKS often charge a considerable commission on currency exchanges; one way to avoid this is to use an official exchange office such as **Change Point** or **Change Spot**. These places charge no commission. They also tend to be open much longer hours than the banks (from 9am to 9pm in some cases). Such exchange offices in Jerusalem can be found mainly on Jaffa Road and Ben Yehuda Street. There are also several small Arab exchange offices just inside Jaffa and Damascus gates in the Old City.

In Jordan, central Amman is full of small exchange offices, but there are not so many outside the capital. You can use one of the big hotels, but beware of the commission they may charge.

TRAVELLER'S CHEQUES AND CREDIT CARDS

TRAVELLER'S CHEQUES can be exchanged at banks but commission is charged per cheque. Better to cash them at exchange offices, where no commission is charged at all.

Major credit cards, such as VISA, MasterCard, Diners Club and American Express are widely accepted throughout Israel, Jordan and Sinai in shops, restaurants and hotels. If you have your PIN number you can draw cash from ATMs.

CURRENCY

ISRAEL'S NATIONAL currency is the new Israeli shekel (NIS), referred to simply as the shekel. It is also the currency in the Palestinian Autonomous Territories, although there are plans to introduce a Palestinian national currency in the near future. Jordan has dinars (JD), while the currency in Sinai is the Egyptian pound (LE). These currencies are only valid in their home countries so, for example, you cannot spend excess Israeli shekels in Jordan. Exchange rates between the three tend to be very bad. This means, for example, that it is wise to use up all your shekels before leaving Israel and then to exchange dollars for dinars or pounds on arriving in Jordan or Egypt.

DIRECTORY

EXCHANGE OFFICES

Change Place
112 Ha-Yarkon St, Tel Aviv.
(*(03) 523 3207.*

Change Point
40 Jaffa Rd, Jerusalem.
(*(02) 625 5572.*
2 Ben Yehuda St, Jerusalem.
(*(02) 624 0011.*
106 Ha-Yarkon St, Tel Aviv.
(*(03) 524 5505.*

Change Spot
13 Ben Yehuda St, Tel Aviv.
(*(03) 510 0573.*
140 Dizengoff St, Tel Aviv.
(*(03) 524 3393.*

MoneyNet
Paulus VI St,
Nazareth.
(*(06) 655 2540.*

Israeli Banknotes

Israeli banknotes come in four different denominations: 200, 100, 50 and 20 NIS. The most recent series of notes is in the style of the 20- and 100-shekel notes shown here.

Two hundred shekels (200 NIS)

One hundred shekels (100 NIS)

Twenty shekels (20 NIS)

Israeli Coins

The shekel is divided into 100 agorot. There are coins to the value of 10, 5 and 1 shekels, as well as 50 and 10 agorot.

Ten shekels   Five shekels   One shekel   Fifty agorot   Ten agorot

Jordanian Currency

The Jordanian dinar is divided into 1,000 fils and, confusingly, also 100 piastres (100 fils therefore equals 10 piastres). Notes come in denominations of 20, 10, 5, 1 and ½ dinars. Coins exist to the value of 500, 250, 100, 50, 25, 10 and 5 fils, and 10, 5 and 2½ piastres.

20 dinars

10 dinars

5 dinars

½ dinar   100 fils   5 piastres

Egyptian Currency

The currency in Egypt is the Egyptian pound (abbreviated to LE). The pound is divided into 100 piastres. Notes come in denominations of LE 200, 100, 50, 20, 10, 5, 1 and 50 and 25 piastres. Coins exist to the value of 50, 20, 10 and 5 piastres.

Twenty Egyptian pounds (LE 20)

Five Egyptian pounds (LE 5)

Communications

Israeli post office logo

Israel's POSTAL SERVICE is generally efficient, but letters to Europe and North America can still take a week or more to arrive. This, however, is quicker than the Jordanian or Egyptian postal systems, which are highly unpredictable. Calling overseas is very straightforward from Israel, and it is similarly easy to call overseas in Sinai, but telephone communications from Jordan are considerably more complicated, and expensive.

PUBLIC TELEPHONES IN ISRAEL

Israel's PUBLIC TELEPHONES are almost all operated by the national phone company, Bezek. They take prepaid phonecards, which are sold at post offices, shops and lottery kiosks. They are available in denominations of 10 units (12 NIS), 20 units (24 NIS) or 50 units (48 NIS). Calls made from 10pm to 1am and all day Saturday and Sunday are 25 per cent cheaper than the standard rate. Calls made between 1am and 8am are 50 per cent cheaper. To dial abroad using Bezek, the international access code is 014.

Bezek competes for custom with other telephone companies, including Golden Lines (012 to dial abroad) and Barak (013 to dial abroad). These rival services are often cheaper than Bezek, although it does depend on the country you are calling. You can also make discounted calls from Solan Telecom, whose offices are found throughout Israel.

An Israeli lottery kiosk, where phonecards can also be bought

Israeli telephone and phonecards

Visitors can rent mobile phones on arrival at Ben Gurion Airport. Rental rates start at about US$1 per day. Israel's mobile network does not have reciprocal roaming arrangements with many countries. Anyone who plans to take their mobile with them should check with their home service whether it can be used in Israel.

PUBLIC TELEPHONES IN THE PALESTINIAN TERRITORIES

In THE WEST BANK and Gaza Strip, the Palestinians have their own telephone network with their own phonecards. These Palestinian phonecards can be purchased in Arab post offices and some shops. They cannot, at present, be used in Israeli phones.

PUBLIC TELEPHONES IN JORDAN AND SINAI

Jordan's TELEPHONE network is creaky, but it is in the process of being upgraded. International calls can be made from public cardphones, for which the cards are purchased from nearby shops. However, phonecards for international calls only come in the denomination of JD 15. A better option is to use one of the many unofficial telephone bureaus, where you write the number you want on a piece of paper and the desk clerk makes the call. These calls are charged by the minute and, with a great many offices competing for custom, rates are reasonable.

The Egyptian telephone network in Sinai also uses phonecards. These come in denominations of LE 15, 20 or 30 and they can be bought at post offices.

POSTAL SERVICES

Using ISRAELI POST OFFICES is a very straightforward procedure. The exception is if you are sending parcels or bulky items; this entails a series of security inspections. When it comes to posting letters, the yellow post boxes are for local correspondence and the red are for the rest of country and abroad. Post office opening hours are generally 7am to 7pm from Sunday to Thursday and 7am to noon on Fridays. Postal rates vary according to the type of post and its weight, but a standard airmail letter to Europe or the US costs the equivalent of half a US dollar.

The Palestinian Authority also has its own postal service, and issues its own stamps, but it is not as efficient as the Israeli service.

Red Israeli post box

A letter posted in Jordan can take anything up to two weeks to reach Europe and a month to the US. It can help to speed things up if you post

Jordanian stamps

Israeli stamps

Egyptian stamps

your letters at a five-star hotel or a main post office, rather than a post box on the street. Post offices are closed Friday.

NEWSPAPERS, RADIO AND TV

Eglish-language readers are well catered for in Israel. The leading English-language publication is the daily *Jerusalem Post* (no Saturday edition). This is worth picking up on Fridays for its extensive cultural supplements and entertainment listings. The weekly *Jerusalem Times* is a Palestinian publication, which is usually available only in East Jerusalem and Arab areas of the Old City. In Jordan, look out for the *Jordan Times*, published daily except for Fridays. Foreign newpapers

Local English-language press

and magazines, such as *The Times*, *The Washington Post* and *Newsweek*, are widely available, and are usually just one or two days old.

Israeli TV has two state channels, both of which show a large number of subtitled English-language programmes. Most hotels also offer satellite channels such as BBC, Sky News and CNN. In Jordan, Channel 2 devotes a lot of screen time to US programmes, and has English-language news nightly at 10pm. Most hotels have satellite TV.

Israel Radio broadcasts news in English each weekday evening at 6:16pm.

INTERNET CAFÉS

Despite being an extremely computer literate society, internet cafés are few and far between in Israel. This is possibly because most Israeli families have a computer with internet access of their own at home. There are just three internet cafés in Jerusalem, and only a handful more dotted around the country. Jordan has an excellent venue for sending and receiving emails in **books@cafe**, located in central Amman. There are further internet cafés in Jordan at Wadi Musa (Petra), Madaba and Aqaba. In Sinai there is an internet café near the Fayrouz Hilton in Sharm el-Sheikh. Internet services are also offered at two shops in Dahab. Online time is usually charged by the half hour.

Newspaper seller in Tiberias, Israel

Sporting and Specialist Holidays in the Holy Land

WITH TERRAIN THAT RUNS from reefs rich in marine life to sometimes snow-capped peaks, and from coniferous forests to stony desert, the region offers a wide assortment of outdoor activities. Added to this, Israel is very much an "outdoors" society. As a consequence, the region is criss-crossed with hiking trails and treks, rivers are busy with rafts and canoes, parks offer opportunities for horse riding, and deserts for exploration by camel. All this is primarily for the locals but visitors can enjoy these facilities too.

Diver with shoal of sergeant major fish on reef in the Red Sea

DIVING AND SNORKELLING

EXPERIENCED DIVERS claim that the Red Sea offers some of the world's best diving. The various scuba diving centres in Eilat, Aqaba and Sinai organize courses for beginners, as well as for more experienced divers who wish to qualify for the various international licences. Most centres hire out all the diving equipment you need (the daily rate is about $25–35), including underwater photographic equipment. In Eilat, reputable diving centres include **Aqua Sport**, which organizes daily boat excursions along the Sinai coast to less-dived locations, **Marina Divers** and **Village Divers**. In Sinai, some of the better outfits include the **Sheikh Coast** at Dahab, the **Nesima Dive Centre** at Sharm el-Sheikh, and **Sinai Divers** based in Naama Bay.

Another way of viewing the rich marine life and beauty of the reefs is to go snorkelling. This has the advantage of being cheap and of not requiring any complicated equipment or specialized training. Dahab and Naama Bay are the best spots.

WATER SPORTS

POSSIBILITIES EXIST for rafting and canoeing on the Jordan River north of the Sea of Galilee; these activities are supervised by **Abu Kayak** in the Jordan River Park, at Bethsaida, and by the **Ha-Goshrim Kibbutz**, further north, close to the Lebanon border.

The windsurfing is good in the Gulf of Aqaba, particularly on the coast between Eilat and the border at Taba; there are plenty of places to rent boards, many of them near the small marina by the Club Med hotel. The region's centre for water sports is Eilat, with everything from snorkels to jetskis for hire, plus a multitude of other activities, including paragliding and glass-bottomed boats. The larger Sinai resorts, Sharm el-Sheikh and Naama Bay offer similar facilities.

The Mediterranean coast is more exposed with dangerous currents, but there are water sports activities at Tel Aviv and a few other coastal towns, such as Netanya.

Windsurfing in the Gulf of Aqaba

DESERT HIKING AND CLIMBING

A LARGE NUMBER of specialist organizations lead hikes throughout Israel. A good starting point for finding out about such trips is to visit the **Society for the Protection of Nature in Israel (SPNI)**; its offices/bookshops in Tel Aviv and Jerusalem carry a wide range of specialized maps and useful publications such as *A Guide to Hiking in Israel* by Joel Roskin. The SPNI also runs plenty of hikes itself.

The best hiking in Jordan is, without doubt, in and around Wadi Rum. There are trails lasting anything from a couple of hours to several days, all of which are described in the essential *Treks and Climbs in Wadi Rum* by Tony Howard. While not as magnificent as Wadi Rum, the Sinai interior is starkly beautiful and well worth exploring; this can be arranged at most hotels in Nuweiba or Dahab. In Sinai and Wadi Rum there is also the option of day-long treks on camels.

Rope-assisted descents of spectacular gorges in the Dead Sea region of the Judaean Desert are organized by the **Metzoke Dragot Centre**. The same company also offers climbing, hiking, and jeep or truck excursions into the desert.

BIRDWATCHING

ISRAEL AND SINAI lie on one of the principal bird migration routes between Europe and Africa and, as such, are

Trekking in one of the canyons of the Judaean Desert

something of a birdwatcher's paradise; interested parties should visit the **International Birdwatching Centre**, opposite the bus station in central Eilat for more details.

HORSE RIDING

M ANY KIBBUTZIM keep stables and hire out horses by the hour, half-day or day; try **Vered ha-Galil**, just north of the Sea of Galilee, **Kibbutz Nahsholim** just off the Mediterranean coastal highway or **Herod's Stables** at nearby Caesarea.

It is also possible to ride at Petra, although this is limited to a 1 km (half a mile) canter to the site entrance, while the **Captain's Restaurant** in Aqaba organizes horseback trips to Wadi Rum.

Tourists on horseback at Petra

WORKING ON A KIBBUTZ

N OT AS POPULAR as it once was, Israel's pioneering, socialist-style kibbutz movement continues to employ young volunteers (who must be aged between 18 and 32) from abroad to carry out manual work. Typical work involves picking fruit out in the fields, working on a factory product-ion line, or being attached to a dining room, kitchen or laundry. The kibbutz will normally expect a minimum commitment of two months, during which time volunteers work for their keep, receiving accommodation, meals, toiletries and a small personal allowance of about $50 per month, plus one day a week holiday. Whatever facilities the kibbutz has are available to volunteers; these may include such things as a swim-ming pool or a sports hall.

Would-be volunteers usually apply through a special kibbutz office in their home country, although there are

Celebrating the harvest festival on a kibbutz

also kibbutz offices in Tel Aviv, through which applications can be made; addresses are given in the directory below.

JOINING AN ARCHAEOLOGICAL DIG

V ISITORS WHO FANCY some hands-on experience at one of the region's many archaeological sites can sign up with the "Dig for a Day" programme, organized by **Archaeological Seminars** of Jerusalem. A three-hour excavation is accompanied by seminars and a site tour and costs about $20 per person. However, the programme operates during July and August only.

DIRECTORY

DIVING AND SNORKELLING

Aquamarina
Aquamarina Hotel, Aqaba.
☎ (03) 201 6250.

Aqua Sport
Coral Beach, Eilat.
☎ (07) 633 4404.

Marina Divers
Coral Beach, Eilat.
☎ (07) 637 6787.

Nesima Dive Centre
Sharm el-Sheikh, Sinai.
☎ (062) 601 713/4.

Sheikh Coast
Dahab, Sinai.
☎ (062) 640 320.

Sinai Divers
Naama Bay, Sinai.
☎ (062) 600 697.

Village Divers
Coral Beach, Ellat.
☎ (07) 637 2268.

WATER SPORTS

Abu Kayak
Jordan River Park,
Beth Saida.
☎ (06) 692 1078.

Ha-Goshrim Kibbutz
Route 99, the Golan.
☎ (06) 681 6034.

DESERT HIKING AND CLIMBING

Metzoke Dragot Centre
Metzoke Dragot,
Dead Sea.
☎ (02) 994 4222.

Society for the Protection of Nature in Israel
13 Heleni ha-Malka St,
New City, Jerusalem.
☎ (02) 624 4605.
4 Ha-Shfela St,
Tel Aviv.
☎ (03) 638 8674.

BIRDWATCHING

International Birdwatching Centre
PO Box 774,
Eilat 88106.
☎ (07) 633 5339.

HORSE RIDING

Captain's Restaurant
El-Nahda St,
Aqaba.
☎ (03) 316 905.

Herod's Stables
Caesarea.
☎ (06) 836 1181.

Kibbutz Nahsholim
Off Highway 2,
Dor.
☎ (06) 639 5504.

Vered ha-Galil
Korazim, Galilee.
☎ (06) 693 5785.

WORKING ON A KIBBUTZ

Kibbutz Programme Centre
18 Frishman St, Tel Aviv.
☎ (03) 527 8874.

Meira's
73 Ben Yehuda St, Tel Aviv.
☎ (03) 523 7369.

Project 67
94 Ben Yehuda St, Tel Aviv.
☎ (03) 523 0140.
10 Hatton Garden,
London EC1, UK.
☎ (020) 7831 7626.

JOINING AN ARCHAEOLOGICAL DIG

Archaeological Seminars
34 Habbad St, Jewish
Quarter, Jerusalem.
☎ (02) 627 3515.

TRAVEL INFORMATION

THE EASIEST WAY to get to Jerusalem and the Holy Land is to fly direct. Jerusalem is served by Ben Gurion Airport, and there are also international airports at Eilat, Amman in Jordan and Sharm el-Sheikh in Sinai. There are frequent flights to Ben Gurion and, being a busy tourist destination, it is possible to get

El Al aeroplane at Ben Gurion airport

cheap deals, especially if you are prepared to travel with a smaller, lesser-known airline, or take advantage of a charter package. There are no direct sailings to Israel from mainland Europe; the only sea route is from Athens via Cyprus. Travelling overland is an arduous business as all European trains terminate at Istanbul.

Ben Gurion, Israel's main international airport

FLYING TO ISRAEL

THE ISRAELI national airline is **El Al**. It has direct flights to Ben Gurion Airport from most major European cities, as well as from New York, Los Angeles, Chicago, Miami, Baltimore and Orlando in the United States. Ben Gurion is also served by a great many foreign airlines, including Air France, Alitalia, British Airways, Lufthansa and Swissair; and American Airlines, Delta, Tower Air and TWA.

Fares are seasonal. The high season is during the Jewish and Christian holiday periods, in particular Passover, Easter and Rosh ha-Shanah *(see pp34–7)*. At such times fares are at a premium and it can often be hard to find seats.

It is always worth looking into flights to Eilat's Ovda airport. This largely caters for charter traffic, and it is on these flights that the cheapest fares are to be found. The drawbacks are that there are often restrictions on the dates

you may travel and you have to make your own way up to Jerusalem and back, a bus journey of between four and five hours each way.

BEN GURION AIRPORT

NAMED AFTER the first prime minister of Israel, Ben Gurion Airport lies southeast of Tel Aviv, just off the road to Jerusalem. Services at the airport include duty-free shops, a telecommunications office, car-hire outlets and tourist information and hotel reservation desks. There is no

domestic terminal; Jerusalem and Tel Aviv both have small city airports for internal flights.

Ben Gurion reputedly has the tightest security of any airport in the world. The time taken to inspect each and every item of baggage means that passengers must check in three hours before departure. However, anyone flying with El Al can check in luggage the day before at special offices in Jerusalem, Tel Aviv and Haifa. Passengers who do this need only turn up at the airport an hour and a quarter before departure.

GETTING TO AND FROM BEN GURION AIRPORT

BEN GURION AIRPORT is at Lod, about 22 km (14 miles) from Tel Aviv and some 45 km (28 miles) from Jerusalem. Private taxis take about 45 minutes to Jerusalem, or you can take a shared taxi, or *sherut (see p276)*, which is much cheaper. These leave from just outside the arrivals hall. They do not set off until they are full, but it is rare to have to wait more than 10 or 15 minutes. The *sheruts* run through the night and will drop passengers anywhere in the city.

Egged buses Nos. 945 and 947 depart every half hour from around 5:30am until 9pm for Jerusalem's Central Bus Station on Jaffa Road. While this is the cheapest method of getting from the airport into the city, the bus station is more than a kilometre from

Newly arriving tourists disembark at Ben Gurion Airport

the centre of the New City, and most people will then have to catch a further bus or taxi on to their hotel. The buses do not run on Shabbat – sundown Friday to sundown Saturday.

To get to the airport from Jerusalem, book a taxi the day before departure or reserve a seat in a shared taxi with **Nesher Taxis**. Most hotels can usually organize this.

FLYING TO JORDAN AND SINAI

JORDAN'S PRINCIPAL airport, and the home base for the national carrier **Royal Jordanian Airlines**, is Queen Alia International. Royal Jordanian has direct services between Amman and most major European capitals. It also flies, via Amsterdam, to New York and Chicago.

Other major carriers flying into Amman include Air France, Alitalia, British Airways and KLM. There are no non-stop flights from the US – instead you have to fly via a European hub. There is a second airport, known as Marka, about 5 km (3 miles) east of central Amman, but this handles only short-hop flights to Israel and Egypt.

Compact Queen Alia International Airport, Jordan's main air transport hub

There is also a further airport about 10 km (6 miles) north of Aqaba, but it receives few international flights.

Flights to Amman are not cheap. In general, it is much more economical to fly into Ben Gurion or Eilat in Israel and take a bus across the border. The airport at Sharm el-Sheikh in Sinai lies about 17 km (11 miles) north of town. It is served by Air Sinai and Egypt Air, but these are not direct flights; they involve a change of plane in Cairo.

GETTING TO AND FROM QUEEN ALIA AIRPORT

QUEEN ALIA AIRPORT is about 30 km (19 miles) south of Amman. Comfortable Airport Express buses depart hourly between 7:15am and 9:15pm

for Downtown from just outside the arrivals terminal. Other buses head for the northern parts of town. Be sure to check the destination before boarding. Baggage is charged extra. Alternatively, you can catch a private taxi, but bear in mind that the official going rate is some 15 times the fare on the bus.

FLIGHTS WITHIN THE HOLY LAND

WITHIN ISRAEL domestic flights are operated by **Arkia**. In Jerusalem these flights use Atarot Airport, 7 km (4 miles) north of the city centre. They connect to Tel Aviv (Sde Dov Airport), Eilat and Haifa. With distances in Israel being so short, it only makes sense to fly internally to or from Eilat.

El Al and Royal Jordanian both fly between Ben Gurion and Amman, while El Al and Air Sinai connect Ben Gurion with Sharm el-Sheikh and Cairo. Fares are not cheap, but you can, of course, save a lot of time by flying.

DIRECTORY

AIRPORTS

Ben Gurion
(03) 971 0111.

Eilat (Ovda)
(07) 637 5880.

Queen Alia International
(06) 445 1000.

NATIONAL AIRLINES

Arkia
8 Shlomtsiyon ha-Malka St, Jerusalem.
(02) 622 5588.
11 Frishman St, Tel Aviv.
(03) 524 0220.

El Al
12 Hillel St, Jerusalem.
(02) 677 0200.
32 Ben Yehuda St, Tel Aviv.
(03) 526 1222.

Eilat.
(07) 633 1515.
Amman.
(06) 562 2526.

Royal Jordanian Airlines
Seventh Circle, Amman.
(06) 560 7300.

OTHER AIRLINES

Air France
Jerusalem.
(02) 625 2495.
Tel Aviv.
(03) 511 0000.
Amman.
(06) 566 6055.

Alitalia
Jerusalem.
(02) 628 4896.
Tel Aviv.
(03) 520 0000.
Amman.
(06) 463 6038.

American Airlines
Tel Aviv.
(03) 510 4322.

British Airways
Jerusalem.
(02) 628 8654.
Tel Aviv.
(03) 510 1581.
Amman.
(06) 582 8801.

Delta Air Lines
Jerusalem.
(02) 673 8842.
Tel Aviv.
(03) 620 1101.

KLM
Amman.
(06) 465 5267.
Jerusalem.
(02) 628 6643.
Tel Aviv.
(03) 521 9999.

Lufthansa
Jerusalem.
(02) 624 4941.

Tel Aviv.
(03) 514 2350.

Swissair
Jerusalem.
(02) 624 0094.
Tel Aviv.
(03) 511 6666.

Tower Air
Jerusalem.
(02) 625 0255.
Tel Aviv.
(03) 519 1919.

TWA
Jerusalem.
(02) 624 1135.
Tel Aviv.
(03) 795 5355.

AIRPORT TAXIS

Nesher Taxis
21 King George V St, Jerusalem.
(02) 625 2223.

Getting Around Jerusalem

Street sign

MOST OF JERUSALEM'S major historical and religious sites are concentrated in the Old City, which has to be explored on foot, as it is almost-a completely vehicle-free zone. Elsewhere, the city bus network functions efficiently and will get visitors to more or less everywhere they might want to go. This is just as well, as taxis tend to be prohibitively expensive for frequent use. The one time when visitors might have to resort to taxis is on Shabbat, when public transport stops running from sundown on Friday to sundown on Saturday.

Israeli shared taxi, or *sherut*

Yellow Palestinian taxi

JERUSALEM ON FOOT

THE OLD CITY is very much a pedestrian zone. Its narrow streets and alleys do not allow for vehicles. This makes it a wonderful area to explore. Flat-soled footwear is essential, as many of the ancient streets are either cobbled or unevenly paved. There are some areas of the New City that are also easy and rewarding to get around on foot, notably Yemin Moshe and Nakhalat Shiva, but elsewhere wide roads and aggressive traffic can make walking very unpleasant.

Finding your way around poses little problem as street signs are in at least two languages (either Hebrew and English, or Arabic and English). In the Old City, they are in the scripts of all three.

TAXIS

IT IS EASY to find a taxi in Jerusalem. You can either book one by phone, hail one on the street, or find one at

an official rank. Restaurant and hotel staff will always phone a cab for you.

Taxis are white if they are Israeli and yellow if they are Arab. There is little difference between them. Occasionally an Israeli driver may refuse to drive to an address in Arab East Jerusalem, while an Arab driver may balk at venturing into parts of West Jerusalem. Arab or Israeli, Jerusalem taxi drivers have a bad, but very well-deserved, reputation for over-charging. Although the taxis have modern meters (which can print out a receipt on request), drivers are not in the habit of using them. They will often claim that the meter is not working. You should insist that it is used. If it is not, you will pay a variable fare, which will be dependent on your haggling skills, but which will almost certainly be substantially more than the meter would have indicated. Note also that taxi fares are officially higher between 9:30pm and 5:30am.

White Israeli taxi

SHARED TAXIS

ONE SLIGHTLY UNUSUAL means of transport in Jerusalem (and throughout the Holy Land region) is the shared taxi. Known to the Israelis as a *sherut* and to the Arabs as a "service" (pronounced "servees"), shared taxis are a cross between a bus and a taxi. They operate fixed routes like a bus, but they run far more frequently and, like a taxi, they can be hailed on the street. At the start of the route drivers wait until every seat is taken before setting off. Points of origin and final destinations are displayed in the front window (although in the case of "services", this will be in Arabic only). There are no set stops; passengers indicate to the driver when they wish to be let off. Fares are a little more expensive than the equivalent bus ride but much cheaper than a taxi.

Israeli shared taxis are often white vans, while the Arabs favour large sedans, usually Mercedes or Peugeots.

BUSES

JERUSALEM'S CITY BUS system is run by Egged, the national carrier, which claims to be the world's largest bus company after Greyhound in the United States. Tickets are bought from the driver on boarding. The fare is the same for all destinations – the equivalent of just over one US dollar.

Buses are identified only by a number displayed in the front window, and destinations are not usually written. Major bus routes include: bus No. 1 from **Egged Central Bus Station** to Jaffa Gate and on to Mount Zion and the Western Wall bus station in the Old

Taxi rank on Omar ibn al-Khattab Square inside Jaffa Gate, the Old City

City's Jewish Quarter; bus No. 20, which runs between Jaffa Gate and Yad Vashem, passing along Jaffa Road; and bus No. 27, which runs between the Hadassah Hospital, along Jaffa Road past the central bus station, terminating at Nablus Road Bus Station in East Jerusalem near Damascus Gate.

Most buses run between about 5:30am and midnight. There are no night buses and no services on Shabbat.

East Jerusalem is served by Arab-run buses, which are not nearly so efficient as their Israeli counterparts. It is unlikely that many visitors to the city will find it necessary to use these buses.

THE NO. 99 BUS

ONE OF THE BEST things the first-time visitor to Jerusalem can do is to take a ride on the No. 99 bus. This bus follows a circular route that in just under two hours takes in most of the important sites outside the Old City. It departs every half hour between 10am and 2pm, and again at 4pm (Friday between 10am and noon only), from Safra Square on Jaffa Road. Tickets can be bought on the bus, but it is wise to book in advance as it is often full. Bookings can be made at Egged Central Bus Station on Jaffa Road, or at the city tourist information office.

A ticket is valid for a whole day and you can hop on and off wherever you like (bearing in mind the infrequency of services). It is also possible to get a two-day ticket. The driver may provide commentary, but this is as likely to be in Hebrew as English.

USEFUL INFORMATION

Egged Central Bus Station
208 Jaffa Rd.
[(02) 530 4704 *(information on all public bus routes, including No. 99).*

El-Ittihad Taxis
East Jerusalem.
[(02) 628 4641.

Ha-Palmakh Taxis
20 Shay Agnon Ave.
[(02) 679 2333.

Rehavia Taxis
3 Agron St.
[(02) 625 4444.

Jerusalem's Central Bus Station

THE NO. 99 BUS ROUTE

The circuit made by this bus passes more than 30 Jerusalem landmarks, which are usually pointed out by the driver.

Jaffa Gate *(see p96)* ①
YMCA *(see p118)* ②
King David Hotel *(see p118)* ③
LA Mayer Museum of Islamic Art *(see p126)* ④
Jerusalem Sherover Theatre *(see p260)* ⑤
St Andrew's Church ⑥
Mar Elias Monastery ⑦
Yad Vashem *(see p134)* ⑧

Israel Museum *(see pp128–33)* ⑨
Knesset *(see p127)* ⑩
Mount Scopus ⑪
St George's Cathedral *(see p122)* ⑫
Damascus Gate *(see p64)* ⑬
Rockefeller Museum *(see p123)* ⑭
Church of All Nations *(see p110)* ⑮
Mount Zion *(see p112)* ⑯

KEY

— Old City walls

═ No. 99 bus route

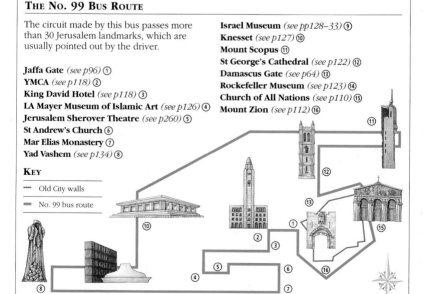

Public Transport in the Holy Land

BY FAR THE BEST and most popular way of getting around Israel and the Holy Land is by bus. Every town and city has a bus station, and inter-urban services tend to be frequent and very affordable. In comparison, rail networks in this part of the world are extremely limited: Israel has just two lines, and Jordan one, which is of little use, running, as it does, north to Damascus. There are no railways at all in Sinai. Sea transport is limited to just one route, across the Red Sea between Jordan and Sinai.

Long-distance Egged buses parked at Jerusalem central station

LONG-DISTANCE BUSES

NEARLY ALL long-distance bus routes in Israel are operated by the Egged company. This virtual monopoly at least has the advantage of making bus travel straight-forward and simple. Except for the Dead Sea region, services are frequent. For example buses depart from Jerusalem to Tel Aviv every 15 minutes, to Haifa every 45 minutes, and to Tiberias every hour. There is rarely any need to book in advance; you can simply turn up at the city bus station and get a ticket for the next service out. The only time that you might need to book in advance is if you are travelling to Ein Gedi, Masada or Eilat, as there are only about four buses a day that head in this direction.

Given the small size of the country, journeys are never very long (the longest is from Jerusalem to Eilat, which lasts around five hours). Egged buses are comfortable and air-conditioned, with plenty of space in the baggage holds.

There are passes for an unlimited number of journeys, which are valid for one or more weeks. These are called Israbus cards. For information on these passes and reduced fares for students, contact the

bus stations or **Egged Tours**, which has sales offices in all major towns and cities.

The one drawback to Israeli buses is that there are no services on Shabbat. This means that you should not plan to travel any time from late Friday afternoon to early evening Saturday. There are no buses either on Jewish holidays (*see pp34–7*). This can prove highly disruptive for any visitors caught unawares.

TRANSPORT IN THE PALESTINIAN TERRITORIES

WITH THE CONSTANT new developments in the administrative situation, public transport in the Palestinian territories is forever changing. In general, there are two options: Arab buses or shared taxis (*see p280*). Arab buses depart from two stations in East Jerusalem, one on Nablus Road (mainly for city services), the other on Suleyman Street, opposite the Old City walls. From one of these two, visitors can catch services for West Bank

Palestinian towns such as Bethlehem, Hebron, Jericho and Ramallah.

Arab shared taxis depart from a parking lot just outside the walls opposite Damascus Gate. They serve all the same destinations as the buses, but they are faster and depart far more frequently.

In general Arab buses do not go to Israeli towns, and vice versa. It is possible to catch an Israeli Egged bus to Bethlehem, but it drops you off on the highway outside town necessitating a 20-minute walk into the centre.

An older, long-distance Egged bus

TRAVELLING BY TRAIN

ISRAEL'S VERY LIMITED railway system comprises just two lines: one from Tel Aviv to Jerusalem and a second from Tel Aviv to Nahariya. The latter runs up the northern Mediterranean coast to near the border with Lebanon. Although the line serves several important destinations, including Haifa and Acre, the drawback is that there are few services each day and on Jewish holidays trains are very crowded. Stations also

The line up the north coast of Israel, slow but scenic

Bright yellow taxis amid the busy traffic of central Amman

RED SEA FERRIES

AQABA IN JORDAN and Nuweiba in Sinai are linked by a ferry and a catamaran. Both of these make one sailing each way, once a day. The ferry, which also carries cars, takes three hours, while the catamaran completes the trip in around one hour. Booking in advance is not necessary unless you are travelling with a car. It is possible to obtain a Sinai Permit *(see p267)* on board both vessels.

tend to be some distance from the town centre, often requiring a taxi ride to reach them.

The other line, between Tel Aviv and Jerusalem, passes through some particularly lovely scenery, but at the time of writing is not in operation. However, there used to be only one or two trains a day, and they were extremely slow. The plan is to upgrade the line and return it to regular service by the year 2004.

TRANSPORT IN JORDAN

THERE ARE several national bus companies in Jordan. The main one is **JETT**, which runs blue-and-white air-conditioned buses between Amman and Aqaba, the King Hussein (Allenby) Bridge and Petra. Booking your seat in advance is advisable. The JETT bus station in Amman is on King Hussein Road. Ten minutes' walk downhill on King Hussein is the Abdali bus station, which is where all the other Jordanian bus companies depart from for routes north and west, including services to Ajlun, Jerash and the King Hussein Bridge. All non-JETT buses to the south (including services to Kerak, Petra and Aqaba) leave from the Wahdat station, some 5 km (3 miles) south of the city centre.

The one destination that is hard to reach from Amman is the Dead Sea. There are no scheduled bus services. The only way to get here is by minibus or shared taxi.

Shared taxis are common in Jordan and far more frequent and convenient than buses. A shared taxi ride from Amman

to Aqaba takes about five hours and one from Amman to Petra about three.

The only regular rail service in Jordan is the three times a week train up to Damascus. It runs on the Hejaz Railway, built at the turn of the 20th century by the Turks but more famous for being repeatedly blown up by Lawrence of Arabia and his Arab fighters *(see p209)*. The trip takes about nine hours but you must have a visa in advance to enter Syria.

To get about in Amman there are city buses, but the destination is indicated only in Arabic. Taxi drivers tend to be honest and use the meter, making this an acceptable way of getting around. Only late in the evening or for longer journeys (such as to and from the airport) will you have to agree upon the price beforehand.

TRANSPORT IN SINAI

THE RESORTS of the east coast of the Sinai peninsula are served by the buses of Egypt's East Delta Bus Company. Services are not particularly frequent with no more than about half a dozen buses a day. All of these buses are either coming from or heading to Cairo (which is between seven and nine hours away). Only one or two of these buses pass by St Catherine's Monastery, so you need to check timetables carefully.

A very informal shared taxi service also operates in Sinai, but it can take time for the cars to fill up and the drivers can be alarmingly reckless.

Travelling Around by Car

Road sign in three languages

WITH WELL-MAINTAINED ROADS, light traffic away from the big cities and Israel's coastal highway, short distances between towns and some enchanting scenery, the Holy Land should be a pleasure to drive around. The one black spot is other road users. Both Israelis and Arabs can be reckless behind the wheel, and road fatalities are high. While this should not put you off driving, you do need to be cautious. On the positive side again, Israel is full of small places of beauty and interest, located well off any bus route, and having a car at your disposal can really open up the country.

CAR HIRE

Sign for a car rental company

MOST MAJOR international car hire companies are represented in Israel. Most have offices (or counters) at Ben Gurion Airport, in Tel Aviv and in Jerusalem. For the sake of convenience, it is better to use one that has a representative at the airport. To rent a car, you must have a full, clean driving licence (an international driving licence is not necessary). Cars are rented only to those over 21 years old, although some companies require that you be 23. Prices vary dramatically and it is recommended that you shop around before settling on a deal. Local companies, such as **Eldan**, frequently offer the best rates. Be aware that rental charges are usually quoted exclusive of insurance and collision waivers.

Note that it is not allowed to take cars hired in Israel over into Jordan or Sinai.

Car hire is not very popular in Jordan and Sinai because there are so few roads to explore. It also works out as very expensive when compared with getting around by other forms of transport, such as the bus or hiring a taxi for a day or two.

Petrol stations in Jordan, Sinai and even certain parts of Israel, particularly the Negev and Dead Sea areas, are few and far between. You are strongly advised to fill up your tank before setting off on any long journeys.

THE RULES OF THE ROAD

DRIVING IN ISRAEL is on the right-hand side of the road. At unmarked junctions drivers give way to traffic on the right, and overtaking is done on the left. The speed limit in towns is 50 km/h (30 mph) and 90 km/h (55 mph) on out-of-town roads. On some motorways the speed limit is 100 km/h (60 mph). Seat belts must be worn. Children under 15 must sit in the back and children under four must be restrained in a suitable child's seat.

ROAD SIGNS IN ISRAEL

ALTHOUGH THERE IS a lack of cautionary and warning signs on Israel's roads, all places of interest are well indicated. Signs are in both Hebrew and English (and sometimes in Arabic too). A problem arises, however, with the lack of consistency in the transliteration of place names from Hebrew and Arabic into English. You could be following directions for Beersheba one minute and for Be'er Sheva the next. These are, of course, the same place. In this book we have tried to present place names as you will see them spelled on Israeli road signs but local inconsistencies mean that this is not always the case.

No entry sign

School sign

Two-way sign

Right-hand bend

Tourist site sign

Parking sign

DRIVING IN THE PALESTINIAN TERRITORIES

CARS IN ISRAEL and the Palestinian Autonomous Territories have licence plates of different colours. Israeli cars have yellow plates, while Palestinian cars' plates are blue or green. It is inadvisable to drive a car with yellow, Israeli plates into Palestinian areas, particularly frequent troublespots such as Hebron and Ramallah. Cars hired in Israel are usually not insured for the Palestinian Territories. Conversely, driving a car with Palestinian plates in Israel will make you the object of a great deal of unwelcome attention from the security forces.

DRIVING IN JORDAN

WHILE DRIVING is on the right, Jordanians seem to consider most other road rules open to interpretation. Overtaking takes place on both sides of the road and right of way goes to he or she

Petrol station in Israel

Typically heavy traffic on the seafront promenade in Tel Aviv

who hesitates least. Roads are often in a poor state of repair. Many are badly surfaced, and road markings are often absent.

Speed limits are generally 100 km/h (60 mph) on open roads and 40 km/h (25 mph) in built-up areas. Care is needed on desert roads, where drifting sand can put the car into a spin if hit at speed.

Direction signs are frequently positioned right at the junction, offering no advance warning and making it all too easy to drive past your turn-off.

DRIVING IN SINAI

THERE ARE VERY few roads in Sinai, so routes to drive are limited. They do, however, pass through some stunning scenery. Traffic is light but what traffic there is, is mainly composed of buses and large shared taxis; these generally travel at high speed, paying little heed to other road users. Car drivers must constantly be on the lookout and be prepared to take evasive action.

Other than on recognized trails, off-road driving is not encouraged as it can damage the fragile desert environment. Several such trails begin in the region of Nuweiba (see p218).

DRIVING IN CITIES

TRAFFIC IN and around Tel Aviv and, to a lesser extent, Jerusalem is nightmarish. You should aim to avoid rush hour, which is roughly 7–9am and 4–6pm. That said, it is not unknown to encounter traffic jams in Tel Aviv at 1am.

HITCH-HIKING

KNOWN IN ISRAEL as *tremping*, hitch-hiking used to be a common way of getting about the country. It was particularly popular with soldiers heading home or returning from leave. But recently hitch-hiking has become increasingly unsafe. Women soldiers are now banned from hitching and we recommend visitors do not hitch-hike either.

CYCLING

PARTS OF ISRAEL are excellent places for cycle touring. The best regions are Galilee and the Golan Heights, where the scenery is at its most varied and the altitude serves to moderate the extreme summer temperatures. Even so, from June to August it is best to plan to cycle only in the mornings, to avoid the afternoon heat.

In Tiberias, it is possible to hire bicycles by the day to explore the shores of the Sea of Galilee (see pp162–4). In Jerusalem you can rent bicycles by the day from **Walk Ways**, who will deliver to your hotel. For general cycling advice and to enquire about joining organized rides, enthusiasts could also try contacting the **Jerusalem Cycle Club**.

Cycling in Jaffa

General Index

Acknowledgments

DORLING KINDERSLEY would like to thank the following people whose invaluable contributions and assistance have made the preparation of this book possible.

SENIOR MANAGING EDITOR
Louise Bostock Lang.

MANAGING ART EDITOR
Jane Ewart.

EDITORIAL DIRECTOR
Vivien Crump.

ART DIRECTOR
Gillian Allan.

PUBLISHER
Douglas Amrine.

MAIN CONSULTANTS
Felicity Cobbing, Andrew Humphreys, Jonathan Tubb.

TRANSLATOR
Richard Pierce.

MAPS
Rob Clynes, James Macdonald (Colourmap Scanning Ltd).

PRODUCTION
Marie Ingledew.

ADDITIONAL CONTRIBUTORS AND CONSULTANTS
Jonathan Elphick, Professor Jonathan Magonet, Peter Parr, Amir Reuveni, Wolfgang Tins.

VISUALIZER
Joy FitzSimmons.

ADDITIONAL ILLUSTRATIONS
Richard Bonson.

ADDITIONAL PHOTOGRAPHY
Steve Gorton.

DESIGN AND EDITORIAL ASSISTANCE
Gillian Andrews, Sam Borland, Esther Labi, Lee Redmond, Marisa Renzullo.

PROOF READER
Stewart J Wild.

INDEXER
Hilary Bird.

SPECIAL ASSISTANCE
Sheila Brull, Egyptian Tourist Authority, Giovanni Francesio and Mattia Goffetti at Fabio Ratti Editoria, Efrat Goller at Keter Publishing, Tony Howard and Di Taylor at N.O.M.A.D.S. (New Opportunities for Mountaineering and Desert Sports), Israel Ministry of Tourism, Jordan Tourism Board, Amalyah Keshet and Tal Sher at the Israel Museum, Deborah Lipson at the Tower of David Museum of the History of Jerusalem, Hila Reuveni, Shelly Shemer at the Israel Wine and Gourmet Magazine. Special thanks to Massimo Acanfora Torrefranca.

ADDITIONAL PICTURE RESEARCH
Julia Harris-Voss.

PHOTOGRAPHIC AND ARTWORK REFERENCE
Dale Harris, Ben Johnson, Albatros, Jerusalem.

PHOTOGRAPHY PERMISSIONS
The publisher would like to thank all the churches, museums, hotels, restaurants, shops, galleries and sights too numerous to thank individually, for their co-operation and contribution to this publication.

PICTURE CREDITS
t = top; tl = top left; tlc = top left centre; tc = top centre; tr = top right; cla = centre left above; ca = centre above; cra = centre right above; cl = centre left; c = centre; cr = centre right; clb = centre left below; cb = centre below; crb = centre right below; bl = bottom left; b = bottom; bc = bottom centre; bcl = bottom centre left; br = bottom right; (d) = detail.

The publisher would like to thank the following individuals, companies and picture libraries for permission to reproduce their photographs:

ANCIENT ART & ARCHITECTURE COLLECTION: 26cb, 27ca, 28cr, 39c, 39br, 40t, 42cl, 45ca; R Sheridan 22t, 39bl, 42tl, 44b, 48cb, 103cla, 103cl; G Tortoli 25cra; ANDES PRESS: Carlos Reyes-Manzo 21cr, 277t; AKG, LONDON: 40crb, 44t, 48t, 52bl, 209br; Erich Lessing 18cl, 19ca, 20br, 27b, 28b, 43cb, 43b, 44cb, 88ca, 169c, 192t, 192ca, 192br; Jean Louis Mou 57t; FABRIZIO ARDITO 18b, 24t, 33cra, 76tl, 99b, 106 tl, 159t, 193b, 198t, 200t, 208t, 209t, 209cb, 214t, 214c, 215b, 266t, 267t, 268tl, 268tcr, 268tr, 268c, 272c, 272b, 274c, 274c, 274br, 275c, 276t, 280tbr, 280c, 284cl, 284cb; ASAP, JERUSALEM: 116ca; Eyal Bartov 32tl, 32cl, 33t, 33ca, 33bl; Lev Borodulin 231c; Bridgeman Art Library 22cl, 25cr, 49bl, 69c; C.Z.A. 50ca; Shai Ginott 32clb, 56bl; Avi Hirschfield 77c, 77cb; Hanan Isachar 128tr, 133cra, 282b; Itsik Marom 32bl, 33cl, 33clb, 33cb; Garo Nalbandian 3 (inset), 22bl, 22br, 103cr, 106ca, 106cb, 222b, 223b; Richard Nowitz 106tr; Nitsan Shorer 278t; Vivian Silver 51t; Israel Talby 32cr, 278b; Andina Tovy 278c.

BRIDGEMAN ART LIBRARY: *Christ Carrying the Cross* Eustache Le Sueur (1651) 29b, 30b, *Jerusalem from the Mount of the Olives* Edward Lear (1859) 31t, *The Finding of the Saviour in the Temple* William Holman Hunt (1854–60) 31b, 38, 224b; Bibliothèque Municipale de Lyon 46clb; British Library 18cr, 19t; Galleria Borghese *St Jerome Writing* Caravaggio (1604) 175b; Giraudon 24cl; Musée Condé, Chantilly 26b; BRITISH LIBRARY: 20t.

CAMERA PRESS: Fred Adler 279t.

JO DORAN: 86c.

E.T.ARCHIVE: 47t, 47br; MARY EVANS PICTURE LIBRARY: 9 (inset), 30t, 30c, 31c, 46bl, 46br, 55 (inset), 227c.

ffOTOGRAFF: Patricia Aithie 15t, 48b, 57b, 58, 65t, 94b, 95t, 100ca, 101t, 111b, 118t, 118c, 121br, 125t, 134c, 134b, 177c, 229c, 254t, 256tr, 259cra, 260b, 274bl, 280tl, 284t; Charles Aithie

20–21c, 29clb, 57tr, 110b, 117ca, 257crb; GINO FRONGIA 14, 22–23c, 32cla, 66c, 68tr, 98tr, 100tr, 101ca, 154tl, 167b, 170b, 230c, 268b, 270tl.

CRISTINA GAMBARO: 5ca, 60ca, 60cb, 63t, 65c, 89b, 95b, 105t, 159c, 162b, 177t, 182t, 270tr, 272tl; EDDIE GERALD: 28cl, 60b, 66tl, 76cla, 76c, 77ca, 81t, 102b, 103t, 103bl, 107cb, 116cb, 120t, 121bl, 148, 152t, 154tr, 154ca, 154bl, 162tl, 163t, 163c, 175cra, 185, 204b, 212b, 218b, 222cb, 223ca, 255c, 256cb, 261t, 261c, 261b, 262c, 262b, 271t, 271c, 271b, 274t, 280tr, 282c, all 284cra, all 284cr, 284crb, 284b.

SONIA HALLIDAY: Laura Lushington 133bl; ROBERT HARDING PICTURE LIBRARY: 23cr; ASAP/Nalbandian 56t, 96br; Gascoigne 26c; HOLMES PHOTOGRAPHY: 225, Jean Holmes 47crb, Reed Holmes 208b, TONY HOWARD: 208ca.

IMAGES COLOUR LIBRARY: 220–221; HANAN ISACHAR: 1c, 4b, 5t, 5clb, 17b, 23t, 23cra, 23crb, 29t, 33crb, 34t, 34c, 34b, 35ca, 35br, 36cra, 36b, 37c, 37b, 53cb, 59t, 84, 87t, 88cb, 89t, 89cra, 90ca, 90cb, 96bc, 106b, 146ca, 150c, 151b, 152c, 152b, 152b, 155ca, 155cb, 155b, 156t, 156b, 158t, 162cb, 169t, 174ca, 174cb, 180t, 185, 192cl, 194–195, 197b, 202c, 225t, 252b, 254b, 257cra, 285b; ISRAEL MUSEUM: 42cbl, *Destruction and Sack of the Temple of Jerusalem* Nicolas Poussin (1625–6) 43t, 43cr, 47cra, 51b, *Apple Core* Claes Oldenburg (1929), 123t, 128tl, 128cla, 128cra, *Red-Blue Chair* GT Rietveld (1918) 129t, *The Rabbi* Marc Chagall (1912–13) 129ca, 130tl, *Jeanne Hebuterne seated* Modigliani (1918) 130tr, 130b, 131t, 131c, 131b, 132c, 133t, 133cl, 133c, 133cr, 181c; Adam Bartos © ARS, NY and DACS, London 2000 *Woman Combing Her Hair* Alexander Archipenko (1914) 128bl, 132b; David Harris 129cb, 129bl, 130c, 133br; Ann Levin 132t.

PAUL JACKSON: 154b, 155t, 201bl, 203br.

MAGNUM PHOTOS: 52t.

NHPA: Henry Ausloos 33br; RICHARD NOWITZ: 2–3, 16t, 72–73, 88b, 89c, 91c, 146b, 147t, 147cb, 149b, 153t, 158c, 158b, 166, 168ca, 169b, 173b, 176b, 177b, 180br, 181bl, 184, 193t, 199b, 201br, 206b, 210, 213t, 218t, 223t, 223bl, 225b, 226–227, 228t, 241b, 255t, 259ca, 267b, 275b; Air Photos, Israel 166.

CRISTINE OSBORNE PICTURES: 147b, 205c, 224t, 224c, 277c.

PLANET EARTH PICTURES: Kurt Amsler 213b; POPPERFOTO: 49br, 50c, 50bl, 50br, 51c, 52br; David Ake 53t. ZEV RADOVAN: 4–5t, 18tr, 19cb, 20cl, 20bl, 21t, 21tr, 26t, 27cb, 40bl, 40br, 41cb, 41b, 49t, 65b, 69b, 74, 75t, 126c; FABIO RATTI: 70c, 99ca, 113b, 190t, 190b, 191t, 191b, 269b; RETROGRAPH ARCHIVE: 52c; REX FEATURES: 17c.

PETER SANDERS PHOTOGRAPHY: 24bl, 24br, 25t, 68tl, 68c; SCIENCE PHOTO LIBRARY: CNES, 1990 Distribution Spot Image 10ca; THE ORIGINAL SHAKESPEARE COMPANY 35bl; EITAN SIMANOR: 37cra, 42b, 54–55, 162tr, 230b, 262t; JON SPAULL: 147ca, 186t, 186b, 187t, 187b, 264–265, 283c.

VISIONS OF THE LAND: American Colony Hotel 49cb; Tony Malmqvist 211b, 216t, 216c, 216cb, 216bl, 216bc, 216br, 217tl, 217tr, 217cra, 217cb, 217bl, 217br, 219c, 219b, 276c; Beni Mor 27t, 61t, 62b, 86tl, 86tr, 87b, 97c, 110c, 111t, 112t, 112b, 157b, 160t, 160b, 161t, 161b, 164t, 164b, 170t, 171t, 171b, 172t, 183b, 198cl, 209ca, 276cl; Garo Nalbandian 24–25c, 33cla, 57crb, 61cb, 66b, 67cr, 67b, 70b, 71cr, 96t, 96clb, 102t, 102c, 103cb, 103br, 108tl, 108tr, 109t, 109b, 120b, 121t, 165t,

173t, 178–179, 189b, 199tl, 199tr, 199c, 200c, 200b, 202t, 202b, 203tr, 203tl, 203cla, 204t, 205cb, 205b, 206t, 206c, 207t, 207cl, 207cr, 207b, 214b, 215t, 222t, 222cla, 222b, 231t, 240t, 240c; Basilio Rodella 41ca, 60t, 61ca, 62t, 62c, 64t, 64c, 64b, 67t, 70tr, 71tr, 71b, 76b, 77b, 80t, 80c, 80b, 82t, 82c, 82b, 83t, 83c, 83b, 86ca, 88t, 100tl, 110t, 113t, 117cb, 118b, 119b, 122t, 122bl, 122br, 123c, 123b, 126t, 126b, 127c, 127b, 134t, 157c, 164cr, 165b, 170c, 172b, 176t, 180c, 180bl, 181t, 181ca, 182b, 183t, 188t, 188b, 229t, 260t, 276b; SPNI Collection/Yossi Eshbol 183c, 219t; Studium Biblicum Franciscanum Archive 192–193c, 193cr; Ilan Sztulman 5crb, 228c, 242tr, 242tl, 242tc, 242cla, 242ca, 242cra, 242cl, 242cr, 242clb, 242bl, 242bc, 242br, 243t, 243tl, 243tr, 243cla, 243cra, 243c, 243cb, 243bl, 243bra, 243br, 244tl, 244cl, 244cr, 244cr, 244b, 245bl, 245clb, 245bc, 245cbc, 245brc, 245br, 253t, all 258cla, 258crc, 258clb, 258cb, 258bcl, 258bc, 259tl, 259tc, 259tr, 259trr, 259cla, 259c, all 259crb, 266b, 281c, 282t.

WERNER FORMAN ARCHIVE: British Museum 19b; PETER WILSON: 15b, 32tr, 32br, 144–145, 151t, 163b, 168b, 189t, 198–199, 203b, 204cb, 205t, 208cb, 209bl, 212t, 270b, 285t.

Jacket: All VISIONS OF THE LAND except Richard Nowitz front t, back t; ffOTOGRAff: Patricia Aithie front c.

Front Endpaper: All commissioned photography except ffOTOGRAff: Patricia Aithie tr; EDDIE GERALD tcl; HANAN ISACHAR c; RICHARD NOWITZ tl, bcl, bl; ZEV RADOVAN brc.

Hebrew Phrase Book

Hebrew has an alphabet of 22 letters. As in Arabic, the vowels do not appear in the written language and there are several systems of transliteration. In this phrasebook we have given a simple phonetic transcription only. Bold type indicates the syllable on which the stress falls. An apostrophe between two letters means that there is a break in the pronunciation. The letters "kh" represent the sound "ch" as in Scottish "loch", and "g" is hard as in "gate". Where necessary, the masculine form is given first, followed by the feminine.

IN EMERGENCY

Help!	Hatzilu!
Stop!	Atzor!
Call a doctor!	Azminu rofe!
Call an ambulance!	Azminu ambulans!
Call the police!	Tzaltzelu lamishtara!
Call the fire brigade!	Tzaltzelu lemekhabei esh!
Where is the nearest telephone?	Efo hatelefon hatziburi hakhi karov?
Where is the nearest hospital?	Efo bet hakholim hakhi karov?

COMMUNICATION ESSENTIALS

Yes	Ken
No	Lo
Please	Bevakasha
Thank you	Toda
Many thanks	Toda raba
Excuse me	Slikha
Hello	Shalom
Good day	Boker tov
Good evening	Erev tov
Good night	Laila tov
Greetings (on the Sabbath)	Shabat Shalom
Have a good week (after the Sabbath)	Shavu'a tov
morning	boker
afternoon	akhar hatzohoryim
evening	erev
night	lyla
today	hayom
tomorrow	makhar
here	po
there	sham
what?	ma?
which?	eizeh?
when?	matai?
who?	mi?
where?	efo?

USEFUL PHRASES

How are you?	Ma shlomkha/shlomekh?
Very well, thank you	Beseder, toda
Pleased to meet you	Na'im meod
Goodbye	Lehitraot
(I'm) fine!	Beseder gamur
Where is/Where are?	Efo...?
How many kilometres is it to...?	Kama kilometrim mipo le...?
What is the way to..?	Ekh megi'im le...?
Do you speak English?	Ata/at medaber/medaberet anglit?
I don't understand	Ani lo mevin/mevina
Could you speak more slowly, please?	Tukhal/tukhli ledaber yoter le'at, bevakasha?

USEFUL WORDS

large	gadol
small	katan
hot	kham
cold	kar
bad	lo tov
enough	maspik
well	beseder
open	patuakh
closed	sagur
left	smol
right	yamin
straight	yashar
near	karov
far	rakhok
up	lemala

down	lemata
soon	mukdam
late	meukhar
entrance	knisa
exit	yetzia
toilet	sherutim
free, unoccupied	panui
free, no charge	khinam

MAKING A TELEPHONE CALL

I'd like to make a long-distance call	Haiti rotze/rotza lehitkasher lekhutz lair
I'd like to make a reversed-charge call	Haiti rotze/rotza lehitkasher govaina
I'll call back later	Etkasher meukhar yoter
Can I leave a message?	Efshar lehashir hoda'a?
Hold on	Hamtin/hamtini (Tamtin/tamtini)
Could you speak up a little, please?	Tukhal/tukhli ledaber bekol ram yoter?
local call	sikha mekomit
international call	sikha benleumit

SHOPPING

How much does it cost?	Kama zeh oleh?
I would like…	Haiti rotzeh/rotza...
Do you have..?	Yesh lakhem...?
I'm just looking.	Ani rak mistakel/mistakelet
Do you take credit cards?	Atem mekablim kartisei ashrai?
Do you take traveller's cheques?	Atem mekablim traveller's cheques?
What time do you open?	Matai potkhim?
What time do you close?	Matai sogrim?
this one	zeh
that one	hahu
expensive	Yakar
inexpensive/cheap	lo yakar/zol
size	mida
shoe size	mida (midat na'alyim)
white	lavan
black	shakhor
red	adom
yellow	tzahov
green	yarok
blue	kakhol

TYPES OF SHOP

antiques shop	khanut atikot
bakery	ma'afia
bank	bank
barber's	maspera
bookshop/newsagent	khanut sfarim/ve'itonim
butcher's	atliz
cake shop	ma'adania
chemist's	bet merkakhat
clothes shop	khanut b'gadim
greengrocer's	yarkan
grocer's	makolet
hairdresser's	maspera
jeweller's	khanut takhshitim
market	shuk
post office	snif hadoar
shoe shop	khanut na'alyim
supermarket	supermarket
travel agency	sokhnut nesiyot

SIGHTSEEING

bus station	takhana merkazit
bus stop	takhanat otobus
church	knisia
closed	sagur
library	sifria
mosque	misgad
park	park
synagogue	bet haknesset
taxi	monit
tourist information office	merkaz hameida letayar
town hall	bet ha'iria
train station	takhanat rakevet

STAYING IN A HOTEL

I have a reservation	Yesh li azmana
Do you have a free room?	Yesh lakhem kheder panui?
double room	kheder zugi
room with two beds	kheder im shtei mitot
room with a bath or a shower	kheder im sherutim ve ambatia o miklakhat
single room	kheder yakhid

key	mafteakh
lift	ma'alit
Can someone help me with my luggage?	Mishehu yakhol la'azor li im hamisvadot?

EATING OUT

Have you got a table free?	Yesh lakhem shulkhan panui?
I would like to book a table	Haiti rotze/rotza lehazmin shulkhan
The bill please	Kheshbon, bevakasha
I am vegetarian	Ani tzimkhoni/ tzimkhonit
menu	tafrit
fixed-price menu	tafrit iskit
wine list	tafrit hayeinot
glass	kos
bottle	bakbuk
knife	sakin
spoon	kaf
fork	masleg
breakfast	arukhat boker
lunch	arukhat tzohoryim
dinner	arukhat erev
starter	mana rishona
main course	mana ikarit
portion	mana
rare	mevushal me'at
well done	mevushal hetev

FOOD AND DRINK

almonds	shkedim
apples	tapuakhei etz
apricot	mish mish
aubergine/eggplant	khatzilim
beans	shu'it
beef	bakar
beer	bira
bread	lekhem
broad beans	ful
broccoli	brokoli
butter	khem'a
cabbage	kruv
cake	ugha
carrot	gezer
cauliflower	kruvit
cheese	gvina
cherries	dudvanim
chicken	off
chickpeas	khumus
chips/fries	chips
chocolate	shokolat
coffee	kafe
cold cuts	pastrama
coriander	kuzbera
courgettes/zucchini	kishuim
crabs	sartanim
cucumbers	melafefonim
dessert	kinuakh
draught beer	bira mihakhavit
dry	yavesh
eggs	betza
figs	te'enim
fish	dag
French beans	shu'it yerokha
fried	metugan
fruit	peirot
garlic	shum
grapes	anavim
grey mullet	buri
grilled	al haesh
grouper	lokus
hard-boiled eggs	betza kasha
herbal tea	tei tzmakhim
hot (spicy)	kharif
ice	kerakh
icecream	glida
kebab	shipud
lamb, mutton	keves
lemon	limon
liver	kaved
meat	basar
milk	khalav
mineral water	myim mineralim
nuts	egozim
olive oil	shemen zyit
omelette	khavita
onion	batzal
orange juice (freshly squeezed)	mitz tapuzim (tiv'i sakhut)

oranges	tapuzim
peaches	afarsekim
pepper (condiment)	pilpel
peppers (capsicums)	pilpelim
pickles	khamutzim
plums	shezifim
potatoes	tapukhei adama
prawns/shrimps	shrimps
red snapper	denis
red wine	yain adom
rice	orez
roast	betanur
salad	salat yerakot
salmon	salmon
salt	melakh
sandwich/filled roll	lakhmania
sauce	rotev
seafood	peirot yam
smoked	me'ushan
soup	marak
spinach	tered
spinach beet (Swiss chard)	alei selek
squid	kalamari
steak	steik
strawberries	tut sade (tutim)
stuffed vegetables	memulaim
sugar	sukar
tea	tei
tomatoes	agvaniot
trout	forel
turkey	hodu
vegetables	yerakot
vinegar	khometz yain
water	myim
white wine	yain lavan

NUMBERS

0	efes
1	akhad
2	shtaim
3	shalosh
4	arba
5	khamesh
6	shesh
7	sheva
8	shmone
9	teisha
10	eser
11	ahadesreh
12	shtemesreh
13	shloshesreh
14	arbaesre
15	khameshesreh
16	sheshesreh
17	shvaesreh
18	shmona'esreh
19	tshaesreh
20	esrim
21	esrim veakhad
30	shloshim
40	arba'im
50	khamishim
60	shishim
70	shiv'im
80	shmonim
90	tish'im
100	mea
200	matyim
300	shlosh meot
1,000	elef
2,000	alpyim
3,000	shlosha elef
4,000	arba elef
10,000	asara elef

TIME

one minute	daka
one hour	sha'a
half an hour	khetzi sha'a
Sunday	yom rishon
Monday	yom sheni
Tuesday	yom shlishi
Wednesday	yom revi'i
Thursday	yom khamishi
Friday	yom shishi
Saturday	shabat
week	shavu'a
month	khodesh
year	shana

DORLING KINDERSLEY *TRAVEL GUIDES*

TITLES AVAILABLE

THE GUIDES THAT SHOW YOU WHAT OTHERS ONLY TELL YOU

COUNTRY GUIDES

AUSTRALIA • CANADA • FRANCE • GREAT BRITAIN
GREECE: ATHENS & THE MAINLAND • THE GREEK ISLANDS
IRELAND • ITALY • MEXICO • PORTUGAL • SCOTLAND
SOUTH AFRICA • SPAIN • THAILAND

REGIONAL GUIDES

BARCELONA & CATALONIA • CALIFORNIA
FLORENCE & TUSCANY • FLORIDA • HAWAII
JERUSALEM & THE HOLY LAND • LOIRE VALLEY
MILAN & THE LAKES • NAPLES WITH POMPEII & THE
AMALFI COAST • PROVENCE & THE COTE D'AZUR • SARDINIA
SEVILLE & ANDALUSIA • SICILY • VENICE & THE VENETO
GREAT PLACES TO STAY IN EUROPE

CITY GUIDES

AMSTERDAM • BERLIN • BUDAPEST • DUBLIN • ISTANBUL
LISBON • LONDON • MADRID • MOSCOW • NEW YORK
PARIS • PRAGUE • ROME • SAN FRANCISCO
ST PETERSBURG • SYDNEY • VIENNA • WARSAW

TRAVEL PLANNERS

AUSTRALIA • FRANCE • FLORIDA
GREAT BRITAIN & IRELAND • ITALY • SPAIN

DK TRAVEL GUIDES CITY MAPS

LONDON • NEW YORK • PARIS • ROME
SAN FRANCISCO • SYDNEY

DK TRAVEL GUIDES PHRASE BOOKS

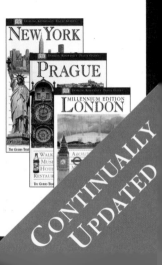

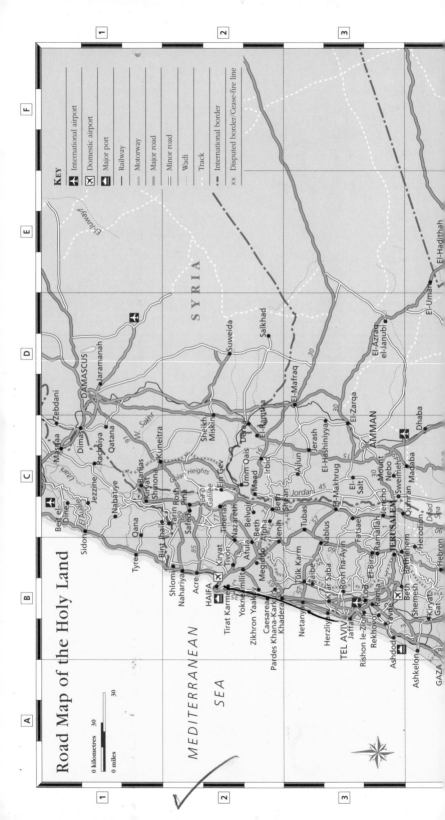

Road Map of the Holy Land

0 kilometres 30

0 miles 30

Key

✈ International airport
☒ Domestic airport
⚓ Major port
━━ Railway
━━ Motorway
━━ Major road
━━ Minor road
⋯⋯ Wadi
⋯⋯ Track
━·━·━ International border
xx Disputed border/Cease-fire line

MEDITERRANEAN SEA

SYRIA

DAMASCUS
Jaramanah
Zebdani
Masha
Dimas
Ragheibla
Qatana
W. Sakhr
Kuneitra
Banias
Kiryat Shmona
Rosh Pina
Golan Heights
Ein Gev
Sea of Galilee
Sheikh Miskin
Suweida
Salkhad

Sidon
Jezzine
Nabatiye
Beit el-Dine
El-Aale
Qana
Bint Jbeil
Tyre
Safed
Tiberias
Nazareth
Belvoir
Beth Alpha
Afula
Megiddo

Umm Qais
Maad
Deraa
El-Ramtha
Irbid
Ajlun
Jerash
El-Hashiniyya
El-Mafraq
El-Zarqa
AMMAN
El-Salt
Sweimeh
Madaba
Mount Nebo
El-Azraq el-Janubi
Dhaba

Shlomi
Nahariya
Acre
HAIFA
Tirat Karmel
Yokneam
Zikhron Yaakov
Caesarea
Pardes Khana-Karkur
Khadera
Netanya
Herzliya
TEL AVIV
Jaffa
Rishon le-Zion
Rekhovot
Yavne
Ashdod
Ashkelon
GAZA

Kiryat Tivon
Jenin
Beth Shean
Tubas
Nablus
Tulk Karm
Taibe
Rosh ha-Ayn
Kfar Saba
Lod
Ramla
El-Bira
Beth Shemesh
Kiryat Gat

Jordan
El-Makhrug
Jericho
JERUSALEM
Bethlehem
Herodion
Qumran
Dead Sea
Hebron

El-Umari
El-Hadithah

El-Iuwait